CENTER FIELD

James R. Walker and Robert V. Bellamy Jr.

UNIVERSITY OF NEBRASKA PRESS · LINCOLN AND LONDON

SHOT

A History of Baseball on Television

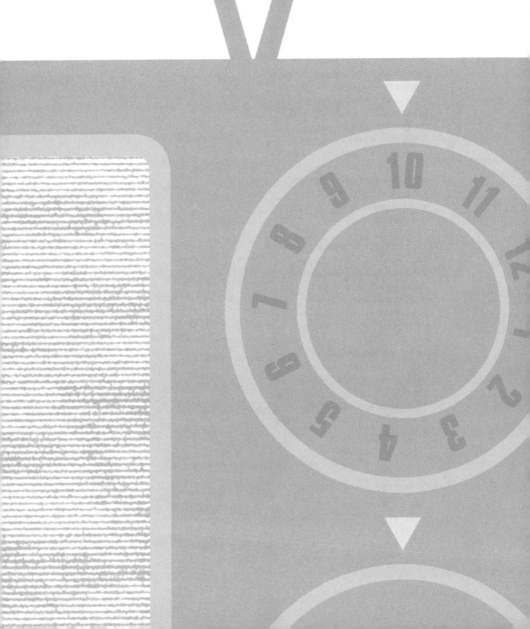

Earlier versions of the following chapters appeared in NINE: A Journal of Baseball History and Culture by permission of the University of Nebraska Press. © by the University of Nebraska Press: chapter 1, "The Experimental Years," appeared as "Baseball on Television: The Formative Years, 1939–51," in vol. 11, no. 2 (2003); chapter 3, "Team Approaches to Television in the Broadcast Era," appeared as "Baseball and Television Origins: The Case of the Cubs," in vol. 10, no. 1 (2001); chapter 7, "National Broadcasts in the Cable Era," appeared as "Foul Tip or Strike Three: The Evolving 'Partnership' of Major League Baseball and Television" in vol. 3 (1995); chapter 10, "Television and the 'Death' of the Golden Age Minors," appeared as "Did Televised Baseball Kill the 'Golden Age' of the Minor Leagues? A Reassessment," in vol. 13, no. 1 (2004); and chapter 12, "Baseball and Television Synergy," appeared as "Whatever Happened to Synergy? Major League Baseball as Media Product," in vol. 13, no. 2 (2005). ¶ ©

Library of Congress Cataloging-in-Publication Data ¶ Walker, James R. ¶ Center field shot: a history of baseball on television / James R. Walker and Robert V. Bellamy Jr. ¶ p. cm. ¶ Includes bibliographical references and index. ¶ ISBN 978-0-8032-4825-0 (pbk.: alk. paper) ¶ 1. Television broadcasting of sports—United States—History. 2. Baseball—United States—History. I. Bellamy, Robert V. II. Title. ¶ GV742.3.W35 2008 ¶ 070.4′497960973—dc22 ¶ Set in Quadraat by Bob Reitz. ¶ Designed by R. W. Boeche.

Contents

Illustrations

Table

Acknowledgments

Jim Walker

Rob Bellamy has been my collaborator on many ventures since our paths first crossed at the University of Iowa in 1980. His spirited insights and decade-long dedication to this project helped make it a reality, while his sharp wit made working on it more fun than it should be.

I would like to thank the staff at the National Baseball Hall of Fame Library for their help in locating and providing at modest cost many of the photographs used in this book. In addition, the Hall of Fame's television files, collected over decades, also made a major contribution to this volume. Steve Gietschier, senior managing editor of the *Sporting News*, gave me entry to the SN archives' extensive clippings file on television and related topics, and offered many helpful suggestions. He also reminded me that history should be more than "the lies told by the living about the dead." The staff at the Wisconsin Historical Society and the Joyce Sports Research Collection at the University of Notre Dame also provided considerable assistance in accessing their important holdings. I would like to thank Margaret Schmidt and her students for their many helpful comments on the initial drafts of several chapters.

I am most grateful to Saint Xavier University for providing the sabbatical leave that allowed me to complete my portion of this book. Joel Sternberg, my friend and colleague at SXU, provided me with many articles containing essential information on early televised baseball. Our conversations about this project over the years were immensely valuable.

Finally, I dedicate my portion of this book to my wife, Judith Hiltner, whose belief in and support for my scholarly efforts have made them possible.

Rob Bellamy

Jim Walker has been a great friend and coauthor for over twenty-five years. Our relationship is one I value and am thankful for having. Thanks also to Jim's wife, Judith Hiltner, for her skillful copyediting. Special thanks to the late Bill Kirwin of NINE: A Journal of Baseball History and Culture for giving us an outlet to try out early chapter drafts at the always delightful NINE Spring Training Conference and within the pages of the journal.

As most authors know, our work would not turn out as well (if at all) and would not be nearly as fulfilling without the support of our loved ones. Thanks to my wife, Catherine Cecil Bellamy, for her essential love and support.

My daughter, Kate Bellamy, deserves special thanks. She is truly an inspiration for all that I do. She has been amazingly tolerant of the Pirates, although they have not had a winning season in her lifetime. Like her mother, she has also been a real trouper when it comes to my travel, writing schedule, moodiness, and idiosyncrasies. Kate, this one is for you.

Introduction

The Game in the Box

In an end-of-the-millennium feature on "The Top 100 Things That Impacted Baseball in the 20th Century," *Baseball Weekly* listed television as second only to Jackie Robinson's signing. Television was cited for exposing Major League Baseball (MLB) to a much larger audience, generating a financial windfall for owners, increasing the value of franchises exponentially, and, with the development of cable, changing "the way Americans followed the game."[1]

We agree with *Baseball Weekly*'s analysis. And today, a few years into the twenty-first century, television's impact on each of these elements—team revenue enhancement, franchise values, and ways we follow the game—has become even more prominent. More importantly, Major League Baseball owners finally may have learned how to partner with, rather than fight, television, making the game's dysfunctional "marriage" to television more harmonious.

Perhaps the greatest impact of television on Major League Baseball was to make MLB a common synonym for "baseball." Although the big league game had a privileged position before the video medium, the U.S. television industry has focused most of the nation's attention on the MLB version of the game. Nightly ESPN *Sportscenter* highlights record nearly every significant MLB "dinger," "punch-out," and defensive "web gem," while only the most extraordinary moments from the minor leagues, college or high school baseball, or international competition receive any exposure. In the United States, virtually every MLB game is telecast over some combination of broadcast, cable, satellite, or Internet. But minor league games are rarely telecast, college games are cablecast during the College World Series, and international games come to prominence only during the MLB player–dominated World Baseball Classic. Though television has magnified both the best and worst that Major League Baseball has to offer, it has offered only a distant glimpse of much of the rest of the sport.

Despite the intense coverage the medium gives MLB, baseball's relationship with television has been more difficult than that of any major sport.[2] The 2005 and 2006 World Series set new records for all-time low-est ratings (11.1 in 2005; 10.1 in 2006).[3] The 2005 result was particularly disturbing because the two competitors—the Chicago White Sox and the Houston Astros—represented two of the nation's top ten television markets. However, the rating for the 2006 All-Star Game (9.3) was up 15 percent from 2005.[4] Despite mixed results, Fox Sports renewed its multibillion-dollar contract with MLB, maintaining its exclusive cover-age of the World Series and All-Star Games in addition to one of the two League Championship Series (LCS) through 2013. In renewing the contract, Fox affirmed that postseason games are an "invaluable pro-motional platform—for both our new series and returning hits such as *House, 24, Prison Break, Bones, The Simpsons,* and *Family Guy.*"[5]

Analysts have offered several explanations for the relative decline of MLB as a national television attraction, including aesthetic, marketing, economic, and historic reasons. On the aesthetic level, baseball's play-ing field, characterized by wide dispersion of players, makes it a difficult sport to televise because the cameras cannot follow all of the action. Curt Smith, a popular historian of baseball and broadcasting, argues that baseball is perhaps the worst sport for television because the breaks in the action are boring for viewers. However, for viewers at the stadium, the same breaks are welcomed, giving fans opportunities to hash over questionable calls, go to the restroom, or buy brats and beer.[6]

MLB owners have been blamed justifiably for misunderstanding mod-ern-day marketing, particularly integrated marketing, which is the coor-dinated combination of advertising, promotion, and public relations.[7] Critics lament that baseball has not developed a strong fan base among the young or among African Americans of any age, and has not effec-tively promoted its stars.[8]

Although aesthetics and marketing are concerns, MLB's status as a national television attraction has also been influenced by primary struc-tural problems that are economic and historical. Baseball has always been the sport with the most games (product) to sell. Baseball offers 162 regular-season games per team compared to 16 for the National Football League (NFL) and 82 for the National Basketball Association (NBA) and the National Hockey League (NHL). The abundance of product reduces the national network ratings for the game, excepting once-a-year events such as the All-Star Game and the World Series. And even these long-standing ratings successes are in decline.

The Lineup Card

We have written this book to interest baseball fans, scholars of baseball and the media, and anyone curious about the twentieth-century history of these two significant bulwarks of American culture. Our purpose is to provide for the first time in one volume:

1. A history of MLB's nearly seventy-year relationship with television, emphasizing how a pretelevision entity like baseball deals with the most powerful of all media.
2. An analysis of the business dealings between MLB and television entities from the 1940s to the present. We focus particularly on the changing symbiotic relationship of sports and television, how and under what circumstances the mutually beneficial relationship has shifted over time.
3. A consideration of how the game has changed for television viewers. How did television adapt its production limitations to a game that has often been described as "unfriendly" to television? How has the baseball announcer adjusted to the demands of the medium?
4. A look at how the MLB and television relationship is evolving. How is MLB leveraging what it calls "Advanced Media"? Will the rise of the Internet, satellite radio, and broadband high-definition television create more revenue imbalance in the game, therefore widening the economic gap between large- and small-market teams? Or, does the posttelevision era offer MLB a way to build and share more prosperity?

We have divided the book into five thematic sections that include chapters exploring the most important issues in the baseball-television relationship.

The Local Game

Part I will explore the earliest days of baseball on television. Here we will present a prehistory of the MLB-television relationship. In this period (1939–52), baseball was the indisputable national pastime and thus one of the first sports to be covered extensively by the new medium. During this era, television evolved from an experimental medium reaching only a few hundred receivers to a national phenomenon in millions of households. Since no one could foresee the impact of television, baseball owners' reactions to the new medium were mixed, ranging from fear that the "box" posed dangerous box-office competition, to a belief that television would be the greatest boon ever for the game.

The emphasis of this section of the book is on local telecasting of games. National television networks did not develop until the late 1940s, and could not deliver a live coast-to-coast signal until 1951. There was no coherent MLB-wide national television policy for regular-season games until 1966. Excepting the World Series and the All-Star Game, each owner determined his team's television policy. As the television industry diffused into almost all U.S. households during the 1950s, the medium presented different challenges and opportunities in different markets. Though some of these differences were based on geography, many reflected decisions made by individual teams, controlled by owners who either embraced the new medium or disdained it.

The National Game

Part II will consider the national television arrangements that MLB has made over nearly sixty years, focusing particularly upon the World Series. Despite declining ratings, the Fall Classic remains the "crown jewel" of the game, justifying impressive rights fees that seem to be out of line with the Series' audience appeal. The World Series and, to a lesser degree, the All-Star Game are events that draw casual fans to the televised game. These "big ticket" games also stimulated networks to introduce innovations in production techniques or announcing configurations.

Regular-season MLB games first came to national network television in 1953 with ABC's *Game of the Week*. These weekend games lifted Dizzy Dean and Leo Durocher to national prominence. For millions of Americans, the colorful commentary by "The Lip" and "Ole Diz" was their initiation into televised baseball.

By the time NBC became the first truly national home of the game of the week in 1966 much had changed. Slick, professional Curt Gowdy became NBC's national voice of the game. But by this time, the NFL was replacing baseball in the hearts and minds of the majority of American sports fans. Beginning in the mid-1970s, NBC and ABC attempted to raise the profile and popularity of the game through prime-time telecasts. Though baseball's prime-time telecasts never matched the popularity of the NFL's, they demonstrated that broadcast networks still valued MLB, even as many individual owners began their long and counterproductive "war" against the newly empowered players.

The birth of the cable era enhanced the value of baseball's television rights. Technological, regulatory, and judicial changes in the 1970s allowed cable television to connect to an increasing number of U.S. households and become a serious competitor for the dominant broadcast television industry. Cable was hungry for popular first-run programming, and baseball was a major contributor. Although inequitable distribution of cable revenues increased the gap between "have" and "have-not" teams, it provided MLB with a substantial new source of revenue and marketing opportunities.

Television and Baseball's Dysfunctional Marriage

What has television done to baseball? What has television done for baseball? These are the questions we will explore in part III. Unlike many earlier commentators, we do not believe that television has harmed baseball.

Over the past fifty years, television has been blamed for a range of baseball's problems, including the retraction of the minor leagues and the relocation of two of New York City's two National League teams to the West Coast in 1958. As traumatic as these events were to minor league teams and to the supporters of the Brooklyn Dodgers and the New York Giants, it is simplistic and erroneous to attribute these changes solely to the effects of television.

Television had a large impact on baseball, as it did on all existing media and on television's business partners. The owners' "television-enhanced" revenues altered irrevocably the economics of the game. As baseball became a more lucrative business, the players demanded a fairer share of industry revenues. Owners found it increasingly difficult to deny basic labor rights to the players as they and the public watched television money swell club profits. Television publicized the labor/management dispute more emphatically than radio or the tradition-bound print media had ever done.

Television also stimulated more scrutiny of baseball by lawmakers. Protecting the "national pastime" proved a popular pastime for members of Congress. Minor league contraction, the shift of franchises, and the threat of baseball moving from "free" to pay television have all provided plenty of fodder for legislative and judicial posturing. Although baseball has maintained its Supreme Court–granted antitrust exemption, the franchise owners and their commissioner are no longer treated with the deference they enjoyed before the rise of television.

Television has redefined baseball and all other major sports. Baseball is no longer regarded as a national trust. It has become just another business. Many "purist" fans lament the loss of baseball's innocence and status as the "national pastime." However, baseball purists are not likely to rein in the forces of an advanced capitalist economy. Major League Baseball is a large and growing business.

Like all businesses, baseball seeks to maximize revenue and profits. It has become more than a sport; it is now a media commodity and media partner. This relationship is complex, dynamic, and symbiotic. In the past sixty years, MLB has become a major provider of sports product valued by broadcast and cable networks, and essential to regional sports networks (RSNs) on cable and satellite systems.

One of the major buzz phrases of the 1990s and into this decade has been "synergy." Jointly, industries with synergy would become a more powerful economic and cultural force than they could have become separately. In the sports-media world, synergy applied to the contractual relationships between media companies and sports teams, including occasional co-ownership. In part III, we examine MLB's unique synergistic partnerships with television industry.

How the Game Was Covered

Part IV explores what viewers actually saw or heard on their television sets. Though radio announcers have been the subject of considerable attention in many biographies, the challenges faced by the television announcer in adapting to the medium have received less discussion. We examine how baseball announcers, schooled in the radio era, prospered in the new medium. We also introduce a "MAT" (medium, announcer, and team) theory of announcing that helps explain why some announcers became legends while others labored in relative obscurity. Finally, we document announcers' struggle for control of the telecast as their words competed with images for the viewers' attention.

As many biographies attest, the public recognizes and applauds its favorite announcers. But they are not the most important members of the television crew. Anonymous directors of the baseball telecast control the important visual dimension of the telecast. As a problematic television sport, baseball has always been a challenge for the director. The large and asymmetrical size of the field, the small size of the ball, and the shifts of action from and within the infield and outfield have all bedeviled television production of baseball. No previous study has documented how directors and their crews have met these challenges since the first televised games. We examine the evolution of production practices from the two-camera setups with hand-lettered graphics in the 1940s to today's productions featuring a multitude of cameras, digital replay, and "FoxBox" graphics.

Epilogue: Baseball in the Advanced Media Age

We conclude our book by examining the rapidly changing world of new media. Though television has changed baseball, the medium also has changed. Thirty years ago, a viewer had only two venues for televised baseball: the local team on a nearby broadcast station or a game featuring out-of-market teams on a national Saturday afternoon or Monday night telecast. If they are willing to pay, today's fans can also watch most or all of their home-team games on their RSN available on cable or satellite. They also can watch several games a week on ESPN, ESPN2, and, beginning in 2008, TBS and TNT. For more money, fans with DirecTV satellite or cable service can watch hundreds of out-of-market games on MLB's "Extra Innings" package, or they can receive the out-of-market games via the MLB.com web site. MLB.com also includes archived games that fans can watch as many times as they desire. Fantasy baseball games can be played on hand-held devices that combine a mobile phone, music player, and camera. Game highlights and scores are available from scores of Internet sites, the local newspaper, local radio and television cable and broadcast sportscasts, a twenty-four-hour cable sports news service (ESPNEWS) and, soon, a twenty-four-hour-a-day Baseball Channel.

The explosion in game presentation and game information availability continues. The television industry is merging with the Internet, making it less dependent on its traditional broadcast or cable delivery systems. Advanced media are giving baseball an opportunity to address some of the problems that television helped generate. Our account of MLB's efforts to exploit these changes will conclude our history of television and baseball.

Why a Book on Televised Baseball?

There are several reasons for the relative paucity of baseball and television studies. First, serious baseball scholarship, and sports scholarship in general, have only recently gained credibility in mainstream academia. Departments of economics, English, history, sociology, and mass communication, and schools of business now employ and produce a growing number of scholars who recognize the cultural and economic significance of sports.

Of course, baseball does have a voluminous and longstanding print-industry history. However, until recently, those offerings were designed for a general, or even juvenile, reader. Not until the 1970s and 1980s did literature on baseball move beyond nostalgic reminiscences and fiction to explore the intricacies of the game. The advent of personal computers, fantasy baseball, and an increasingly well-educated fan base made publications on statistical analysis a major new category of baseball literature. These factors also contributed to an increase in serious historical accounts of Major League Baseball.

With the advent of free agency in the mid-1970s, the amounts of money made and spent in MLB increased dramatically. Business publications and presses responded to the increasing cultural fascination with the political economy of the sport. The business of baseball joined history and quantitative analyses as a third major topic for baseball publications.

A history of baseball's relationship with television became essential once baseball research was legitimized as an academic topic. However, academic resistance is not the only reason no history of televised baseball has been written. Another factor is baseball's myth of nostalgia, a source of the game's charms and its problems.

The Myth of Nostalgia

Baseball has the most historical resonance of any sport in the United States. The game boasts a 150-year history in the U.S. and recognition as the "national pastime." It played a significant role in the assimilation of the great wave of immigrants between 1880 and 1920. Baseball is mythologized in "fathers and sons" traditions handed down from generation to generation. But baseball's myth of nostalgia is a costly one.

Looking backward alienates the young, who would rather anticipate the future. Younger fans do not follow the game with the passion of their parents and grandparents. Many young people view baseball as "old-fashioned," "slow," and only one of many sports, entertainment, and leisure activities. Mature fans exacerbated their disaffection by pining for baseball's "good old days" before free agency, multimillion-dollar multiyear contracts, television, or "cookie-cutter" stadiums.

Television has long been one of the major "villains" in baseball's nostalgic narrative. Television is accused of "ruining" the game by inadequate coverage, slowing the game down with too many commercial breaks, and exacerbating the revenue disparity between rich and poor teams. Players also are criticized in nostalgic interpretations of baseball's fall from primal innocence. Such nostalgic mythmaking is a long-standing tradition in baseball and can border on the ridiculous.

In 1960, forty-year-old White Sox pitcher Gerry Staley declared that "TV Makes Sissies!" Staley believed that younger pitchers "don't want to look bad on television" and "don't want people to think they're like the villains in wrestling matches." He claimed that they "are scared of the batter" and "a lot of 'em are 'sissies,' nowdays."[9] And if creating sissies was not enough, television also "ruined" catchers. After White Sox manager Al Lopez criticized catchers for poor positioning, forcing them to catch the ball with one hand rather than two, he homed in on the source of the problem. "Do you know what I think? I think today's catcher is a television actor. He's conscious of the cameras and wants to look good. Well, maybe he does, but he doesn't catch good."[10] (Or perhaps, young catchers just wanted to save their throwing hands from abuse by taking advantage of the larger catchers' mitts of their era.)

Free agency brought a more serious round of criticism. For over thirty years, owners and the more sycophantic baseball writers have contributed to fan alienation by blaming greedy players for the declining state of the game. Who wants to "buy" a product that the seller is always knocking?

The aura surrounding radio's "Golden Age" baseball coverage has contributed to the myth of nostalgia. Many essays have focused on the "glory days" of baseball heard on the radio. Though we are not suggesting that Red Barber, Vin Scully, Mel Allen, Jack Buck, Harry Caray, Ernie Harwell, Bob Prince, and many others were not important in the lives of millions of fans, the emphasis on baseball as a *radio sport* has been self-defeating. An emphasis on radio stars who, with a few exceptions such as Scully and Caray, are unknown to most of today's fans, makes baseball seem even more "unhip" and out of touch. Audience ratings have always demonstrated that fans preferred their baseball on television when given a choice. But those writing about the two media have usually waxed nostalgic for the radio version.

Our Approach

Some of the seminal works on baseball history were largely based on oral history. These books are essential to our understanding of the social and cultural development of the game. The most comprehensive account of baseball and broadcasting has been Smith's work on baseball's broadcasters, which focuses on pretelevision announcers.[11] In addition, fans have been able to enjoy biographies and autobiographies of many of the most famous local and national broadcasters, primarily from the radio era.[12] This growing body of work is an important contribution to the literature of baseball history. As important as they are to fans, announcers are but one part of that story.

We document a part of baseball's history that has been mostly ignored: the story of television's impact on baseball during their nearly seven decades together. Included here is both what the game looked like to the television viewer and the behind-the-scenes corporate and government decisions that directly affected the type and amount of television coverage made available to the fan. However, we do not intend to discuss all applications of video. Excluded in this history are the many uses of television as part of the in-game experience at the ballpark, the use of video as an instructional tool for players, and television advertising and promotion for a specific team or a nationally telecast series of games. We will draw much of our review from dozens of books and over fifteen hundred newspaper, magazine, and Internet articles published throughout the history of televised baseball. In addition to these secondary sources, we incorporate into our history information from primary documents in media archives, the National Baseball Hall of Fame Library, the *Sporting News* archive in St. Louis, and interviews with both baseball and television executives.

Our primary goal is to produce the first book-length account of the relationship between Major League Baseball and the U.S. television industry. Though we have no doubt committed errors of omission, we will be gratified if our effort provokes more studies of the very important dynamics of that relationship.

We tell a story of interest to multiple audiences. Fans of the game will gain a fuller appreciation of how the baseball telecast they currently view evolved over the decades. We also hope that scholars of both baseball and the television industry gain a deeper understanding of this dynamic economic and cultural relationship.

The Local Game

1

The Experimental Years

Although NBC's May 17, 1939, telecast of a college game between Columbia and Princeton from Baker Field in New York is widely considered the first televised baseball game, there are several other claims to the title. As with many "firsts" in history, the prize goes to the event that was "first" in publicity rather than the chronological first. The NBC telecast was announced in advance and publicized in New York.[1] Earlier experiments and demonstrations received little or no exposure.

Before the Beginning

Illustrations showing fans watching baseball on television appeared regularly in the popular press in the 1920s and '30s. As baseball was America's most popular sport, baseball telecasts exemplified the promise of television, and the medium's promoters jumped on it. In one 1922 image from *Science and Invention*, a professorial looking man stares intently through his monocle at a television a few inches away, as two colleagues in the background look on. A 1935 *Radio-Craft* cover features an illustration of three men, fists clenched, watching a receiver designed to improve upon the small picture size of early television by providing a private screen for each viewer. Illustrations were easy to create, but covering actual games was very difficult given the low-resolution mechanical systems of the era.

The earliest dated reference to a televised game appears in *Television News* in December 1931. The magazine's cover announces "baseball game successfully televised," but the story inside is based on a single photograph from a Japanese magazine. The article features an artist's rendering of the photo, and "judging by the original photograph . . . the televiser utilized for picking up the baseball game was a stationary affair

1. The anticipation of TV baseball is as old as television itself, as this 1922 image shows.

. . . focused across the home plate."[2] The image could not have been very clear since the systems at that time used only 60 scanning lines, whereas the standard U.S. television today has 525. Consequently, a shot of a player could devote only about 4 lines to reproducing the player's face. About the same time in Boston, television developer Hollis Baird reportedly used a mechanical television system to televise games played at Fenway Park. The camera was positioned on his rooftop and pointed across the street at the ballpark.[3]

In February 1937, the *Sporting News* reported that Connie Mack was asked about the upcoming season by newsman Boake Carter on Philco's experimental TV station in Philadelphia, making the seventy-four-year-old Mack television's first documented baseball interviewee. Although

2. A 1931 illustration of a game reportedly televised in Japan.

the grand old man of baseball was not quoted about television, he did claim that radio "broadcasting of games has helped attendance, rather than hurt it, on the same basis that the newspapers stimulate baseball attendance in ratio to the space they devote to the game."[4]

In late March of 1939, Mutual Broadcast Network telecast from a Los Angeles studio an interview with the manager and several players of the Pacific Coast League's Los Angeles Angels. The Sporting News suggested that the studio interviews were a step in the right direction, but that "the time may be rather distant when the fan can sit at his home and not only hear an account of the games but witness the players in action as well." Less than two months later, NBC's experimental station, W2XBS, in New York would dash that prediction by airing the first televised baseball game. The Sporting News' photograph of the Angels' interview shows the players in white socks and dark leggings. Apparently, the players were not told to appear in street shoes instead of spikes that might damage the studio floor. Fortunately, the television camera is tilted up to hide the feet of these "Shoeless Joes."[5] These few documented events suggest that baseball was the focus of some television experimentation, making it likely that other appearances of baseball personalities, and perhaps even games, went unreported before NBC's first baseball telecast.

NBC's First Game: "A 42nd Street Flea Circus"

Early experiments aside, the first widely publicized televising of a baseball game took place on May 17, 1939. The summer of 1939 was the time of the New York World's Fair, and the fair's theme was the "World of Tomorrow." For NBC and its parent company, RCA, the world of tomorrow would be seen on television, and "tomorrow" meant the very next day.

Throughout that summer and the next year, RCA used the remote truck of its experimental station, W2XBS, to cover outdoor events throughout New York City. The summer mobile-unit schedule included a six-day bicycle race, the arrival of the king and queen of England at the World's Fair, the Nova-Baer prizefight, a musical ride of the Canadian Northwest Mounted Police, and the Eastern Grass Court Tennis Championships. In all, W2XBS would telecast fifty-nine remote programs in what RCA called "Television's First Year."[6] Sports and other remote events, along with studio programs and films, fed W2XBS's ambitious first year of programming.

The impetus behind RCA's packed programming schedule on W2XBS was a push for its 441-line system of television. RCA hoped that the Federal Communications Commission (FCC) would accept its system as the de facto standard in the United States. RCA had used the same strategy in radio two decades earlier. Ultimately, the FCC rejected RCA's standard, however, adopting the National Television System Committee's 525-line system. But from April 1939 until the approval of the NTSC standard in 1941, RCA filled the New York ether with remote programming from locations all over the city.

As the most important sport of the era, baseball had to be included, and quickly. A 1940 survey of 2,050 World's Fair visitors found that baseball was the most popular television sport, gaining 384 votes to football's 343 and boxing's 275.[7] For their second remote telecast, only three weeks after NBC first televised the opening of the World's Fair, the network therefore turned its primitive iconoscope camera to the national pastime with Bill Stern, NBC's best-known sports personality, presiding.

As a sports commentator, Stern was not the epitome of accuracy. Red Barber described how Stern would work himself out of a tight situation on the radio: "He [Stern] never admitted he made a mistake. When Stern would do a football game and name the wrong ball carrier, he would simply pretend the wrong man lateralled the ball to the right man. College football never had so many single and double and triple laterals as when Stern had the mike."[8] Despite his creative reporting, three things are certainly true about Bill Stern: he was one of the most popular figures in radio sports in the middle of the twentieth century, he was the announcer of the first televised baseball game, and at that first game, he had no idea of what he was doing.

Played at Columbia University's Baker Field, the first televised baseball game was the nightcap of a doubleheader won by Princeton 3 to 2 in ten innings. There were about four hundred receivers in the New York area, although most of the audience probably viewed the game at the RCA television facility in Rockefeller Center. The telecast was not "big league" in any way, and it wasn't just that the competitors were college teams. Produced by television program manager Thomas H. Hutchinson and directed by Burke Crotty at a cost of $3,000 for NBC's experimental station W2XBS, the coverage used only one low-resolution iconoscope camera on a twelve-foot platform positioned on a hill along the third base line. The camera was stationed far from the action, and its lens could provide only a distant view of the game. Every time the ball was put in play, the camera had to pan quickly to the left to follow it. The *New York Times'* radio reporter, Orrin E. Dunlap, described the dizzying view: "the lone camera sees the pitcher as he winds up on the mound and then quickly swivels to the home plate to catch the play with the batter, catcher, and umpire flashing into view. If it's a hit the camera follows it down to first base; if a home run it makes the circuit with the runner."[9]

The ball was so small that it was impossible to see it on the tiny television screens of the day. "Too often when the specklike ball was struck 'it ne'er was found.'"[10] Since the camera could not include both the pitcher's box and home plate, it "was focused on the mound for the wind-up and quickly followed the ball to the batter and catcher."[11] The camera had no long lens capable of magnifying the action so the players, in the words of the *Times*, looked like "little white flies." *Variety* suggested that without the announcer's commentary, the production would have resembled "a 42nd street flea circus."[12]

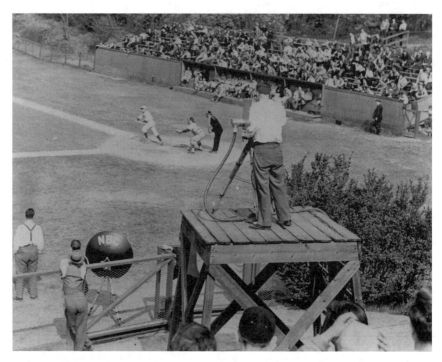

3. A single camera captured NBC's first baseball telecast, a college game in May 1939. National Baseball Hall of Fame Library, Cooperstown NY.

By positioning the camera to the side of the main action—the pitcher throwing the ball and the batter swinging—the director failed to follow one of the rules of good television: action should be staged at the center of the screen with motion coming toward and away from the viewer, rather than from side to side. But this was 1939, and there were few fast rules for good television.

Although the video coverage was disappointing for both technical and artistic reasons, the announcing was even worse. Stern worked with no monitor or audio connection to the director and thus had no idea what the camera was showing at any given time. With no chance to coordinate his commentary with the video action, Stern simply called the game as though it was on radio, describing all of the action whether the audience could see it or not. The cardinal rule for today's televised baseball announcers is that their coverage should enhance the action the viewer sees rather than provide verbal repetition of the video coverage. But this

8

4. The primal scene: a photograph of a TV image from NBC's first game.
Photo by Ralph Morse/Pix Inc. / Time Life Pictures / Getty Images.

was another rule yet to be codified, and even the egotistical Stern knew that coverage could be much better. After the broadcast he lamented, "in that one game, we learned a complete lesson about how not to televise a sports event."[13]

The New York Times' Dunlap offered his own suggestions for improvement, outlining a prophetic plan for camera assignments: "Baseball by television calls for three or four cameras, the views of which can be blended, as the action calls for it. There might be one 'eye' fixed on the home plate; one off first base to cover the infield; one in the outfield and another perched atop the grandstand for a bird's-eye view of the entire field. Still another might be given a roving assignment to survey the dugout, the bleachers, also to follow the ball in flight and telecast various sidelights." But even if coverage improved, Dunlap thought that the television experience would still be second best: "the imprisoned baseball fan becomes restless; his eyes tire. He knows he is missing so much. His eyes cannot wander off to look at the landscape, the near-by trees and apartment-fringed skyline of upper Manhattan. . . . In fact after

5. Bill Stern conducts the first postgame interview.
National Baseball Hall of Fame Library, Cooperstown NY.

an inning or two the viewer may feel like singing that old refrain, 'Take Me Out to the Ball Game.'"[14]

Others, however, worried that televised baseball might eventually become too good. One of the college coaches told Stern that he expected television to become so successful that eventually there will "be nobody watching the games from the sidelines."[15] *Life* magazine offered a photograph of the game declaring that the "reception that day was rather fuzzy," but "within ten years an audience of 10,000,000, sitting at home or in movie theaters, will see the World Series."[16] *Life*'s estimate was, if anything, conservative. The World Series would first be telecast in 1947, and an estimated thirty-eight million Americans would watch some part of the 1950 World Series.[17]

Bill Stern is also credited (by Bill Stern) with covering the first Major League baseball game "early in the war."[18] But like some of his radio commentary, Stern's account of this television first is a fiction. The first televised Major League game was on August 26, 1939, and its announcer, unlike Stern, was not a national figure at the time. He was an articulate storyteller from the Old South who had just come to Brooklyn after five years at Cincinnati. He began the first televised Major League game with "This is Red Barber speaking. Let me say hello to you all."[19]

Although he worked for the Dodgers' Larry MacPhail, Barber was no stranger to NBC. In the mid-1930s NBC had scouted the then WLW-Cincinnati announcer, bringing him to New York to discuss an announcer's position. Alfred H. Morton, NBC's program department manager, viewed Barber as an "ambitious young man of 29" with "a determination to be the outstanding sports announcer in the country." Indeed, Barber told NBC that he did not see himself as a general announcer, "but as a specialist in sports." Although initially impressed, the network concluded that Barber was "a little too much of a prima donna for us" and "just a trifle conceited."[20]

The First Major League Game

Like the first college game, the first Major League Baseball TV games were telecast by NBC's experimental station W2XBS. As part of the push for its television standard, RCA created its first remote television facility in 1937, allowing the station to telecast events in the New York area. At a cost of $125,000, the facility consisted of two buses: one for the transmitting and one for the production equipment.[21]

RCA's ally in this first Major League broadcast was Barber, who brought the idea to Larry MacPhail, general manager of the Brooklyn Dodgers. NBC's Alfred "Doc" Morton approached Barber and the Dodgers only after the Yankees and Giants turned NBC down.[22] But MacPhail always believed in the power of radio to promote baseball, and he saw television as baseball's newest salesman. Before the arrival of MacPhail, the three New York teams had a five-year ban on radio broadcasts because they believed game broadcasts reduced attendance. MacPhail ended the radio embargo, and the other teams followed quickly. According to Barber, when asked if he would like the honor of the first Major League telecast, MacPhail said, "I'd love it."[23]

6. *Red Barber interviews Leo Durocher at* NBC's *first* MLB *game in August 1939.*
AP/Wide World Photos.

For the cost of a new television receiver placed in the pressroom and price of admission for the crew, RCA secured the right to telecast the August 26, 1939, doubleheader between the Brooklyn Dodgers and the Cincinnati Reds from Ebbets Field and to use the Dodgers' chief radio announcer. Barber recalls only the first game being telecast, but other sources indicate that both games were carried.[24] RCA advertised the game in the August 24th *Brooklyn Eagle*, urging Dodger fans to "See Big League Baseball for the first time by Television at any RCA Victor Television Dealer's Store."[25] Dodger fans were partially disappointed in what they saw on the dealer's tube. The Reds, who would take home their first pennant in twenty years that fall, won the first game 5 to 2, while the Dodgers rebounded in the nightcap for a 6 to 1 victory. Many more fans watched the game in the stands (33,535) than on the estimated four hundred sets in the New York area.

For the players, the new medium was hardly noticed. In 1987, a Penn State University graduate student asked players and officials who participated in the game to write him with their recollections. Most could not remember much about the first televised MLB contest. Gabe Paul, Reds publicity director at the time, reported, "there was very little reaction by the players to the event."[26] However, one player, Reds outfielder Harry Craft, reported seeing some of the game with other players: "The screen was full of snow and the players were silhouettes. We recognized them by their mannerisms, batting stance, swing, running, fielding, and throwing. We wondered if they would ever, ever be able to clear up the picture, and see all the action on the field—but I for one, never dreamed of anyone walking on the moon but Buck Rogers."[27]

A Better Approach for Baseball

After its poor first effort at Baker Field, RCA knew that one camera would not be enough to cover baseball, so it added another. One camera was placed at field level in the stands to the left of home plate, while the second camera was positioned in the upper deck above third base. Beside it sat Red Barber. The additional camera, closer placement, and the addition of telephoto lenses resulted in a far better review of the first MLB game telecast in the *New York Times*: "The spheroid which appeared only occasionally as a white streak across home plate at Baker Field was clearly followed at Ebbets Field when pitched, hit for a line drive or as it bounced across the grass. Baseball becomes a natural for television. . . . All in all, the baseball enthusiast sitting in a comfortable chair at home gets a more intimate glimpse of the players than do the majority in the grandstands."[28] The game also was enthusiastically received at RCA's World's Fair television building where an overflow crowd watched. A Broadway theater that had advertised the game was reportedly "swamped by the inquisitive."[29]

For his part, Barber found the announcer's task daunting that day and not particularly rewarding. He was moved from his radio announcer's booth "catbird seat" and into the direct sunlight in the stands. Although he had audio contact with the director, he had no monitor so he could not see what the audience viewed. The director, Burke Crotty, "every once and a while . . . would holler at me through the earphones that the camera was on second base now or it was on the pitcher. But only once in a while."[30] The earphones also went out occasionally, leaving Barber to infer what the viewer saw by noting which camera had its red light on and its direction. Despite the problems, Barber reminded viewers several times during the telecast that the viewers were seeing "an historic first."[31]

After the game, Barber rushed from his upper-deck perch to the field to interview Dodger player-manager Leo Durocher, who had gone 0 for 3; Reds manager Bill McKechnie; and several players, who were eager to appear on the new medium. For his part in the historic first broadcast, NBC later sent Barber a silver cigarette box inscribed, "To Red Barber Pioneer Television Sports Announcer in grateful appreciation National Broadcasting Company August 26, 1939." NBC also sent Barber a bill for $35 to cover the cost of this souvenir.[32]

Although commercial television's official launch was nearly two years away, Barber still played TV pitchman for three Dodger radio sponsors: Wheaties, Socony-Vacuum Oil Co., and Ivory Soap. Exploiting the visual side of television, he waved a stack of stage money to signify the $1,000 that could be won in a Procter and Gamble contest, and later demonstrated the culinary art of breakfast preparation by making a bowl of Wheaties with sugar, cream, and a banana. Since the ads in these games were aired at no charge, they did not violate existing FCC's rules prohibiting commercial sponsorship of television programs.

Advertisers leasing outfield wall billboards also benefited from TV exposure, when cameras framed the action against their backdrops. The trade publication *Broadcasting* reported that "the Gem razor ad in the right field, showed up as well on the television receiver screens as in the park," noting that "sponsors of ball games will have to take over the billboards at the parks as well, or see other advertisers get as much benefit from telecasts as they do."[33] *Variety* suggested that the Calvert billboard was the "first liquor commercial on a major network," since the National Association of Broadcasters (NAB) had a prohibition against such ads at the time.[34] In the next decade, cameras would be placed and shots framed to avoid such commercial freeloading. Eventually, ballpark signage would be incorporated into the television image. Today, signs are placed on the wall behind home plate at many ballparks, so the ads can be seen from the center field camera during much of the game.

More Games Follow

The second televised professional baseball game took place three thousand miles away in the other American mass media hub, Hollywood. Don Lee Broadcasting station w6xao telecast the opening Pacific Coast League contest on March 30, 1940, between the Hollywood Stars and the Seattle Rainiers, making it television's first minor league game. And a few other Hollywood stars showed up, including actor George Raft, and radio comedians George Burns and Gracie Allen. Two starlets posed for the camera with Stars' manager Bill Sweeney, bringing "a little typical Hollywood oomph to the broadcast."[35] Although there were only about three hundred receivers in the area, the broadcast still caused a stir. To keep traffic flowing, police dispersed a crowd that gathered in front of a Long Beach shop that was showing the game. These Southern California pedestrians would be some of many fans to gain their initial experience of televised baseball from a receiver in their local retailer's display window. As in the first Major League game, the home team, in this case the Stars, took it on the chin, losing to the Rainiers 11 to 4.

N BC's second Major League telecast was also its first grand opening. Two sixty-second commercials for Ivory Soap were part of the Dodgers and Giants contest from Ebbets Field on opening day, April 19, 1940.[36] Ivory's parent company, Procter and Gamble, was a co-sponsor of the Dodger radio broadcasts. In one spot, the TV pitchman demonstrated the soap's foaming action in a glass of water. In the second, he used red and white gloves to show how Ivory cleans hands. Although the benefits of the first television advertisements were minimal, considering the tiny potential audience, they demonstrated from the outset that televised baseball and advertising would be partners.

This second Major League game was broadcast in New York City and retransmitted to fifty patients at the Metropolitan Sanitarium in Mount McGregor by a General Electric relay station near Schenectady, New York. This made the telecast baseball's first networked game. One day earlier, the opening International League contest featuring Montreal at Jersey City was telecast from Roosevelt Stadium. Telecasts of Major League games from Ebbets Field continued sporadically during the 1940 season, along with college games from Columbia and Fordham Universities.

Major League telecasts increased to a rate of one or so a week the next season. On June 11, 1941, NBC's W2XBS telecast the first night game using two side-by-side cameras on the second deck at Ebbets Field above the third base dugout.[37] The game was scheduled to start at 8:45, much later than a typical night game, presumably so the iconoscope cameras could to be calibrated exclusively for night baseball. The trade magazine *Radio & Television* reported that the "results are amazingly good . . . skeptical set owners, who had expected to see dark grey [sic] figures cavorting on an ebony field, were pleasantly surprised, for the illumination was apparently as brilliant and more uniform than natural sunshine."[38] However, the Dodgers would have preferred a better result, dropping an 8-to-1 decision to the Pirates. Three weeks after the first night game, commercial television would begin, and telecasters would start charging for their time.

Commercial Television Debuts at the Ballpark

The first program on the first day of commercial television, July 1, 1941, was a baseball game. The 2:00 p.m. game, once again from Ebbets Field, featured the Dodgers against the Philadelphia Phillies. The telecast over NBC's newly christened commercial station, WNBT, included what is usually credited as the first paid television commercial. At a cost of $4, the Bulova Watch Company presented a video version of its radio time signal, showing "a standard test pattern, fitted with hands like a clock and bearing the name of the sponsor."[39] Bulova then signed a thirteen-week contract for daily time signals.

Other sponsors came aboard, including Adams Hat Stores. Adams told NBC that it wanted to be the "first to go on record to give you an order for television facilities covering all the sports events [including baseball] on contract."[40] WNBT charged advertisers $90 for each hour of weekend afternoon programming, meaning that the typical two-and-a-half-hour Saturday afternoon baseball game would cost sponsors $210 in time charges.[41] Television's twenty-year experimental period finally appeared to be ending. However, the events of December 7, 1941, quickly brought to a conclusion television's first period of commercial operation.

Although television did not go completely black during World War II, it did revert to its experimental past. A few stations remained on the air with only a few hours of programming a week. Starting with a rodeo in October 1943, WNBT offered regular remote broadcasts, including prizefights, track, hockey, and basketball from Madison Square Garden, using the newly developed orthicon camera pickup tubes, which operated better in lower light. The telecasts were not sponsored and were "chiefly for the enjoyment of wounded servicemen in hospitals in the New York area."[42] Baseball remained part of the show with a few live games televised in New York, starting in 1944. WNBT telecast two MLB games, one from the Polo Grounds and one from Yankee Stadium. NBC called the Yankee Stadium telecast a "failure" because of radio frequency interference.[43] When live transmission was not possible, games were filmed. The American Network filmed the *Esquire* All-American Boys baseball game and aired the film the same evening on WABD, New York.[44]

Emerging from War Time

By 1945, televised baseball had become a weekly event aired primarily to entertain veterans in New York–area hospitals. In June, Supreme Allied Commander Dwight Eisenhower attended a Giants-Braves game at the Polo Grounds, and an improving medium covered the event. The broadcast was a success, despite the overcast and rainy day, because television's faster camera lenses and improved pickup tubes produced better images in lower light. The future president waved "a greeting to the hospitalized veterans . . . demonstrating again the famed Eisenhower smile."[45] Later that month, NBC telecast the contest between the Yankees and the Detroit Tigers, marking the return of Burke Crotty, NBC's prewar pioneering director, from the army. But despite improved image quality, technical problems forced NBC to cover most of this game with one camera rather than the two assigned to it.[46]

In Chicago, technical problems initially proved an even greater barrier. WBKB had widely publicized the Cubs' home opener on April 20,

1946, as the season's first telecast. But it "resulted in nothing more than a second-rate audio play-by-play with a test pattern on the screen."[47] Although Bill Eddy, WBKB station manager, had run several tests prior to the game, when the actual coverage began, interference from the power system for the elevators in the station's headquarters overpowered the transmission. WBKB's plans had called for one announcer to do the play-by-play from Wrigley Field, while a second handled a between-inning summary from the studio. Only the game audio and the studio summary were broadcast.

The snafu was only temporary. WBKB successfully telecast Cubs home games during the second half of the 1946 season, starting July 13 at Wrigley Field against the Dodgers and continuing at the rate of about four games a week until the end of the season. The first Cubs television announcer was Jack Gibney, WBKB's staff announcer, and Reinald Werrenrath Jr., head of the station's special events division, directed the telecasts.[48]

Although more regular television coverage of baseball began in 1946, the most significant TV sports event of that year was the June 19 heavyweight boxing championship between Joe Louis and Billy Conn, the first title fight ever televised. The much-anticipated rematch between the champ and the boxer who had almost defeated him in 1941 was a bit of a bust. Lewis stopped Conn in the eighth round. NBC transmitted the fight on its infant network, linking stations in New York (WNBT), Philadelphia (WPTZ), and Washington (W3XWT). The fight's coverage generated considerable publicity for televised sports and dramatically revealed the potential of networking major events. Members of Congress and the Truman administration watched the fight in DC, while TV dealers were "swamped" with requests for rental sets in New York, a metropolitan area that already had three thousand receivers.[49]

In September 1946, CBS used a boxing exhibition in its New York studio to demonstrate its color television system. The New York Times reported that the "fast boxing contest" yielded "good visual results."[50] Televised sports also received a boost when the Army-Navy football game was televised by RCA to an estimated audience of 235,000 in the Philadelphia area, while "only" 100,000 saw the game in person.[51]

7. Two NBC cameras covered the game from the third base stands at Ebbets Field in 1940. Photo by NB Universal Photo Bank.

Although these events demonstrated its rich potential, televised sports, especially baseball, also began to draw criticism for its approach to the game. Much of that disapproval came from *Variety*, the voice of the established entertainment vehicles of stage, screen, and radio. *Variety*'s review of the May 26, 1946, telecast of the New York Giants–Boston Braves game illustrates how the expectations for televised baseball were rising.

The NBC telecast used two cameras, both from the third base side. One focused on the pitcher and the infield, while the second covered the batter. When the pitcher released the ball the director switched to the camera covering the batter. If the hitter connected, the director switched back as the "pitcher's" camera followed the ball in the infield or outfield. Although the ball was still too small to be seen, the viewer "is able to follow the game with ease." But the director still missed some plays. Fortunately, the small audience for televised games made this "the right time to experiment."[52]

According to Variety, baseball owners should not worry about televised baseball's taking "a big slice out of their gate receipts. WNBT's telecasts of the N.Y. home teams' games prove their fears to be groundless." Though acknowledging that the televised picture was better than the distant view most fans experienced at a game, Variety observed that "it's virtually impossible at the present developmental stage of video for a person watching the game from his home to get even a small share of the feeling and color that's made baseball the national pastime."[53] Variety believed that owners had nothing to fear from TV; the new medium would "hypo" the game by attracting new fans to the ballpark, just as radio had.

By August 1946, NBC had added a third camera for its coverage of the Red Sox–Yankee game at the Stadium, and Variety's review of the video coverage was more positive. The "image orthicons were not hindered in the least by low-hanging clouds and the players were easily recognized," while camera direction "was about as nearly perfect as it could be."[54] The director was also making better decisions by shifting occasionally from the "pitcher-batter-defense sequence" and staying focused on key players such as Ted Williams. Variety's complaints focused on the play-by-play commentary by Don Pardo, who much later gained fame as the announcer on Jeopardy and Saturday Night Live. According to the publication, Pardo "evidently hasn't looked at many ball games" and "was only annoying." But Variety still damned televised baseball with faint praise, concluding that televised baseball was just "outstanding filler for afternoon hours with light listenership."

A Postseason First and Full-Season Sponsorships

By the end of the 1946 season, televised baseball was expanding. The Sporting News reported that Gillette, a radio sponsor of the World Series, had contacted Commissioner "Happy" Chandler about possible television coverage of the Series, but an agreement was never reached.[55] Viewers would have to "wait until next year" to experience World Series play. However, for the first time a playoff game was televised. Game two of the possible three-game 1946 National League playoff between the Dodgers and the Cardinals (MLB's first tiebreaker playoff) was telecast by WNBT from Ebbets Field on October 3, 1946.[56] The third game was scheduled for telecast the next day, but the Cardinals eliminated the "Bums" by taking the first two games, 4 to 2 in St. Louis and 8 to 4 at Ebbets Field. As a result, television's first postseason series was over almost before it started.

By the end of the 1946 season, the major players in the fledgling television industry—NBC, CBS, and DuMont—were lining up sponsors for the next baseball season. For the owners, the next year would bring their first substantial revenues from television, and they moved rapidly to make sure they would not have to share the spoils. In September 1946, the Sporting News reported that the owners had attempted to insert a clause in player contracts that would deny the player any revenue from the sale of television rights, establishing full control over this potentially rich source of revenue.[57]

In New York, three stations announced plans for televised baseball in 1947. Continuing their long line of televised baseball firsts, the Dodgers were the first New York team to sign in early November, but with CBS rather than their longtime TV partner NBC. CBS lined up Ford and General Foods as sponsors for seventy-seven home games.[58] CBS's three-year contract included plans for colorcasts as well as networking telecasts if permission could be obtained from other clubs. Less than a month later, DuMont contracted with the Yankees to telecast all seventy-seven home games and eleven road games from Philadelphia, Boston, and Washington, pending clearance from the home teams.[59] NBC was also interested in the Bronx Bombers, but lost out to DuMont, despite an $80,000 NBC bid, because the Yankee management was annoyed about a rumored NBC offer to the Giants. Ultimately, NBC signed with the Giants, the only remaining New York club, paying them $50,000 to cover the team's seventy-seven home games.[60]

During the 1947 season, ten of the sixteen Major League teams would telecast some home games, marking the dawn of regular locally produced baseball. By 1948, every Major League team except the Pirates was broadcasting some of its games on local television. Televised baseball's experimental phase was over. The telecasts would be fully commercial, and sponsors would begin to shape the coverage and the game itself.

The First Seasons of Televised Baseball

By 1947, in the wake of the Second World War, the television industry in the United States was finally taking hold. Manufacturing resources geared up for wartime production of radar and other electronics now were channeled into the production of television receivers. The nation's economy was recovering from the double curse of labor shortages and scarce raw materials. Indeed, Americans needed new industries, like television, to limit the impact of the postwar recession caused by cutbacks from wartime production. Burgeoning labor and raw materials could be turned to the construction of new television stations in the vast number of communities that had no stations. The radio industry wisely saw television, not as a competitor, but as an extension of its prosperous industry.

For the public, television was not a new phenomenon, but a long delayed one. The medium had been developing since the early 1920s, and its long period of gestation had created a pent-up demand. After a decade and a half of economic depression and world war, television had arrived! Talk of television was everywhere. Americans—either gazing through storefront windows, frequenting the local tavern, or visiting a friend or family member's home—finally discovered this "window to the world" they had been reading about for more than two decades.

What television lacked in 1947 was not public interest, but programming to interest the public. Radio had experienced the same evolutionary process in the early 1920s, when stations, desperate for any kind of programming, paraded local talent—much of it forgettable—before the microphones for an audience that was less than discriminating. Within a few years, major market stations and the first radio networks were employing the best available talent in their metropolitan areas, greatly

8. *A dying Babe Ruth, icon of the newspaper and newsreel age, receives a TV from RCA. AP/Wide World Photos.*

improving the quality of radio programming. Television would follow a similar pattern, although the radio industry's control over early television stations and networks would quicken the pace of this transformation.

In this chapter, we will examine the evolution of televised baseball during its formative period from early 1947, when local stations provided all of television's programs, to 1952, when coast-to-coast live network programming became the norm for the television industry. We will focus on (1) how baseball contributed to the development of television, (2) the first sponsors of televised baseball, (3) the extent of television's coverage of the game, (4) the evolution of TV's production techniques, and (5) the responses of audiences and critics to viewing the "national pastime" on the small screen. For its first few years, television would rely on baseball and other sports to help fill program schedules, giving consumers a strong reason to invest in the new medium.

Growing a New Medium

Since networks provided little programming, most stations created their own programs in the late 1940s. Stations needed programming that was cheap to produce and that filled substantial time. Baseball fit the need. For stations in most major and some minor league markets, baseball was the solution to the dearth of daytime programming at least during the game's six-month season. Baseball was also cheaper to produce than studio programming. In this very early period, many new stations relied on their mobile units to produce much of their programming because their studios were under construction. In early 1948, Otis Freeman, operating engineer at DuMont's WABD in New York, estimated that at least half of all television station programming came from remotes. Remote telecasts of sports in general, and baseball in particular, provided stations with readily available events and offered great "entertainment value per dollar cost."[1]

Initially, televised baseball was a bargain. Because audiences were small, most owners charged little, if anything, for television rights. For the 1948 seasons, the Braves and Red Sox actually refused an offer of $30,000 for the teams' TV rights. Because there were so few receivers in the Boston market in "fairness to the [radio] sponsors" they could not accept any additional rights money.[2] The 1949 Cubs charged stations only a $5,000 service fee to carry the team's games.[3] Such owner generosity would fade rapidly.

In 1947, the first season of regular television coverage, nine of the eleven active television stations in the United States covered either Major League or Minor League Baseball, with two stations carrying both American and National League games. Games of ten Major League teams were telecast, including the St. Louis Cardinals and Browns, the Philadelphia Phillies and Athletics, the New York Yankees and Giants, the Brooklyn Dodgers, the Chicago Cubs, the Washington Senators, and the Detroit Tigers. During June and July of 1947, nearly half of all television time was filled with baseball telecasts.[4] The next year, Ohio's franchises, the Cleveland Indians and Cincinnati Reds, and Boston's two teams, the Braves and Red Sox, joined the TV parade. With less than 1

9. Baseball sold televisions even if the images on the sets were fake.
Security Pacific Collection, Los Angeles Public Library.

percent of U.S. households owning a receiver, advertising revenues were trivial; stations simply wanted low-cost programming to sustain their broadcast signal for consumers considering the new medium.[5]

In 1949, as set ownership jumped to 2.3 percent of U.S. households,[6] *Broadcast News'* new survey of televised baseball reported significant changes. Now thirty-one out of seventy-seven stations in the United States were televising the baseball games of fifteen of the sixteen Major League teams. Only the Pittsburgh Pirates remained outside of the electronic eye's vision. Over half of the stations telecasting baseball were covering minor league teams, including Columbus, Dayton, Louisville, Newark, New Orleans, Toledo, and the future big league markets of Dallas–Fort Worth, Los Angeles, Miami, Milwaukee, Minneapolis–Saint Paul, New Orleans, San Diego, and Seattle.[7] Women's baseball was also part of the TV package. WENR-TV in Chicago telecast National Girls' Professional Baseball games for fifteen weeks under the sponsorship of Nectar Beer.[8] Locally produced televised baseball was at its zenith.

Television did not create baseball, but baseball helped to create television. Newly minted television stations were not the only ones that needed baseball to fill their broadcast hours. Television manufacturers needed appealing programs to push consumers to buy their first sets.

Programming had to be very attractive because television receivers were a major investment. The typical twelve-inch receiver sold for $300, $3,000 in 2006 dollars. The first television receiver under $100, the three-inch screen (!) Pilot, was introduced in 1949. In 2006 dollars, that minuscule glimpse of televised baseball cost $800. To compensate for the small screen size, a common addition to televisions in this early period was a magnifying lens that could make the twelve-inch image look like a twenty-inch. In most American families of that era, it was the father's decision whether to buy or wait for prices to drop. Televised sports, especially baseball—the dominant sport of the time—was a key factor in that decision. The infant television industry needed baseball. As RCA chairman David Sarnoff observed years later, "we [television makers] had to have baseball games and if they had demanded millions for the rights, we would have had to give it to them."[9] Televised baseball helped move sets from the showroom to the living room at no direct cost to the dealer.

Manufacturers knew that sports sold the new medium. Illustrations and still photos of baseball action, although never actual television images, were a staple of print ads for television receivers. In the last half of 1949, sports accounted for nearly 20 percent of all programming in New York, making it the most plentiful program type.[10] Never was the sport so important to the medium, both its broadcasters and its manufacturers, than in these first summers of television.

Televised Baseball's First Sponsors

Since the percentage of homes that had receivers was low, early sponsors of televised baseball were not focused on audience size. Most advertisers were simply extending their longstanding radio sponsorships to include television, hoping to benefit from a positive association between their products and the exciting new medium. A summary produced by NBC in 1949 reported that televised baseball's sponsors included five brewers (Falstaff, Goebel, Ballantine, Burger, and Narragansett Brewing), two tobacco companies (P. Lorillard and Co. and Chesterfield Cigarettes), two automakers (Ford and Buick), one oil company (Atlantic Refining Co.) and one radio-TV manufacturer (Philco).[11] The "big three" baseball sponsors (beer, tobacco, automakers, and related industries) would underwrite much of televised baseball for a generation. Time magazine observed that "beer and cigarettes are today as much a part of the league and the national game as bat and ball."[12] Home runs were no longer home runs, but a "Ballantine Blast" or a "White Owl wallop." Beer was such an important sponsor that Yankee announcer Mel Allen even took lessons at a Newark brewery in how to pour a beer on camera without any overflowing. (According to Yankee telecast director Don Carney, the secret was to keep the beer at the proper temperature.[13]) By 1950, advertisers were spending over $20 million to sponsor baseball on radio and television, much of the money going to television to cover its much higher production costs.[14]

And what did sponsors get for their advertising dollars? NBC's sponsor of New York Giants games, Chesterfield, received six thirty- to fifty-five-second filmed commercials that aired ten minutes before game time, at the end of the second, fourth, sixth, and eighth innings, and after the game recap. In addition, there were "short" Chesterfield plugs at each half inning. Chesterfield's signage at the ballpark was shown on camera, and the announcer was often shown "lighting up." Between games of a doubleheader, the telecast switched to WNBQ's studio for a ten-minute program, "Chesterfield Baseball Quiz," in which fans attending the game competed for cartons of the sponsor's product.[15] Assuming fifty-five seconds for each filmed commercial and about twenty seconds for each between-inning plug, the sponsor got about ten minutes of commercial time during a typical two- to two-and-a-half-hour baseball game. That much advertising time could fit into the first two innings of a regular-season telecast today. The modern era of televised sports—with saturation advertising and wall-to-wall promotion—was decades away.

How Much Television Is Enough Television?

As the new decade dawned, the question was not just how television should cover baseball, but how much of it should be covered and what that coverage was doing to the game. As was true in an earlier radio era, baseball in the late 1940s had a difficult time figuring out what to show and when to show it. If Major League Baseball showed too much too often, game attendance would drop. But the lesson of radio was that though broadcasting might discourage some traditional fans from attending games, it could also be used to develop new fans: women and working-class men who had limited interest in or time for spectator sports, and especially the children that baseball needed to perpetuate to grow the national pastime. Television might do the same, but the risk was much greater.

The television experience was in some ways better than watching a game at the ballpark. Even with the limited black-and-white cameras of the early 1950s, every viewer was closer to the players than any ticket holder. Television's tightest image was a medium closeup that framed the starting pitcher from the chest up. The pitcher's own catcher could not see him that close. Television also focused the viewer's experience by limiting the visual field to a prearranged sequence of shots, designed to isolate key moments of action. The viewer saw what was, in the view of an experienced director, the most important image at any moment in time. Viewers lost the freedom to let their eyes wander the field of play, but gained a more accessible view of the game. Television might annoy longtime fans who were comfortable following the game on their own, but the medium would help a new generation of fans to learn the game. But how many games should be telecast? Like much of the decentralized decision making that characterized baseball in the 1950s, the answer to that question depended on which team you watched.

In New York and Chicago, you could watch a lot. "Big Apple" televised coverage started in 1947 when the Dumont network offered the Yankees significant television rights fees, paying them $75,000 for the rights to regular-season home games. The Giants signed with NBC and the Dodgers with CBS. Almost immediately, the three New York teams were televising every home game. New Yorkers could watch at least one and usually two games almost every day of the baseball season. Because of an abundance of stations, by 1948 the selection in Chicago was almost as plentiful: all Cubs home games were televised as well as most White Sox day games. In the late 1940s, the Cubs invited all comers, with as many as three stations covering the same game, creating a "forest of TV cameras" at Wrigley Field.[16]

But after coverage peaked in the late 1940s, viewing opportunities were much more limited in other markets. The cities with the most competing television stations (New York and Chicago) had the most televised baseball. Because they had no need to run network shows, independent (not affiliated with a network) stations like WGN in Chicago and WPIX and WOR in New York could show baseball both day and night. In cities with few stations, including most smaller and medium markets, there was no room in prime time for baseball because each of the major networks had locked up each station's evening programming. Night baseball games were getting kicked off the prime-time stage.

The Network Dilemma

The growing strength of television networks reduced the demand for televised baseball. Starting in 1947, the first networks (ABC, CBS, NBC, and DuMont) linked stations on the East Coast and later the Midwest. Stations, affiliated with the two dominant networks (NBC and CBS) and now nationally linked, grew from twelve in 1948 to ninety-five in 1952.[17] Major networks were committed to airing programs that would benefit the entire network, not just their owned and operated stations. NBC and CBS could not sell a national audience to advertisers when their own stations in New York, the nation's largest market, were carrying the Dodgers (on WNBT) or the Giants (on WCBS) instead of the network's programs.

As early as May 1948, NBC saw that "the conflict between night baseball on WNBT only and network programming is a rather serious one."[18] When prime-time commitments forced NBC to eliminate telecasts of

Giant night games, the network could not meet its commitment to the sponsor, Chesterfield, to carry sixty-six games.[19] NBC solved its dilemma by transferring its night games after July fifth to independent WPIX. By July, the network had decided to release Chesterfield from any commitment to sponsor Giants games in 1949, noting that "with the growth of television, it would appear that, since our main operation would consist of networking, telecasts of baseball games may be outside of our program schedule possibilities" for "the next four or five years."[20] Commitments to night baseball games, even if they produced strong ratings in New York and Chicago, were a threat to a network's national presence.

One solution to the network dilemma was to carry games during the day, which the networks did not program at the time, and farm out the night games to other stations. In 1948, NBC carried the Giants' day games and allowed their night games to be carried by WPIX. NBC tried to continue the strategy in 1949, but its Giants sponsor, Chesterfield, no longer wanted to divide its promotion of the team's telecasts between two stations. NBC also made inquiries about carrying Dodger or Yankee games in 1949, but without success.[21] CBS had an option for the 1949 season and was able to place night games on another station, but by 1950 the network dropped baseball, and Dodger games shifted to independent station WOR. DuMont had also abandoned baseball in the early 1950s, with its Yankee games shifting to WPIX. Independent stations like WPIX and WOR in New York and WGN in Chicago began to specialize in local sports coverage. By 1953, WPIX claimed to telecast "more sports than any other station in the country," having aired more than one thousand sportscasts during its brief history.[22] As the new decade dawned, the networks shifted their baseball interests to the World Series and All-Star Game, and eventually a national game of the week (see chapters 4 and 5).

Team Reactions to Television

Although Clarence "Pants" Rowland, president of the Pacific Coast League, and Clark Griffith, owner of the Washington Senators, threatened to reduce or eliminate televised games because of sagging attendance, other clubs signed long-term deals.[23] In early 1951, the Yankees signed with WPIX for five years. Next, the Dodgers signed with Schaefer

Beer for five years with options for two additional years. WOR telecast the games. The first five years of the Dodger television and radio rights brought the club $3 million (most of it for television), prompting Walter O'Malley, Dodger owner, to claim that television, "despite an initial harmful impact, would become a 'potent ally' of baseball by reaching people who aren't fans, and luring them into ball parks."[24] Clearly, $3 million was persuasive evidence that television might be a "potent ally."

Between 1949 and 1952, teams reacted to the perceived threat of television in a variety of ways. Some telecast all of their home games; some telecast only their more numerous day games; others restricted the number of TV games, whether day or night (see appendix A).[25] In Philadelphia, the Phillies and Athletics telecast about three-quarters of their home games, parceled out among three stations (WPTZ, WCAU, and WFIL). The White Sox began their longstanding pattern of telecasting all home day games, while the Tigers telecast thirty-five home games each year. In Boston, the Braves telecast all home games in 1949 and 1950, and then dramatically reduced their TV offerings to thirty-two home games in 1951 and 1952. The Reds and Senators also slashed their TV games after 1950. St. Louis viewers saw few games on the tube, as both the Cardinals and Browns telecast only a handful of home contests. At the extremes, six teams—the Yankees, Dodgers, Giants, Cubs, Red Sox, and Indians—telecast all of their home schedule, while the Pirates telecast no games at all.

By 1952, with television in more than a third of U.S. homes, baseball's TV presence was starting to decline.[26] Concerns about a 30 percent decline in Major League attendance from 20.9 million in 1948 to 14.6 million in 1952 were moving some owners to reduce their coverage of the game.[27] The perceived "television threat" (see chapter 9) would lead to less game coverage throughout the 1950s, and the almost complete elimination of TV games by four relocating franchises, the Athletics, Dodgers, Giants, and Braves. Having televised extensively in their original markets, these franchise owners seized the opportunity to rein in television in their new homes. Eliminating games would have outraged their old fans, but did not disturb their new customers, who had not yet cultivated an appetite for televised Major League Baseball (see chapter 3).

10. *Older stadiums were not designed for television coverage. This high home cameraman at Cleveland Stadium uses a glove for foul ball protection.* © Bettmann/Corbis.

Evolving Production Techniques

In its first couple of years, televised baseball struggled with teams to gain access to decent camera locations and press-room amenities that the established media, newspapers and radio, took for granted. For Harry Coyle, the nastiest ballpark was "Yankee Stadium, they were the worst bastards." His Dumont crew had no control room during the first year they telecast games from Yankee Stadium. The director worked from a canvas-covered cage.[28] Bill Garden, program director for NBC, had to plead with Newell-Emmett, the ad agency handling the Giants games, for enough press passes for his crew and access to the press club lunches, so they didn't have to "subsist on a diet of sandwiches or hot dogs and coffee . . . a good method of developing ulcers." Noting that "the press coop is provided cold cokes and beer," Garden also wanted a "few cold ones" for his control room crew sweating under the Polo Grounds' stands.[29] Jack Murphy, a director of early Yankee telecasts, confirmed that baseball writers were often hostile. "It took a long time to break down the prejudices of the press corps" because "we were strangers poaching on their territory."[30]

The typical telecast needed about ten crew members: a director, a crew chief, video engineer, an announcer, an assistant for the announcer, two or three camera operators, and an "emergency man" to handle unexpected problems, including personnel incapacitated by excessive heat or a well-placed foul ball.[31] At the very least, the production crew needed a production van or in-park control room, two or three camera chains (camera, control unit, monitors), two off-the-air receivers, a microwave relay transmitter, an audio amplifier, several microphones, several telephone headsets, and assorted other equipment, including hundreds of feet of cable. The extra personnel and equipment meant much higher costs for television compared to radio. NBC estimated that each 1948 Giants game cost $1,725 to produce, about $15,250 in 2006 dollars.[32] Both production crews and costs would grow as televised baseball matured.

In this period, television's coverage of the game was quite diverse. Although most stations used just two cameras, DuMont's WABD (Yankees) and NBC's WNBT (Giants) covered their teams with three. The placement of cameras varied wildly. In St. Louis, KSD-TV covered the Cardinals, the Browns, and the first televised All-Star Game in 1948 with two side-by-side cameras on the first base line, which was dictated by the absence of space behind home plate for camera placement. The first base cameras had to pan constantly to follow the flight of the ball, creating a dizzying broadcast. Since there was no control room, the director sat just behind the two cameras choosing the shots by looking at the camera viewfinders.

Chicago station WBKB, under the management of television pioneer Capt. William Eddy, took an alternative approach, placing first two then three cameras on the third base side. Always an innovator, Eddy had been experimenting with television since the war and studied camera placement in motion pictures (WBKB was owned by Paramount).[33] Eddy learned that action coming toward or away from the screen was more dynamic than action moving side to side. Applying this principle to televising baseball, he reasoned that the action of the most exciting plays in baseball—runners moving into scoring position at third base or actually scoring—should be given the best angle.[34] WBKB's two cameras were in a wonderful position to show that action, but were forced to pan every

Local Station Television Coverage of Major League Baseball, 1949

Station	Team(s)	#Cameras	Location of Cameras
KSD	Cardinals/Browns	2	2 side by side midway between home and 1st base
WBKB	Cubs	3	all 3rd base side of home
WBZ	Braves/Red Sox	2	2 in press box, on 1st base side of home
WGN	Cubs	3	2 behind home and 1st base dugout
WPTZ	Athletics/Phillies	2	20' high behind home and 80' high behind home

Source: John P. Taylor, "Baseball Television," *Broadcast News*, September 1949.

time they focused on the most common activity in baseball: the pitcher throwing to the catcher. Eddy's publicized his innovative approach in a brochure that got the attention of NBC, but reviews of WBKB's idiosyncratic camera placement were "unfavorable."[35]

KSD-TV and WBKB's camera placements were unusual; most directors placed one or both of their cameras behind home plate with a shot that showed the pitcher, catcher, batter, and umpire when no one was on base, and widened to include second base when a runner was on second. However, this "high home" camera(s) could be at any height, from near ground level to stadium rooftop. By 1949, this became the standard shot in baseball and the shot that occupied the most screen time. It would be twenty years before the center-field shot of the same quartet would replace it as the most important shot in baseball. The first base camera could cover effectively two of the more common actions in baseball: runners moving from first to second and fly balls to left field. The above table illustrates just how varied the camera placement was.

Outside the United States, the approach to the TV game could be even more imaginative. In 1952, *Sport* magazine reported that televised Mexican League games featured cameras actually on the field of play. One camera was "directly behind the home-plate umpire, with the cameraman posted in a big, round plexi-glass shell." Similar shells protected on-field cameras located near first and third base. There were also two cameras in the outfield.[36]

Because most cameras were equipped with fixed lenses rather than the zoom lenses that today are standard on even consumer video cameras, every time the camera operator wanted to move in closer he had to turn a turret of three or four lenses of different focal lengths offering different degrees of magnification. Even though the average game was only a couple of hours, the constant changing of lenses was exhausting. Camera crews frequently included an extra camera operator who relieved the "starter."

The coverage of baseball evolved constantly. By 1949, a significant and growing minority of stations (nine of thirty-one) used at least one Zoomar lens. Although the new lens required more light and was less clear than a fixed lens, it was much better at following the ball because it could rapidly adjust between wide and telephoto shots. Control rooms were also improving. Six stations, mostly in New York and Philadelphia, built a permanent control room at their stadiums, eliminating the need for a remote truck.[37] Many other stations installed permanent camera stations and cabling in their stadiums. This investment in permanent facilities shows that stations, at the time, were committed to baseball as a regular part of their programming.

Since local telecasts were not accessible beyond their markets, most neophyte directors could not learn their craft by observing telecasts of other teams. Instead, they turned to national trade publications or visits to stations in other markets. In July 1949, *Broadcasting* offered a detailed description by Red Thornburgh, director of sports for WLWT in Cincinnati, of his station's approach to televised baseball. WLWT used three cameras: camera one with a Zoomar lens was placed in the upper grandstand behind home plate, and cameras two and three were located side by side about forty feet above the field midway between home and first base. These cameras had four fixed lenses. Camera one with its Zoomar lens provided the basic cover shot of much of the game's action, while cameras two and three were assigned to cover base runs, closeups of the batter and pitcher, crowd shots, and the scoreboard. Noting what many TV directors would discover to their chagrin, Thornburgh observed that "baseball is the most difficult sport to televise since the action is spread out over a wide area."[38]

By 1951, coverage of the Brooklyn Dodgers had shifted to independent station WOR, where producer Jim Beach brought a new approach. First, he added a fourth camera at ground level by the third base dugout and the next year a fifth camera by the first base dugout. These new cameras offered closer shots of both right-handed and left-handed batters, both dugouts, and the runner crossing home plate. Beach and a colleague even pushed for a center-field camera, but abandoned the plan because of "engineering difficulties" and the confusion that the center-field perspective might cause fans.[39]

Directors were now using a technical director to make the actual camera switches. This allowed for more rapid switching between cameras and the greater use of special effects, such as superimposing players' names as they came to bat or split-screen shots that could show both the runner leading off first and the pitcher checking the length of the runner's lead. With more cameras, directors could include more crowd reaction shots or focus on "a celebrity in the box seats."[40] Starting in 1951, the World Series and later the All-Star Game were telecast coast to coast. Television directors thus watched how others approached the TV game and adapted new strategies to their own station's coverage. Also, a few years' experience enabled camera operators and directors to react more quickly to the game's unexpected turns, so the camera's eye missed fewer significant moments. By the early 1950s, the quality of television's coverage of the game had improved dramatically.

Responses to the TV Game

Responses to the first versions of the televised game were a split decision. The public liked what it saw, but the critics were, well, critical. The May 1948 Hooper ratings found that "baseball is currently the most popular video fare with New York TV set-owners," with the May 8 Saturday-afternoon Yankee game attracting 38.4 percent of the city's set owners.[41] In June 1948, three of the five highest-rated programs in New York, including the top-rated broadcast, were Yankee telecasts.[42] Philadelphia viewers flocked to their sets during a July 1948 doubleheader between the Athletics and White Sox—70 percent of set owners watched the games. The Philly fans expressed a preference for night games over day because the ball was "easier to follow on the screen under artificial lights."[43] And from the very beginning, fans preferred to be "viewers" rather than "listeners." A 1950 survey of thirteen hundred barber shop customers in Chicago found that 72 percent preferred watching the games on television compared to 22.8 percent who preferred listening on radio.[44] The lack of strong competing programming and the novelty of seeing the game for the first time undoubtedly contributed to this early viewer enthusiasm.

Viewers were not just watching at home. Indeed, most probably saw their first games while sitting in front of some liquid refreshment at their local bar. In Chicago, a survey of public places, mostly bars, during six Cubs telecasts found that 71 percent of owners had their sets tuned to the game, with an average of almost ten patrons per set.[45] With in-home receivers still a novelty, bars by the hundreds in major cities urged drinkers to "see the baseball games here." Taverns without TVs quickly got one; one despairing saloon keeper reportedly rushed into a Queens appliance store crying, "I've got to have a set now, today or I'm ruined."[46] At this point, baseball's owners considered "tavern ball" a more serious threat to attendance than in-home viewing.[47]

Authorities were also concerned that televised baseball was drawing youngsters into local pubs to catch a glimpse of the games. To provide an alternative, WBKB provided the Chicago Park Board with receivers for ten playgrounds. Cubs owner Phil Wrigley also committed resources to purchase additional sets. Captain Eddy, director of WBKB, said that the project was designed "to keep kids out of bars."[48] The local Catholic diocese also purchased receivers so youngsters could watch at their local church. If alcohol wasn't strong enough to tempt the young, there were reports of a "new racket" in Los Angeles: "televised baseball gambling." Bettors could wager on whether the next pitch would be a strike or ball, or if the batter would smash it into the stands.[49]

Though the general public seemed satisfied with their twelve-inch view of the game, professional commentators were far more critical. Baseball writer Red Smith called the televised game a "peep show" that was more akin to looking at the game through a knothole than from a ballpark seat: "Until they develop a television camera that can embrace the entire field, showing all of the diffuse action of a game with detail fine enough to follow the flight of the ball, the video version of baseball cannot be better than a makeshift substituted for the real thing."[50]

The small screens of the era made it difficult to follow the flight of the ball. Joe DiMaggio, with one of the best batting eyes of all time, found it difficult to see the ball on TV.[51] Baseball writers and players, the game's most skilled observers, both found the TV game restricting: the director alone selected what would be shown at any given moment. Media critics also raised objections. John Crosby, television critic for the *New York Herald Tribune*, saw the television crew's role as "not much different from that of a novelist; they must pick up and emphasize the significant detail from the mass of the extraneous." Their efforts succeed only "intermittently," producing "not so much a baseball game as an impressionist version of one."[52]

The most frequent, and usually critical, observer of televised baseball was *Variety*, the major trade paper of both the entertainment industry establishment (radio, film, and theater) and the emerging television industry. During televised baseball's first seasons, *Variety* wrote frequently and pointedly about the game, and television professionals read its reviews with considerable interest.

Variety Offers "Tough Love"

The opening of the 1947 season brought the first full season of televised baseball to the air. From New York, *Variety* could view coverage of three different teams by the three major players in television at the time: CBS (WCBS), DuMont (WABD), and NBC (WNBT). *Variety's* first piece on the new season briefly examined the coverage of all three, complimenting both CBS and NBC for their camera positions behind home plate, and especially NBC's view up the middle of the battery, shortstop, second baseman, and center fielder. But television's limitations were apparent from the start, and *Variety* concluded that "if the weather is good, this new gadget . . . is not going to keep 'em away from the ball park."[53] *Variety* openly criticized the WABD production team for its ignorance of the game. "For instance, with men on base the camera often can't make up its mind whether to follow the ball, the batter, or a base-runner. The answer is simple—follow the ball." Sometimes, the director, the man who "makes or breaks the broadcast," focused on the mundane, a runner trotting home from third, missing a close play at third on a runner coming from first. The director also needed to show the scoreboard more often and earlier in the game because "the scoreboard is a fascinating device to a ball fan, something no announcer's announcement of the scores can replace."[54]

As televised baseball's first season and World Series ended, so did *Variety*'s flirtation with the affirmative. In a May 1948 article titled "No Runs, Few Hits, What Errors!" *Variety* launched its broadside at video ball, claiming that all "three Manhattan television stations are turning in an ordinary, routine version of baseball," and that N BC's camera work had regressed from its first season.[55] In its most detailed and hostile analysis yet, the show-biz organ identified major problems in televised baseball and offered a few solutions as well.

Among *Variety*'s many grievances:

> Too many closeups, a "peep show" mentality that forces viewers to miss action seen in a wider shot. This leads to more jarring camera pans as the cameraman works to keep up with the action.

> Poor coordination between the director and announcer, leading to frustrated announcers unable to get the pictures they want to talk about.

> Following the batter as he runs toward first base, rather than the ball in play.

> Not enough "color" shots of the players in the dugout, fans in the stands, pitchers in the bullpen, and the scoreboard.

> Dull coverage of the long, slow walk of relief pitchers to the mound.

> Over concentration of coverage on the home-plate action at the expense of other field action.

> Creeping commercialism in the telecasts. While DuMont only superimposed Ballantine beer's logo over the between-innings action, N BC used a commercial every half inning. "That's only a minimum of 18 commercials a game." (Modern-day viewers would

delight at such a modest number, but in 1948 this precedent was just being established.)

Television personnel do not understand baseball and need to become "fans" of the game.

Variety made four suggestions for improving television coverage, some of which reflected their allegiance to the film industry. First, put a knowledgeable source in the control booth by placing "a former big leaguer, or someone who knows a lot of baseball, alongside the camera director to call shots for him." Second, send television production personnel to "film" school. Have directors and camera operators "study the newsreels of baseball and football which are so far ahead of video in their screening of team games. . . . The newsreel boys could be asked to let the video men sit in with them to practically go to school and learn." TV studio cameramen could be sent to "Hollywood in relays and let the lens experts out there show them what, why, and how." Third, use the medium shot more and the closeup less. "Medium shot holds those eye-straining fast camera 'pans' to a minimum," and reduces the need for lens changes, "which are hard on the eyes." Finally, simplify commercials. "Agencies should learn that for video the simple commercial is the best commercial."

With this critique, *Variety* had poked the caged television tiger once too often, and this time the tiger growled back. Perhaps it was the suggestion that television could learn from the "newsreel boys" or maybe it was the call for a former big leaguer to seize control of the telecast. In any event, the empire that was NBC retaliated two weeks later in the pages of *Variety*. William Garden, NBC's television field director, stated that *Variety* had "presented a very unfair and inaccurate picture of the situation."[56] Garden offered a point-by-point rebuttal of *Variety*'s criticisms. Announcers were provided with a monitor so they could coordinate with what was shown on the screen. Shots of the fans, bullpen, scoreboard, and the like add interest, but should not compromise coverage of the game action. NBC does follow the ball and not the runner moving to first. Directors *do* understand the game; in fact, one big leaguer was at Garden's side for one game and reported that this "is excellent baseball coverage." NBC employs "men who know baseball as well as how to handle the technical tools of their trade." Wide shots are used when the bases are loaded, but closeups are used at other times because of the amount of detail lost in wider shots. Small screens make for small images when closeups are eschewed. Finally, in response to the suggestion that newsreel techniques be studied, Garden wrote, "ridiculous!" Newsreels offer five or ten minutes of highlights that can be carefully and leisurely selected during the editing process; television must cover every play as it happens. Nevertheless, in an editor's note accompanying Garden's rebuttal, *Variety* still lamented the overuse of the closeup, arguing that "the baseball fan says he'll trade the mole on the pitcher's chin for a wide angle view of the infield." Despite its experience with worse coverage in Boston, *Variety* still believed that New York's video ball offered "a dim view."

Variety's review of the opening week of the 1949 season reported no improvements in telecast quality, as "local outlets continue to provide video's cramped version of the national game." *Variety* claimed that the directors' insistence on using closeups resulted in stations "missing at least 10 plays a game." The viewer must often rely on the announcer to find out what is happening, and "when the announcer is the source of information on a telecast the picture is falling down on the job." *Variety* even suggested that talented Red Barber should control the television broadcast as he already was doing in radio. "The camera director is head man, but as far as the viewer is concerned it would be better if Barber were at the control board telling the director what views to pick."[57] *Variety*'s suggestion would be picked up by the "Old Redhead." Using a model of a baseball field that had pairs of switches and lights at key locations, Barber was able to get key shots on the screen (see chapter 14). Eventually, Barber would abandon his cumbersome control panel, but *Variety* would continue its pointed critiques.

Building a New Vision of Baseball

In its formative period, televised baseball grew from a novelty to a mainstay of early station-based television programming during the baseball season. As the networks grew from regional to national between 1947

41

and 1951, they withdrew from baseball coverage.[58] The network focus shifted from regular-season games to the game's marquee events: the All-Star Game and the World Series. In cities with stations that were not affiliated with a network, baseball continued to receive daily coverage during the season. But in most cities, as the networks dominated first prime time and later daytime programming, baseball coverage was shifted to weekend games. With the rise of the network game of the week in the mid-1950s, these local games would receive new competition.

By the late 1940s, baseball dominated the spring, summer, and autumn television schedules as it never would again. Not until the cable revolution of the 1980s would as high a percentage of Major League games reach the screen. By the mid-1950s, the roots of the antitelevision argument were in place: baseball was not well suited for television, TV hurt the box office, and it was killing the minor leagues (see chapter 10). At first, baseball seemed made for television, but after a few "honeymoon" years both television and baseball would find their marriage a troubled one.

Team Approaches to Television in the Broadcast Era

Economist Andrew Zimbalist argues that to understand the economic condition of Major League Baseball one must look at the "ongoing technological revolution in telecommunications and the ever more concentrated and interlocked structure of the broadcast industry."[1] We would add that even in a time of rapid change in the global telecommunications and entertainment industries, history continues to matter just as much as the "ongoing revolution."

Market and Revenue Inequities

More than any other major professional sport, MLB has been affected by the ongoing restructuring of the U.S. television industry because of baseball's historical reliance on local broadcast revenues. These revenues vary widely primarily due to the differences in market size. At the advent of local, commercial broadcasting in the 1920s, baseball was the only established professional sport. MLB's first contracts with broadcasters were local contracts. The emphasis on localism prevented the creation of a national broadcast game of the week until 1966 and led to the regionalization of playoff coverage as recently as 1995.[2] For these reasons, MLB teams have always placed great emphasis on local and regional radio and television money. By the late 1990s, these monies contributed approximately one half of broadcast revenue, far more than for the other U.S.-based professional sports leagues.[3] Localism is so pronounced that it is one of the primary reasons why MLB has had so much difficulty developing consistently successful national television packages (see chapter 6). Since local television and radio revenue is not shared equally, the result is wide revenue disparities between the teams.

Television's increasingly powerful regional sports networks (RSNs), which use local team telecasts as primary programming and marketing elements, have exacerbated revenue disparity. RSNs like YES and Fox Sports Pittsburgh serve as competitors to local broadcasters for local team rights. The result is an increase in both the number of games telecast and in the fees paid to the local team. Not surprisingly, the primary beneficiaries are those teams that represent the largest television markets.

The increasing prominence of RSNs has sparked broadcaster complaints that the shift of games to basic cable RSNs reduces the public's access to games. This charge is partially supported in 1993 and later Federal Communications Commission reports on sports siphoning. Of the 3,715 local or regional games scheduled in 1998, 2,059 were on cable outlets and 1,656 on broadcast stations.[4] In addition, the superstations that use MLB teams as major programming elements (e.g., WGN–Chicago Cubs) shift more games from broadcast to cable television. Although fading as a problem for MLB, superstations contributed to revenue disparity by providing affiliated teams with another revenue stream that is only partially shared with the other franchises.[5] This siphoning of games from broadcast to cable and satellite delivery has continued to increase in the years since the FCC studies.

Revenue sharing between the large- and small-market franchises has been a key issue in MLB at least since the advent of player free agency in the mid-1970s. Shared revenues for MLB increased to around $220 million in 2003 as a result of MLB's "luxury tax" on the payrolls above a certain threshold.[6] Nevertheless, small-market teams (e.g., Kansas City, Milwaukee, Pittsburgh) continue to argue that a more equitable distribution of revenue is essential to achieve competitive balance and profitable operation. They also argue that MLB's long-term best interest is served by the maintenance of a strong and competitive league structure. As might be expected, large-market team owners argue that they paid a premium to purchase teams in large markets and therefore should expect to generate more income.

The seriousness of the revenue-sharing dispute was demonstrated in 1994 when fifteen smaller market teams threatened to deny access to television crews representing the larger market franchises, invalidating local and regional television agreements.[7] Although this threat ended when the owners agreed to a partial revenue-sharing plan, the present revenue-sharing scheme provides only a modest amount to teams. For example, the Pittsburgh Pirates received approximately $7 million in revenue-sharing money for 1998 out of a total pool of $100 million, a figure that grew to $13.3 million by 2002.[8] Although revenue-sharing provides some relief, it does not address the vast revenue disparities in the game. These disparities are increasing as such teams as the New York Yankees and Mets and Boston Red Sox have created their own RSNs that allow them to further maximize revenues. Smaller market teams have much less market leverage in establishing team-owned RSNs, and even if they make the investment, the return is largely determined by market size (see chapters 8 and 12 for a more detailed analysis of RSNs and their growing importance to MLB teams).

Another historical factor is MLB's media fear: the belief that if fans received games through media coverage attendance would decline. Baseball historian Paul Adomites reports that even before the broadcast era, newspaper coverage and telegraphic accounts of games to bars and poolrooms were hotly debated by team owners as "giving away the game."[9] Radio was feared even more, prompting New York City teams to ban broadcasts in the 1930s, while other teams imposed serious limits. Only in the case of the Cubs, and shortly after the Cardinals, was radio fully embraced as a marketing tool.[10] As recently as the 1990s, the effect of cable coverage on home attendance was still a concern in Pittsburgh.[11] In fact, the still-present "blackout" rules that limit the telecast of out-of-town games when they compete with local-team home games are a remnant of media fear.[12]

Overview of the Broadcast Era

Although (media) market size remains a key factor in the imbalances among MLB's franchises, it does not completely explain those imbalances. Though markets like Cincinnati and St. Louis are considered "good baseball towns" because of fan interest and media revenues, markets of roughly the same size (Milwaukee, Pittsburgh) are considered marginal baseball towns. This is surprising in the case of Pittsburgh, where local television ratings in some years have been among the highest in the league.[13] In other cases, teams that share a single market (Chicago Cubs and White Sox, Los Angles Dodgers and Angels) have often differed greatly in revenue and fan support regardless of team performance.

One of the most important ways to understand such differences is to examine the origins of the individual teams' relationships with the television industry. Appendix A consists of six tables reflecting team approaches to television from 1949, the first year yielding complete information, to 1981, the first year of MLB's initial national cable contract with the USA Network. The information was assembled from annual summaries published each April in the *Sporting News*. Except for relocated franchises, most teams followed a consistent pattern in the total number of games televised and the proportion of road games televised after 1953, when telecast of road games became more common. In reviewing the tables in appendix A, we found several clear trends:

Big City, Big Schedule: Teams in New York (the Giants, Yankees, Dodgers, and Mets) and Chicago (Cubs and White Sox) telecast the most games, including a high percentage of their home games and a substantial portion of their road contests once they began road telecasts. The presence of independent stations in these cities hungry for programming created a strong demand for these games. Because of the large television market, teams could demand substantial rights fees from stations, offsetting any financial losses suffered if attendance declined.

Relocation Restrictions: Most teams that relocated in the 1950s (the Braves, Athletics, Dodgers, and Giants) dramatically reduced their television coverage, initially eliminating all games and then restricting television to a handful of road contests. Gradually, the number of road contests increased.

Road Warriors: Several teams (the Orioles, Phillies, Reds, and Tigers) telecast a substantial number of games (forty to seventy), but these were predominately road contests. After 1954, the Cardinals telecast only road games for several years. The Pirates, the last holdout from game telecasting, eventually limited telecasts to road games only for many seasons.

Expansion Limitations: Most expansion teams telecast only road games (Angels, Colt .45s-Astros, Padres, and Mariners). The Canadian franchises (Expos and Blue Jays) were an exception, but they also tended to telecast only a few games.

Limited Telecasts and League Parity: The percentage of games telecast was surprisingly consistent over time, with an average of 27 percent of American League and 29 percent of National League games aired locally between 1949 and 1981.

The Road's the Rage: The number of road telecasts rose over time. In the American League, the figure rose from 39 percent in 1954-60, to 59 percent from 1961 to 1968, to 69 percent from 1969 to 1981. The National League percentages were 42 percent (1954–61), 54 percent (1962–68), and 70 percent (1969–81). The pattern of predominant road coverage was especially strong for teams in new markets: relocated franchises and expansion teams. In general, MLB tried to solve its television "problem" by shifting telecasts from home to road games, assuming that fans were more likely to stay home when the telecast competed directly with the game at the local ballpark. On the other hand, road games provided both revenue and promotion for the teams.

Although we did not include the data in our tables, a review of the *Sporting News* summaries also indicated a preponderance of weekend games in many markets. In the period before national cable, most television stations were network affiliates and could more easily accommodate Saturday and Sunday afternoon games that did not conflict with their network's programming. This allowed weekend games to be telecast by a local "flagship" station and its regional network of stations.

These general coverage trends over the first three decades of televised baseball show that individual teams attempted to answer the question of how much television was enough in many different ways. In the next section, we will examine how many of these approaches can be explained by four models for managing the extent of local radio and television coverage.

Local Models

One of the most important ways to understand differences in game telecast policies is to examine the origins of the individual teams' relationships with the television industry. Four models describe the typical relationships between an MLB team and television: the pinned-ins, the hinterlands, the embracers, and the relocators.

The "Pinned-In" Pirates

The Pittsburgh Pirates figure prominently in almost any account of MLB economics. Even with a new ballpark (PNC Park) featuring the requisite "luxury amenities" and corporate sponsorship in place, observers continue to question the team's long-term ability to compete or even exist.[14] Pittsburgh is considered too small and too poor a baseball town even while its population "twin," St. Louis, is considered a medium-to-large and healthy baseball market. Although Pirate attendance is relatively low it reflects a greater percentage of its metropolitan population than many large-market teams. On television, Pirate games as recently as the late 1990s had the second-highest local ratings of all MLB teams.[15] Pittsburgh traditionally has boasted one of the highest percentages of residents who have watched a game on television in the past year, reflecting the older-than-average age of its population. Despite such seemingly positive figures, television is the problem in Pittsburgh. As former team executive Dick Freeman explained in a newspaper article, small teams generally can compete with large-market clubs in attendance, but television audiences are problematic because "you can't overcome differences in population."[16]

The fact is that the Pirates did not take steps to extend the fan base of the franchise in the early days of television. By 1955, the Pirates were one of only three teams that were not televising any games.[17] The other two nontelevision markets were Kansas City and Milwaukee, both considered marginal and both of which lost a team in the 1960s. All three cases illustrate how television can affect the basic structure of the game. By 1958 the Pirates were one of only six MLB teams that telecast no home games, ignoring a critical marketing tool in extending the "local" fan base into the "hinterlands."[18] The team was concerned about the effect of home-game telecasts on attendance despite the mounting evidence (i.e., Chicago, New York) that the effect was at worst negligible and, at best, a major promotional bonanza. As appendix A reveals, the Pirates limited road telecasts to between thirty and forty in the first twenty years of Pittsburgh television. The Pirates also failed to develop much of a broadcast television network; there were never more than five affiliates in addition to its flagship station during in the same twenty-year period.[19]

Another important factor depressing the Pirates' television market is the city's geographical location—pinned in by other major league teams to the northwest (Cleveland), southwest (Cincinnati), northeast (New York), east (Philadelphia), southeast (Baltimore, Washington), and, since 1977, north (Toronto). Unlike the Cardinals and to a lesser degree the Chicago teams, the Pirates could only extend their market so far. Their failure to do even this in the early days of television has had serious ramifications for the team's fortunes since then. Despite evidence that fear of local telecasts was a shortsighted blunder that made a tough marketing situation worse, as recently as the 1990s the team still was limiting home-game telecasts.[20]

The effect of being geographically pinned in was exacerbated by the team owners' failure to better exploit both the radio and television media. This parochial mind-set was self-defeating and is now essentially irremediable. The Buccos remain at best a small regional phenomenon, evidenced by the failure of legendary local announcers such as Rosey Rowswell and Bob Prince to gain national prominence. In fact, Prince's hiring by ABC for its mid-1970's *Monday Night Baseball* package was a failure. Prince was too much a "homer" and acquired taste to break through at the national level.

Although there are unique circumstances in each market, the pinned-in model is relevant in examining the situations in Milwaukee, Minnesota, and possibly Tampa Bay. Although the Pinned-Ins are not able to alter geography, these teams can recognize that different approaches to television marketing are necessary in their markets.

The Cardinals and the Hinterlands

More than any other team, the St. Louis Cardinals successfully used radio and later televised road games to expand the market for its baseball product. Until 1958, the Cardinals were the most western and, until 1962, the most southern National League team. Thus, during the first several decades of broadcasting for vast portions of the United States the Cardinals were geographically the closest team. Advertising-supported broadcasting was the most effective means of promoting the team across its vast potential market. Although revenue from broadcast rights to the games was limited at first, radio and later television developed new Cardinal fans and stimulated attendance. The team was second only to the Cubs in embracing radio.[21] The Cardinal radio network stretched across 124 affiliates in fourteen states, with flagship station KMOX in St. Louis reaching listeners in eight states at its peak.[22] By 1998, the radio network still included about 100 stations spread over nine states, while the television network included over two dozen outlets in eight states.[23]

Many of the stations in the Cardinals' vast network were in smaller communities that developed local stations only after the FCC greatly increased the number of AM station assignments after World War II. Hungry for low-cost programming, these stations became loyal members of the Cardinals' radio network. The strong network boosted the careers of such legendary broadcasters as Baseball Hall of Famers Dizzy Dean, Harry Caray, and Jack Buck. In turn, the flamboyant styles of Dean and Caray helped to build a Cardinals fan base over mid-America.

The Cardinals were also the most aggressive franchise in using road telecasts to complement their vast radio network. The team telecast only a handful of home games before road telecasts of MLB games became more common starting in 1954. As appendix A shows, after 1953 they were strictly Road Warriors, telecasting only road games through 1981. This allowed the team to exploit the promotional potential of television without providing an attraction that might siphon off paying customers.

In addition to selling Cardinals baseball, both home and road radio broadcasts and road telecasts sold beer. Griesedieck Brothers Brewery first sponsored the Cardinals' broadcasts, and then the team itself was purchased by Anheuser-Busch in 1953. Baseball broadcasts succeeded in selling two products, both of which could be enjoyed at home or at the park: baseball and beer. Augustus A. "Gussie" Busch Jr. saw baseball as a key ingredient in the expansion of his Budweiser brand. After the purchase, Busch touted his fortunate decision. "Development of the Cardinals will have untold value for our company. . . . This is one of the finest moves in the history of Anheuser-Busch."[24] Busch was right. Only four years after the purchase of the Cardinals, Anheuser-Busch became the largest producer of beer in the United States. Busch had an early understanding of the now widely recognized "circles of promotion," by which a medium promotes a sports team through its news and sports programming, and the sports team helps support media outlets.[25] Busch's ownership of the Cardinals was a precursor to the symbiotic sport team–media relationship so valued by conglomerates today.

By using media to develop a market well outside metropolitan St. Louis, the Cardinals secured large-city status for itself, despite its relatively modest size, and hastened the departure of the competing St. Louis Browns in 1954. Other examples of teams using the hinterlands model include the Cincinnati Reds, Colorado Rockies, and, at least until recently, the Los Angeles Dodgers.

The Cubs Embrace Broadcasting

Whereas the goal of Cardinals broadcasting was the geographic expansion of the team's fan base, the goal of the Chicago Cubs under longtime owners William Wrigley and his son Philip K. Wrigley was expansion over the airwaves. The Wrigleys knew the value of radio in marketing chewing gum and saw the medium's potential for Major League Baseball. By the mid-1920s, when most owners thought that radio broadcasts of Major League games decreased ballpark attendance, William Wrigley opened his park to virtually any station interested in covering the games.[26] Wrigley, like Larry MacPhail of the Reds and Brooklyn Dodgers, believed that radio broadcasts did not give away the product but increased and diversified interest in it. Indeed, Wrigley did not locate the value of radio in the small rights fees he would receive from exclusive licensing of the Cubs broadcasts to one station. Rather, radio's contribution came from promoting both the largely winning Cubs teams of the 1930s and early 1940s and the wonders of "the friendly confines of Wrigley Field." For Wrigley, more stations carrying the Cubs meant more potential listeners and more potential Cub fans.

Longtime Giants broadcaster Russ Hodges, who got his start in Chicago, described the many announcers who covered Chicago teams:

> Chicago was wide open in all other respects, so it shouldn't have
> been a surprise to me that there were almost no radio restrictions
> there either. But I must admit it was something of a shock to find
> the press boxes at Comiskey Park and Wrigley Field crawling with
> play-by-play announcers. There was nothing exclusive about my
> new job. I was one of five different guys sitting behind five different
> microphones broadcasting over five different stations. We worked
> side by side, so close together that we never had to worry about
> dead air. No matter which station they tuned, the fans could always
> hear somebody talking.[27]

Daytime Major League Baseball also provided stations with inexpensive,
commercially sponsored programming. The dominant commercial fare
of daytime radio was soap operas targeted to women and late-afternoon
adventure programs aimed at children. Stations that could not offer these
successful commercial genres frequently saw daytime as "sustaining time"
(i.e., not advertiser supported), to be filled with less popular programming that maintained the station's signal until sponsored programming
could be obtained. Cubs baseball provided broadcasters not blessed with
successful soaps or children's fare with programming that could produce
commercial revenue by attracting male listeners, both young and old, and
women who enjoyed the national pastime more than soaps.

With the advent of television, P. K. Wrigley followed his father's radio
plan. As early as 1945, Wrigley commissioned Chicago television pioneer Capt. William Eddy to develop techniques for covering baseball.
Eddy produced a manual for producing baseball telecasts that greatly
influenced the early coverage of the game. During this mid-1940s experimental period, Wrigley also gave the Cubs' television rights to Eddy.[28]
WGN-TV's initial purchase of television equipment included facilities
for remote production, including a large van called the "Blue Goose."
This mobile unit was a self-contained television control room that could
microwave live transmissions from anywhere in the Chicago area. Thus,
at its sign-on on April 5, 1948, the station was fully prepared for live
baseball coverage.[29]

Cubs games were televised frequently in 1948, and, starting in 1949,
all of the team's home games were on TV.[30] The home telecast promoted
not just the team, but the "friendly confines" of Wrigley Field, laying the

groundwork for the ballpark's emergence as a "national treasure" in the 1980s. As seen in appendix A, the Cubs added a handful of road telecasts to their abundant home offerings starting in 1960. The road telecasts jumped dramatically to more than sixty games a year starting in 1968.

In 1951, WGN placed a camera in the outfield stands to deliver the center field shot of the pitcher, batter, catcher, and umpire to its television audience. This preceded the shot's adoption in network broadcasts by two years.[31] WGN gained exclusive coverage of all Cubs home games and the daytime, usually weekend, games of the White Sox in 1958. By 1961, WGN was using a team of twenty-one production personnel and four-color cameras to telecast 130 daytime Cubs and White Sox games.[32] WGN was also among the first stations to telecasts games in color (see chapter 14).

Throughout the 1950s and 1960s, Phil Wrigley sold the Cubs' television rights for minimal fees, reasoning that he was creating fans. As late as 1963, the Cubs' rights for both radio and television were only $500,000, half of the fees earned by the Mets and Dodgers, and $350,000 less than the fees earned by the crosstown White Sox.[33] But the rights fees could be undervalued as long as new fans got hooked on the Cubs and came out to the ballpark.[34] The team's unique position of playing all of its home games during the day became a means of developing new fans among daytime television viewers. A generation of Cub fans was born when they came home from school and turned on the game, unless mom already had it on.

In the 1980s, the Cubs' new owners, the Tribune Company, would apply a similar strategy to extend the team's fan base, using Cubs telecasts over cable superstation WGN as a means of building a national market. As part of its national strategy, Cubs baseball would provide relatively cheap, original, daytime cable programming in an era when most cable programming, even in prime time, consisted of network reruns, old movies, and inexpensive talk shows. Its daytime home games also would give it an advantage over other superstation teams (the Braves on WTBS, Mets on WOR, Yankees on WPIX) in developing a regional or national fan following. For most weekday home games, the Cubs faced no TV competition from other big league teams.

WGN also knew the power of the star announcer. In the early 1980s, the White Sox had alienated fan favorite and baseball announcing legend Harry Caray by developing a plan that would put many Sox games on pay television. As soon as his contract expired, he jumped at WGN's offer to become the voice of the Cubs. The new cable superstation gave Caray his first national audience. In the 1950s, Caray's colorful style and the Cardinals Radio Network had made St. Louis mid-America's team. Thirty years later, Caray's style and WGN's national reach would expand "Cubdom" from Chicago's North Side to much of the United States. In doing so, the Cubs would join the Cardinals in "delocalizing" the team and in opening up a dominant position in its home city.

The increased value of the Cubs franchise is clear evidence of their successful cable television strategy. The Tribune Company bought the Cubs in June 1981 for $20.5 million.[35] After over two decades of superstation promotion, the value of the franchise has increased to at least $400 million. This is over $130 million more than the value of the crosstown White Sox, who have a much newer ballpark and who won a World Series in 2005.[36]

The Chicago White Sox, despite their 2005 championship, remain second-class baseball citizens in Chicago in terms of both media and fan attention. Despite more on-field success than the Cubs, the White Sox's television strategy limited their coverage to a small number of day games during television's formative period. The White Sox also suffered from a more limited radio network and a financially strapped ownership. Shallow-pocketed Sox owner Bill Veeck was a master of ballpark promotion, but he had a shortsighted approach to television. His 1977 business organizational chart featured a business manager who handled TV advertising sales as just one of his five major responsibilities, which included ticket sales, park operations, and accounting.[37] Later experiments with pay TV failed and cost the team its only star announcer. The White Sox situation deteriorated to such a low point in the late 1980s that the team's continued presence in the city, the nation's third-largest television market, was saved only by a last-minute and highly controversial state government action on a new ballpark that kept the team from moving to Tampa Bay. The White Sox owners allowed the team to become a pinned-in franchise both in Chicago and in the hinterlands.

The Cardinals and Cubs are both good examples of how television can be leveraged to expand fan support, generate positive promotion, and promote other businesses (Budweiser, Wrigley's gum). The Atlanta Braves are another example of how a team used a superstation to extend its fan base well beyond its metropolitan area, making Skip Caray almost as famous as his father (Harry) in the 1980s and 1990s. However, unlike the Cubs and Cardinals, the Braves did not embrace television in the earlier days of the medium when the club was located in Milwaukee. Atlanta became a television embracer only after the team's acquisition by pioneering cable television entrepreneur Ted Turner.

The Cubs and the Braves are also prime examples of the trend to merge media product and distribution (see chapter 12). Before its sale to real estate tycoon Sam Zell, the Tribune Company media conglomerate owned the *Chicago Tribune*, the city's dominant newspaper; WGN-AM, the rights holder for all Cubs games; and local powerhouse WGN-TV, a pioneering superstation that made the Cubs a national commodity for over a quarter of a century.[38] The Braves were owned for years by Turner's growing cable television empire before Time Warner, one of the world's largest media corporations, acquired his assets.

The Relocators of the 1950s and 1960s

No media technology to date, including the Internet, has diffused as rapidly as television. From a near zero base in 1946, television was in over 87 percent of U.S. households by 1960.[39] Not surprisingly, this unprecedented acceptance by the public triggered great concern in existing media industries (radio, motion pictures, and newspapers). It also troubled industries such as professional sports, which were just now coming to terms with radio, about which baseball ownership was still highly skeptical because of its possible impact of "giving away" product.

As we have seen, the approaches of the always contentious group of MLB owners diverged widely, from the essentially open-gate policy of Wrigley to the antitelevision position of the Pirates' ownership. Another model of teams' approach to television developed with the relocation and expansion of MLB franchises in the 1950s and early 1960s. Although this model was not as obvious as the other three models and overlaps them somewhat, there is no question that television was an important factor in baseball's relocation and expansion years.

We are not saying that television was the primary factor in these two changes. The move to the suburbs encouraged by new highways and an expanding automotive culture, the subsequent decline of the inner-city neighborhoods where many parks were located, and the decay of public transportation in many cities were more important factors. In addition, the commercialization and expansion of jet travel encouraged the expansion of MLB's national footprint. Nevertheless, television became a convenient "villain" for explaining many of the moves of the 1950s and 1960s as well as the decline of the oversaturated minor leagues (see chapter 10), not to mention any number of perceived social ills beyond baseball or sports.

The movements of the Braves from Boston to Milwaukee (1953) and the Athletics from Philadelphia to Kansas City (1955) reveal much about how owners regarded television. In leaving two of the then five largest cities in the country for much smaller virgin territory in the Midwest, both the Braves and A's adopted a policy of extremely limited local telecasting of games (see appendix A). In retrospect, both moves demonstrated ignorance of contemporary media and marketing dynamics. To give up such large media markets for two of what remain among the smallest Major League and television markets is counterintuitive. The subsequent movement of both teams to the perceived riches of the South and West (Atlanta and Oakland, respectively), after only thirteen years in their Midwestern cities, reflects the negative consequences of these moves. Fortunately for the great fans in Kansas City and Milwaukee, the residual effect of the Athletics' and Braves' sojourns in their cities became the impetus behind local business leaders restoring their MLB status in 1969 and 1970, respectively.

Of course, the owners of the franchises (Lou Perini in Boston-Milwaukee and Arnold Johnson and the Connie Mack heirs in Philadelphia-Kansas City) saw the situation much differently in the 1950s. To them, as well as to the owners of the St. Louis Browns, sharing a "declining" market with another franchise—Red Sox, Phillies, Cardinals—that had established local dominance did not make good business sense. Milwaukee and Baltimore offered new parks outside the downtown area. Milwaukee, Baltimore, and Kansas City all had a long tradition of successful minor league and, in the case of K.C., Negro League baseball. In addition, neither Kansas City nor Milwaukee offered nearly as much competition from other sports teams and other leisure-time activities as did Philadelphia and Boston. The slow and limited availability of local television broadcasts of A's and Braves games until well into the 1960s clearly indicates that the owners saw television as a drain on their attendance rather than a marketing tool. Even the much more successful Orioles were somewhat stymied in maximizing television by the fact that Baltimore was pinned in by Philadelphia, Washington, and Pittsburgh.

Yet the most famous and controversial franchise shifts in baseball's long history were the 1958 relocations of the Brooklyn Dodgers and New York Giants. So much has been written about these teams, which shared the nation's largest media market with the Yankees, that their stories are a major component of the myth of nostalgia that is one of MLB's charms and curses.

The history or hagiography of these two teams reveals many of the same issues that led to the departure of other teams, including antiquated parks, stagnant or declining attendance (particularly in the case of the Giants), suburbanization, and the rise of television as Americans' dominant leisure-time activity. However, the move of these teams to California was triggered by a television motivation often overlooked in histories of the Los Angles Dodgers and San Francisco Giants: the lure of pay television riches.

The concept of pay television predates the commercial introduction of the medium in the United States. Zenith's chief corporate executive, Eugene McDonald, whose company's Phonevision was the first of the pay television systems, did not believe that advertisers could support enough quality programming to make television competitive with radio and motion pictures.[40] McDonald's analysis was wildly off the mark because he did not take into account the huge consumer boom of the post–World War II years. He could not envision people being so captivated by the new medium of television that programming would not have to be of movie "quality" to attract huge audiences and mass advertisers.

Sports telecasts were mentioned in the early Phonevision materials as possible programming, and McDonald solicited support from Walter O'Malley in early 1953.[41] This was after O'Malley had said that pay television might be a good idea for baseball in markets (Cincinnati, Detroit, Pittsburgh) where there was limited or no television coverage of games.[42] However, Zenith placed much more emphasis on motion pictures in its experiments. The corporation finally gave up on Phonevision in the mid-1960s, by which time it was evident that broadcast television was prospering in an advertising-supported model.[43]

Subscriber-Vision, Telemeter, and Telemovies were other proposed pay television systems that appeared soon after Zenith's push for Phonevision began. By far the most important for baseball was Subscription Television, Inc. (STV). STV was a wired version of Skiatron's over-the-air Subscriber-Vision system. A wired system could jump some of the hurtles faced by a pay television service that used an FCC licensed broadcast station to distribute its signal.[44]

Hollywood and baseball were key components of STV's plans. Whereas Phonevision's tests were in Chicago and Hartford, Connecticut, and Telemeter's were in the Toronto suburbs, STV, Inc. had a decidedly California orientation. Among its executives was Sylvester "Pat" Weaver, the highly acclaimed and innovative former chief programmer for NBC and creator of such seminal programs as The Today Show and The Tonight Show. STV also attempted to entice the major motion picture studios into partnerships.[45] The studios, reeling from the breakup of the studio system by the federal courts and from the rapid diffusion of television, were seen as natural partners in the creation of a new form of box office.[46]

As in most of the early pay television systems, there was much more hype than reality to most of STV, Inc.'s plans. However, by the mid-1950s the company was generating significant attention through its announced project to wire the Los Angeles and San Francisco markets, linked to the move of the Dodgers and Giants to the West Coast.[47] Although there were no ownership links between Skiatron and either team, the promise of pay television was often cited as a reason for the departure of the teams from New York.[48] Of course, O'Malley's lamentations about having "too many" Dodger games on broadcast television and his support for pay television fueled the disgust of both New York baseball fans and pay television opponents.[49] Even the threat by Brooklyn's powerful congressional representative, Emmanuel Celler (Democrat), of federal legislation to stop pay television did not keep the Dodgers and Giants from moving or, for that matter, stop pay television.[50]

The criticism and threat of legal actions did contribute to a setback in Skiatron's plans for several years as it suffered delay after delay in getting STV operational. As early as September 1958, the Giants, now in San Francisco, announced that home games would appear on STV in 1959.[51] This announcement was premature by over five years, as STV did not get its three-channel system in operation in San Francisco and Los Angeles until July 17, 1964. On that date, the Cubs-at-Dodgers game became the first MLB game on STV. Of the approximately twenty-five hundred television receivers with STV hookups in Los Angeles, 61 percent paid $1.50 each to watch the game.[52] Although a small audience saw the game, pay television and baseball had their first partnership. It was to prove short lived.

Ultimately, the fact that California was the center of the motion picture industry was responsible for the demise of STV's plans. The National Association of Theater Owners (NATO) launched a statewide antipay television campaign. In November 1964, California voters approved by referendum a ban on pay television by wire within the state.[53] This initiative was found to be unconstitutional in federal court, but the delays it caused, combined with the rising popularity of "free" (advertiser-supported) television, weakened the demand for pay TV.[54] At the same time, the movement of most broadcast network production from New York to Hollywood provided new and lucrative opportunities for the major studios in "free" television. This shift also depressed what had always been a more theoretical than actual demand for pay television. Pay television as a major force in the medium had to wait another decade (see chapter 8).

Although baseball history has not been kind to Walter O'Malley for abandoning Brooklyn, few can deny his credentials as a profit-maximizing capitalist. Not only did a move to Los Angeles open up new territory in what was then the nation's fastest-growing metropolis; it also gave him a real estate and stadium deal that was the envy of his peers as well as a possible windfall of extra "attendance" through pay-per-view. Baseball history also has been unkind to Horace Stoneham, not only for leaving New York, but also for being O'Malley's virtual stooge. By moving the Giants to the smaller San Francisco market, he gave the Dodgers a West Coast rival and reduced the teams' travel costs. Although the later history of Stoneham's ownership makes it clear that he and his front office were not nearly as astute as O'Malley's in revenue generation and team building, the lure of pay television as well as a new city was not an easy one to turn down.

Although the Dodgers and Giants were not to be the beneficiaries of a pay television windfall, they hardly embraced free television. Telecasts by both teams for the next twenty plus years were limited in number and mainly restricted to a few away games (see appendix A). Clearly, the idea that television broadcasting was the equivalent of "giving away the game" had a long life span in Los Angeles and San Francisco.

MLB's first-ever planned expansion in 1961–62 was not predicated on television, but does offer some interesting insights into how important the medium was becoming to baseball and to big league sports in general. The American League's 1961 expansion into Los Angeles and Washington is instructive. Gene Autry, a major show business figure, but, more importantly, the owner of a major L.A. television station, was chosen to own the Major League Angels. It has been widely reported that Autry came to the owners seeking television rights to Dodger games and ended up with his own franchise.[55] This is one of the first examples of a television station owner becoming a baseball franchise owner. Of course, placing another team in what was to become within ten years the second-largest television market was a canny strategy for the American League whether or not Autry was the owner. Only in recent years, during the ownership by Arte Moreno of the now Los Angeles Angels of Anaheim, has this prescience become evident.

Washington immediately received a replacement team when the Griffith family moved the original Nationals or Senators to Minnesota. Though Washington was a large television market and an original American League team, the birth of the new Senators was also a strategy for keeping members of Congress from becoming overly critical of baseball's business practices and longstanding antitrust exemption. If MLB had abandoned the nation's capital, the passage of the Sports Broadcasting Act of 1961, which excluded baseball from its purview because of the sport's antitrust exemption, would have been much more difficult. Although Washington was abandoned eleven years later for what turned out to be thirty-three years, baseball by 1972 was in a relative economic slump, beset by labor trouble, and considered to be an old and tired game surpassed by pro football in American consciousness. In addition, the poor on-the-field performance of the new Senators and the changing demography of the District of Columbia left relatively few Washingtonians, both in and out of the Congress, to bemoan the team's move to Dallas-Ft. Worth.

Meaning of the Models

Major League Baseball is a pretelevision and therefore premodern sport that continues to have a problematic relationship with television—the indispensable life force of "big-time" corporate sport. This dysfunction is often expressed in terms of "haves" or "have-nots." Journalists Jack Sands and Peter Gammons, for example, used a retail analogy to describe what they consider to be a three-tier structure of MLB teams:

> "The Supermarkets," consisting of the teams located in the largest media markets in the United States (i.e., New York, Los Angeles, Chicago).

> "The Convenience Stores," consisting of the teams in medium-size markets (e.g., St. Louis, Baltimore, Cleveland) that have managed through public-funded facilities and savvy marketing to carve out a lucrative niche for their product.

> "The Lemonade Stands" such as the Pittsburgh Pirates and Kansas City Royals. Due to some combination of small market size and weak fan base such teams are unlikely to compete with other teams without major revenue sharing.[56]

Since this analysis appeared over a decade ago, the economics of MLB have greatly improved. The presence of Fox and ESPN as television partners is of particular importance. Fox's willingness to continue to pay a premium price for MLB is related to its continuing emphasis on sports product as the key element in its domestic and international growth. ESPN, which must have major sports events on both a national and international level in order to grow, adds a considerable amount to baseball's national television pool. As the national revenue that is equally shared becomes larger, the importance of local television money is diminishing. Of course, as long as there are such wide disparities in local rights fees, the situation will remain problematic.

The strengthening of the commissioner's power to deal with revenue inequities in recent years is starting to have a substantial impact on media revenue inequities. Major League Baseball Advanced Media's (MLBAM) success in offering compelling video and audio content on the Internet, with all its revenue equally shared by the thirty MLB teams, is a major success and a model for other sports leagues. This book's epilogue will examine MLB's initiatives in "advanced media" in detail. As the Internet morphs into a combination of all existing media forms, MLBAM could be an avenue to equal media sharing, including television, although it is difficult to imagine that the owners of the largest market teams had this in mind when they approved the agreement.[57]

MLB officials are increasingly committed to enhanced marketing and globalization as key elements in the game's revival. MLB has rich opportunities to develop its value in Asia and Latin America. The inaugural World Baseball Classic (WBC) in 2006 is in many ways a culmination of MLB's international plans.

Although MLB has yet to overcome its television "problem," it clearly is working hard to do so and to figure out the best blend of international, national, regional, and local television coverage for the game. The increasing co-ownership of teams and television networks and the increasing retention by teams of both television and radio rights indicate the growing importance of television to MLB's continuing success, even while such co-ownership can exacerbate team revenue inequalities.

We hope that documenting the historical underpinnings of the current inequities in the television revenue streams of the thirty MLB teams may help loosen the grip of nostalgia that has often hindered an understanding of the business and media side of MLB. At the very least, we trust that our discussion of the pinned-in, the hinterlands, embracers, and relocators models has made the case that, while market size is the most important influence on local television revenues, other factors, which teams control, should be part of any analysis of baseball's economic inequities.

The National Game

2

Televising the World Series

The canceling of the 1994 World Series by interim baseball commissioner Bud Selig is often regarded as the nadir of Major League Baseball in the past twenty years. Fans and baseball writers did not understand how a business owned by billionaires and played by millionaires could let a labor dispute interrupt its shining moment on the national stage. The vitriolic reaction to the canceling of the 1994 World Series points out the prestigious place the Fall Classic still occupied in the popular psyche, even as the twentieth century was fading into the twenty-first. Although baseball was clearly not the foremost sport, as it had been in the first half of the twentieth century, the World Series was still seen by millions as a sacred rite of October. For the mass media, the World Series, from its very beginning, has been the defining climax to a very long baseball season.

Starting in 1903, when newspapers were the dominant mass medium for most Americans, the World Series has provided a dramatic focus for baseball that each new medium has used to help sell itself to the pubic. Graham McNamee's coverage of the World Series helped stoke the fire for the new mass medium of radio in the 1920s. The first nationwide broadcast of the World Series by the newly minted National Broadcasting Company in 1927 promoted both radio and what broadcast historian Erik Barnouw would call "The Golden Web" of the national radio networks.[1]

By 1947, television would offer its first World Series, and greatly expand its coverage in the East and Midwest in 1948. Coast-to-coast live coverage began in 1951. But the significance of the World Series in promoting television does not end there. In 1955, RCA used the World Series to sell the first generation of color televisions. Later the Series would help sell large-screen projection televisions, and more recently, high-definition television receivers. With each new broadcast technology the American family was asked: wouldn't it be great to experience the World Series, the national pastime's ultimate event, in the comfort of your own home on your own radio, your own television, in color, on a giant screen, or in high definition? Millions of times, the American family has answered: yes!

Television's First World Series

Although the *Sporting News* reported in 1946 that Gillette was interested in expanding its radio coverage, begun in 1939, to include televising the 1946 World Series, coverage actually began with the 1947 World Series between the New York Yankees and Brooklyn Dodgers.[2] The all–New York confrontation meant that all games could be covered in each team's home city. The telecasts were limited to nine stations in four markets: New York, Philadelphia, Washington DC, and Schenectady. All three of New York's stations (WABD, WCBS-TV, and WNBT) carried the games produced for the Mutual network. Overall, an estimated fifty thousand television sets brought the game to between six hundred thousand and seven hundred thousand viewers.[3] Even with these modest television audience figures, the *Sporting News* believed that the medium's first World Series had "been seen by more people than any other sports event in history."[4]

The World Series coverage convinced many families to purchase their first TV. The *Sporting News* reported that the coverage pushed New York–area interest in receivers "to what was described as the most unprecedented demand since the early days of radio."[5] Indeed, some manufacturers, hoping to stimulate receiver sales, advertised that the contests would be telecast even while the contract for the coverage was still being negotiated. The ads put pressure on broadcasters to carry the games or face the public's wrath.[6] In addition to television manufacturers and their dealers, New York bars were major beneficiaries. When the Series games aired on their receivers, tavern owners reported a 500 percent increase in business over a typical weekday afternoon. Some taverns took reservations from regulars for the choicest seats near the set.[7]

11. *New Yorkers watch the 1952 World Series. Many fans saw their first game at a tavern. Photo by Francis Miller / Time Life Pictures / Getty Images.*

New York was a fortuitous location for the first televised World Series. At a time when TV networking was very limited, the Yankees-Dodgers World Series got maximum publicity from the New York–based national press and was seen by many of the nation's corporate leaders. Even members of the recently created United Nations were invited to view the World Series. A special guide to baseball was produced in English, French, Spanish, and Russian to help UN delegates and employees understand the sport.[8]

No Beer, Please

Although the Television Broadcasters Association lobbied Commissioner A. B. "Happy" Chandler to allow the telecasts, the televising of the World Series was not a certainty until mid-September. Chandler approved the telecasts despite opposition from a minority of owners.[9] But there was still the unsettled matter of the rights fee. Initially, Commissioner Chandler had demanded an additional $100,000 for the rights. Many observers thought Chandler's original demand was extravagant, considering radio rights to a vastly larger nationwide radio audience was no more than $175,000.[10] Liebmann Breweries of Brooklyn met Chandler's lower $100,000 demand (provided the Series was an all–New York affair), but the commissioner declined the brewery's offer on the "grounds that it would not be good public relations for baseball to have the Series sponsored by the producer of an alcoholic beverage."[11] Since beer and baseball had been and would continue to be strongly linked, the commissioner's rejection seemed inconsistent. But baseball's leadership, or at least Commissioner Chandler, viewed the World Series as a special event, one that should not be compromised by commercial expediencies. Ford Motor Co. then offered to meet the commissioner's $100,000 price, but only if he would give them sponsorship for the next ten years for $1 million.[12] But even baseball's less than "TV savvy" leadership knew that the rights in the future would be worth far more than that.

Ultimately, Gillette and Ford cosponsored the games. The rights fees cost $65,000, a generous figure considering so few could actually see the telecasts. The commissioner rejected a last-minute offer of $85,000 from an auto accessories chain. For their rights fees, the two sponsors got commercials of varying quality. Most Ford and Gillette commercials relied on slides and were acceptable, but the live commercials were another matter. According to *Variety*, poor lighting in Gillette's commercials produced at CBS's Ebbets Field studio gave the models five o'clock shadows even after shaving.[13]

The Reviews Are In

By 1947, televised baseball had moved out of its experimental period. Coverage of Major League home games became commonplace. The home games of all three New York teams had been telecast that season. By the time of the World Series, crews were experienced, although production techniques were still fairly primitive. DuMont produced three games (numbers two, six, and seven), while NBC produced games one and five and CBS produced games three and four. NBC used only two cameras: a "cover shot" above and behind home plate and one on the first base side to provide closeups of the players and to follow the ball to the outfield.

Even at this early stage, the benefits of television were evident, but reviews of the Series coverage were mixed. R. W. Stewart of the *New York Times* thought baseball action was "more difficult to capture on the tele-screen than that of other sports" and especially difficult at Yankee Stadium. However, "despite the limitations of the scene reproduced by the electronic cameras, those in the tele-bleachers were getting a more intimate view of the game than those actually in the ball park."[14]

The show business voice *Variety*, which was often critical of televised baseball coverage, noted that "despite the limited scope of tele cameras, which seriously hindered the audience's view of the field at times," and despite its difficulty handling the dark late-afternoon shadows, "tele proved conclusively that it's better than radio—and even better than a seat on the first base line—when it comes to dramatic moments."[15] In particular, *Variety* raved about TV's coverage of Dodger Cookie Lavagetto's winning pinch-hit double in game four and the closeup of Eddie Stanky "blowing his top" after a questionable call. For these instances, television "was certainly better than any description of the action that could be furnished by radio announcers Red Barber and Mel Allen, who can be classed with the best." But *Variety*'s praise was tempered. Television is "convenient and more comfortable but it's not the same as being there." Directors were also chided for using too many closeups and missing key action. "Closeups have their place," noted *Variety*, "but not when the ball is in play. Most viewers want to see the game, or play, as a whole."[16]

Networking at Twenty Thousand Feet

The 1948 World Series between the Boston Braves and the Cleveland Indians presented a very different set of problems. Gillette purchased exclusive sponsorship for $175,000, nearly three times what Gillette and Ford paid only a year before.[17] In becoming the exclusive sponsor of the World Series, Gillette would make the Fall Classic the centerpiece of its sports advertising over the next two decades. For a generation of baseball fans, the razor company's "look sharp, feel sharp, be sharp" slogan and animated parrot would be linked annually to the World Series. The Mutual Broadcasting System, the radio network that had both radio and television rights, offered the games to all interested television stations on its World Series network. But what stations would be networked?

The Stratovision Experiment

By 1948, the U.S. television industry featured separate eastern and midwest television networks with no link between them. By September, it was clear that if Cleveland and Boston were the Series combatants, then all stations in eight eastern cities (Boston, New York, Philadelphia, Baltimore, Washington, Richmond, Schenectady, and New Haven) would carry games one, two, six, and seven from Boston, and seven Midwest cities (Cleveland, Buffalo, Toledo, St. Louis, Detroit, Chicago, and Milwaukee) would carry games three, four, and five from Cleveland.[18] Could the two regions be linked, so that fans in both regions could see all seven games? The answer was maybe.

The "maybe" took the form of an experimental television relay system called Stratovision. This revolutionary system was a joint venture of Westinghouse and the Glenn L. Martin Company under the direction of their young inventor Chili Nobles. Stratovision used a refitted B-29 bomber as a relay between originating and receiving stations. The B-29, flying at twenty thousand feet, could send a television signal about 250 miles, enough to bridge the East and Midwest networks for the World Series. If it worked, viewers on the East Coast and in the Midwest would get to see all seven Series games. Stratovision would gain a publicity windfall for its technology.[19]

Initially, the Federal Communications Commission denied Stratovision's petition to use television channel six for the World Series relay because of potential interference with television stations already using that channel. Broadcast stations can share a channel, but they must be geographically separated and their power limited to prevent interference. But Stratovision persisted and convinced the FCC to grant a waiver for game six of the World Series originating in Boston. Station WMAR-TV in Baltimore took the game feed from the East Coast network and relayed it to the Stratovision B-29 flying over western Pennsylvania, where it was relayed to WEWS in Cleveland for transmission on its Midwest network. But the transmission had several problems. The picture received by

WEWS would not stay in sync. The station's own signal on channel five interfered with the Stratovision signal on channel six. WEWS responded by shutting off its own signal, but the problems persisted. They were unable to provide an acceptable signal for the Midwest network.[20] On October 11, 1948, Cleveland fans rejoiced at the Indians 4–3 victory in Boston, wrapping up the Series, but they never saw the live action clearly.

What Cleveland and the Midwest network could not receive clearly was viewed with interest by fans in dozens of towns in Ohio and Pennsylvania. Their television receivers took the World Series feed directly from the airplane. One enterprising radio dealer in Indiana, Pennsylvania, drew a crowd of twenty-five hundred to watch the televised game in the rain.[21] Because the East Coast–Midwest link failed to work during the Series, the Commissioner refunded $35,000 of Gillette's original $175,000 rights fee. By the time Stratovision's problems were solved, land-based coaxial cable networks were well underway, making Stratovision obsolete. In 1951, AT&T would complete the coaxial cable network, allowing coast-to-coast television coverage of the World Series.

Bringing the World Series to the People

Although Stratovision failed to deliver a stable connection for the 1948 Series, other distribution experiments were more successful. Gillette, in a master promotional stroke, worked with the Boston Park Commission to set up one hundred RCA-donated receivers in the Boston Commons. An estimated ten thousand Beantowners use the sets to see the Braves Field games on television.[22] In Chicago, WGN set up five projection televisions for a crowd jamming the Nathan Hale Court outside of the Tribune Tower. All three licensed Chicago stations presented the games from Cleveland and WNBQ, which, while not officially on the air yet, was also allowed to offer the telecasts.[23] In Cleveland, station WEWS combined the audio feed of the game with a studio video presentation of a baseball diamond to show the progress of the Boston-based games.

The B&O Railroad used the World Series to show that television could be received on trains, with only a few minor interruptions for tunnels. The demonstration provided a photo "op" for the FCC's first female commissioner, Frieda Hennock, who the *New York Times* referred to as

12. Gillette made sure Bostonians could watch the 1948 World Series
by placing receivers on the Boston Commons. AP/Wide World Photos.

a "pretty blonde." The B&O reception on a train from Washington to
Jersey City was favorably reviewed; an Associated Press (AP) report said
that "technically, it was surprisingly good, so good that the Baltimore
and Ohio Railroad may install it as a regular feature on its better trains.
But, as a way to watch a ball game, make mine Braves Field."[24]

The Coverage: A Boston Massacre

What bothered the AP reporter was likely the very poor coverage of the
Braves' home games. *Variety* absolutely hated the Boston coverage of the
first, second, and sixth games of the 1948 World Series. WNAC's coverage
of the first World Series, seen widely outside of New York, "provided its
viewers with a dull version of probably one of the quietest opening world
series games on record. The camera work was without imagination and
completely failed to transmit the color or flavor of the game." *Variety* reported that WNAC never showed the crowd or even the outfield. Announcer
Red Barber often called for shots "of some particular action on the field

but the camera director simply ignored him."[25] It later added, "What that WNAC camera crew did to him in the opener was murder."[26] The *Washington Post* concurred, saying that the coverage "left much to be desired." The cover shot showed only the pitcher at the top of the screen and only the batter's head at the bottom. The bat, catcher, and umpire were missing from the scene. Cameras were late covering plays to the infield, and even put-outs at first base were missed. In contrast, the Cleveland games covered by station WEWS received very positive comment, as they offered "good camera mobility, with little dullness and no confusion."[27]

The 1949 World Series: Experimental Approaches

By 1949, coaxial cables joined the East and Midwest, and for the first time all cities with Major League teams could view all the World Series contests live. Commissioner Chandler, still uncertain about the long-term prospects for television, continued his year-to-year sale of TV rights. Once again Gillette obtained exclusivity, but the price increased to $200,000. For the first time, TV rights exceeded radio rights ($175,000). The radio rights fee would never again approach television's, as radio's "golden age" would gradually come to an end. Gillette also won the right to match any other offer for the next year's contest.[28]

Although industry sources speculated that Gillette would restrict the telecasts to just one network, the sponsor offered the games to any station connected to AT&T's video cables if the station was willing to pay the line charges. However, there was one significant catch. Gillette would not pay stations to carry the Series games, even though it would include all of Gillette's commercials. Thus, despite the potential for record audiences, telecasters would not profit from the World Series. Stations were in a bind. They did not want to set a precedent by carrying sponsored programming without charge. But station managers knew it would be a local public relations nightmare if they did not carry the Series and their competitors did. Several managers claimed that the plan was "unfair to other advertisers," and they refused to "run the Gillette business for nothing." However, all but a few stations eventually caved in to Gillette's demand. A station manager from Toledo lamented the arrangement "as one of the worst chisels that has been worked, but you can hardly refuse to carry the series."[29] A. Craig Smith, vice president in charge of advertising, defended Gillette's plan. The sponsor could not afford to pay every station for its time and allowing only one station in a market to carry the Series would trigger protests from the slighted stations.

The plight of station managers illustrates the mounting popular pressure to televise the World Series. Although only about 1 million American homes had televisions in 1949, an estimated 17.5 to 20 million viewers saw some part of the second Yankee-Dodger World Series in three years.[30] Millions of "setless" fans visited a neighbor who had one or went to the local tavern to see the games. Among those viewers were members of the U.S. Senate. Vice President Alben Barkley had a television set installed in his office so his colleagues could sneak a peek during slower moments of the proceedings.[31]

The Series' success in selling receivers produced shortages in some markets. Admiral, RCA, Philco, and Emerson restricted their allocation of receivers in the New York area because "the shortage is more serious now than at any time since we entered the television business."[32] But even as set sales soared, MLB was exploring another more potentially lucrative form of video distribution for the World Series.

The Theater Experiment

In 1949, Chandler authorized experimental distribution of World Series telecasts to movie theaters. Ultimately, six movie houses in five cities (Brooklyn, Boston, Chicago, Milwaukee, and Scranton) charged admission to see the projected video of the Series. In Brooklyn, the Fox Theatre paid $10,000 for the rights, and about fifteen thousand attended its video projection of the games. Admission was $1.20 for the weekday and $1.50 for the weekend games, substantially higher than the ordinary weekday matinee price of $.55. The theater owner even offered ballpark concessions; popcorn, peanut, and soda vendors worked the aisles. Attendance for the Series averaged three-quarters of the house capacity. The theater owner saw the experiment as "something between a double and a triple," but not a home run.[33]

One of the theater owner's problems was competition from bars. Tavern owners were offering the same product, though on a smaller screen, for the cost of a beer. Both corner pubs and fine hotels' watering holes reported booming business during the Series. Some taverns required a cover charge during the games. Others stopped sales of cheaper draft beer, offering only premium-priced bottled brews. Patrons abstaining from libations were asked "politely" to leave. But the bar owners could not control the rate of consumption. The New York Times quipped that "never did so many nurse so few beers for so long" as the fans watching the opening game of the 1949 World Series.[34]

Creative Coverage

The 1949 World Series coverage offered a few new TV tricks. DuMont covered the Yankees' home games and CBS the Dodgers'. For the first time, both networks used a split screen to show both the pitcher throwing home and the runner leading off first base. DuMont put the shot of the runner in a small circle on the upper-right corner of the picture, while CBS gave roughly equal portions of the screen to both pitcher and runner. In addition, DuMont put a camera in the Yankee bullpen for the Stadium games. Although not the center field camera that is so dominant in today's televised baseball, the Series' "bleacher shot" from about the middle of right field offered a view of the pitcher, batter, catcher, and umpire from a totally new perspective. However, DuMont used the shot sparingly because the new vantage point proved confusing for viewers accustomed to the behind-the-plate perspective.

The Series' growing TV reach meant comments on the new techniques might come from cities throughout the East and Midwest. Variety summarized the mixed reactions of viewers from New York ("solid job"), Chicago ("didn't measure up to our local coverage"), Detroit ("good job, but plenty of gripes heard"), Boston ("fans stunned by overall pickup quality"), Cleveland ("Series not so good, 'ours was better'"), Cincinnati ("cameras performed 'swell job'"), and St. Louis ("compared favorably").[35] Attention focused on the new split-screen technique and the outfield camera. Some viewers praised the innovations, while others found them puzzling. Reviewers were generally positive about announcer Jim Britt, who successfully adapted his commentary to the varied interests and loyalties of the national audience.

"The Greatest Advertising Force on Earth"

In 1950, big money televised sport came of age, and the new wealth it produced would contribute to the firing of Commissioner Chandler. The webbing of America continued at a steady pace. Fourteen cities were added to the coaxial network, which now reached seventy-six stations in forty-nine communities. The network went as far west as Omaha and as far south as Jacksonville, connecting five million sets to the World Series. Audience projections for the Series ranged from twenty to thirty-eight million viewers.[36] Audiences of this size interested more than one suitor.

DuMont and its sponsor, Chevrolet, entered the bidding against Gillette and its network, Mutual, the Series' broadcast rights holder since 1939. The offers started at $500,000, two and a half times what the TV rights brought in 1949. They moved up to $650,000, then $770,000, and finally $800,000. At each point, Gillette used its right to match the highest offer, negotiated the previous year, to equal the latest DuMont-Chevrolet challenge. The negotiation clock ran out on August 21, Chandler's deadline, and Gillette won the rights. The television rights combined with $175,000 for radio rights, negotiated early as part of a six-year radio contract, pushed Gillette's World Series price tag to nearly a million dollars.[37] In only the fourth year of Series telecasting, television rights fees were more than four and half times radio's. Gillette allowed ABC, CBS, and NBC to network the games. An angry DuMont refused to participate, retreating to lick its wounds.

The total costs, including promotions, for the World Series and All-Star Game consumed $1.5 million of Gillette's $5 million advertising budget. A. Craig Smith, Gillette's head of advertising, however, was convinced the Series was worth it: "The World Series is the greatest advertising force on earth."[38] Chandler had initially expressed interest in continuing the theater experiment that had generated about $32,000 the previous year, but the Gillette windfall made theatrical distribution less important, and no theatrical exhibition was approved. The dalliance with direct payment was over. Advertising would support the World Series as it did the rest of television.

A Commissioner's Mistake

The four-and-a-half-fold increase in television rights fees spurred an immediate response from the players. The owners had agreed to use the Series radio rights to help fund the players' pension, begun in 1947, but the television bonanza was ticketed for the game's central fund, which was distributed to all owners. The players wanted their share. In September, Fred Hutchinson of the Tigers and Marty Marion of the Cardinals sought a 50 percent cut of the future World Series television revenues for the players, requesting a hearing with Commissioner Chandler on the matter. Although some players wanted direct payment from the World Series' TV pot, most believed that all of the $800,000 should go to the pension funding. The new funds would reduce the age at which benefits began from fifty to forty-five.[39]

Initially, Chandler indicated that he would meet with the players during the Series, but when Marion tried to confirm a meeting time the commissioner did not respond. Marion went public with the story, arguing that the players "deserved a hearing and the commissioner refused to even answer me."[40] Chandler responded that a meeting would be held in due course, dismissing rumors that the players might strike before the Series. Reflecting the management paternalism of the era, he reported, "we discussed the whole thing quite amicably . . . and I'm sure the player representatives are satisfied with whatever decision eventually may be made."[41]

Chandler kept his word. After setting a meeting with the owners for November 16 to discuss the distribution of the World Series revenues, he met with the players' representatives at his Kentucky home on November 8. He recommended that the bulk of the $975,000 received from the Series be put in the player pension fund. Armed with tax and insurance experts, Chandler convinced the players that it was in their interest to defer paying taxes on their Series share by putting money into the pension plan. On November 16, in less than three minutes, the owners ratified the agreement he made with the players.[42] However, less than a month later, they would unanimously agree that Chandler should be replaced.

With a three-quarters majority needed, the owners failed to reelect

13. *Happy Chandler's World Series rights package would anger many owners.*
Ford Frick (on the left) would replace Chandler.
National Baseball Hall of Fame Library, Cooperstown NY.

Chandler to a second term by votes of nine to seven, eight to eight, and nine to seven. They then voted sixteen to zero to seek a new commissioner. The meetings were covered in *Life* magazine, which published a series of photographs, some shot through a keyhole, of the owners debating Chandler's future.[43] On December 12, 1950, "Happy" Chandler went quickly from happy to "shock and pained surprise."[44] Dan Topping, owner of the Yankees, and Cardinal owner Fred Saigh, a longtime Chandler critic, spearheaded the dump Chandler movement. Topping gave only a vague explanation for the owners' shocking move. "Why did we do this? I'd imagine it was an over-all thing. They didn't think he was doing a good job."[45] Years later, Chandler offered his analysis of the events: "I negotiated the first television contracts (multi-year) and put the money in the pension fund for the benefit of the players. The owners didn't think much of that."[46]

Chandler vowed to finish the remaining sixteen months of his term, in part because he wanted "to complete certain commitments concerning certain world series television which will make the pension fund a working and substantial factor in our game."[47] Chandler was a baseball outsider who suffered in the long shadow of Judge Landis. In 1947, he had provoked considerable animosity by allowing the Dodgers to integrate baseball by promoting Jackie Robinson to the big league club. However, his "pro-player" handling of baseball's World Series bounty was the straw that broke the owners' backs. Chandler made good on his vow to not quit, at least for the moment. On the day after Christmas, he offered his own "shock and pained surprise" gift to the owners.

A Commissioner's Revenge

Chandler wanted to provide funding for the player pensions and saw World Series rights as the long-term solution. He started in November by signing away radio rights to Gillette through 1956 for $1,370,000. Then, on December 26, 1950, the lame-duck commissioner announced a six-year $6 million deal for Series television rights with Gillette and Mutual. Chandler indicated that the money from TV and radio rights would be "applied in large part to the baseball player's annuity and insurance plan."[48] The deal represented a $200,000-a-year, 20 percent increase over the fee for the 1950 Series. But the deal also included the All-Star Game, which had generated $184,000 in rights fees in 1950. Essentially, Chandler had frozen the television rights for the next six years at 1950 prices, when only 9 percent of American homes had television.[49] With competitive bidding, surely the rights fees would continue to grow, reflecting the growth of the new medium and its potential audience.

A few owners, such as the Comiskeys (White Sox), Roy Mack (Athletics), and Horace Stoneham (Giants), thought it was a "good deal," while Warren Giles, president of the Reds, said it would take six years to evaluate. Since Chandler was giving most of the money to the players' pension fund, the owners were less concerned about the value of the deal. In an article criticizing the shortsighted deal, Dan Parker of the New York Mirror quipped, "of course, the magnates can't work themselves up into a rage . . . after all, it's the ball player's money."[50] But Chandler's main antagonist, Fred Saigh, still blasted the deal, arguing that "television is in its infancy . . . rights worth $1,000,000 today may be worth several millions two or three years from now. Furthermore, signing such a contract so soon after [Chandler's] repudiation by the owners seems in poor taste."[51] Although clearly biased against Chandler, Saigh's assessment of the World Series' future value would prove correct. The percent of U.S. households with televisions grew from 9 percent in 1950 to almost 72 percent in 1956 at the end of the contract, meaning the rights to the World Series and All-Star Game were "worth several millions."

Saigh also implied that "NBC or CBS or others do not have a chance to bid on television or radio" because of the affiliation of Chandler's hometown radio station with Mutual.[52] NBC also believed the commissioner's station "had much to do with Mutual's influence with Chandler's office." Internal NBC memos show that the network considered offering affiliation to Chandler's low-powered station WVLK in Versailles, Kentucky, to enhance its influence with the commissioner in its attempt to secure rights to the World Series. The idea was discarded after an NBC analysis showed that its network coverage in the area was "entirely adequate" and so adding the station would only alienate existing radio affiliates.[53]

Despite his earlier resolve to serve his full term, Happy Chandler stepped down as commissioner on July 15, 1951, about a year before his term would have expired. Former ghostwriter for Babe Ruth and National League (NL) president Ford Frick replaced Chandler on September 20th. Chandler's ouster signaled a significant shift in the power of the commissioner's office. The Judge Landis era, when an all-powerful baseball commissioner could wield his "best interests of baseball" powers without fear of owner retaliation, was over. The owners hired the commissioner, and they could fire the commissioner, or at least force him out. Handling the new medium of television was now part of the job, and the next commissioner had better do it in the interest of those who hired him. Frick was anxious about television from the start. In 1947, the then NL president opinioned that television, a golden opportunity for many, "within a few years is going to be another big problem for us."[54]

Improving Coverage

The coverage of the 1950 World Series would be split between WOR, Mutual's affiliate in New York, and WPTZ in Philadelphia. ABC, CBS, and NBC would carry all the telecasts. After experimentation with an outfield camera and split screens the previous year, television's coverage of the 1950 World Series reverted to a more conservative approach, pleasing some critics. For *Variety*, the World Series coverage "answers all questions," and WOR-TV's "video pickup was strikingly efficient in the last two games from Yankee Stadium." WPTZ's coverage of the first two games from Philadelphia "was marked by the use of an overhead camera that captured dramatic shots of the infield." Instead of the 1949 split-screen shot of the first base runner and pitcher, a new camera position behind third base showed the runner and the pitcher in the same frame. The outfield camera from the 1949 Series also was dropped. The big story, however, was the excitement generated by a new piece of technology.

A new reflectar lens could show very tight closeups of the players. *Variety* called it "the most important advance in TV baseball coverage."[55] In the third game, the lens captured the grim expression of Phillies pitcher Ken Heintzelman, as his club, down two games to none, fought back. It also brought "the players into far more intimate contact with the viewer than would a seat in the field boxes," *Variety* opined. Television could now give the viewer an even closer view of the game. The medium couldn't deliver the "peanuts, popcorn and Cracker Jacks" of the live game, but it could transmit an enhanced visual experience.

Unfortunately, the Series' opening game was interrupted when a power failure near Shibe Park killed the video portion for about twenty minutes. Such frustrations were not uncommon in early television. Later, audio was lost on the network feed for several minutes. Once again Jim Britt was on hand for the Series; this time joined by Jack Brickhouse, who "occasionally leaned to the effusive side and was not always the best judge of where fly balls were going," the New York Times judged.[56]

The First Nationally Televised World Series

During the 1951 season, it seemed increasingly likely that fans would witness the long-anticipated coast-to-coast telecast of the World Series. In August, AT&T announced that its new $40 million transcontinental microwave relay facilities would be completed by September 30th, in time for the Series. The network was completed even earlier. Its first transmission was of the Japanese peace conference in San Francisco on September 5.[57]

The new national broadcast coincided with a fresh approach to World Series coverage. For the first time, one network (NBC) would cover the World Series. As part of a four-year deal, Gillette granted NBC exclusivity for the World Series. In exchange, NBC gave Gillette sponsorship of the Rose Bowl, whose television rights the network controlled. NBC's expanding national network meant the games would be within the television reach of eighty-five million Americans. For the next twenty-six years, NBC would be the network of the World Series. Moreover, the "no pay, no play" controversy ended. Gillette agreed to pay stations their full rate for two hours to carry the first four games. However, coverage beyond two hours and the telecasts of games five, six, and seven, if played, was gratis.[58]

NBC's exclusivity represented a significant shift in the corporate perception of the World Series. Telecasting the Series was no longer viewed as a public service, making the games available to the widest number of Americans by using as many stations as possible. It was now just programming: bound to the interests of its network and sponsor(s) just like any other television programming.

But First, "A Shot Heard Round the World"

The newly completed nationwide coaxial cable network would shine a national spotlight on baseball. But a hard-charging baseball club from

14. *San Franciscans stand in the rain to catch a glimpse of the first coast-to-coast baseball telecast: game one of the 1951 Dodgers and Giants playoff.* © *Bettmann/Corbis.*

Coogan's Bluff, New York, would make sure the first light would not be cast at the World Series. On August 11, the Dodgers had a thirteen-and-a-half game lead; the pennant race looked like a "laugher." The Giants won their next sixteen games, however, shrinking the Dodger lead to five games. The turnaround continued in late September as the Giants won five in row and the Dodgers lost six out of eight. The teams were tied with two games to go. Both won their last two contests, forcing a three-game playoff.[59] With the national network now ready, the baseball brass and the networks scrambled to cover the three-game playoff for the entire country.

On October 1, 1951, CBS transmitted coast to coast the first game of the famed three-game playoff between the New York Giants and Brooklyn Dodgers. But it was not a simple operation. CBS got the game rights but needed to get the signal from ABC, which had already made arrangements for national distribution. ABC got the game coverage from WOR-TV, which had telecast the Dodgers' regular-season games. Rights to the second and third games were purchased by NBC from WPIX, which carried the Giants' home schedule. For the three playoff games, CBS and NBC shared the new microwave relay connection across the United States and exchanged time to allow each network to carry its game(s) to completion.[60]

As most baseball fans know, the playoffs ended with Bobby Thompson's "shot heard round the world," but they were also the first baseball games seen live across the nation, making Thompson's historic homer the first shot seen coast to coast. Video of the Dodgers and Giants' classic clash made it to the West Coast in the autumn of 1951. The two teams themselves would follow in the spring of 1958, pursuing greener television pastures.

A Period of Stability

Coast-to-coast baseball continued with the 1951 World Series, produced by New York station WOR-TV and telecast nationally on NBC. *Variety* was impressed with "TV's Slick Performance" and particularly pleased that the Series was presented "with a minimum of added frills."[61] Most coverage came from the high home position, with cameras also on the first and third base sides to show more detailed shots of the batter. WOR-TV seemed to be heeding its critics' longstanding call to "follow the ball at all times" by using a wide-angle lens to show all of the infield in the basic cover shot of the game action. The Zoomar lenses provided more detailed coverage of the outfield action. "After several years of televising regular pennant games, the TV sportscasters have developed an excellent camera technique for baseball." Televised baseball had finally finished its years of experimentation and found its standardized technique.[62]

With sponsor, network, and production technique set for the near term, the televising of the World Series in 1952, 1953, and 1954 fell into a familiar pattern. N BC predicted that the 1952 Series might reach seventy million viewers. The only affiliates unconnected to transcontinental network lines were in Albuquerque, New Mexico, and Brownsville, Texas.[63] During the Series, *Life* magazine ran two photos that captured the national focus on the televised World Series. One showed working men at a crowded New York tavern, their eyes staring upward at the TV above the bar (see figure 11 earlier in this chapter). The second photo focuses on a group of suited MIT scientists viewing the game in their faculty lounge.[64] Professor or plumber, everyone watched the World Series.

The coverage of the Yankee-Dodger 1953 World Series was a "workmanlike job" without gimmicks, such as the split screen, which had characterized earlier efforts. But also absent from the Series was the Zoomar lens, which was now standard in most regular-season television coverage of baseball. Two cameras were placed behind home plate, one on the third and one on the first base side of the field. Other cameras were used for graphics or commercials. Behind the mike, the low-key approach of Vin Scully, who had been mentored by Red Barber, counterpointed the style of Mel Allen, the "purveyor of purple prose."[65] *Variety* noted that Allen called "his plays sharply and accurately" and maintained an objective view.

The 1954 World Series, the first in five years without the Yankees, provided an opportunity for a new Series announcer, Russ Hodges. The coverage followed familiar patterns, although a camera was placed in the Giants' locker room to catch the team's celebration after its surprising four-game sweep of the highly favored Indians. Zoomar lenses reappeared as part of the seven-camera coverage. WXEL's director, Clay Dropp, was applauded for his intimate knowledge of Cleveland's Municipal Stadium, gained from years of directing the coverage of Indians games.[66]

Confining the Commercial

In the early 1950s, the professors and plumbers watching the World Series saw more Series and fewer commercials than today's viewers. A

15. *A Chicago cabby makes sure his fares can follow the 1956 World Series.*
© *Bettmann/Corbis.*

review of the first two innings of game six of the 1952 World Series, the oldest known kinescope of a complete game, reveals that viewers enjoyed limited commercial interruption by the Series' one sponsor, Gillette.[67] There is no commercial break between the pregame coverage and the start of the game. A single forty-five-second filmed commercial is shown at the end of the first half inning, and a fifty-second animated spot airs between the top and bottom of the second inning. At the end of the first inning is a twenty-second shot of the Gillette Blue Blade logo superimposed over a shot of the infield. At the end of the second, the Gillette logo appears for about ten seconds while Allen recaps the game action. Thus, the pregame and first two innings of the game contained only slightly more than two minutes of advertising content. The same time slot for game five of the 2006 World Series included fourteen minutes of commercials and network promotions, nearly a sevenfold increase. No wonder *Variety* considered the Gillette commercials of this earlier era "well delivered."[68]

All-Star Game Origins

Although our principal focus in this chapter is the World Series, the origins of baseball's mid-summer classic also deserve attention. The All-Star Game was never the main focus of network competition for baseball's premier games because the event was limited to a single contest, played in the weekday afternoon, when viewing levels are much lower.[69] The commissioner's office began soliciting network interest in telecasting the game in 1948. Walter Mulbry, MLB's secretary-treasurer, contacted NBC on May 4th and directly asked: "Is the National Broadcasting Company interested in submitting a bid in behalf of a sponsor for the television rights of the 1948 All-Star Game, to be played in Sportsmen Park, St. Louis, 13 July?"[70] NBC telegrammed the commissioner's office a week later declining the offer because "we have no cable connection with St. Louis as yet. Our only method of doing it would be by film which is not saleable at the present time."[71] The network also had a commitment to cover the Democratic convention, which coincided with the game. NBC recommended that the game be handled locally, and that is what happened.[72] Under Gillette's sponsorship, Mutual Broadcasting's St. Louis affiliate, KSD-TV, produced the first All-Star Game telecast on July 13, 1948, during which the American League (AL) won its third straight contest, 5 to 2.[73]

Networking was more advanced in 1949, but once again NBC declined to cover the game, deferring this time to its network rival, CBS. NBC decided against covering the game because it was "economically unsound," but wanted the commissioner's office to understand "that this decision of ours will not affect any future opportunities we may have to work with you on baseball." NBC believed that the $50,000 the commissioner was rumored to be asking for the rights was too much for a single afternoon game, but the network still had its eye on capturing rights to that fall's World Series.[74] On July 12, 1949, CBS telecast network television's first All-Star Game. The American League continued its win streak, topping the National's in an 11-to-7 slugfest that featured twenty-five hits, seven doubles, and two homers.[75]

In May 1950, the commissioner's office once again offered NBC the All-Star Game, and the network had to decide if it wanted "to compete with Gillette" for the rights while believing that "the All-Star Game is not as important as the World Series."[76] Ultimately, Gillette did secure the rights and contracted with NBC to carry the games on its network's stations. It was the beginning of a two-decade partnership between the network and its All-Star Game sponsor. The television stations of Gillette's radio partner, Mutual Broadcasting, also carried the game. NBC billed Gillette for two hours of its daytime rate, and Gillette paid WGN in Chicago to produce the telecast from Comiskey Park.[77] NBC's first All-Star Game was also the first to go into extra innings. On July 11, the National League broke the American League's four-year winning streak with at 4-to-3 victory in eleven innings.[78]

The 1951 contest began NBC's quarter-century run as the exclusive network of the All-Star Game. Rights to the game were now included with the World Series rights as part of Gillette's six-year television contract negotiated with lame-duck Commissioner Happy Chandler. NBC farmed out coverage of the Briggs Stadium contest to Detroit station WWJ, who charged $826 ($6,700 in 2006 dollars) to produce the telecast.[79] WWJ used only three cameras, but NBC thought the station did "a bang-up job."[80] The television script, produced by Gillette's advertising agency, Maxon Advertising, directed announcer Jack Brickhouse to tell viewers that 1951 was "the two-hundred fiftieth birthday of Dynamic Detroit . . . birthplace of modern mass production . . . Arsenal of Democracy . . . and home grounds of the fighting Detroit Tigers. So, this year's All-Star classic represents organized baseball's birthday present to a great American City . . . Detroit."[81]

Although Gillette saluted the home of the Tigers, the National League disappointed Briggs Stadium's predominately American League fans with a decisive 8-to-3 victory over the AL's best. From 1951 through 1965, Gillette would continue to sponsor the All-Star Game as part of its contracts with Major League Baseball, while NBC would provide the networking and ultimately its own production team, headed by legendary director Harry Coyle.

The Coming of Color and a New Contract

The 1955 Yankees-Dodgers World Series saw the first use of color in a baseball telecast. RCA had only one color remote van, but the Series'

16. An injured Pee Wee Reese watches his teammates on television. Reese would become Dizzy Dean's telecast partner. National Baseball Hall of Fame Library, Cooperstown NY.

all–New York location made it possible to colorcast all of the games. The response to TV's first color World Series was overwhelmingly negative. The first-generation color cameras could not compensate for the harsh late-afternoon shadows produced in both ballparks. NBC's president, Robert Sarnoff, received the following telegram blasting the color coverage: "YOUR COVERAGE OF WORLD SERIES POOREST EVER SEEN IN THIS AREA PICTURES TOO DARK LOSING LOTS OF FRIENDS FOR YOUR COMPAY [SIC]." NBC responded that the problems were "the fault neither of the television equipment nor of the crew, but are inherent in the nature of such outdoor telecasts."[82] But the Series got some positive press for reducing crime. During the Series, the Felony Court in Manhattan reported a dramatic dip in traffic from fifty to sixty new cases a day to just twenty. Court officers credited the World Series with keeping "the ne'er-do-wells nailed to radios and television sets."[83]

In 1956, Gillette spent $2.74 million in advertising and promotion expenses for the Series. For its outlay, it reached an estimated audience of

100 million, over 60 percent of the U.S. population—one of the best bargains in advertising history.[84] Never again would the World Series reach so many viewers for so little. To keep the Series for the next five years, Gillette would have to spend much more. The World Series was still the crown jewel of American sports, however, and Gillette wore the crown proudly.

In color or black and white, the televised Series was so important that Secretary of State John Foster Dulles caught some of the games with other delegates at the UN. In Chicago, one cab driver had Admiral television install a set in his taxi so riders could watch the games. In Stamford, Texas, Mrs. W. B. Johnson, who had missed only one inning of the Series on radio or television over the previous thirteen years (to take a friend's phone call) refused to answer the phone or the doorbell.[85] On October 8, 1956, the attentions of UN delegates, taxi riders, Mrs. Johnson, and much of the rest of the country were rewarded with the only perfect game in postseason history. It was television's first big league perfecto and the first since 1922. In game five, Don Larsen, "the imperfect man," pitched "the perfect game," delivering the required twenty-seven Dodger outs without a runner reaching base.

Escaping Chandler's Shadow

The Chandler-negotiated World Series–All-Star Game contract with Gillette ended in 1956. Television was now in more than 70 percent of American homes, and both the owners and the players wanted a bigger slice of the World Series pie.[86] They got it. The players challenged the owners' contention that they owned the World Series rights and that it had been solely up to the owners' discretion in 1954 to allocate 60 percent of the rights to the pension fund. The owners argued that they could not "allocate" 60 percent of the proceeds to the player pensions if they did not own them already. The players then asked to be included in the negotiations for the new contract. Once again the owners rebuffed them, arguing that negotiation of the television and radio rights were the province of the commissioner. Commissioner Frick agreed to consult with the pension committee, which included two players (Bob Feller and Robin Roberts), about the contract. Despite their conflicts, both sides were encouraged by the new deal that baseball finally negotiated with NBC and Gillette.[87]

The five-year, $16.25-million deal nearly tripled the previous combined TV and radio rights deal. Frick stressed that his office had "received a number of offers competing with the network's bid," but provided no details about the competition. In the new deal, Mutual, the broadcast rights holder of the World Series since 1939, was out. NBC would handle both radio and television.[88] Otherwise, there was little change. The stable bond with Gillette, forged on radio in 1939, and with NBC on television in 1951, would continue at least through 1961. The players received 60 percent of the rights fee. They used their new riches to expand the pension plan, adding both medical and widows' benefits.

The second Frick-negotiated contract in early 1960 looked a lot like the first. NBC and Gillette re-upped the TV and radio rights, this time for $3.75 million a year over five years. The contract included the World Series and one of the two annual All-Star Games; NBC would get the rights to any second All-Star Game for an additional $250,000. The pension fund would get 60 percent of the fee, the players receiving an additional $250,000 in 1960 and 1961 and another $500,000 for the five years of the new contract. In recognition of the possible development of Branch Rickey's proposed Continental League, the contract gave the commissioner the right to cancel if a third major league became eligible for the Series.[89] Frick's first contract produced a threefold increase in rights fees, consistent with the growth of the potential television audience, but the second did little more than keep pace with inflation. The bidding process was noncompetitive. Commissioner Frick apparently concluded that rights fees had reached their peak, even though television penetration in the United States had grown 17 percent since the last contract.[90] Since only 40 percent of the fees went to the owners, getting top dollar seemed less important than maintaining a comfortable relationship with NBC, one of the country's two largest broadcast companies.

Evolving Technology and Wider Distribution

World Series telecasts of the 1960s featured some technological advances, but otherwise it was business as usual. The NBC team had been in charge of production since 1951 with the same director, Harry Coyle. Color and the center field camera, introduced by Coyle in 1957, were now standard. Instant replay made its first appearance. NBC began to use portable cameras to interview politicians and celebrities attending the games (see chapter 14). The 1966 World Series between the Dodgers and Orioles saw a significant improvement in instant replay. Simple replaying of videotape was replaced by a videodisc system capable of recording twenty seconds of action and then replaying it with both stop action and slow motion. Viewers could now see close plays a second, third, and even fourth time.[91] Television offered a perspective not available to the naked eye. For every armchair umpire, TV was better than being there. Gradually, most stadiums would add giant video displays, so fans in the stands could see some of the replays they were used to watching in their living rooms.

The Series games were reaching an increasingly international audience and actually becoming more of a "world" Series. NBC's coverage reached 225 stations in the United States and almost as many outside of it (211) in Canada and Latin America. Kinescopes of the games reached 35 Armed Forces Radio and Television Service stations around the world. For the first time, the British saw the Series: the final game edited down to forty minutes. However, baseball's unique jargon was a bit mangled. The Irish-accented BBC announcer referred to a "double hit," a "treble," and the "left outfielder." But the Series audience was still not a worldwide one. In a curious item, the *Los Angeles Times* reported that Spain ignored the World Series completely, with no references to it in any of the newspapers or broadcast media.[92] No mention was made of how Liechtensteiners reacted to the games.

A New Contract, A New Advertising Model

On the surface, the $12.6 million contract announced by new commissioner William D. "Spike" Eckert in May 1966 for rights to the 1967 and 1968 World Series and All-Star Games seemed a significant improvement and a new direction.[93] For the first time, the network worked without Gillette's exclusive sponsorship. The company's twenty-eight-year run of World Series sponsorship came to an end. The event was simply becoming too expensive for a single sponsor. Now a network would buy the rights and sell commercial availabilities to a variety of advertisers. The number of minutes of advertising per hour would increase steadily. A single sponsor paying a flat fee for the entire Series had little reason to expand the number of commercials, since its commercials would be seen many times during the game's numerous inning breaks. But a network paying a flat fee could directly increase its revenues by simply adding more commercial slots. It also would benefit from additional promotions for its other programming. The days of a mere thirty-second break between World Series innings would never return.

The 68 percent increase in rights was certainly above inflation. The increase could no longer be justified by television's continuing growth since the medium was already in 93 percent of U.S. homes.[94] But CBS was paying $2 million a year for one NFL championship game.[95] This was substantially more than the $1.48 million per game that Major League Baseball would earn in a four-game World Series (declining to as little as $843,000 per game for a seven-game Series).

In the *New York Times*, Leonard Koppett accused the owners of undervaluing the World Series rights they had to share with the players in order to help them cut a better deal with NBC for its game of the week. He suggested that the players feel "somewhat betrayed by the current arrangement" because "no one doubts that rights to the World Series alone could have brought more than $6-million."[96] Koppett also noted that the owners were moving to eliminate the sixty-forty formula and instead offer the players a fixed amount for the pension fund from the World Series–All-Star Game rights.

Enter Marvin Miller, a former economist for the United Steelworkers. The 1966 election of Miller as executive director of the Major League Baseball Players Association (MLBPA) brought a very different attitude to the negotiating table. In the past, the players had either represented themselves or used counsel favored by the owners. Here was a labor man with years of experience in tough negotiation with management. One of the first of many Miller/owner conflicts (see chapter 9 for a discussion of owner/player conflicts in the 1970s) focused on how television money could be used to support the Players Association.

The new television contract with NBC had made player contributions to the pension fund unnecessary. Miller and the players proposed that the $394 each player was contributing should be transferred to the MLBPA to support a new permanent national office. The owners countered that this would violate labor laws. For their part, the owners wanted a fixed fee to subsidize the pension fund, which would enable them to reap the benefits of any future rights increases. Miller knew what the owners were up to. Miller reasoned that "by getting away from the 60–40 split the owners are counting on reaping future increases in TV money for themselves."[97]

A compromise gave both sides their key demands. Players would no longer contribute to the pension fund and would pay annual dues of no more than $344 per player to support the Players Association office. The owners would give a flat sum to the pension fund with no percentage tie to World Series–All-Star Game broadcast rights.[98] The new inflow of funds from these games had helped precipitate an owner/player conflict. Now television's extra money helped to smooth over the differences.

The new deal with the players meant there was no longer any reason to separate the game of the week and postseason rights. The complete package for 1969–71 produced a $50 million deal, a 35.5 percent increase over the last deals for the same rights in 1967–68 (see chapter 6). The players' pension cut was fixed at $4.1 million per year, an 8.5 percent increase over the $3.78 million from the previous contract. Clearly, Miller's contention that the owners would benefit from the abandonment of the sixty-forty split was correct.[99]

The 1969–71 rights package brought to a close the era in which postseason and regular-season packages were negotiated separately. From now on, the World Series and All-Star Game would become the major prizes in the national baseball package, their revenues split evenly among the owners. Major League Baseball would learn by observing the NFL's skillful playing of one network against another that competition for premium sports events produces far more television revenue than even the most comfortable relationship with a single network. It was a lesson MLB should have learned from its own experience with competitive bidding for the 1949 World Series. Baseball's premium games would become more valuable with the addition of new playoff rounds and the gradual shifting of games from daytime to prime time over the next four decades.

Origins of the Game of the Week

By 1953, Major League Baseball needed a coherent television policy. Each club wanted to preserve its current television revenues and increase future revenues. Each had its own history with television. At one extreme were the Brooklyn Dodgers, who exploited television from the very first televised MLB game. Their fan base was in a metropolitan area that had more people and stations than any other in the nation. At the other extreme were the Pittsburgh Pirates, yet to telecast their first game in a city with only one television station. MLB did have a commissioner with "best-interests" powers (although substantially limited after 1945), but Ford Frick was a former newspaperman who viewed television as a devil one day and as a savior the next. He was convinced that the television version of baseball must not be "too" good. For Frick, "the view a fan gets at home should be worse than that of the fan in the worst seat in the stadium."[1]

With eighty-three-year-old Clark Griffith as their elder statesman, the baseball owners in 1953 were guardians from a different era. They presided over an MLB structure that had not changed in half a century. There were still sixteen teams in ten cities, none of them in the South or West. The owners, shaped by the hardships of the Depression and the Second World War, focused more on containing costs, primarily player salaries, and preserving their paternal rule. Exploiting new technology was of lesser interest. In 1950, Clark Griffith "predicted that both the American and National leagues will ban television next season."[2] Clearly, he underestimated the power of ready cash. In 1953, the owners were feudal lords whose teams played behind the walls of their early-twentieth-century baseball castles, but they were hearing the thunder of television's first cannon fire.

In this era of stagnant minds, new ideas would have to come from outside MLB's leadership, and that is in fact where the game of the week was born. The idea of a weekly broadcast game had found earlier success in both televised football and national radio coverage of baseball. The NCAA national football game of the week had shown that top teams could draw substantial national audiences to what had been local and regional contests. The ease of access that television brought drew new audiences to the game. Focusing on one major contest per week made each game special. Liberty Broadcasting's and Mutual's daily games had developed a national audience for Major League Baseball, by offering quality MLB games that eroded local allegiances to minor league teams. The TV game of the week coincided with a major transformation of MLB that would first bring franchise relocation (Braves, Browns, Athletics, Dodgers, Giants, Senators) and then expansion (Angels, Senators-Rangers, Mets, Colt .45s-Astros, and more to follow). From 1953 to 1965, the game of the week's first era, Major League Baseball became much more major, and Minor League Baseball much more minor.

Network television was also changing. The completion of the coast-to-coast AT&T television link in 1951 signified the beginning of the network era of U.S. television. The four national networks (ABC, CBS, DuMont, and NBC) could now deliver a national audience to national advertisers as radio had done since the 1920s. The networks now began to expand their programming into daytime, nighttime, and weekend hours formerly programmed by their affiliates. NBC was especially successful, developing Today in 1952 for the early morning hours and The Tonight Show in 1954 for post–prime-time viewing.

In less profitable hours, local stations willingly ceded time to their networks, but weekend afternoons were rich in profit potential. Networks would have to offer strong programming that delivered a substantial audience. The formula for success was televised sports that appealed to working males who were part of the available weekend afternoon audience. DuMont had successfully televised professional football starting in 1951. However, in the early 1950s, baseball was still the province of the local Major League market stations. Outside of these markets, televised baseball was rare, although radio coverage was an established success.

A Foot in the Door

Into the television-policy void created by MLB's aging leadership stepped two men, one who brought rhetorical bluster from the U.S. Senate and the other who worked quietly with a few owners to shape a new television reality. "Big Ed" Johnson was both a senator (D-CO) and the president of the Western League. When the New York baseball writers met at the Waldorf Astoria Hotel for their thirteenth annual dinner in January 1953, Johnson summoned ghosts of the American Revolution, warning the Minors to "wake up; the Majors are coming to your ball park. They are no longer satisfied with the blood-letting in their own territory; they are conniving with a super-salesman [television] to take the last drop of blood in the minor league territory, also. Who will fire the shot to be heard 'round the baseball world'?"

Johnson threatened to "testify before Congress and the courts that major league baseball is a cruel and heartless monopoly motivated by avarice and greed."[3] Indeed, Johnson led congressional investigations into baseball's broadcast invasion of the minors (see chapter 10), but though these hearings produced a lot of thunder no legislative lightning emerged. While Johnson barked publicly to New York's baseball writers, a far less imposing figure, Thomas McMahon of the DuMont television network, was working with individual owners to telecast baseball's first regular-season national games in the summer of 1953.

Initially, Johnson's "blood and thunder" speech thwarted McMahon's progress. By January 1953, McMahon thought he had a done deal. But the owners he had lined up for places on the national stage were concerned about Johnson's accusations that they were holding the banner for "avarice and greed." McMahon's plan was to negotiate with individual teams to obtain national rights to their local games for national telecast. Games would be blacked out in the local market to allay owners' fears about siphoning off paid attendance. By negotiating with individual teams and not Major League Baseball as a whole, McMahon would avoid a potential antitrust suit from the Department of Justice. To counter the possible negative effect on the Minors, McMahon would offer them a piece of the national television pie. He would set up a corporation to sell the national MLB telecasts, giving stock shares to minor league teams. Further, because the games would be played on Saturday afternoons, the Minors that scheduled most of their contests for the evening should not be greatly affected.

Stoic in the face of Johnson's bluster, McMahon saw the development of a national telecast as inevitable. "It simply makes sense—as well as sure-fire profits all around."[4] McMahon was right. The Johnson threat faded, and MLB got a national game of the week. But the first game of the week would air with only three teams under contract and not on the DuMont network.

The First Game of the Week

The American Broadcasting Company needed both programming and a reason for new affiliates to become links in their broadcasting chain. The early 1950s was the era of the big two and little two television networks. While the "established networks," NBC and CBS, competed for ratings and profits, the "weak competitors," DuMont and ABC, struggled for affiliates and survival.[5] After the freeze on television licenses ended in 1952, the number of new stations grew dramatically. Although NBC and CBS added their share of new affiliates, competition between DuMont and ABC for new partners was a matter of life and death. The DuMont network's demise by the mid-1950s was due in part to its failure to develop a fully national network of affiliates. For ABC, Major League Baseball would be a boon, even if the games were blacked out in Major League markets. The network could offer medium- and small-market stations America's most popular sport, played at its highest level. Even if the initial ratings were modest, it was a significant edge in the race for new affiliates. ABC would act on DuMont's initial plan by the opening day of that very season.

With Vice President Richard Nixon set to toss out the first ball, the season was scheduled to open on April 13, 1953, in Washington, DC. The Senators would host a Yankee team that was four years into a five-year run as world champions, and ABC planned to send the game across the nation to fifty-eight stations. Nixon was substituting for President Dwight Eisenhower, who was still on a golfing vacation in Augusta, Georgia. But the grand debut never happened.

The Senators were rained out, and ABC had no backup game. Two days later Nixon watched as "Ike" tossed out the first "opening day" pitch thrown by a Republican president in twenty years. The television audience was local. By the time the canceled opening game could be made up, ABC's telecast would be in competition with other local telecasts of Major League games. On shaky political ground because of Johnson's hearings, ABC decided to skip what would have been its first national regular-season game.[6]

ABC continued to press quietly for a weekly game. It eventually was able to sign just three of the sixteen Major League teams (the White Sox, Indians, Athletics) to a contract for seventeen Saturday afternoon home contests. Johnson's speech and the subsequent Senate hearings had caused the New York Giants to turn down a lucrative $100,000 offer for six games.[7] All of the New York teams and the entire National League would sit out the first contract, although the Yankees could appear as the visiting team. By the middle of July, Johnson's bill was dead, and he was looking for a way to "work something out that would be reasonable . . . that would preserve both broadcasting and baseball, both great American institutions."[8]

ABC's coverage began on Memorial Day 1953 with the first game of an Indians–White Sox doubleheader from Chicago. But publicity for the event was minimal. It was noted in a brief article in the *Washington Post* and not at all in the *New York Times*. Because of the blackout of Major League cities, ABC was sending the games, by mid-season, to only eighteen affiliates, almost all of them in the MLB-deprived southern and western United States.[9] Although the number of teams and affiliates was modest, ABC had stuck its foot in MLB's seemingly closed door and, amazingly, done it in the middle of a congressional inquiry. With each passing year, the number of teams participating, the number of stations telecasting, and the number of viewers watching increased. The *Game of the Week* became a television institution and one of the most popular programs in rural America.

Star Power

One of the major reasons that the audience for the *Game of the Week* grew steadily was ABC's corraling of Dizzy Dean, the baseball broadcaster best suited to connecting with the southern and western baseball markets. The year 1953 was Dizzy Dean's year. He achieved the ultimate recognition for his playing career, induction into the Baseball Hall of Fame, and the ultimate prize in broadcasting: a national network series. Dean had always been a media star with a star's ego, a star's ambition, and a star's ability to connect personally with ordinary people. As a broadcaster, he had already moved from small-market St. Louis and its perennial losers, the Browns, to the nation's largest market, New York, and its most successful team, the Yankees. In the process, he made country-boy storytelling and his personal version of the English language succeed in the nation's most cosmopolitan city. Now he had a national stage, albeit, for the moment, a small one.

In 1954, ABC aired the first full season of the *Game of the Week* on more than five times as many stations as in 1953, nearly one hundred stations by the end of the season.[10] Four new teams—the Phillies, Giants, Senators, and Dodgers—joined the White Sox and Indians from 1953's package. Dean's charisma and the additional stations translated into increased ratings. When only the non–Major League markets that carried the game are considered, the *Game of the Week* was the nation's fourteenth-highest rated program—a very strong showing for a non-prime-time weekend series on a weak network. Sponsorship was also growing. Falstaff beer was the chief sponsor, but in markets where Falstaff was not sold, local stations paid for the game and found their own advertisers. These included other brewers (Blatz, Schlitz, Utica Club), soft drinks (Coca-Cola, Pepsi Cola, Seven-Up, Dr. Pepper), auto makers (Chevrolet, Pontiac), and sports sponsorship giant Gillette.[11]

In 1954, it was a spring-training game from Clearwater, Florida, that received more attention than any regular-season contest. The game between the White Sox and the Phillies was stopped after three innings, not by rain, but by contract. ABC's *Game of the Week* contract prohibited games within a seventy-five-mile radius of Major League cities. However, ABC assumed that consent from the White Sox for the telecast of the exhibition game meant it could telecast that game nationally. Both the Chicago and Philadelphia general managers objected. The network canceled the game coverage, but the word did not get to all the appropriate personnel until after the third inning. Viewers watched as the game suddenly disappeared, causing a minor embarrassment for ABC. The incident also demonstrated just how intent Major League Baseball was in 1954 on keeping national television competition out of its local markets.

With the *Game of the Week*, ABC succeeded in establishing a television franchise, but it was still one of the "little two" networks. Now that the threat of government intervention was over, Major League Baseball sought a bigger stage for its product. And Dizzy Dean was too huge a personality to be limited to even one hundred stations. For the next eleven years the CBS "eye" would give MLB and Dean a higher platform for the *Game of the Week*. The series would become an institution in small-town America.

CBS Takes Control

ABC had cracked open the door to national coverage; CBS would nudge it wide open. The *Sporting News'* announcement for the 1955 CBS version of the *Game of the Week* listed twenty-six games, to be telecast over one hundred stations, about the same as ABC. The *Game of the Week* was blacked out in Major League markets and in minor league markets where games were in progress. However, the rest of the country got the games. The minor leagues protested, threatened, and sued unsuccessfully. The major leagues expressed concern, broached the possibility of sharing *Game of the Week* revenues with the minor leagues, but ultimately let teams negotiate separate contracts with CBS.

As it had since 1947, Major League Baseball argued that developing a unified approach to negotiating the *Game of the Week* contract would constitute collusion and violate antitrust laws. But the television door was opening ever wider. By 1956, CBS was still sending twenty-six games, but now to over 175 stations. All three New York teams, as well as the Red Sox, Indians, White Sox, and Reds, were part of the package. When visiting teams are included, thirteen of the sixteen Major League teams appeared, led by the Dodgers with ten and the Yankees with eight appearances. In Hawaii, where no live telecast was available, one station broadcast a filmed version of Saturday's game on Sunday afternoon. In the markets where it could be seen, the *Game of the Week* was a hit.

CBS was also expanding and promoting its product. Taking an idea from local television, the network added a fifteen-minute "Baseball Preview" before the game, featuring Dean. It also added coverage of special events such as a Yankee–White Sox old-timers game before the regular game. Short announcements on each week's telecast and features about special games began to appear regularly in the Sporting News. The CBS games included Carl Erskine's no-hitter against the Giants, the first triple play broadcast nationally, and the first game covered by the backup announcers because of a rainout.

Openly critical at its inception, the Sporting News (SN) now accepted large Falstaff beer ads promoting the Game of the Week. Dean's comings and goings were routinely publicized in SN. Columns described his golf games, his time on his Texas ranch, and the declaration of "Dizzy Dean Day" by the governor of Arizona. He was becoming an important national celebrity. "Ole Diz" even showed up on CBS's chief rival, NBC, appearing on The Dinah Shore Show. He sang his signature tune, "The Wabash Cannonball," and even danced with Shore and guest Frank Sinatra. But, as has often been noted, imitation is the sincerest form of television. Thus, it was not long until a competing game of the week was in the works.

NBC Joins the Fray

In early 1957, the other half of the "Big Two," NBC, took on CBS with its own game of the week, called simply Major League Baseball. Although the Dancer, Fitzgerald, Sample ad agency, representing Falstaff, had already signed many teams for the CBS telecast, NBC found four Major League teams (the Braves, Pirates, Cubs, Senators) with games to sell. According to NBC's play-by-play choice, Lindsey Nelson, the network's affiliates were demanding programming that could compete against Ole Diz on CBS.[12] Like the CBS games, the NBC games were blacked out in all Major League markets and in minor league markets that had games in progress. In addition to a limited variety of teams in its first year, NBC also had a smaller reach. Its game of the week was carried by 116 stations in thirty-seven states, compared to CBS's games on 163 stations in forty-two states.[13]

17. NBC countered Dizzy Dean's success on CBS with its own publicity hound, Leo Durocher (left), pictured with Lindsey Nelson. National Baseball Hall of Fame Library, Cooperstown NY.

Although Nelson was a seasoned and highly skilled announcer, Dean's star power meant NBC would need a star of its own to compete on Saturday afternoons. They found their headliner in Leo Durocher, one of baseball's most outspoken figures. Durocher had spent a decade waging the New York baseball "wars" as manager first of the Dodgers and then the Giants. He was an active self-promoter and a broadcast celebrity in his own right. If Dizzy was country kin, then Leo was his citified cousin. He was married to film and television personality Lorraine Day and friends with Frank Sinatra and many other show-business figures. In one late 1950s Chesterfield cigarette magazine ad, Durocher appeared wearing a smoking jacket, something that would never hang on Ole Diz's shoulders, at least in public. Durocher had been associated with televised baseball as long as anyone; he was interviewed by Red Barber as part of the very first Major League telecast in 1939. But he was an announcing novice. Where Dean had a decade's experience as a baseball announcer on radio before taking on television's first weekly national telecast, "the Lip" had never covered baseball regularly.

Durocher was nearly Dean's equal in generating publicity, however. He often appeared in the *Sporting News*. There readers could learn of Durocher patching up an old rift with former Dodger outfielder Carl Furillo stemming from his days as the Giants' manager, confessing that he never learned how to keep score because he simply remembered each play in the game, or explaining why you need both a slow and a fast grounds crew to gain advantage during rain delays.

Comparing the CBS and NBC versions of the game of the week in May 1957, the *Sporting News* found "Columbia's pair used a lighter, livelier touch—one which was more colorful, talkative, reminiscent, anecdotal and more personal." Durocher was clearly an ex-manager: "he anticipates strategy . . . guesses what may be done; concedes misses. He is a keen observer and a sharp analyst at all times." However, "his voice level is sometimes a bit high and shrill."[14] Durocher stayed with NBC through the 1959 season, when he left to pursue coaching opportunities. He was replaced by Fred Haney, manager of the pennant-winning 1957 and 1958 Milwaukee Braves.

Whatever Durocher's limitations, CBS recognized that it no longer had the national coverage of the game to itself. The network beefed up coverage, adding a small "videon" camera behind home plate that approximated the umpires' view when calling balls and strikes. But improved coverage and a lively Dizzy Dean could not restore all of the ratings siphoned off by NBC. Faced with legitimate competition on Saturday afternoons, CBS took the next logical step: an additional game on

Sunday afternoon. As the network began to negotiate with clubs for a Sabbath series, both the minor leagues and the commissioner of Major League Baseball started to cry foul.

Sunday Baseball Begins

By 1957, broadcasting was pumping $9.3 million in rights fees into Major League Baseball, including the World Series–All-Star rights ($3.2 million), two Saturday games of the week ($1.26 million), and local rights fees ($4.84 million). And more was on the way. Facing Saturday competition from NBC, CBS announced plans in December 1957 to expand to Sunday afternoon. Immediately, the minor leagues fired an angry salvo. George Trautman, president of the minor leagues, gave voice to the rage that his minor league colleagues felt at the next push to open the national television door. "Apparently Columbia has but one thing in mind and that is the preservation of Columbia and the destruction of the minors."[15] MLB commissioner Ford Frick requested that Congress "provide legislation that will take us out of the clutches of the Justice Department and give us the right to regulate such telecasts."[16]

But CBS soon signed four American League (the Indians, Orioles, White Sox, Yankees) and two National League teams (the Phillies and Reds) to contracts for Sunday games. As ABC had done in 1953 and NBC in 1957, the network argued that the games would not harm minor league attendance because they would be blacked out on stations within fifty miles of where those teams were playing. CBS estimated that only 103 stations would carry the games, compared to the 159 that aired the Saturday contests.

The minor leagues were not persuaded. The National Association appealed to U.S. Representative Emmanuel Celler (D-NY), chairman of the House Judiciary Committee, for relief.[17] As we will see in chapter 11, the leadership of the Minors received a hearing from Celler's committee but was given no legislative relief.[18] Although the protest continued, the Minors soon realized that congressional action was not likely.

As in 1953, the congressional storm passed, and CBS's Sunday *Game of the Week* premiered on June 1, 1958. NBC announced plans for a second Sunday game in December 1958, and was soon asking viewers to "join

18. In 1960, Jack Buck would become ABC's first play-by-play announcer.
Thirty years later, he would headline CBS's national team.
National Baseball Hall of Fame Library, Cooperstown NY.

us for all fifty games this year," while its rival cried "see two games every weekend on the CBS-TV Game of the Week. . . . There's a big game every Sunday too."[19]

In 1960 ABC announced that Gillette would sponsor its Saturday Major League telecast. Each of the national television networks now had a piece of the national pastime, and baseball fans (in non-blacked-out markets) had access to 123 network games during the twenty-five-week season.[20]

ABC's Second at Bat

By 1960 what we have called the first generation of television, a medium dominated by three major commercial networks, was reaching its own prime time.[21] Although clearly the weakest of the three webs, ABC was slowly gaining ground with filmed prime-time action shows, and had begun to see sports as a primary programming strategy to bolster its fortunes (see chapter 9).

Although ABC developed the first national weekly baseball telecast in the 1953 and 1954 seasons, its weak affiliate position prompted its sponsor, Falstaff beer, to move the game to CBS for the 1955 season. ABC's second taste of Major League Baseball, during the 1960 season, was also destined for a short run. The network entered into discussions with some teams about a prime-time game on Saturday night, but it settled for a late-afternoon edition. ABC's new game of the week was a relatively minor part of an $8.5 million contract with Gillette that included two staples of TV sports: boxing and NCAA football games. ABC had only recently won the NCAA rights away from NBC for a record $6.25 million.[22] The package provided Gillette with year-round sports sponsorship.

Given its relatively weak position and the existing network hierarchy, ABC chose not to compete directly with the earlier-established CBS and NBC Saturday telecasts. Instead, it telecast its games starting at 4:00 p.m. in the East. In programming parlance, ABC hoped to attract an outflow of the baseball fans captured by CBS's and NBC's earlier games, but avoid head-to-head competition with its stronger rivals. Since ABC needed late-starting games, it contracted with the San Francisco Giants to provide thirteen Saturday home games, which formed the core of its Saturday baseball schedule. The remaining Saturdays featured tape-delayed games from Kansas City (six), Washington (three), and Philadelphia (three). As with the other network games, all Major League and minor league cities with teams playing were blacked out within a fifty-mile radius. The Giants stood to make about $400,000 from the new deal, with minimal effect on their own attendance. Although this was a pittance compared to the $6.25 million that ABC paid the NCAA for college football rights, for the Giants it was like found money. Although ABC's late-afternoon strategy may have appeared savvy, the network still suffered from a weak affiliate lineup, a limited number of teams, and well-established competition for the national baseball audience. ABC ended its second attempt at a game-of-the-week experiment after only one year, replacing it with what would become a television sports legend: *Wide World of Sports*.

Despite its game-of-the-week problems, ABC was still willing to tele-cast baseball if the stakes were high enough. The network "scooped" its stronger network rivals by obtaining rights from the Orioles to telecast Roger Maris's 154th game in 1961. This was Maris's last chance to tie or break Babe Ruth's sixty-home-run record in a season that was the same length as Ruth's was when he set the record. Although the game was a blackout in Major League cities, viewers in about 150 markets saw Maris hit his fifty-ninth homer, but fall one short of Ruth's 154-game mark.[23]

"Fifty Games This Year"

The passing of ABC's Saturday game of the week was not of great conse-quence to televised baseball. The two most powerful networks continued to carry games on both Saturday and Sunday for the twenty-five-week Major League season. But a major regulatory change was underway.

The power that Commissioner Ford Frick long had sought for Major League Baseball, control over its television package, was codified with the passage of the Sports Broadcasting Act of 1961. The act gave all major sports the ability to negotiate television rights packages with the major television networks as a league rather than as individual franchises (see chapter 11). Instead of many individual teams competing with each other to sell rights to three networks, a professional sports league could now negotiate with the three television networks in a winner-take-all com-petition. Given this important legal change, the old system of multiple network games of the week was doomed. Although it would take MLB a few years, it would soon discover what the NFL had already knew: when networks compete, major sports profit.

New Announcers for the National Telecasts

The Saturday and Sunday telecasts on CBS and NBC continued through the 1964 season. Dizzy Dean remained the star at CBS's *Game of the Week*, but his sidekick since 1953, Buddy Blattner, was dumped after a falling out with Dean. In 1960, CBS replaced Blattner with future Hall of Fame shortstop Pee Wee Reese. At NBC, Durocher's replacement, Fred Haney, lasted only one year and was replaced by Joe Garagiola, who would be-come a fixture at NBC. In 1962, Lindsey Nelson left the national game to begin a seventeen-year run with the Mets. Nelson's replacement was Bob Wolff, the longtime Washington Senators (1947–60) and Minnesota Twins (1961) announcer. Wolff handled play-by-play and Garagiola color commentary for NBC's game of the week for the 1962–64 seasons.

Tepid Coverage

Game coverage changed very little in the early 1960s. Staffed with veteran directors and production crews and blessed with steady ratings, CBS and NBC had little reason to modify anything. Although the networks, especially ABC, were developing new techniques for other sports, including instant replay, slow-motion replay, and tighter camera shots, Major League Baseball games seemed more focused on the live action. Replays were seen as potential interruptions. Whenever new technology was applied to the game of the week, it often provoked a negative reaction from MLB's old-guard leadership.

A prime example occurred in the middle of the 1959 season. When NBC used an 80-millimeter lens on its center field camera during a Yankee–Red Sox game from Fenway Park, Commissioner Frick charged that the new lens could "cause all kinds of trouble."[24] The very long lens made it possible to see clearly the catcher's signs. Thus, the commissioner feared that teams could "steal" the catcher's signs and tip off their batters to the coming pitch. Indeed, announcers Mel Allen and Phil Rizzuto, who were using the NBC video to call the game for WPIX in New York, were accurately calling each pitch during the game by focusing on the close-up images of Yankee catcher Yogi Berra and Red Sox catcher Sammy White provided by the new lens. Frick immediately requested that NBC discontinue the use of the lens. Tom Gallery, the sports director at NBC, hastily capitulated to the commissioner's request, conceding that "of course, Mr. Frick is right. Actually, we had been experimenting mainly with the idea of bringing close-ups of horse racing and football events. In baseball, our aim was only to use the lens in the All-Star game. . . . It will not be used again in our games-of-the-week."[25]

Frick then wrote to all of the Major League clubs, advising them that they should include clauses in future television contracts restricting the use of such lenses. What might enhance a televised football game or horse race was seen by the commissioner as a threat to baseball's integrity because it might allow one team to steal the other's signs. Instead of restricting team access to the televised game, which would have eliminated the potential problem, Frick simply restricted the access of the television viewer to an interesting nuance of the game. Louis Effrat of the *New York Times* speculated that Frick might be more concerned about another "danger . . . that those who watched proceedings on their television screens would be getting 'for free' considerably more than what those who paid their way into the ballpark received."[26]

In retrospect, the 80-millimeter lens controversy revealed the mindset of two veteran figures, baseball's Ford Frick and sports television's Tom Gallery, both schooled in the established rules of televised baseball. Innovation could only be tolerated as long as it did not affect, or even appear to affect, the game on the field. Television was ancillary to the stadium experience. It should be good, but not be too good, since a superb television experience might convince some paying customers to stay at home. Television was still the threat that must be managed, rather than an opportunity to exploit.

By 1964, both CBS and NBC were limiting their September Sunday MLB games in deference to professional football and its higher ratings. NBC's "fifty games this year" had eroded to forty-six. As television became a dominant economic force in the world of sport, baseball's conservative approach would hamper its development, while football's partnership with television rapidly improved its fortunes.

Finally, a National Game of the Week

By 1964, change was in the air, maybe even radical change. Tom Moore, president of ABC, suggested, according to Red Smith, a "revolutionary" approach, "modestly referring to his proposals as the Moore Plan." MLB should cut its schedule to sixty weekend games over a thirty-week season, ending the "overexposure" that had caused baseball's decline since 1948.[27] Teams could cut their costs by reducing their rosters to only their best players.

Needless to say, the baseball establishment was not receptive to a television executive's suggestion that it eliminate nearly two-thirds of its product. "Now, isn't that too bad!" cried sports columnist Jim Murray, "Tv [sic] has invited itself to the dinner but doesn't care for the entrée. It is a house guest which wants to change the wall paper."[28] Red Smith charged: "Ever since the hucksters of television got their grubby little paws into sports, it has been inevitable that sooner or later, they would want to rewrite the script for their own convenience and profit."[29] In August, baseball's traditionalists saw a much more tangible threat when a major television network, CBS, purchased the crown jewel of the sport, the New York Yankees (this early version of baseball-television synergy is analyzed in chapter 12).

Although much of the national attention at the time focused on the Yankees purchase, behind the scenes MLB was shifting the responsibility for negotiating national television contracts from individual clubs to a committee headed by John Fetzer, the Detroit Tiger owner and a broadcast executive with thirty years of experience. The new Major League Television Committee realized that it was to the sport's advantage to negotiate a winner-take-all-contract that would provoke strong competition among the three television networks. The result was the contract for the 1965 season, which thrust Major League Baseball into the lap of the most aggressive player in sports television: ABC.

The Monday Night Baseball That Never Was

Although ABC would ultimately land a Saturday game of the week, the Major League Television Committee first floated a proposal for a much more ambitious *Monday Night Baseball Spectacular*. In addition to increasing game-of-the-week revenues, a prime-time game would "enhance baseball's image at a time when professional football was receiving increasing national exposure on the screen."[30] Despite a "lukewarm" reaction from the networks, the committee, using former head of NBC sports Tom Gallery as its chief consultant, issued a detailed proposal to the major networks in August of 1964.[31] If it had been implemented, baseball's Monday night game would have appeared a half decade before its more famous football cousin.

The plan outlined a schedule of twenty-six weeks of Monday night games, commencing with an opening-day contest from Washington, DC attended by the president of the United States. All twenty Major League teams agreed to participate in the package. Two games would be telecast each week: the first for stations in the East and Midwest time zones and the second for the stations in the Mountain and Pacific time zones. For sixteen of the twenty-six weeks, the games would consist of twi-night doubleheaders, the first game to be telecast to the East and Midwest and the second to the mountain states and Pacific coast. A backup game would be provided except for games from the West Coast where cancellations were rare.

The Television Committee erred in allowing only a month for the networks to submit their bids, which made it difficult for them to line up the necessary advertising support and clear their prime-time schedules. Because of network resistance to a prime-time game, the committee shifted its focus to a more conventional Saturday afternoon package.

ABC's Third Strike

Significantly, ABC's new Saturday afternoon contract was the first in which games would be broadcast on a truly national basis. For each game, blackouts were limited to the home- and visiting-team markets, and the network's backup games could be aired in these markets. This nearly doubled the potential audience for the games, making the game of the week a truly national television event.[32] Sunday games were gone, but ABC would present two games, one targeted to most of the country and a second game transmitted to states in the Mountain and Pacific time zones. A third backup game was included in case of rainouts of the primary games. ABC agreed to pay participating clubs $300,000 each regardless of how often they appeared—the first communal sharing of game-of-the-week rights fees. Developed by the NFL, this "corporate socialism" model, in which teams equally shared all of the network spoils, had finally come to Major League Baseball, albeit with one significant exception.

The New York Yankees were contractually obligated to their new owner (CBS) through the 1965 season. The network paid the team $550,000 for its own version of a game of the week. Thus, ABC would begin its new national package absent the most successful franchise in baseball history.

19. *Roone Arledge broke with many televised baseball traditions.*
Here he hires Jackie Robinson. AP/Wide World Photos.

The contract with ABC included an option for a second year that would pay teams $325,000, making the two-year package worth more than $12 million.[33] But the second year money would not come from ABC.

For ABC, the contract resembled Coca-Cola's plan for New Coke, a product that would invigorate an established brand without alienating its loyal customers. And the ponderously named ABC *Presents Major League Championship Baseball* worked about as well as New Coke. While Dizzy Dean continued to entertain small-town America with the big-city

Yankee home games on CBS, ABC tried to bring its dazzling approach to televised sports to the nation's most traditional game. Tom Moore, ABC president, crowed that the network planned to do "something truly revolutionary for baseball," to give viewers coverage that "won't be like baseball telecasts that we have seen up to now"; and they were "going to like the results."[34] The network promised to use the isolated replay camera that "adds to football's appeal," arguing "it will do the same thing for baseball."[35] Though initially the addition of the Major League markets to the potential audience of their game of the week seemed to be a boon, ABC soon learned that it was difficult to compete against both "Ole Diz" and the local team's telecasts with an out-of-market game.

CBS's eleven *Yankee Baseball Game of the Week* telecasts consistently beat ABC in the ratings when both networks had games. As one NBC executive put it, "Dean killed 'em."[36] The exclusion of the Yankees from the ABC package removed one of the few Major League teams with a truly national following. Over its first nine games in 1965, ABC claimed that its average rating dropped from 6.56 to 4.18 on the weeks in which it had to compete with the CBS-Yankee telecasts.[37]

The major problem for ABC was that it lacked exclusivity for its national games. By 1965, most Major League teams were telecasting some of their Saturday afternoon games locally. The baseball owners wanted to preserve all of their local television revenues and still tap the kind of "big-time TV money" that the networks gave the NFL and NCAA. But ABC's glitzy coverage was not enough to overcome the home team's advantage.

ABC presented extensive analyses to the commissioner's office that showed the dramatic effects of local-game competition on the network's ratings. For example, on April 17, 1965, the ABC telecast of an Orioles—Red Sox game received a New York market rating of 3.0 while the locally originated Mets-Giants game received an 8.0 rating. When the Mets game ended, the ABC game's rating jumped to 8.0. These local conflicts varied greatly from week to week. During the first ten weeks of the contract the number of markets with competing local games ranged from three to fourteen.[38]

ABC's Roone Arledge accused the baseball owners of uncooperative scheduling. "The owners weren't helpful at all. They sold us the rights and just sat back to collect their money. They refused to adjust many schedules, so our national games were always competing with local ones."[39] Used to calling the game-coverage shots, the owners resisted ABC's innovations. Arledge complained that "the owners were spoiled people. They were used to local TV setups that they could control, as if TV was just a public relations arm of the clubs. They never seemed to get used to dealing with the network that had paid for a product and expected to get something in return."[40]

The owners were joined by another wing of the baseball establishment, the writers. ABC provoked the wrath of baseball writers by entering the dugout with cameras and microphones for pregame interviews. The writers, outraged at the invasion of what they considered their exclusive territory, protested to the commissioner's office.[41]

With Dizzy Dean holding on to his loyal rural viewers and local MLB broadcasts grabbing the urban ones, ABC's ratings for its game of the week were a disaster. One industry source estimated that the network lost over $1 million during the program's one-year run.[42]

Despite the handicaps, ABC improved the production quality of the games, providing viewers with more camera angles and making substantial use of an isolated replay camera, slow-motion replay, and stop action—techniques that were increasingly common in the coverage of other sports, but rare in televised baseball. ABC's announcers included competent professional broadcasters (Keith Jackson, Chris Schenkel, Merle Harmon) and well-known former players as analysts (Jackie Robinson, Tommy Henrich, Leo Durocher, and, after his release by the Mets in mid-summer, Warren Spahn).

Variety's review of ABC's first Saturday-game coverage hinted at the network's potential to revolutionize what the viewer would see. However, it chided the network for being overly cautious in the use of its high-tech toys, noting that they were not employed until the third inning. Michael Katz of the New York Times agreed that the coverage was not revolutionary, observing that only once did the isolated-replay camera show something not seen in the live shot. Concerns that the umpires would be "shown up" by the replays were unfounded, as instant replays either validated

20. Baseball commissioner Ford Frick (left) looks at his NFL and NBA counterparts. The NFL's Pete Rozelle (in the middle) would use television more effectively than any other commissioner. National Baseball Hall of Fame Library, Cooperstown NY.

their calls or the video itself was inconclusive. In addition, the center field camera equipped with the long lens reemerged, and the catchers' signs were easily picked up by color analyst Durocher. Play-by-play man Schenkel "assured the viewers that there were no monitors in either dugout."[43] However, *Variety* saw a basic incompatibility between the pizzazz of ABC sports and the slow pace of the national pastime: "From here on, excepting the stretch drive, it looks like a contest between the game's inherent dullness and all the resourcefulness network sports chieftain Roone Arledge can muster from his troops."[44]

Although not a ratings success, the ABC contract was a financial success for MLB. It demonstrated that the packaging of all national games and winner-take-all bidding could produce greater revenues than those produced by several competing network games. According to *Washing-*

ton *Post* columnist Shirley Povich, the new contract helped send the value of a "big league franchise soaring."[45]

However, television was still seen as a problem. The issue this time was competitive imbalance. As he left office in 1965, Commissioner Frick lamented that baseball had not "solved TV yet, nor the related problem of the economic balance between the clubs." Noting that "baseball has made more strides in the last year to solve its problems than at any time in the 35 years I've been in the game," he argued that revenue sharing should be expanded to include all local as well as national television revenues. This pooling of all TV moneys would help bring competitive balance to baseball.[46] However, the disparity among clubs in local and regional television revenues would only grow over time. It is a "problem" yet to be solved by baseball.

For MLB, the next step would be a supernational package, including both a single Saturday game of the week and the most attractive nationally televised games: the World Series and the All-Star Game. By 1966, Major League Baseball was ready for the next step. It would take it with a new commissioner and an old television ally, NBC.

6

The National Television Package, 1966–89

History has not been kind to the fourth commissioner of Major League Baseball, retired air force general William D. Eckert. It wasn't just that he had no background in baseball; "Spike" Eckert was "obscure even within the Pentagon."[1] Amazed at his appointment, one writer quipped: "Good God! They've named the Unknown Soldier."[2] A sampling of newspaper headlines captures the press's shock at his selection from among 150 suggested candidates: "Eckert Surprise Commissioner Choice" (*Chicago Daily Defender*), "Baseball Takes Flier—-Hires General" (*Los Angeles Times*), "Out of the Blue" (*New York Times*). Having decided to pass on baseball for the 1966 season, an admittedly sour ABC official ridiculed Eckert's weak preparation for the post: "baseball goes off and hires this Neanderthal, who wouldn't know Madison Avenue from Madison, Wisconsin."[3] While the NFL was headed by the prototype of the television-age sports commissioner, Pete Rozelle, MLB had picked a neophyte, and an inarticulate one at that. One review of his short reign featured the following common complaint: "Eckert was disastrous as baseball's leading spokesman, delivering speeches in a mumbling monotone. Speech coaches advised him to use notecards instead of wading through text, and soon he was famous for shuffling the cards out of order and delivering spectacularly disjointed talks."[4]

Perhaps the owners only wanted a figurehead who could be easily controlled, but at a time when the sport was losing popularity, Eckert, labeled the "great stone face" during his air force days, was an unfortunate choice for the public face of the sport.[5] Appointed for a seven-year term on November 17, 1965, he would last only three. Although his accomplishments as commissioner were as minimal as his time in office, on his watch the first comprehensive national television contract commenced. With it, "the grand old game" entered the modern television age.

By mid-October 1965, ABC was nearly through with baseball. Having just made a winning $15.5 million bid for NCAA football, the network could only afford MLB at a bargain price, even if it had not already soured on the sport. Since ABC had not picked up its option and the CBS contract with the Yankees had expired, for the first time MLB could sell the rights to its complete national baseball product in one package. Because the owners still refused to provide exclusivity for the Saturday afternoon game, the weekly game was not a major attraction for networks. NBC and CBS, like ABC, were only interested at a greatly reduced rate. But the World Series and All-Star Game were different matters. Knowing this, the owners for the first time insisted that the rights to these showcase events would be sold only in a package with the game of the week. As *Baseball Digest* put it, "O.K., fellers, if you want the World Series and the All-Star Game—and all of them did—you've also got to buy the Game-of-the-Week."[6]

Local Revenues, Yes; Exclusivity, No

The owner's resistance to providing exclusivity for the game of the week can be traced to the substantial revenues they had been generating since the late 1940s from their local television contracts. Unlike the NFL, each of whose teams played only one game a week and which thus could package its total product relatively easily, Major League Baseball had established the priority of the local package first. The national game of the week had always been seen as additional revenue, rather than a central component of a team's television revenues. The significance of a national game of the week evolved slowly and only started to benefit financially weaker franchises with the advent of equal distributions of revenues in the 1965 ABC contract.

Although the large-market owners had lost that round by agreeing to share the network treasure equally, they were not going to cede any more television territory to "smaller-market" franchises. Thus, the owners would not protect the game of the week from local competition, even if the cost was the elimination of competing televised Saturday afternoon games. From the network's point of view, the weekly game's previous popularity simply may have been due to Dizzy Dean's popularity, which was a product of the era when blackouts restricted the game of the week to smaller television markets. The networks were more concerned with the World Series' and All-Star Game's primary position on the national sports stage. The game of the week would not gain exclusivity until 1984, at a time of enormous change in the television industry.

NBC Becomes the Network of Major League Baseball

On October 18, 1965, at the Edgewater Beach Hotel in Chicago, the MLB Television Committee, consisting of four club presidents (John Fetzer—Tigers, Walter O'Malley—Dodgers, Robert Reynolds—Angels, Roy Hofheinz—Astros) met with the three television networks sports heads (Carl Lindemann—NBC, Roone Arledge—ABC, Bill MacPhail—CBS). MLB offered three scheduling options for the game of the week: Monday night, Saturday afternoon, or a combination of Saturday afternoon and weekday night games. To the networks' surprise and dismay, the 1966-68 rights to the game of the week were packaged with the rights to the 1967 and 1968 World Series and All-Star Games. NBC already had the rights to the 1966 World Series–All-Star Game as part of an earlier four-year deal negotiated with Commissioner Ford Frick. ABC, still stinging from its 1965 game-of-the-week misadventure, asked for more time. When that was not granted, ABC stated that it would only be interested in bidding on the World Series–All-Star Game part of the package. CBS submitted a bid for both events, and its World Series–All-Star Game bid of $6 million per year nearly matched NBC's. However, its $2 million bid for the annual rights to the game of the week was only a third of NBC's. In the end, it was no contest. NBC won the rights for $30.6 million: $6 million per year for the game of the week and $6.1 million for the 1967 World Series–All-Star Game package and $6.5 million for the 1968 package. The impetus for NBC's generous bid was its urgent need for a win in the sports' rights derby, after losing NCAA football rights to ABC earlier in the year.[7]

Major League Baseball's new network topped the previous high for television rights: the NFL's $28.2-million two-year deal with CBS. Although the contracts were not directly comparable (two years of weekly games for the NFL and three for MLB), the total revenues for MLB increased 60 percent over earlier national baseball contracts. MLB also broke into prime time for the first time. NBC agreed to telecast three prime-time games on the Memorial Day, July 4th, and Labor Day holidays in addition to twenty-five Saturday afternoon telecasts. For the network, the new NBC *Game of the Week* package was an improvement since the Yankees would participate. Although the Phillies also were expected to participate, constraints in the existing television contracts prevented their sharing in the game-of-the-week revenues.

Despite its new network contract, however, Major League Baseball had real image problems on Madison Avenue. By blacking out most major markets, MLB's game of the week had succeeded in ruralizing its viewers. Dizzy Dean was a cultural icon, but not in that part of America that advertisers wanted to reach. After springing for a record contract, NBC's Lindemann articulated the network's desire to change televised baseball's audience demographics: "Increasingly, because of its marvelous ability to self-promote, the NFL was a hit with upper-income, well-educated, suburban viewers—a sponsor's dream, and at the same time, Madison Avenue was more and more saying, 'God, baseball's becoming a turn-off to the affluent. It has a terrible following: the rural, low-income, the elderly, grade school graduates. What television sponsor wants them?' Dean's problem was that was exactly the kind of people who adored him."[8]

Ole Diz's reign as the central figure in televised baseball was doomed because the game was now pumped into all Major League cities, and no longer restricted to small-town and rural America. His cornball country-boy style did not match the desired demographics for the national baseball audience. Thus, NBC's first move in attempting to change televised baseball's demographics was to ignore the man most universally identified with its past. Despite considerable pressure from Falstaff beer, still a major game-of-the-week sponsor, NBC took a pass on Dean. He had not seen it coming. When Pee Wee Reese speculated that the new NBC deal might be a problem for the CBS team, Dean told him: "Don't worry

21. By 1966, sponsors thought too many of Dizzy Dean's fans looked like these seated old-timers. National Baseball Hall of Fame Library, Cooperstown NY.

about it, pod-nuh. We'll be all right."[9] Well, one of them was, but not Dean.

NBC's attempt to reposition MLB's game of the week was part of a larger trend in network television in the 1960s and 1970s. As television became the dominant commercial medium, pressures from the advertising community began to push network television programmers to consider the quality of the audience (demographics) as much as its total size.

Not surprisingly, the most desired audiences were the ones who had the most money and for whom product choices were not fixed, making them susceptible to advertising's influence. The demand came from Madison Avenue for younger, more upscale viewers. Males were also in demand for certain product categories (beer, cars and related products, men's toiletries). These were precisely the groups that had the most entertainment options and out-of-home interests, making them the most difficult audience segments to capture. Older rural viewers were loyal television viewers, but they also were easiest to find in the demographic breakdowns included in the Nielsen national ratings.

A New Lead Announcer

NBC retooled by hiring Curt Gowdy, who had extensive experience with broadcasts of football on three networks and with World Series and All-Star Games for NBC. Raised in Wyoming and nicknamed the "Cowboy," Gowdy was a Boston Red Sox announcer from 1951 to 1965. For a decade, from 1966 to 1975, he would be the voice and face of network baseball, as the lead announcer of NBC's game of the week and of every World Series and All-Star Game. His reputation was well established; he was a solid broadcast professional whose personality did not get in the way of the game. In the words of one critic, Curt Smith Gowdy was "restrained, newsy, interesting. Just enough chatter."[10] He was the anti-Dean. Gowdy was also a replaceable part. If he asked for too much money, or developed an uncontrollable ego, another solid broadcast professional could replace him. The low-key Gowdy would never be the source of televised baseball's appeal; the focus would be on the game. NBC also saved money by using Gowdy as their announcer for its two major sports: MLB and American Football League football.

In its brief game-of-the-week experience, ABC had learned that "being a *Dean* fan didn't necessarily translate into being a TV *baseball* fan."[11] But with one important exception, advertisers no longer wanted the core Dean fans. Falstaff wanted Dean on the broadcast, if not as lead announcer then as Gowdy's partner. But the "Cowboy" wisely resisted. "No, sir, I told'em. Look, Diz is a boyhood idol of mine. I love the guy, but I can't sing 'Wabash Cannon Ball' and all that craziness—our styles are different."[12] Although Gowdy's Red Sox favorite, Ted Williams, was given some consideration, NBC, at the urging of Falstaff, hired Dean's "pod-nuh," Pee Wee Reese, as Gowdy's color announcer, providing some connection to past games of the week. With Gowdy and Reese, NBC thought it had the best match of the new and the old.

Clearly influenced by ABC's innovations, NBC beefed up its coverage.

Five or six color cameras would follow the action, with increased use of instant replay, stop action, and split screen. NBC Sports' director, Chet Simmons, promised, "our fans are going to see baseball like they've never seen before."[13]

The owners, reacting to the bad press they received as a result of their previous year's problems with ABC, were far more cooperative with NBC. NBC and MLB were both pleasantly surprised by the 1966 ratings for the *Game of the Week*. The telecasts had an average 9.1 rating, up 58 percent from ABC's 5.9 in 1965. NBC attributed the increased ratings to its use of color telecasts, a close National League race, less local television competition from the clubs, and the Yankees joining the new package. But NBC also was a stronger network than ABC in the mid-1960s. It had more powerful affiliate stations, and a higher percentage of its affiliates typically carried its programming. Any programming that shifted from NBC to ABC was likely to do better. In addition, the Yankees were not siphoning off NBC's viewers for eleven Saturdays, as they had with ABC in 1965.

NBC's three prime-time games were successful, and the Labor Day Giants-Dodgers meeting produced a 15.8 rating, the highest ever for a regular-season game.[14] The successful prime-time experiment would pave the way for, first, five and then fifteen night-time regular-season games, as well as the All-Star Game (first in 1967) and the World Series (first in 1971).

Even before its successful 1966 season, NBC had already been assured a profit by signing three advertisers for $5 million each for the national package, which had cost them only $9.75 million.[15] The average game-of-the-week rating would increase in 1967 to 9.4 and then show a gradual decline, from 8.6 in 1968 to 8.5 in 1969, and finally to 8.1 in 1970.[16]

A Reserved Lefty Signs

NBC scored a major promotional coup when it signed Sandy Koufax to a ten-year, million-dollar contract after an arthritic left elbow forced his retirement from the Dodgers following his twenty-seven-win 1966 season. Widely considered the best pitcher of his era, Koufax was initially part of the "A" game mix with Gowdy and Reese. However, he eventually became Jim Simpson's partner on the "B" game, which served as insurance against rainouts and was broadcast into the "A" game's home markets. The telegenic but reserved Koufax completed six years of the contract before retiring from television in early 1973. In summing up his time with NBC, Koufax confessed that he "never was comfortable being on television."[17] Lindemann thought Koufax was "one of the nicest guys I've ever known, and also one of NBC's worst mistakes."[18]

Koufax's replacement was former base-stealing champ Maury Wills. Wills was a "banjo" hitter who actually played the banjo as part of his off-season Las Vegas lounge act during his playing career. Although Wills "wanted the job in the worst way," his television "act" was not well reviewed.[19] Writer Melvin Durslag thought Wills knew about "as much about journalism as Edith Bunker [a character in the hit TV series All in the Family] knows about stealing second."[20] Nonetheless, Wills lasted until the end of the 1978 season.

Unlike Koufax, Reese had always seemed comfortable with the medium, but NBC's comfort level with him was waning as its three-year contract with MLB came to an end. With the game of the week trying to become more urbanized, announcers with rural, regional dialects and sensibilities, like Reese and Dean, were no longer as acceptable to national networks. At the conclusion of the 1969 season, Reese was therefore dropped by the network and replaced with the much younger and photogenic ex-Yankee Tony Kubek who moved up from the "B" game. Kubek's two decades with NBC's national telecasts would be the longest of any announcer. For some critics, Kubek and his partner Gowdy epitomized the era of bland generic announcers: competent professionals who neither offended nor excited most viewers.

Same Network, New Commissioner

Although the ratings were declining, cooperation between the network and MLB was increasing. In early August 1967, Fetzer's television committee negotiated a new three-year, $50 million contract with NBC for the 1969–71 seasons even though the old one would not expire until the end of the season. For the moment, MLB seemed to have forgotten the financial value of open competition among the networks. However, the new contract provided a 45.5 percent increase in national TV revenues over the previous three years. For the first time, every MLB franchise would participate in the game of the week, including the Phillies. Commissioner Eckert was a secondary figure in forging the new contract. The Associated Press story indicated only that he "also participated in the negotiations," while NBC Sports just said that he was "present during the Chicago negotiations."[21] The next commissioner would have much more to say about the national contract.

Having quickly grasped the limitations of "Spike" Eckert, even as just a figurehead commissioner, the owners dismissed him in late 1968. Although acknowledging Eckert's flaws, Leonard Koppett of the New York Times saw the firing as not just a change in leaders, but a change in the structure of baseball. He concluded: "In the present structure of Organized Baseball there is no need, no desire and really no room for a commissioner."[22] The position of commissioner of baseball would be filled, but not with a larger-than-life Judge Landis figure. Although the myth of the all-powerful, "best interests of baseball" commissioner was still embraced by the public, MLB needed a corporate administrator to help manage what was becoming a complex entertainment business.

The owners would not make the mistake again of choosing an inexperienced executive. Instead, they went with one of their own lawyers, Bowie Kuhn. He would serve half a year as interim commissioner and then win a four-year term of office in August 1969. The owners, perhaps wary of another mistake, reduced the commissioner's term of office from seven to four years. Kuhn appeared to be everything Eckert wasn't: a clever, decisive, baseball insider. He did not back away from controversy. And he would not be left out of the television negotiations.

Kuhn's First Contract

With Kuhn's permanent appointment, There was some shifting of power back to the commissioner's office. In particular, "more responsibilities for such daily matters as television negotiations and supervision of umpires will come under the commissioner's jurisdiction."[23] Indeed, although the owners were consulted, the next television contract announced in May 1971 was a product of Commissioner Kuhn's negotiations with NBC.

22. Bowie Kuhn would head baseball during the difficult decade of the 1970s.
National Baseball Hall of Fame Library, Cooperstown NY.

As in 1967, NBC was the only network involved, but this time it produced no television bonanza. The $71.75 million, four-year contract for 1972–75 represented only a slight increase per year over the $50 million, three-year contract signed in 1967. Adjusted for inflation, it represented no increase at all. The per-team cut would be even less when 1969 expansion teams became eligible for a piece of the national TV pie, now cut into twenty-four slices. The contract also allowed NBC to televise up to fifteen prime-time games, up from the five televised in 1971.

At least one owner, Jerry Hoffberger of the Orioles, publicly criticized the Kuhn-negotiated TV contract: "in other words, we have sold more of our product for a longer period for . . . less money." Hoffberger reported that owners had authorized Kuhn to "negotiate a new contract on approximately the same terms as the existing one." But he had only consulted the owners by telephone. "I say that's a hell of a way to run a railroad."[24]

The negotiations were not well publicized because it was in the own-

ers' interest to keep the split of the rights fees between the World Series–All-Star Game a mystery to the Players Association. Since the players' pension contribution had historically been 60 percent of the World
Series and 95 percent of the All-Star Game fees, withholding of this
information from the players made it impossible for them to know if
the owners would treat them fairly in their next round of negotiations,
scheduled for 1972. The owners seemed to be saying "trust us." Marvin Miller, executive director of the Players Association, seemed to reply,
"I'll see you in court."

On July 5, 1971, the Players Association filed an unfair labor practice
charge against the owners with the National Labor Relations Board, con-
tending that the Players Association "cannot negotiate on a new benefit
plan without knowledge of N.B.C.'s payments for the World Series and
the All-Star Game in the new four-year pact."[25] The owners countered
that the pension payment since 1967 had been based on a flat payment
($5.45 million per year in the current contract) and that the contract
breakdown was no business of the players. The MLBPA argued that the
pervious agreements had followed the historically established propor-
tions and that it wanted the information to inform its next contract negotiations as it had past ones. Red Smith saw the wrangle as part of a
pattern of irrational hostility by the owners toward their players: "A man
looks at the facts and asks himself what can they be thinking, these guys
who own baseball. Do they have some kind of death wish? Do they set
out deliberately to antagonize their players, to stir discontent, foment
strife, invite strikes, just for the pleasure of making trouble for themselves and damaging their own business?"[26]

Behind it all was the players' suspicion that NBC was paying the
lion's share of the contract for the World Series and All-Star Games,
with the *Game of the Week* as an insignificant "add-on." If that were the
case, the players would demand more for their pension fund in the next
contract. The dispute ended in late October when the owners wrote
the Players Association indicating that they would give the contract
breakdown to the players. The owners still claimed that all television
revenues belonged only to them, but "elected to furnish this information in the interest of promoting . . . a harmonious relationship with

the association."[27] Subsequent years would see little harmony. Kuhn's first experience in negotiating the national television contract revealed that he would be battling on two fronts: with the owners who hired him to promote their interests and with the players who increasingly distrusted those owners.

NBC's major changes for the *Game of the Week* focused on the expansion of the Monday night games from three in 1970 to five in 1971 to ten in 1972, and finally fifteen in 1973. Then, under the influence of ABC's *Monday Night Football*, which had pioneered the packaging of prime-time sports as big-time entertainment, NBC experimented with guest announcers, starting in the 1973 season. Inspired by the American League's new "designated hitters," one wag referred to the guest announcers as NBC's "designated hucksters." Although initially NBC was planning on using entertainment celebrities such as Pearl Bailey, Dinah Shore, and Woody Allen, they finally settled on legendary baseball personalities, including Dizzy Dean (the first guest), Joe DiMaggio, and Satchel Paige. Gowdy and Kubek "weren't overly enthusiastic about the idea," according to the *New York Times*.[28] Their concern was understandable, since announcers depend on each other for a smooth broadcast. Introducing a third person, who was not familiar with the working styles of the regular broadcasters, could produce embarrassing moments and an excess of chatter. Because it used three announcers, *Monday Night Football* was often accused of an overabundance of talk. However, its trio of announcers had time to hone their routine into a polished act. Gowdy and Kubek would have no such opportunity. NBC also added a pregame show: *Joe Garagiola's World of Baseball*.

Garagiola was already a major television personality with a long run on *Today*, the daytime game show *Memory Game*, and substantial contributions to the game of the week in the early 1960s. Garagiola's sharp insights into the game spiced with self-effacing humor were well received by fans and critics. Dave Brady of the *Washington Post* saw him as "the unqualified hit of last year's bid to punch up the Monday night show."[29] His star was on the rise. In the 1974 season, he gradually became the permanent third man in the booth for NBC's Monday night game.

23. Game-of-the-week announcers could become network stars. Here Joe Garagiola hosts an NBC game show. National Baseball Hall of Fame Library, Cooperstown NY.

Sharing the National Package

Kuhn's first network television contract had hardly been a hit with the owners, so for the second he returned to competitive bidding in hopes of enlarging the television pie. He also saw that the NFL benefited from splitting its package and selling parts to two networks. For football, the two-network "strategy" was a product of the development of the American Football League (AFL) as a rival to the NFL in the early 1960s. Two leagues needed two networks. After the two leagues merged, the NFL still wanted multiple sources of national TV revenue and maximum exposure for the sport. In 1970, it added the third network with the launch of ABC's *Monday Night Football*. Since MLB's national package had never been split along league lines, a different arrangement was needed.

The second Kuhn-negotiated contract, signed in March 1975 for the 1976–79 seasons, called for NBC to share the package with ABC. Despite rumors to the contrary, John Lazarus, Kuhn's chief negotiator, had assured NBC that it still had exclusive rights, though Lazarus was secretly negotiating with ABC. After arriving late for a meeting to discuss the package, Lazarus told NBC that "we just sold half of the package to ABC."[30] The next year Lazarus left MLB for a vice president's position at ABC. NBC was outraged. The network saw Major League Baseball, especially the World Series, playoffs, and All-Star Game, as a birthright. Now it would have to share it with ABC, a network that had been openly hostile to the game since its 1965 game-of-the-week flop.

For $42.8 million, NBC would keep its traditional Saturday game and its lower ratings. ABC, whose success with *Monday Night Football* and the Olympics had made it the master of prime-time sports, would get the more prime-time Monday night games for $50 million. Although the home team's market continued to be blacked out, for the first time viewers in the visiting team's market would see the Monday night contest. The networks would share the World Series, the two League Championship Series (LCS), and the All-Star Game. In 1976 and 1978, NBC would get the World Series and ABC both the LCS and the All-Star Game. In 1977 and 1979, the assignments would be reversed. For the first time since NBC gained exclusive rights to the World Series and All-Star Game, the radio rights were split from the television rights and sold to CBS Radio for $300,000. Despite the considerable nostalgia for the "golden age" of radio baseball voiced in the popular press, the public's preference for the televised game was eloquently expressed in the national baseball rights' scorecard: $92.8 million for television versus $300,000 for radio. But CBS Radio gave MLB a third media partner with an interest in promoting its sport.

The $92.8 million television contract was a 29.3 percent increase over Kuhn's previous lackluster effort. The commissioner naturally applauded the contract, saying that "the television deal we just closed is the biggest and best by far that we've ever had" and calling the increase "enormous."[31] However, given the high inflation of the early 1970s, MLB needed a $95.3 million deal to equal the value of the 1971 agreement. Like most American consumers in the 1970s, baseball was not keeping up with inflation. The weak economy and advertising market of the mid-1970s was certainly part of the reason for the modest contract, but MLB also ignored a new potential source of television revenue: cable. Although cable penetration in U.S. homes was only 14.3 percent in 1975, changes in regulation and networking soon unleashed its potential.[32]

Kuhn had earlier ruled out giving part of the contract to cable, broadcast television's new competitor. Echoing the reluctance of early generations of baseball leadership to embrace first radio and later television, Kuhn testified before Congress that he would not let the promise of cable dollars "jeopardize our relationships with our broadcast friends." According to the Washington Post, Kuhn argued that baseball telecasts should not be shifted to cable because "over-the-air television broadcast of games is too important in drawing fans to the ball parks."[33] It had taken twenty-five years, but baseball was finally acknowledging the promotional benefits of television. As we will detail in chapter 8, MLB also would change its mind about the benefits of cable in the next decade.

Announcer Shake-Up

A new contract meant new configurations for the announcing teams. With the prime-time games shifting to ABC, many baseball traditionalists feared that the network would install its biggest announcing star, Howard Cosell, widely seen as antibaseball, on the Monday Night Baseball team. During a guest-announcing appearance on NBC's Monday night game in 1973, Cosell, to the horror of Gowdy and Kubek, ripped the game on the field: "Un-FAW-chun-ately, it is im-POS-sible for us to con-TIN-ue to CAM-ou-flage the in-DIS-put-able fact that this game is lagging in-SUF-fer-ably!"[34] In the end, ABC would borrow from Monday Night Football in the first season of Monday Night Baseball, but not Cosell.

Like its football counterpart, *Monday Night Baseball* needed to be bigger than the game it covered to succeed in prime time. Cosell and his *Monday Night Football* partners had shown that creating excitement in the announcing booth was a key to the prime-time sports ratings. For the 1976 season, ABC hired three new-to-the-networks announcers with flamboyant styles to stir up the broadcasts: Bob Prince, Warner Wolf, and Bob Uecker. Prince would do play-by-play, and Uecker would be ABC's version of Garagiola, a weak-hitting, former big-league catcher with a strong sense of humor. Two of the three, Prince and Uecker, are enshrined in the announcer's wing of the Baseball Hall of Fame, and all three men would have long and successful careers in sports television. But the 1976 grouping of three strong personalities in one small announcer's booth was the equivalent of a Hollywood blockbuster with Brad Pitt, Leonardo DiCaprio, and Johnny Depp in every scene. If too many cooks can spoil the broth, too many "star" announcers can spoil the ballgame.

Variety, in particular, was not impressed with the season premiere, especially Uecker's interview of *The Six Million Dollar Man's* Lee Majors in the middle of a game, which it viewed as "one of those fumbling plugola guest shots from the broadcast booth this network has long used to annoy viewers on its Monday night football telecasts."[35] Prince seemed lost in the crowded ABC booth. His unique personality and catch phrases had made him a legend in small-market Pittsburgh, where he was the whole show. With Uecker and Wolf competing to entertain viewers, Prince was forced to focus on standard play-by-play announcing. Still, ABC was not the only network experiencing announcer turmoil.

In 1976, Joe Garagiola replaced Curt Gowdy, NBC's voice of baseball since 1966. The imminent turnover had been foreshadowed during the 1975 season when Garagiola became a full partner with Gowdy. He alternated as lead announcer on the Saturday game each week with Gowdy, and they shared the booth on Monday, with each man doing play-by-play and color for four and a half innings. According to NBC's Lindemann, Garagiola's support came from powerful quarters: Commissioner Kuhn and Chrysler, a major sponsor: "Kuhn was in Garagiola's corner, and his big ace was Chrysler. . . . Joe was their boy. He was under contract to them; he did their commercials. They had one hell of a lot of money invested in him, and they put the heat on N BC to give Joe half of the '75 play-by-play."[36]

In the country's bicentennial year, Gowdy would continue doing N FL and postseason college football games as well as NCAA baseball championships for the network, but he was no longer the national voice of Major League Baseball. The era of the low-key professional broadcaster was over, and that of the celebrity announcer was in full bloom. Enter Howard Cosell.

Monday Night Football made Cosell a national media phenomenon, and ABC's Monday Night Baseball would extend his run through the summer months. The Prince-Uecker-Wolf experiment ended after one year. Cosell joined the ABC team for the 1976 American League playoffs. In 1977, N BC's thirty-year history of telecasting the World Series came to an end, and ABC, with Cosell, Keith Jackson, and Uecker at the mikes, began bringing the Fall Classic to America. During their coverage of the 1977 playoffs, N BC's Garagiola and Kubek could barely bring themselves to mention the coming World Series "on another network." Cosell's open criticism of baseball as slow moving and dull had upset many in the game, including Commissioner Kuhn. In 1975, Cosell had written in the *Chicago Tribune Magazine* that "the game is too dull—it's that simple. . . . One must realize that baseball is no longer the national pastime. To say so is sheer pretension." Television critic Gary Deeb compared Cosell calling a baseball game to "discovering Bob Hope at an antiwar rally."[37]

Kuhn first lobbied Roone Arledge to drop Cosell from the telecasts and then reportedly met in secret with Herb Schlosser, president of N BC Inc., to ask the network to take control of ABC's part of the package. The commissioner apparently believed that the deal could be voided. N BC, still seething from what it believed was M LB deception in handing part of the national package to ABC, would not bite. One N BC executive fumed: "Bowie Kuhn is the most devious man I've ever dealt with. . . . I wouldn't get into a cab with that [nasty expletive]. I can't stand the SO B." Arledge defended his right to choose World Series announcers, which had become the sole prerogative of the networks in the last contract: "Bowie's gonna find himself without a network if he keeps this nonsense up. . . .

The guy cannot tell us how to run our telecasts. I guarantee you I would give up baseball in a second before I'd give up my principles. To tell us that we can't use Cosell is the same thing as Bowie telling a newspaper that they can't assign a certain writer to cover baseball."[38]

"Humble Howard"'s network turned out to be fine for baseball. The rise of the Yankees as World Series participants in 1976 and champions in 1977–78 helped both Cosell and viewers' interest in the televised game. The 1976 Monday night games' ratings jumped 19 percent over 1975, and the All-Star Game on ABC reached more homes (18,860,000) than ever, a 28 percent increase over 1975.[39] ABC's baseball ratings surge paralleled its rising prime-time ratings in the mid-1970s.

Cool Nights, Hot Ratings, and Cold Cash

As if Cosell wasn't enough, baseball traditionalists were assaulted on a second front by the success of prime-time All-Star, LCS, and World Series games. The ratings pattern was clear. The 1967 All-Star Game from Anaheim started at 4:15 in the East and went fifteen innings, turning it into a prime-time All-Star Game. The telecast drew fifty-one million viewers, a record. The next year's prime-time game from the Astrodome bumped that the number to sixty million viewers, while the 1970 Game played at night produced a television rating 60 percent higher than the 1969 day game.[40] The programming rule was simple: there are more available viewers in the evening than at any other time of day, and the more available viewers, the higher the potential ratings.

Athletics owner Charlie Finley, a maverick and an innovator, saw the same problem with daytime World Series games. In a 1963 letter to Ford Frick, Finley criticized baseball for ignoring the working man, and accused MLB of saying, "thanks, friend, we appreciate your support during the season and now that it's time to stage America's Greatest Sport's Spectacle, we are going to stage it at the most inconvenient and unreasonable time for you to see it. We are going to start it on a Wednesday afternoon when you are working at the steel mills, coal mines, factories, or offices. You can get the details when you get home from work." Finley also believed that MLB was missing an excellent opportunity to sell baseball to children, "tomorrow's fans," by in effect telling them, "boys and girls, we love you too—we are starting the World's Series, when you too can't see it—you are all back to school."[41]

But purists, echoing complaints first made about night baseball in the 1930s, said that the game was made for the daytime, and especially its crown jewels, the World Series and the All-Star Game. Baseball and the television networks were just out for the almighty dollar. The critics waxed poetically about little boys stealing a listen to the World Series on transistor radios during their October afternoon classes, while sympathetic teachers looked the other way. Moreover, night baseball in mid-October, after a long season and a round of playoffs, would be played in frigid conditions, unfit for either fan or player. Young fans would not be able to stay up late enough to see the entire game. Nevertheless, after game four of the 1971 World Series, played at night, produced an audience of sixty-three million—the largest ever for a prime-time sports event—weekday World Series games were all moved to nighttime.[42] Even when the evening temperatures were miserably cold, Commissioner Kuhn stoically watched the game warmed only by a sport jacket. The prime-time World Series would be a major part of his legacy. When Bowie Kuhn died in March 2007, MLB honored him with a full-page memorial in USA Today, noting only three specific accomplishments during his long reign as commissioner. "He [Kuhn] brought us expansion, night World Series games, and greater national television exposure [our italics]."[43]

Because weekend World Series games were still daytime events, they faced competition from other sports, especially the NFL on Sundays, suppressing the ratings. With the 1976–79 contract, the networks and MLB wanted the Sunday game moved to prime time, and the move was a ratings success. The 1975 Series game played on a Sunday afternoon had 42.9 million viewers, the 1975 Series game played on a Sunday night had 65 million. In the blunt words of the Los Angeles Times, "If it has to make a choice, baseball will take cold cash over warm weather."[44] The networks were paying big money for postseason baseball; they demanded the best opportunity to maximize their audience. The nighttime postseason was here to stay. More than ever, television was influencing baseball.

24. Baseball and Howard Cosell always kept their distance from each other.
National Baseball Hall of Fame Library, Cooperstown NY.

Cosell and His Critics

Although ABC's initial seasons of *Monday Night Baseball* had produced
a ratings surge, by 1978 the numbers were in decline. The network's
strong showing with its other prime-time programming made baseball's declining ratings even harder to swallow. As negotiations for the
next national package approached, ABC's affiliates in a straw poll voted
199 to 2 to drop *Monday Night Baseball*.

As the contract ran its course, criticism of Cosell's presence on the
game was mounting. Much of it came from newspaper columnists who
enjoyed skewering pompous television personalities. Barry Lorge, TV
sports columnist for the *Washington Post*, cited the "roar of disapproval" at
Cosell's appearance on the 1977 World Series, calling him "a blight on our
national pastime."[45] Shirley Povich attributed ABC's improved ratings in
early 1977, not to Cosell's presence, but to the network's luck in telecasting a series of close games and a hot Yankee–Red Sox pennant race. Povich ridiculed Cosell when Howard's on-air listing of great Tiger players
(Charlie Gehringer, Hank Greenberg, Mickey Cochrane, Rudy York) over-

looked the first player to go into the Hall of Fame: Ty Cobb.[46] When ABC and Cosell returned for the 1979 World Series, one critic suggested that viewers turn down the TV sound and listen to Vin Scully and Sparky Anderson "delve into the nuances of the game" on the CBS Radio broadcasts of the Series.[47] Critics did acknowledge Cosell's skills as an interviewer capable of asking probing questions and often eliciting surprising answers from normally reticent athletes. But they believed that as an announcer he was better suited to blunt, violent sports like football and boxing that were tailor made for hyperbole, not subtle games like baseball. For his part, Cosell thought the critics "were keeping baseball alive" because, as he scathingly put it, they "live for going to spring training and publicizing baseball every day of the year. They are living in the past."[48]

Changes at NBC

Competition from ABC forced baseball traditionalist NBC to change. Don Ohlmeyer, groomed at ABC under Arledge, had become head of NBC Sports in 1977, replacing Carl Lindemann, who moved onto CBS. Some in the media speculated that Ohlmeyer would bring to NBC Sports ABC's disdain for the older network's traditionalist baseball coverage, leading to extensive changes in personnel or the dropping of baseball altogether. The press had widely criticized Ohlmeyer's coverage of the game while at ABC. But preoccupied with planning for NBC's coverage of the 1980 Olympics Ohlmeyer was not focused on major changes in its baseball plan. He insisted on some changes at NBC, however, arguing that the network needed to improve its presentation of baseball's off-field activities to complement its excellent coverage of the game's action. He also believed that NBC's announcers could improve by providing more background on players unfamiliar to national viewers: "I kept trying to drive home to Joe, Tony and the others the point that Mickey Rivers may be an enormous story in New York, but to the guy in Keokuk, Iowa, Mickey is just another outfielder. You've got to give that viewer out there something to root for or against to maintain his interest."[49]

Although there was some speculation that Kubek, and perhaps Garagiola, might not be renewed at the conclusion of their contracts, both were re-signed in 1979 and continued as NBC's "A" game announcers.

25. Although criticized by some, ex-Yankee Tony Kubek would have a long career with NBC. National Baseball Hall of Fame Library, Cooperstown NY.

Meanwhile, at ABC, Al Michaels was promoted from the "B" game to the role of lead announcer, starting in 1980. The network increasingly relied on current or ex-players (Reggie Jackson, Tom Seaver, Johnny Bench, Jim Palmer) to complement Michaels, especially during the playoffs and World Series. Tim McCarver and Don Drysdale subsequently handled the "B" games. By the mid-1980s, Cosell had left baseball, *Monday Night Football*, and most of his regular sports assignments to focus on his issues-oriented program, *SportsBeat*. Until his death in 1995, he would be one of the sharpest critics of televised sports, chronicling its excesses in his best-selling books, *Cosell* and *I Never Played the Game*.

A New Contract Means More Money

Both NBC and ABC also re-signed with Major League Baseball in 1979. The new contract resembled the old in most respects, including each network telecasting the World Series and All-Star Game–LCS packages in alternating years. However, the rights jumped significantly from $92.8 million for the 1975–79 contract to $185 million for the contract running from 1980 to 1983. NBC's portion was $90 million and ABC's $95 million.[50] The increase was substantially more than the $137.7 million needed to equal the inflation-adjusted value of 1975–79 contract. Baseball was beating inflation.

The new network contract reflected new realities faced both by MLB and the broadcast networks. MLB had entered the era of free agency and salary arbitration, now allowing player salaries, for the first time, to rise with demand in the marketplace. The rapid growth in player costs spurred owners to aggressive pursuit of additional resources. One result was that the national broadcast television revenues in the 1980–83 contract doubled those in the previous contract. There was no doubt now that MLB intended to maximize its television revenues.

But why would the networks pay twice as much? The simple answer is that they were starting to lose their iron grip on the television audience. By 1980 cable was in 19.9 percent of U.S. homes. By the end of the decade, it would reach 57.1 percent.[51] The broadcast networks were facing competition for the first time in their history. They needed programming guaranteed to capture big ratings, especially during the autumn when the promotion of the new network season peaked. The World Series, All-Star Game, and playoffs still seemed to be doing just that. Between 1975 and 1982, World Series ratings were at their peak, ranging between 27.7 and 32.8.[52] The World Series and the playoffs were more than ever the key to the national television package. Even if the networks lost money on the package, especially the regular-season games, the promotional platform the postseason provided would produce greater sampling of their other prime-time programs and a better chance for overall network success. Baseball was becoming the equivalent of a supermarket "loss leader" for the networks: postseason games brought customers into their programming supermarket to be enticed by their product displays (promos).

As the postseason gained in value, the regular-season games showed serious audience erosion. NBC's Saturday game ratings steadily declined from 7.6 in 1978 to 6.3 in 1981 and 5.8 in 1983.[53] As we will discuss in chapter 8, the cablecasting of MLB games in prime time on superstations and the USA Network eliminated ABC's exclusive national franchise on prime-time national games. Indeed, the networks always debated the benefits of Monday night games, since they prevented the scheduling of more potentially popular prime-time programming. Since most games were in the summer, however, when viewer levels are always lower, the problem was not acute. The prime-time baseball competition from cable now tipped the balance. Prime-time regular-season broadcast network baseball was on the way out.

In 1980, ABC limited *Monday Night Baseball* to five mid-summer games and shifted eight games to Sunday afternoon contests in August and September. The change allowed the network to carry games during the height of the pennant races without having to jeopardize its much more lucrative *Monday Night Football* schedule.[54] The changes affecting both MLB and network television would be even more manifest in the last network contract of the broadcast era.

Same Networks, Even More Money

The six-year contract signed by NBC and ABC in 1983 moved televised baseball into the megadollar era; the value of the national baseball package went from ending in *million* to ending in *billion*. In April 1983, MLB, ABC, and NBC agreed to a six-year, $1.2 billion package. The package more than quadrupled each team's cut of the package, raising it from $1.9 million to $7.7 million per year. Inflation be damned; this was serious money. By 1983, the full financial effects of free agency and arbitration had hit MLB. The average team payroll for players was $7,219,000, more than five times what it had been in 1977.[55] The new contract meant that the typical team could cover its current player contracts with just the national broadcast television money. But the pressures on the networks were even greater. Cable's explosive growth fueled the dramatic surge in rights fees for all sports. Eddie Einhorn (co-owner of the White Sox), Bowie Kuhn, and Bill Giles (owner of the Phillies)—the so-called KEG (Kuhn, Einhorn, Giles) committee—negotiated the plum deal. Einhorn was a savvy television packager of NCAA basketball and other sports, with an insider's understanding of the television business. He modestly labeled the new contract "one of the major, if not the major sports negotiations of the decade."[56]

Following the pattern of previous contracts, NBC anointed a new number-one announcer. This time it was Dodger legend Vin Scully. In 1982, Scully had joined his announcing mentor, Red Barber, in the announcer's wing of the Baseball Hall of Fame. Scully was not just a local phenomenon. He was a slick professional with experience covering a variety of sports (NFL, Professional Golfers' Association). He would eventually host the NBC game show It Takes Two. Scully and Joe Garagiola would handle the "A" game, while Tony Kubek, never a favorite of Ohlmeyer, was demoted to the "B" game, where he teamed with Bob Costas, a rising star with the network.

Promoting the Coverage

NBC also continued a practice begun in the mid-1970s of actively promoting the quality of its game coverage, by exploiting the experience and expertise of director Harry Coyle. Coyle participated in his first World Series in 1947 and directed every one of NBC's Series telecasts. From 1975 on, numerous press pieces lauded Coyle's innovations as chief director for NBC's baseball productions, including his introduction of the center field camera to a national audience at the 1955 All-Star Game and his development of a fourteen-page "bible" of baseball coverage for his production crew (see chapter 14 for more on his contributions to game production). Coyle's name became so familiar that the tipsy announcer played by Bob Uecker in the 1989 motion picture Major League was named Harry Doyle, a playful reference to the NBC director. NBC was very successful in convincing many writers that their baseball coverage was the best.

Not surprisingly, ABC's production staff felt slighted. Jim Spence, ABC's head of sports at the time, saw the "Coyle is TV baseball's best director" mantra as just "a matter of things being repeated so often that they become accepted as gospel."[57] But the case for NBC's superiority appears to have been established in 1976, ABC's first year of competition with the older network, when ABC was preoccupied with its preparations for the summer Olympics. Chuck Howard, ABC's vice president of program production, admitted that "baseball got stuck in the corner. . . . It was only when we went into the playoffs that our thoughts and energies got fully into baseball."[58]

Exclusivity, Finally

For television's extra cash, MLB offered the networks some important concessions. NBC would get full broadcast exclusivity for its Saturday games, which was especially important as competition from local cable and superstations grew. Teams would hold the starting times of their own broadcast games until after most of the network games had been completed (4:00 p.m. Eastern Daylight Time). In 1984 NBC saw a modest jump in its Saturday game ratings from 5.8 in 1983 to 6.4.[59] But with no protection from the increasing competition of cable, exclusivity was of much less value than it would have been in the pre-cable era.

The real money was in the postseason, and the networks wanted more for their money. They pushed Commissioner Kuhn to request that owners change the LCS from a best-of-five to a best-of-seven format. The owners agreed, but the players insisted that they must approve any expansion of the playoffs and be given appropriate compensation for the extra games. After some discord, the Players Association agreed to expand the playoffs to a possible seven games for an additional $9 million, starting in 1985. Network television's $1.2 billion was buying more influence over the game than ever before. The national television networks were now dictating to MLB how many games it would take to decide the National and American League pennants. The tail was wagging the dog with more vigor than ever.

7

National Broadcasts in the Cable Era

For both Major League Baseball and the broadcast television industry, the 1980s was the decade in which the revolutionary seeds planted in the 1970s began to flower. For MLB, the death of the reserve clause and the birth of free agency in 1975 ended the owners' power to fix labor costs simply by denying Major League employment to any player unwilling to accept his owner's salary offer. For the broadcast television industry, dominated since the golden age of radio by three companies (ABC, CBS, and NBC) and their networks of affiliated stations, the emergence of the first national cable networks and superstations ended the Big 3's complete dominance of national television. In the 1980s and 1990s, both industries would find a brave, new, and much more competitive world.

Changing Worlds Collide

Free agency brought to baseball a highly visible and increasingly important competition for playing talent. Now every winter fans watched their team compete with every other MLB team for the services of a handful of players. Clever player agents often convinced club owners that their team was only one or two key players—the agents' players—away from fielding a pennant-winning club. Although this was rarely the case, major free agent signings made the owner an instant hometown hero, while the more protracted process of developing players through clubs' farm systems rarely created instant fan interest. The scarcity of free agent talent and the constant demand from owners, often very successful in other business ventures, to win now sent player salaries "up with a bullet." In addition, free agency–generated salaries became the reference point used to resolve salary arbitrations for players with fewer than six years of service. As a result, the average player salary grew from $36,500 in 1973 two years before free agency to $140,000 in 1980.[1] By 1988, the average team was paying about $11.5 million in salaries, an average of $440,000 per player.[2] The free agency era triggered overspending by many clubs and the consequent need for ever increasing revenues. Stadium attendance and local television revenues produced some new money, but income was limited by market size and team success. The national television contract, divided equally among MLB teams, was unaffected by these local conditions. As a result, it would absorb a larger and larger share of the increasing player costs.

The growth of cable networks and independent television stations mirrored the explosion in player salaries during the free agent era. By 1980, the number of national cable networks was twenty-eight, and by 1990 it had grown to seventy-nine.[3] At the same time, broadcast networks faced competition from many more independent (non-network-affiliated) broadcast stations. In 1976, there were 1,030 television stations in the U.S, 90 percent of which were affiliated with ABC, CBS, or NBC. By 1985, that number had grown to 1,505, and almost all of these new stations were competing with the Big 3 networks.[4] The era in which three television networks could assume that at least 90 percent of the prime-time audience would tune to their programs—and commercials—was fading fast.

Conventional business analysis dictated that networks with declining ratings should produce programming at lower cost. This would help to compensate for the declining network revenue from advertisers that resulted from the smaller program audiences generated in the new competitive viewing environment. But, in fact, neither programming costs nor network revenues declined. As competition increased, programming that could still attract a mass audience in an era of audience fragmentation became harder to find and more valuable when found. Televised sports, especially the playoffs and championship tournaments, still produced high ratings for audiences that had desirable demographics. In addition, by the late 1980s, more networks, primarily ESPN and Fox, were competing for sports rights, driving up the prices.

Advertisers were also faced with a new reality. Network audience shares were declining, but more and more major companies, including firms in the booming investment industry, needed to reach network sports audiences. As a result, sports sponsors were willing to pay increasingly higher cost per thousands (CPM)—in television, the cost of reaching one thousand viewers. Thus, although ratings declined steadily, especially for regular-season contests, both networks and their advertising partners paid more, much more, for major sports programming, including the MLB national broadcast package.

Sports programming was no longer a guaranteed profit center. Broadcast television networks began to believe that the greatest value of this programming was in building brand equity and ratings for its prime-time offerings. Fox was especially successful in using sports to build its brand equity as a major television network. Following the formula that ABC used in the 1960s, Fox bid aggressively, first for NFL football in 1993, then for NHL hockey in 1994, and finally for MLB in 1995. At its creation in 1986, Fox positioned itself as a youth network, reasoning that younger viewers were more likely to sample programming on a new broadcast network. Next, Fox used major sports packages as an effective means of expanding its audience to upscale male viewers and promoting its prime-time lineups as it expanded its prime-time offerings to seven nights a week. The strategy worked, and by century's end Fox was the prime-time equal of its broadcast rivals.

Although Fox's broadcast competitors had well-established brand equity, they also needed exposure for their prime-time program promos. Baseball's postseason games, with their substantial and steady autumn ratings, were ideally scheduled to help networks build interest in their new fall programming. As a result, the value of MLB's playoffs and World Series soared even as cable's competition eroded the worth of its regular-season games.

The Return of CBS: More Bucks and a New Cable Rival

As MLB's second ABC-NBC shared contract neared its conclusion in 1989, all three established networks coveted baseball's fall promotional platform. However, MLB saw a new partner on the horizon. ESPN, now well beyond its "Australian-rules football days," wanted major sports franchises to further bolster its status as a must-have cable network. MLB's media-savvy commissioner, Peter Ueberroth, wanted to split the post-season and regular-season games into broadcast and cable packages, thus creating a second national television revenue stream for his cash-hungry owners. Although Ueberroth initially suggested that MLB might include the League Championship Series in the cable part of the pack-age, both the commissioner and the cable industry feared Congress's wrath if some of the postseason disappeared from "free" (broadcast) TV. Ultimately, Ueberroth divided the package primarily along regular-sea-son and postseason lines.

Though both NBC and ABC wanted to renew their package, the lat-ter believed it had overpaid in the previous agreement. ABC was disap-pointed when MLB refused to adjust the contract to compensate for the network's baseball losses. For his part, MLB's Commissioner Ueberroth was concerned that ABC had dramatically scaled back its prime-time games: "ABC bought the rights to show 36 games a year [and] it only showed eight [in 1988]. That tells us that we were selling the wrong package to the wrong people. This time we will satisfy cable first."[5]

Because of the postseason's increasing appeal as a promotional plat-form, all three established networks made bids for the 1990–94 rights. CBS won the rights with a $1.1 billion offer (later reported in various sources as a $1.08, $1.06, and $1.04 billion contract), $400 million more than the ABC and NBC bids. ABC said it was "disappointed" to lose "a blue-chip franchise," while NBC claimed it had bid "aggressively" and was "deeply saddened" by the lost of baseball.[6] Indeed, NBC's link to the TV version of our national pastime stretched back to the very begin-ning of regularly televised baseball in 1947. In 1990, that forty-three-year bond ended. Although Ueberroth reported that the bids were relatively close, NBC later claimed that its bid was substantially lower than CBS's. CBS even accused NBC of waging a "disinformation campaign" to ob-scure the extent of its interest and thus gain a negotiation advantage. In the end, Ueberroth went with the highest offer from the network that had the strongest need—the prime-time ratings challenged CBS.

At the time, CBS's prime-time programming had the lowest ratings, and it was desperate for a "major fall presence." CBS president Howard

26. Peter Ueberroth was a media-savvy commissioner, but owner collusion is part of his legacy. National Baseball Hall of Fame Library, Cooperstown NY.

Stringer believed that baseball would "take us out of the doldrums. . . . In that important [fall] ratings period, we are locking up the male viewers who haven't been visiting our shores for a long time." But industry sources believed that CBS had overpaid by perhaps $400 million for its baseball package—about $165,000 for each out in the Major League games it would televise over the life of the contract.[7]

CBS also accommodated MLB's plan to shift most regular-season games to cable. The new CBS contract called for only twelve regular Saturday games, a dramatic drop from the 32 NBC and 8 ABC regular-season telecasts in 1989, the last year of their contract. When asked about the dramatic shift in the regular-games season, Ueberroth laughed and said "the teams sell them locally and get a lot of money."[8] Indeed, the Yankees had recently signed a half-billion-dollar, twelve-year deal with the Madison Square Garden cable network for as many as 150 games a season. With local cable coverage expanding rapidly with the rise of regional sports networks and a national cable network deal on the horizon, the game of the week seemed like an antique. Still, in 1988, America was only a half-wired nation, with just 49.4 percent of U.S. households connected to cable.[9] By 1990, when the CBS run began, over forty million households would have no access to regular-season games on cable.

As we detail in the next chapter, ESPN won the national rights for four years at a cost of $400 million, outbidding Ted Turner's new TNT network.[10] With regular-season baseball airing on multiple nights and multiple national cable networks (ESPN joined superstations WTBS, WWOR, and WGN), CBS saw little to lose in limiting its regular-season games. Commissioner Ueberroth regarded the lost broadcast exposure for baseball as only temporary. "Look, cable is in 60 percent of the country now, it will go up to 70–80–90 percent. People will have cable television the way they have a telephone."[11] But criticism of the CBS game-of-the-week contraction came almost immediately, while the financial consequences of its bloated baseball contract would play out over the next four years.

Although once seen as threat to baseball itself, the game of the week had become a baseball tradition. Baseball's traditionalists saw its shrinkage as an affront to the game and a shortsighted strategy. Middle-aged men raised on Dizzy Dean's weekend telecasts seemed to rise in unison to protest. The loudest voice belonged to Curt Smith, a Dean biographer and author of *Voices of the Game*, a nostalgic look at baseball's broadcast past. In numerous national publications, Smith, a former speechwriter for President George H. W. Bush, attacked the CBS decision. Smith railed that the "new contract will stand as the greatest calamity in baseball's 69-year broadcast history," in that the cabled half of America received 187 regular-season games and the broadcast half only 12. "The new arrangement benefits the affluent while disenfranchising those who are unable to get cable for geographic reasons or who cannot afford it: pensioners, shut-ins, children, and inhabitants of inner cities, farms, and small towns."[12]

151

27. NBC's Bob Costas linked younger fans to baseball's golden past.
National Baseball Hall of Fame Library, Cooperstown NY.

Populist pleas aside, Smith believed baseball was sacrificing its most valuable promotional tool. "History teaches that network television is any sport's best selling tool. It enters every living room, and shapes the viewing habits of a nation."[13] He mocked Ueberroth's suggestion that local broadcasts would make up the game of the week's losses, claiming that local telecasts declined by 8 percent during the commissioner's tenure. For Smith, the game of the week "spoke of an America that was Mayberry—reassuring in a swirl of change—and preserved baseball's identity through its ribbon of narrative."[14]

Smith's argument for the game of the week tapped the same nostalgic reserve that had fueled Ronald Reagan's "Morning in America" message in the 1980s. He was not alone. NBC's lead announcer, Bob Costas, believed that "in a time of mindless hype in sports television, the 'Game' had a certain innocence."[15] But the contract was signed; the deal was done. Although CBS bowed to pressure enough to increase the number of Saturday games to sixteen for the 1990 season, the game of the week was still an afterthought. In the end, Smith was correct in one respect: the contract would be a "calamity," in the short run for CBS and in the long rung for baseball.

CBS Seeks Relief

CBS's staggering financial commitment to baseball was part of its even larger commitment to sports, which included the NFL, NCAA football, the NBA, the NCAA regular-season basketball and tournament, and the Winter Olympics. Don Ohlmeyer, NBC's former sports chief, saw CBS's sports surge as "an incredible change in the balance of power in TV sports," while Sean McManus, the former NBC sports executive who would eventually become president of both CBS Sports and CBS News, applauded CBS's "enormous programming and prestige coup" in building "a virtual monopoly of major sports series."[16] Over the next three years, however, as its sports, and especially baseball, losses mounted, CBS became fully aware of how much its "prestige coup" would cost it.

CBS's baseball bust resulted from a number of factors, some in its control and some not. First, CBS's baseball bid, around $400 million more than the competing ABC and NBC offers, drove up prices for other sports franchises, especially the NFL, during a period when the sports audience was fragmenting. At the same time, the economic recession of the early 1990s reduced the total amount of dollars available for all advertising media. But even still, CBS was especially unlucky with baseball. Its first regular-season games were delayed by a thirty-two-day spring-training player lockout by owners that angered fans and potential baseball viewers. Moreover, CBS's scheduling of its sixteen regular-season games was chaotic: it scheduled a few early-season games and then none at all until mid-season. MLB games alternated between Saturdays and Sundays and were offered at varying starting times to accommodate the network's other sports programming commitments. As a result, regular-season ratings dropped from 5.8 in NBC's last year to 4.6 in CBS's first.[17]

But the postseason was an even bigger problem. Ratings for the 1990 NLCS, between two small-market franchises, Pittsburgh and Cincinnati, dropped 10 percent from the previous year, setting a record for the lowest playoff ratings. Although ratings were better for the World Series, pitting the Reds against the Oakland Athletics, the Reds' four-game sweep cost CBS an estimated $15–20 million in the advertising revenues generated by a seven-game Series. Although estimates of CBS's first-year baseball losses varied wildly, from $55 to $150 million, there was no denying that the network took a baseball bath. Even CBS chairman Lawrence Tisch admitted that the baseball contract was "a mistake."[18] Baseball losses contributed to a 30 percent decline in CBS's earnings, triggering the elimination of three hundred to four hundred jobs.[19] Ironically, CBS's contract with the "national pastime" had given many CBS employees more time to pass.

CBS responded by trying to renegotiate its contract with MLB, but the network received no reduction in rights fees. However, as regular-season game ratings declined again in 1991, MLB allowed CBS to add more on-field microphones and behind-the-scenes cameras.[20] For the 1991 postseason, MLB permitted CBS to eliminate its half-hour pregame show and cut one camera from its coverage.[21] But these changes did little to help CBS correct its "mistake."

Over the last three years of its contract, CBS's World Series luck improved a bit as the Fall Classic went to seven games in 1991, and six in 1992 and 1993. However, these Series also included teams with modest followings (Twins and Athletics) and, even worse for ratings, a Canadian champion (Toronto Blue Jays) in 1992 and 1993. The 1993 Toronto-Philadelphia World Series was the second-lowest-rated Series to that date and the first World Series to rate below the same year's NBA championship series.[22]

In the CBS years, game-of-the-week ratings declined from 6.1 to 3.4.[23] Estimates of CBS's total losses for its return to baseball ran to over $500 million.[24] CBS's losses from baseball and other sports led to its reassessment of the value of sports programming. As for relief from MLB, Commissioner Fay Vincent offered only that baseball "should probably work much more with the networks to increase the revenues for television. We should be more pro-active in the joint marketing of baseball."[25] Although CBS did move from third to first place in prime-time network ratings during its baseball years by, in part, using MLB postseason games as a promotional platform, the massive losses made it evident that MLB owners would see a major decrease in revenues from rights fees.

CBS's losses had made the network less aggressive in its pursuit of sports packages. In 1994, Fox would outbid CBS for the right to televise National Football Conference games, ending CBS's nearly forty-year affiliation with the NFL. Acquiring rights to the NFL was a major boost to Fox, and losing them was a disastrous blow to CBS. The transfer contributed to the defection of several CBS affiliates to Fox. The NFL became the single most important factor in Fox's eventual rise to parity with the Big 3. The 1990–93 national broadcast contract had seriously injured CBS, but its end sparked an even more dramatic meltdown in baseball, as the contract's swollen revenues began to shrink.

The Baseball Network: A Baseball Package Packaged by Baseball

Major League Baseball was set for dramatic change. In September 1992, the owners fired Commissioner Vincent. He had alienated them by undermining their spring-training lockout in 1990 and pushing his plan for franchise realignment. Vincent was replaced by Bud Selig, president of the Milwaukee Brewers. For the first time, the commissioner of baseball would be an owner, bursting any illusion that the commissioner was an independent arbitrator with only the "best interests of the game" at heart. Future owner/player conflicts would be reduced to a simple management-versus-labor contest with no umpire, not even an illusory one.

The disastrous CBS contract also ended the delusion that the major networks could continue to pay more each contract for smaller audiences and fewer regular-season games. When MLB's Television Committee encountered network offers half as high as the previous contract and a similar cable revenue cutback from ESPN, it began looking for a new formula that would reduce the risk for networks and minimize the lost revenue. The committee's prescription was for the owners to enter the television business.

The Baseball Network (TBN), a joint business venture of MLB, ABC, and NBC, dramatically altered the relationship between Major League Baseball and the television industry.[26] Unlike all previous major national sports contracts, TBN dispensed with all upfront money. MLB was responsible for the sale of advertising time, actually competing with the networks for national advertising dollars. For its efforts, MLB would keep approximately 87.5 percent of the revenues, while ABC and NBC divided the rest. The networks got revenue and a promotional platform from baseball with no risk.[27] Eddie Einhorn, minority owner of the White Sox and member of MLB's Television Committee, believed the new approach was "about control of the future. You can't really do a traditional rights deal anymore. You have to devise something different. That's what we did."[28]

The "something different" included much less money for MLB. In just the first year of TBN, each team could expect to receive as much as $6 million less than it earned from the previous CBS deal.[29] This was the first major decrease in network television money ever experienced by a major sports league. The decrease was particularly onerous for MLB because escalating player salaries were driving up team expenses.

TBN regionalized weekly telecasts, and MLB expanded the playoffs with the addition of a two best-of-five League Division Series (LDS) in both major leagues in an effort to generate higher ratings. With the exception of the World Series and the All-Star Game, there would no national network coverage of individual MLB games. The twelve post–All-Star Game telecasts, the four new LDS, and the two League Championship Series (LCS) would all be telecast on a regional basis.[30] The single primary national game of the week was officially dead. MLB would ape the NFL by presenting multiple telecasts, with first ABC and then NBC carrying six weeks of regional packages. The NFL telecasts all of its games, however, and its national ratings are based on a compilation of ratings from fans in each team's local market, maximizing the league's national rating. In contrast, TBN's games would be regional and would include many fans who were not interested in the particular teams competing.

For example, though a northeast regional game featuring the New York Mets and Philadelphia Phillies might appeal to fans of these two teams, it would be of little interest to Yankee, Red Sox, or Oriole followers.

The additional round of playoffs added as many as twenty games to the postseason, dramatically increasing the number of valuable postseason commercial availabilities that TBN had to sell. MLB hoped this would replace much of the revenue lost from the expiration of the CBS contract. Some in the advertising industry were skeptical that MLB would gain much from the new inventory. Answering his own question, Bill Sherman of McCann Erickson asked, "Can the economy support an additional round [of playoffs]? I don't see it happening, at least at the outset."[31] However, the addition of wild-card teams would also keep more teams in the playoff hunt, a fact that the owners expected would increase both attendance and local television ratings.

The supporters of TBN claimed that the deal was the "wave of the future" and a means to increase aggregate ratings and the general attractiveness of the game through regional coverage.[32] However, the general consensus was that MLB had been dealt a major blow to its prestige and its financial health. To a much greater degree than ever before, television had demonstrated its ability to directly impact the structure of MLB.[33] One reporter characterized the new arrangement as "a remarkable shrinkage for the national pastime."[34] Other observers criticized the elimination of a single national game of the week.[35] Curt Smith concluded that baseball was "destroying itself" by treating its broadcast audience "like lepers at a bazaar." The elimination of the national game of the week would mean that "next year will seal the blackout, with not an inning of network TV that kids are awake to watch."[36] But Einhorn saw it differently: "We didn't kill it [the game of the week]—the fans did by not watching it."[37] Some saw TBN as a prelude to the pay-per-view (PPV) offering of LDS and LCS games, a charge denied by MLB owners in testimony to congressional investigators.[38]

Some baseball owners were also concerned about the radical shift away from guaranteed revenue, believing "baseball is assuming too much risk."[39] Sensing an opening, CBS surprised MLB's owners at a May 1993 meeting with a new proposal that would give baseball $120 million for two years and a share of any revenues over $150 million—the amount that CBS had generated in the last year of its previous contract. But for 1994, it was likely that owners would have to settle for less than one half of the $265 million they received in 1993. After debating their television options in a teleconference, the owners rejected CBS's midnight offer and on May 28, 1993, approved its first, and only, nonguaranteed television contract. The Baseball Network was born.

In September, the owners completed their television-inspired overhaul of baseball by realigning its franchises into three divisions in each league and including a wild-card team in a new best-of-five first round of playoffs for 1994. Continuing the theme of change in its relationship with the television industry, MLB signed a new six-year contract with ESPN that cut the number of baseball telecasts roughly in half. The contract generated considerably fewer dollars than the previous one. Cable joined broadcast television in finding MLB not nearly as attractive a product as in previous years.

Less Money Means More Conflict

Ultimately, the immediate impact of the new contract on MLB was a dramatic decrease in the guaranteed revenue that each team received from national television rights. This anticipated drop in revenue led to an industry financial crisis, especially for lower-revenue teams that were more dependent on national television money. MLB, led by small-market owners (including "Acting" Commissioner Selig), resolved to return struggling franchises to profitability quickly by lowering expenses. Since their number-one expense was player salaries, their number-one objective in the next labor agreement became a salary cap to help control labor costs.

As economist Andrew Zimbalist noted, small-market teams had extra leverage because a longstanding agreement allowing visiting teams to telecast from home teams' stadiums expired in 1993. "The small-market teams threatened not to sign a new agreement unless the big-market teams agreed to additional revenue sharing among the owners." The big-market teams agreed to the revenue sharing only if players agreed to a salary cap.[40]

Especially distrustful of the owners after their free agency collusion during the Ueberroth years, the Players Association was in no mood to accept a cap on its members' earning potential. In addition, the MLBPA was upset that owners had developed a radically new approach to its national television contract, including an additional round of playoffs, without consulting them.

One columnist facetiously suggested the player/owner tussle as a potential solution to baseball's declining ratings. "The owners call the players greedy, and the players call the owners liars. Yet, these are the two sides that have to negotiate a deal. You really want to make money, you televise that."[41] But, the real player/owner fight would be less entertaining and much more consequential. Sagging national TV revenues contributed to an impasse that led to a strike by the players in August 1994 and the cancellation of the World Series for the first time in ninety years. The labor dispute spilled into the 1995 season, and only after federal intervention did the owners and players end their most destructive dispute ever. The World Series cancellation was a public relations nightmare, and it took baseball a decade to repair the damage to its image. But the centrality of national television revenues to MLB was never more evident, and the potential consequences of any dramatic reduction in their levels were sizable.

A New Network, an Old Network, and a New Beginning

The Baseball Network lasted only two years. By the summer of 1995, MLB was desperate for guaranteed money and wanted out of the agreement. Because of the strike and postseason cancellation, the first year had been a disaster. TBN returned to advertisers all but an estimated $30 million of $200 million it would have generated in ad revenue without the strike. In 1994, TBN earned baseball's owners only about 11 percent of what they had gotten from CBS in 1993. But the strike's end and a popular 1995 World Series between the Atlanta Braves and Cleveland Indians led to earnings estimated at $180 to $200 million.[42]

MLB's original agreement with ABC and NBC called for an automatic contract renewal after two years if revenue targets of $330 million were met.[43] The strike had made that impossible. Dennis Swanson, president of ABC Sports, believed that the network had a verbal commitment from Selig that the agreement "would be unaffected by the strike," giving TBN another year to meet its revenue target.[44] But MLB's Television Committee had been restaffed with owners who had been suspicious of the TBN arrangement and more interested in upfront money. The networks wanted the TBN to continue because MLB's postseason games gave them a solid promotional platform for their fall programs without any upfront money risk. When MLB refused to meet a network-imposed deadline for renewal, ABC and NBC opted out of the contract. ABC and NBC executives believed that MLB thought it would get a better deal from either CBS or Fox if it could kill TBN. Dick Ebersol, president of NBC Sports, ridiculed the thought of moving baseball to the upstart Fox network: "They're trading the promotion from the No. 1 and 2 networks to a pushcart."[45]

MLB had correctly assessed the market, however. The addition of Fox contributed to the transformation of the Big 3 into a Big 4, creating increased demand for major sports properties. Despite the still fresh memory of CBS's half-billion-dollar baseball losses, both CBS and Fox were willing to offer guaranteed rights fees, assuming all of the contract's risk. They were also willing to consider MLB's desire to bring back a regularly scheduled Saturday game of week, thereby expanding MLB's broadcast reach. In many ways, the next national TV contract would be "back to the future."

Considering ABC and NBC's disgust with MLB over the collapse of TBN, industry analysts concluded that the two networks would not bid on a new contract. The focus shifted to a potential joint offer by CBS and Fox that would split the national package. However, industry sources doubted that CBS's affiliates supported baseball's return.

On November 6, 1995, MLB announced a new five-year, $1.68 billion contract that for the first time included both broadcast and cable networks.[46] The return of the billion-dollar contract and guaranteed money were a welcome relief to many owners strapped for cash after two strike-shortened seasons.

The national broadcast package was split, but it would be divvied up between Fox and NBC, while ESPN and Liberty Media (later Fox Sports

Network) secured cable rights. The total package added about $11 million per year to each team's revenues. NBC, the network most experienced with baseball, paid $85 million per year for two World Series (1997, 1999), three All-Star Games (1996, 1998, 2000), and a share of the League Division and League Championship Series. Fox, the network with no experience in baseball but a growing presence in television sports, contributed $115 million per year for three World Series (1996, 1998, 2000), two All-Star Games (1997, 1999), its share of the first two playoff rounds, and eighteen to twenty regular-season Saturday games. The NBC bid was a shock. Ebersol had fumed in July that NBC was done with baseball "for the rest of this century."[47]

For the Fox Broadcasting network, MLB baseball, combined with its other sports packages, helped legitimize the network as a major broadcast network. Baseball's value to Fox was not ratings driven. The ratings for Fox's Saturday games averaged only 2.8 during its first contract. Ratings for the network's World Series games showed a steady decline from 17.4 in 1996 to 14.1 in 1998 to 12.4 for the 2000 subway series between the Yankees and Mets.[48] But David Hill, Fox Sports Television Group's chairman and CEO, explains why ratings are only part of the picture: "The playoffs are in a great time of the year, just prior to November sweeps, and they are really an ideal platform for the entertainment boys to launch their wares."[49]

The decline in baseball ratings also should be placed in the context of a radically changing television environment. Every type of programming has experienced ratings declines in the era of multichannel television and other new media technologies. Baseball ratings declined less than many other types of programming. For example, the ratings for Fox's Saturday games have declined very little since the end of the first contract (from a 2.8 to about 2.5).[50] The demographic appeal of all television sports, compared to many other program types, also increases the value of each ratings point.

Fox became the exclusive broadcast network provider for baseball in a six-year $2.5 billion contract covering the 2001-6 seasons. NBC once again was left without a piece of the MLB package as the new millennium began.

In July 2006, Fox signed on for seven more years of Saturday baseball (expanded from eighteen to twenty-six games), All-Star, and World Series play, maintaining its position as MLB's exclusive broadcast network through 2013. Fox Sports will carry the ALCS in 2007, 2009, 2011, and 2013, and the NLCS in 2008, 2010, and 2012. The four League Division Series will be aired only on cable's TBS. TBS also will air twenty-six regular-season Sunday games. The price tag of the combined Fox-TBS deal was nearly $3 billion.[51]

Reacting to declining World Series ratings, especially on Saturday night when viewing levels are at their weekly lows, Fox negotiated with MLB to start the World Series midweek, allowing fan interest to build for the weekend games. Once again, the television rights holder had dictated a major sporting event's schedule.

The national broadcast contract has become part of Fox's baseball branding, which supports its RSN's cable-satellite coverage of local teams. In the next chapter and in chapter 12, we will review the growing influence and importance of regional sports networks. Along with NFL and NASCAR affiliations, Fox's baseball branding contributes to the network's high sports profile for both its broadcast and cable networks. For MLB, Fox has been an excellent partner, bringing financial stability and high-quality coverage to the national pastime.

The Pay Television Era

The most important shift in the relationship of television to its viewers has been the ascendancy of pay television. Starting from a tiny, mainly rural base in the 1960s, cable television is nearing ubiquity in the United States. Approximately 90 percent of television households now pay for cable or satellite delivery of television.[1]

Defining Pay Television

Some basic distinctions are necessary. We consider pay television to encompass any television delivery service that requires the consumer to assume the direct cost. We do not use the standard industry practice of limiting the definition of pay television to pay or premium cable (e.g., HBO, Showtime) or pay-per-view cable or satellite offerings of motion pictures, boxing, professional wrestling, and adult content. We adopt a broader definition because the normalization of pay television *in whatever form* has had a major impact on the television industry and on its programming (product).

Although most observers are correct in arguing that television was never actually "free," advertiser-supported broadcast television is available without direct cost to anyone who has a receiver in geographic proximity to its signal.[2] This had enormous implications for the television industry, as it did for its "parent" radio industry. Being able to reach a large heterogeneous audience meant first and foremost that programming almost always had to appeal to the widest possible audience. One of the semi-tongue-in-cheek programming theories explaining the era of the Big 3 (CBS, NBC, ABC) broadcast networks was that of the "Least Objectionable Program" (LOP). This held that LOPs were most likely to have success because they did not irritate the audience enough for viewers to change the channel.[3]

The programming practices of the broadcast era were predicated on the concept of a passive audience. This made good sense when there were limited channels available, few remote control devices (RCDs) to encourage channel "surfing," no direct payment to motivate viewers to seek out more appealing programs, and an oligopolistic economic structure that discouraged the Big 3 from pursuing innovation.[4]

Although the now Big 4 broadcast networks (ABC, CBS, NBC, and Fox) must still appeal to a relatively mass audience, today they must also compete directly within a cable- and satellite-dominated environment. To the vast majority of viewers, broadcast network programming is just one of many television options available. The large number of "basic," "premium," and PPV offerings give the television user an unprecedented range of viewing options at any given time. This is supplemented by the DVD and prerecorded DVR (digital video recorder) options. Though the lack of direct viewer payment forces broadcast networks and their affiliated stations to seek large audiences, they cannot ignore more specialized tastes. A smaller but more economically desirable audience may keep a program on the schedule despite its low overall numbers. This phenomenon was first noticed in the 1980s with such programs as *St. Elsewhere* and is presently seen with the low-rated but demographically desirable *The Office*, among other programs.[5]

Cable programming rarely attracts broadcast-size audiences. However, the dual revenue stream of both advertising and subscriber fees allows major cable companies and satellite providers to generate huge profits with modest audiences. In addition, most cable networks operate more like the radio than the traditional broadcast television industry: constantly repeating programming and basing advertising rates on cumulative audiences rather than just the rating of a given program at a given time.[6]

As cable began to rapidly diffuse across the nation beginning in the mid-1970s, its primary need was for original programming. With budgets not then allowing for much scripted programming, a plethora of talk programs, repeats, movies, and niche programming (religion,

Spanish-language) appeared. Once the FCC rules prohibiting most major sports on cable were eliminated in 1977, sports became a highly desirable target. Sports attracted desirable demographics and were widely available.[7] In 1979, ESPN (Entertainment and Sports Programming Network) began operations with a mix of mainly collegiate and international pro sports (e.g., Australian-rules football, Canadian Football League [CFL]). Within a few years, MLB and other major sports appeared on ESPN as well as other national (TNT, Fox Family, USA) and regional cable and satellite networks. The founding of ESPN can be seen as the true beginning of the pay television era for sports. However, it was not the first time that sports (and particularly baseball) were seen as a programming vehicle for pay television.

The Early Pay Television Pioneers

Television's arrival had been long anticipated by the time of its commercial introduction in the late 1940s. The basic technology had been demonstrated in the 1920s, and experimental stations had started operations before the war.[8] The two major radio networks (NBC and CBS) were actively making plans for postwar television, as were the then new "third" network (ABC) and DuMont, an electronics manufacturer.

Though most observers assumed (correctly) that advertising would foot the bill for television as it had for radio, others saw pay television as the future of the new medium. As detailed in chapter 3, the period of the late 1940s and mid-1960s saw a considerable number of pay television experiments. The most important for baseball was STV, Inc.'s intent to present Dodger and Giant games over its wired system in California. The passage of an anti–pay TV initiative in November 1964 put an end to STV's grand experiment. Wired subscription systems were soon rendered obsolete by the growth of multichannel cable television. A few over-the-air pay television systems (ON-TV, Wometco) did manage to operate until the 1980s and even offered MLB games in some markets (e.g., White Sox), but even they were no match for the explosion in cable systems and satellite delivery that began in the 1970s.[9]

The modest success of most pay-per-view trials in the 1950s and 1960s further eroded the innovation of pay television. Pay-per-view was eventually replaced as the primary method of pay television delivery by the pay-per-channel model pioneered by the Home Box Office (national) and Z Channel (Los Angeles area) services in the 1970s. In both of these cases, restrictive federal regulations designed to protect broadcasters meant that the business had to rely on movies and specials to build the business, as series and sports pay television telecasts were severely restricted until the 1980s.

Baseball and Cable at the National Level

Two separate 1972 rulings by the Federal Communications Commission opened the floodgates for the growth of cable. One set of rules specific to cable television set parameters for the types of programming cable could offer.[10] Although the rules heavily restricted programming, they did open the doors for cable investors to aggressively seek franchises in urban markets already served by broadcast television. The other important commission action of 1972 allowed communication satellites to be used for domestic transmission.[11] This promoted the creation of new national television networks that would use a combination of satellite transmission to cable systems. These and other regulatory and judicial decisions affecting the development of the cable industry will be discussed in chapter 11.

Superstations

The new FCC rules made possible the beginning of the superstation era of television, in which a local broadcast station could lease satellite transponder space to beam its programming across the nation. Pioneered in the mid-1970s by Ted Turner's WTCG-TV Atlanta (soon renamed Superstation WTBS), superstations were of great benefit to such teams as the Braves, Chicago Cubs (WGN), New York Mets (WOR, then WWOR), and to a lesser degree the New York Yankees, then California Angels, and Texas Rangers. Although Turner claimed that the Braves were "America's Team," the influence of superstations is now declining.

National television time, once it reaches a mass audience, is simply too valuable to devote too much time to the regular-season baseball games of a single city's team. Offering baseball games to fans with a limited number of broadcast telecasts fed the success of TBS, WGN, and the others in their early days. However, the rise of regional sports networks, ESPN, and the Internet has made superstation baseball increasingly superfluous. Even the pioneering TBS phased out its Braves package in 2008 in favor of a national package of MLB games.[12] WGN-TV in Chicago remains baseball's only superstation, although this may change with the breakup of the Tribune Company.[13]

The Basic Cable Explosion

Another key breakthrough for cable was a 1977 federal court decision (HBO v. FCC) that invalidated the FCC cable programming rules.[14] Cable operators were no longer restricted from offering programs that might have value on broadcast television. This included series and sports telecasts that had previously aired on broadcast. This decision, more than any other, created the cable sports business. By allowing cable to offer more popular programming, the number of subscribers greatly increased, providing cable systems with more advertising revenue and subscriber fees (i.e., the dual revenue stream).

The growth of cable audiences also hastened the industry's emphasis on niche or specialized audiences who had much less value for broadcasting with its emphasis on mass audiences. Programming that targeted specific demographic or psychographic categories (e.g., children [Nickelodeon], teens and young adults [MTV], Spanish speakers [SIN, now Univision], movie buffs [HBO, Showtime], and news "junkies" [CNN]) were now possible. It was not long before sports became one of the major cable programming genres. Baseball and other major sports attract a highly desirable audience, primarily younger men, that other types of programming have a notoriously difficult time reaching. Although ESPN was to become the most dominant force in cable sports, MLB first dipped its toe into national cablecasting with another more established network.

MLB and USA

The USA Network remains one of the most popular "basic" cable channels. Starting as the MSG (Madison Square Garden) Network in 1977, it was one of the pioneers in using domestic satellite transmission to reach a national audience. This led to the name change to USA Network in 1980.[15]

Beginning in 1981 and continuing for three seasons, USA telecast a *Thursday Game of the Week* that included some doubleheaders and up to about forty-five MLB games a season. Demonstrating once again that MLB owners still had difficulty reaching a consensus on broadcasting policy, four of the then twenty-six teams (Atlanta, Houston, New York Mets, and St. Louis) were not partners in the deal. The Braves had Superstation TBS, and the other three had lucrative local broadcasting rights that took precedence over the relatively small amount of money that USA paid for the games.[16]

The USA contract specified that games could only be telecast to cable systems that serve homes more than fifty miles away from a Major League park.[17] This helps explain why the rights cost so little, and is indicative of the antitelevision strain long extant in MLB. The owners were still seeing televised games, even on a then small cable network, not as promotion and marketing, but as box office competition.

MLB and ESPN

MLB had no national cable coverage from 1984 to 1989. During these six seasons, MLB as an entity continued to rely on its shared broadcast revenue. However, individual teams did continue to be active with superstations and emerging local-regional cable operations.

During these years, ESPN became identified as *the* outlet for major sports, shedding CFL games and obscure college sports. By 1987 ESPN, now owned in part by Capital Cities–ABC, was the largest and most profitable cable network. In that year, ESPN added a package of Sunday night NFL games to go along with its NBA, NHL, and NCAA basketball and football telecasts.[18]

In 1989 MLB entered into a four-year contract (covering the 1990-93 seasons) with ESPN for an estimated $400 million.[19] Despite the fact that ESPN had now passed fifty million homes in reach, network executives saw it as at best a "break even" proposition.[20] ESPN subsequently claimed multimillion-dollar losses on the contract, although its losses were hardly devastating because:

MLB gave ESPN, for the first time, year-round major league sports. Although viewing levels are lower in summer, the huge drop-off due to lack of compelling programming was no longer a problem for ESPN. By airing about 175 games per season, ESPN was gaining in excess of five hundred hours of first-run and desirable programming per year.

ESPN was able to leverage its purchase by creating new nongame programming such as *Baseball Tonight*.

MLB was the last building block in making ESPN the most important brand name in sports media and marketing. Within a few years, the corporation was able to extend the brand via ESPN2, ESPNEWS, ESPN *Magazine*, and ESPNZone bar-restaurants. ESPN would have expanded without baseball, but not so as quickly and with more competition. If ESPN had not made the deal, another cable network would have done been happy to talk with MLB.

As for MLB, a major hurdle had been crossed. Owners now saw cable and satellite delivery of television as a viable source of new revenue and not just as a competitor to the box office and broadcast partners. The relationship of MLB and ESPN continues, and by the end of the present contract in 2013 it will be the longest relationship that MLB has ever had with any telecaster. Despite its losses in its initial contract and an impending labor dispute, ESPN renewed the contract in 1994 for approximately $42.5 million a year.[21] This was a major decline from the previous $100 million per-year contract, even when accounting for the fewer games that ESPN was to telecast. The mid-1990s decline in television revenue in general was the impetus for the creation of The Baseball Network for national broadcast television, and for the owner's resolve to "win" the most recent dispute with the players.

The resolution of the very damaging owner/players dispute in 1995 allowed MLB to recoup some of its lost credibility and money through ESPN. A new five-year contract valued at about $440 million went into effect in 1996.[22] This contract gave ESPN three games a week and, for the first time, postseason games. The shift of League Division Series games to cable is another key event in the history of baseball and television. No longer would baseball's postseason be available to virtually every television household in the nation. To a large degree, those who argued about the siphoning of sports from "free" to pay television were correct. However, because the vast majority of U.S. television households now paid for cable, there was minimal criticism.

ESPN decided to shift some of its Sunday night games to ESPN2 so the older and larger network could carry NFL games. This led to litigation between MLB and ESPN. The issue was resolved, however, when the now Disney-owned ESPN signed a more than $800 million contract with MLB for the 2001–5 seasons.[23] This huge increase in rights fees established the importance of MLB to ESPN and all its platforms: ESPN2, ESPN Deportes, ESPN International, and so on. In addition, ESPN was able to gain additional exclusivity—no local telecast competition—for its Sunday night games.

Posturing by both partners led to speculation that they might not renew their deal. But the latest ESPN-MLB contract covers eight years (2006–13) and provides MLB owners with about $2.4 billion (approximately $300 million a year).[24] The deal gives ESPN rights to MLB for most of its platforms, total exclusivity for all Sunday night games, and other rights for developing multimedia platforms. In addition, ESPN Radio pays separate rights of about $11 million a year, and ESPN.com pays another $30 million a year to Major League Baseball Advanced Media (MLBAM).[25]

The multibillion-dollar cost to ESPN for multimedia MLB rights reaffirms the rising value of new media platforms. In addition, MLB was able to hold back some important national rights from Disney's ESPN. Of these, the Fox national broadcast contract is most prominent. However, other examples include the burgeoning revenue stream of MLB .com, jointly owned by the thirty franchises; the XM Radio contract, which pays about $60 million a year for satellite radio rights; and the MLB "Extra Innings" package, which sells out-of-market games to DirecTV satellite and cable television subscribers.[26] In addition, the current ESPN contract gives MLB the right to sell up to 150 games per season (on a nonexclusive basis) to another cable or satellite operator. TBS-TNT and a new "Baseball Channel" basic cable network will be the location of these games.[27]

The Age of Regional Sports Networks

RSNs are today the main television outlet for local telecasts of home teams. In the past twenty years, RSNs have replaced local broadcasters as the television home of the home team in most of the United States. This stunning change in the baseball television landscape can be explained by several factors independent of the growing cable-satellite penetration in U.S. households:

1. RSNs target the local fan with most of their programming. RSNs enhance their dual cable-satellite revenue stream by targeting parochial fan interest (i.e., the most highly rated telecasts of any team sports event are almost always in the home market of the competing teams). This appeal extends to game coverage and pre- and postgame shows and other team-oriented programs. National cable-satellite companies cannot offer this local focus.

2. Independent television stations, which used local sports to compete with their network-affiliated competitors, have declined in number and reach. The Fox Network, followed by The WB and UPN (now combined into the CW), Univision, Telemundo, PAX (now "I"), and MyNetworkTV have absorbed most formerly independent stations. These networks provide prime-time programs for the former "indies," leaving no room in prime-time for baseball. The few remaining truly independent stations can rarely afford costly sports rights. They are much more likely to program their hours with home shopping or repeats of ancient network series than the games of their local MLB franchise.

3. As we discuss in some detail in chapter 12, RSNs are increasingly allowing team owners to become media owners. Although operating a full-time broadcast station entails a level of financing and government oversight that MLB owners might understandably choose to avoid, owning an RSN enables owners to leverage their investment in a team in a medium that must have rights to the team broadcast in order to prosper. Owning both the team and the RSN is a way to ensure the marketplace success of the lucrative RSN while providing a guaranteed stream of revenue to the team.

The Beginnings of RSNs

The concept of RSNs is similar to that of the STV pay system of the 1950s and 1960s. It presents local programming in specific markets for a fee. The big difference is that RSNs charge a monthly fee rather than per program. "Premium" channels, such as HBO and Showtime, have used this "pay-per-channel" model since the 1970s. This model has the decided advantage of reducing the pressure on any particular program to attract a large audience. The channel can succeed so long as the customer finds value in the entire package, and predictable consumer inertia keeps the cancellation rate low.

The first RSN was MSG (Madison Square Garden Network), which began operations in 1969.[28] Restrictive federal regulation of pay television and cable prevented the development of RSNs in other markets until the late 1970s and early 1980s. During this period, Chicago, Baltimore-Washington, Philadelphia, Houston, and Pittsburgh were among the MLB markets that developed RSNs, many of which are still in operation under different names.[29]

As audiences grew for these new local-regional services, a consortium of major cable companies launched Sports Time, a "super" RSN covering fifteen Midwestern states, in April 1984.[30] The consortium included Tele-Communications, Inc. (TCI), then the largest of the multiple system operators (MSOs), and one of the nation's primary sports advertisers, Anheuser-Busch. The Anheuser-Busch-owned Cardinals as well as the Reds and Royals provided the baseball games for the channel. Sports Time was a major failure, however; it folded in less than a year despite converting to a basic cable service. When it folded, Sports Time had only about forty thousand pay customers and reached only about one million households.[31] The Sports Time failure demonstrated that a super-regional service was not viable in a market accustomed to national and local-regional telecasts.

Despite Sports Time's failure, other more targeted RSNs continued to gain subscribers in the 1980s. Cable industry reporter Richard Tedesco has suggested that many major cable systems were eager to add RSNs to temper growing criticism of the cable rate increases that followed the Cable Communications Act of 1984.[32]

The Move to Basic and the Creation of "Backdrop" Networks

The next phase in the development of the RSN industry was the establishment of the Los Angeles-based Prime Ticket (PT) Network in 1985. Prime Ticket, owned in part by Lakers' and Kings' owner Jerry Buss, was the first major RSN designed to be a basic cable offering.[33] The network prospered in the nations' second-largest media market by fully exploiting cable's dual revenue stream. The success of Prime Ticket led to the establishment of Prime Network (PN) in 1989. In the same year, Cablevision debuted its SportsChannel America (SCA) service.[34]

There was much press speculation that PN and SCA were the new competitors to ESPN because SCA invested over $50 million in a three-year contract for NHL games.[35] However, what both PN and SCA represented was a new model for sports television—the RSN backdrop, which offered programming for affiliated RSNs during the time periods when local sports were not being carried. PN and SCA's national offerings did not replace local programming. Program-sharing arrangements had started among some RSNs in the mid-1980s, and these two networks institutionalized the procedure.

The creation of these two networks hastened the end of the RSNs as pay channels. In order to gain enough viewers to justify program expenditures and gain advertising support, RSNs switched to the basic service model.

SCA's decision to purchase national NHL rights was a failure; the network lost a considerable amount of money. In 1993, SCA merged with PN to form the Prime SportsChannel Networks.[36] By this time, a new sports media powerhouse was in the mix.

The Fox RSNs and New Competition

By the early 1990s News Corp. had decided to make sports a major component of its drive for profits and influence in the television business. News Corp. officials understood better than any other media company that one of the prime attributes of sports is the ability to create and maintain a desirable audience, even as the average audience for most other programs declined.[37] The corporation aggressively sought sports rights for its still new Fox Broadcasting Company, a drive that culminated in its acquisition of NFL rights in 1994 and MLB rights in 1996.

News Corp. followed this same strategy in acquiring most of the Prime and SportsChannel affiliates in 1996–97. The new Fox Sports Net, now called FSN, purchased many of the RSNs that comprised the PN and SCA networks and made affiliate deals in markets where it could not consummate a purchase.[38] Within five years, the various FSNs had local-regional rights to twenty-seven of the thirty MLB franchises.[39]

The FSN-MLB deals should be assessed in the context of the Fox Broadcasting network deals. Though separately negotiated for different events (local versus national) and by different parties (FSN and a team, as contrasted to Fox Broadcasting and MLB), there can be little doubt that the two deals support one another. Fox Broadcasting is willing to pay what many consider an enormous amount for national broadcast rights so as to please team owners, whose cooperation its RSNs need. At the same time, the use of the Fox brand name on the RSNs supports the national network and other entities through literally thousands of hours of promotion. After all, the average viewer probably makes no distinction between the local FSN and the network. It is all "Fox" and all baseball.

Despite this mutual support, the various FSNs have recently lost the rights to several MLB teams, as Comcast, the nation's largest cable operator, has created new RSNs with the participation of team owners. Though the importance of these new RSNs is a subject for chapter 12, the challenge of team-controlled RSNs is worth remarking. The first RSN owned, at least in part, by a team is the still existing New England Sports Network (NESN), owned by the Boston Red Sox. More recently, the Yankees' YES network has opened another lucrative revenue stream for the biggest-spending team in MLB. With RSNs getting as much as $2 per subscriber per month from cable systems, they are cash cows.[40] Owning an RSN also means that teams no longer need worry about rights fees except as a corporate accounting device.

Comcast has long been a major RSN owner in Philadelphia and an investor in the Phillies franchise. It is extending its investment in RSNs to improve its brand recognition and so sell its services. Company executive Steve Burke says that "having your name attached to a local sports network is a huge branding opportunity."[41] New York, Chicago, and Baltimore-Washington are among the markets that now have a Comcast RSN co-owned by a sports team (Mets, Cubs, White Sox, and Orioles).[42]

Of course, not all teams seem to have the means to create an owned or co-owned RSN. Both Kansas City and Minnesota have failed to create successful RSNs.[43] However, the lure of yet another lucrative revenue source is likely to lead to more deals in the next few years.

The Meaning of Pay Television for MLB

MLB, and most every sport, has greatly benefited from the shift of U.S. television from a purely advertiser-supported broadcast model to the dual revenue stream of cable and satellite television. Cable created a new stream of revenue to supplement broadcast money. The proliferation in the number of channels available to most Americans has led to increased competition for MLB's television rights. The effect has been an almost unbroken string of increases in the fees paid for these rights.

Rights fees that increase while audience sizes for most broadcast programming decline is an anomaly that even increased competition cannot explain. Indeed, some of the Big 3 networks walked away from contract renewals with MLB and other sports as ratings declined and costs increased.[44]

Part of the explanation for this seeming anomaly is that pay television (via cable or satellite) has a dual revenue stream of advertising and subscriber fees that makes even relatively low ratings a lucrative proposition. The result is the diversion of more and more baseball games to cable. This is particularly pronounced at the local level where RSNs have supplanted local broadcasts in an increasing number of markets.

The inherent qualities of sports as a form of television programming also help explain why rights fees can increase even as audiences decline. Sports telecasts actually have demonstrated less ratings erosion than most other programming. An example is the consistent 2.5 ratings average of Fox's Saturday afternoon national baseball broadcasts. Although a 2.5 rating would have been completely unacceptable in the Big 3–dominated broadcast era, that figure is considered healthy and lucrative for a summer weekend telecast in a multichannel environment.[45]

Several explanations have been offered for sports' ability to generate and maintain a relatively consistent audience in an age of rapid media change. Perhaps the most important factor is that, as noted earlier, they attract a highly desirable audience of young men who are very difficult to reach with other types of programming. Sports are also much less susceptible to channel surfing and time shifting because they present live action and suspense in a way unmatched by most other programming. Sports telecasts also offer advertisers unmatched opportunities to integrate their messages within the content. "Zap-proof" advertising is so ingrained in sports telecasts that viewers are unlikely to be upset by it. Sports are also considered to be a vital promotional platform for television networks. Fox's ability to promote its programming during the World Series or an RSN's ability to telecast the home team to promote its other offerings have a value that is factored along with ratings into the cost of rights fees. Finally, being known as the local or national home of MLB plays a key role in differentiating a network's brand from all the competition. Baseball and other sports have enormous value as an element of branding strategy.[46]

This is not to suggest that pay television has been entirely positive for baseball. The benefits of superstations and RSNs have been unequally distributed, exacerbating the gap between the "haves" and the "have-nots." Increased revenue also ramped up the always-tense relationship between owners and players. Although new revenue-sharing initiatives have quelled both issues for the moment, there is always the chance they will return with a vengeance.

As for baseball fans, they now have access to much more televised baseball than was once the case. This increased access, however, comes with a cost. Truly "free" (i.e., advertiser-supported) television only exists in about 10 percent of U.S. households. In most of these noncable and nonsatellite homes, MLB telecasts are limited to the Fox Saturday package, the All-Star Game, the World Series, and some, but not all, of the LCS. The home team's games are rarely available on the viewers' hometown stations. To an increasing degree, the fear of pay television's power to siphon games away from "free" (advertiser-supported) television has been realized.

Television and Baseball's Dysfunctional Marriage

3

Television As Threat, Television As Savior

From the beginning, baseball saw television as a threat; television, how-ever, saw baseball as an opportunity. In one of the earliest references to televised baseball, published in January 1925, the *New York Herald Tribune* lamented that baseball on television would prove "Another Menace to Sports." Although the first very crude mechanical television pictures had been demonstrated only recently, the *Herald Tribune*'s W. O. McGeehan predicted that in the future "persons possessing these machines will be able to sit in their homes or offices and watch the World Series . . . with-out having to contribute to the gate receipts." For baseball, the stakes were high. "How long could Colonel Ruppert support Yankee Stadium and Mr. Babe Ruth if there were no gate receipts?"[1]

McGeehan's initial reaction to "these machines" would be reflected in the received wisdom about televising baseball for the next forty years. When McGeehan expressed his concern, radio broadcasting of Major League Baseball had barely gotten started. In New York, the nation's largest market and the home of baseball's most consistently successful franchises, regular-season radio coverage would be delayed until 1939.

The Broadcast "Problem"

The leadership of baseball was dominated by late-nineteenth- and early-twentieth-century "giants" who invented the modern game: Connie Mack, Clark Griffith, John McGraw, Jacob Ruppert, Judge Landis, and later, Babe Ruth's ghostwriter, Ford Frick. Their business sense was formed in the P. T. Barnum era of "the greatest show on earth." Broad-way, burlesque, and baseball were all live events to be experienced in the flesh. Revenue came from ticket sales, concessions, and ballpark billboards. Attendance and revenues for most teams were tiny by modern standards, but the reserve clause controlled labor costs. With a little success, more than enough fans would turn out. Profits were modest, but owners only needed enough profit to support their families: the era of shareholders demanding ever increasing corporate profit was decades away in baseball. In the 1920s, the new medium of radio and the distant prospect of television were considered "problems" to be managed rather than a means to a greater market for the owners' baseball product. However, other forces would soon offer an antithesis to baseball's cautious, conservative, nineteenth-century thesis.

The countering wind came from broadcasters, advertisers, and a new generation of owners who saw the potential power of radio and television. Perhaps most influential among the new owners were William K. Wrigley and his son, Philip K. Wrigley. For two generations they would be the most consistently probroadcast forces among the baseball owners. Unlike some owners, who were former players who obtained teams early in the century, William Wrigley developed his business acumen by selling a product that no one needed, costs only a few cents, and required a mass market to be successful: chewing gum. In a business that required millions of repeat customers to really succeed, mass advertising made that success possible, and new advertising media (radio and later television) were opportunities for even greater profit.

The Wrigleys applied the same approach to their baseball team, the Chicago Cubs. Broadcasts were not "giving away the product" but a two-hour promotion (free advertising) of the product. The Wrigleys welcomed baseball broadcasts, allowing stations to offer competing coverage of Cubs games and, initially, charging nothing for broadcast rights. This approach, honed by the elder Wrigley in the radio age, was the blueprint for the younger Wrigley's television strategy (see chapter 3). But the Wrigleys did not neglect the paying customer. To ensure that the ballpark experience would offer more than the broadcast coverage could, they marketed their Wrigley Field ballpark as "the Friendly Confines," creating a baseball mecca that decades later turned Chicago's Lakeview neighborhood into "Wrigleyville."

But the number of progressive, probroadcast owners was small. From the 1920s to the mid-1950s, most owners saw broadcasting, especially telecasts, as giving the fan "the milk without buying the cow." However, radio and television stations and the advertisers that supported them needed programming that would draw a steady audience. Baseball, the "national pastime" of the era, could not be ignored. Broadcasters and their advertising partners pushed for increased coverage, while hesitant baseball owners and their commissioner forecast declining gate receipts. Umpiring the contest was the Department of Justice's Anti-Trust Division.

At the heart of this debate was a fundamental question: did broadcast coverage reduce, enhance, or have no effect on attendance? The owners had mostly concluded that radio helped. Radio could heighten fan interest, developing a new fan base especially among women and children who dominated the weekday daytime radio audience. In 1939, even the New York broadcast boycott had been lifted. Larry MacPhail brought his proradio policies and smooth, professional announcer, Red Barber, to the Dodgers from the Cincinnati Reds. The Yankees and Giants were forced to open their games to the microphone or risk losing market share in baseball's most competitive city.[2]

But television was a very different medium. Adding sight to sound meant television was one step closer to the ballpark experience. Although the television technology of 1939, the year of the first Major League telecast, provided a visual experience clearly inferior to actually being at the game, it was inevitable that television's pictorial quality would improve. Television couldn't provide the "peanuts, popcorn, and Cracker Jacks," but every game would be "free," if you didn't count the cost of watching commercials.

Different Owners, Different Opinions

During the 1940s, television's experimental period, owners and columnists expressed both the pro-TV and anti-TV points of view. Bob Carpenter, president of the Philadelphia Phillies, thought television would be "the greatest boost the game ever had."[3] Phil Wrigley supported televising games as a promotional device, but, based on baseball's slow acceptance of radio broadcasts, he thought it would take years to get other owners to agree with that position.[4] As early as 1948, Horace Stoneham, president of the New York Giants, saw television as hurting both Giant night attendance and the gate receipts for the team's minor league affiliates, and therefore recommended banning night telecasts.[5] The *Sporting News*, the "baseball bible," saw in television both potential and peril.

In May 1947, the *Sporting News* concluded that "television does not constitute a problem for baseball yet, but it inevitably will." Owners needed to capitalize on the promotional value of the broadcast media by "formulating plans to incorporate their radio and television rights to get the most out of them, not merely in money, but in advertising value. After all, baseball, too, has a product to sell to the public."[6] A few weeks later, it cautioned that television was not another radio. "Listening to a game a man may develop the desire to see it. But seeing it from his easy chair, at no cost and free from parking problems, he might decide that only a darn fool would make the trip to the ball park."[7] By 1949, the *Sporting News* took a more explicit antitelevised baseball position, as its front-page headline reported a "Crack-Down Seen on Major Telecasts—Stay-at-Home Fans Cutting Clubs' Gate."[8] However, *Broadcasting* magazine countered that the attendance figure reported by the *Sporting News* in the same article refuted its own claim.[9] Little research was available, however, to answer the central question: what effect did televising games have on attendance?

After the war, most owners yielded to the push from broadcasters and advertisers for programming. The first full season of televised baseball saw all but one Major League team (the Pirates) offering their games. One industry source reported that baseball accounted for nearly 50 percent of all the airtime for stations carrying the game during June and July of 1947.[10] Never again would the game so dominate the medium. Yet the game itself was booming—postwar America wanted baseball, both its major and minor league versions.

With major and minor league attendance reaching all-time highs in 1948, the early evidence supported an optimistic assessment of television's effects. Televised baseball was clearly boosting the tavern trade, as bar owners installed televisions. But ballpark turnstiles also were turning at a record pace, and some owners believed that television was part of the reason why. Lou Perini, owner of the Boston Braves and minor league Milwaukee Brewers, attributed the minor league club's record 1948 attendance to the televising of seventy-seven home games. Perini suggested in *Broadcasting* that television would "create many new fans, especially women," and that the new medium gave "just enough interest to excited fans so they come to the park and see the real thing."[11] Perini was so optimistic about television that he gave away the initial rights to Braves games for the promotional value of the telecasts alone. And he was not alone. In 1948, Bill Veeck refunded half of the Indians' $100,000 television rights when a sponsor could not be found for half of the Tribe's home games. Similarly, the Cardinals charged only $11,000 for fifty-five TV games.[12]

Cautionary voices could also be heard among the owners and sportswriters. Early television advocate Larry MacPhail, then general manager of the New York Yankees, and a minority of owners expressed opposition to plans for the first televised Word Series in 1947.[13] At a 1949 meeting, the New York chapter of the Baseball Writers Association offered new words to "Take Me Out to the Ball Game":

> Take us home to the ball game.
> Take us home to the wife.
> Get us our slippers; they're just the style,
> Plug in the gadget and spin the old dial.
> Then we'll root for plenty of action.
> If the tube blows out, it's a shame.
> But no matter what happens we'll never go out
> To the old ball game.[14]

By the early 1950s, the initial television optimism was beginning to fade. The postwar baseball boom was over. Both the Minors and the Majors were beginning to see attendance declines that would continue for many years. Had baseball's generous early television policy maimed, or even killed, the golden goose?

Early Answers from a Suspicious Source

Some answers began to emerge in 1950. A twenty-one-year-old psychology student examined the impact of television on sports attendance for his undergraduate thesis paper at Princeton and his masters' thesis at the University of Pennsylvania. He concluded that television had little to do with declining attendance.[15] Jerry Jordan's master's thesis might have gone unnoticed except for a powerful combination of good timing and family connections. Baseball clearly wanted an explanation for its declining attendance, while Jordan's father, Clarence L. Jordan, executive vice president at N.W. Ayer advertising agency, had the connections to ensure that his son's thesis would see the light of day. In 1950, the Radio and Television Manufacturers Association published a summary of Jordan's thesis and made sure it was widely distributed.[16] In the next two years, Jordan's conclusions would be frequently reported in both the broadcast and baseball trade press with, not surprisingly, very different interpretations.

Jordan concluded that baseball fans had a slight tendency to attend fewer games right after the purchase of a first television set, but this novelty effect disappeared rapidly. Given a stable economy, it was the team's performance, and not television coverage, that was the main factor in determining attendance. The impact on minor league teams also was minimal. Television negatively affected only teams close to Major League telecasts, which amounted to less than 3 percent of all minor league franchises.[17] However, the limitations of Jordan's study were substantial. Data collection ended after the 1949 season, when both major and minor league attendance were at record high levels. In addition, his survey of viewers came from just one market, Philadelphia. But most significantly, the full impact of television could not possibly be assessed in 1949 because the medium reached into only 2.3 percent of U.S households.[18] And given that the typical receiver cost $1,550 in 2006 dollars, most of these households were affluent.[19] Thus, the study was conducted much too early to detect any effect on the vast number of middle- and working-class viewers that would adopt television over the next decade.

The broadcast trade press, led by *Broadcasting*, accepted Jordan's conclusions as definitive, endorsing an open television policy. *Broadcasting* reported parts of Jordan's findings on at least seven occasions in 1950 and 1951, concluding that a "complete survey of television's long range effect on attendance at sports events [showed] that the medium does not hurt the gate."[20] But other research did not support this conclusion. A survey of four hundred families in Washington DC reported a decline in baseball attendance of 30.9 percent as well as dramatic declines in attendance at other sports events and at motion pictures for families who owned a set two or more years.[21]

In 1950, NBC entered the debate with a report on television's possible impact on attendance. The network noted that the relatively limited number of receivers in most major cities would weaken any potential effect of televising baseball. In addition, NBC offered graphs showing that attendance at both baseball games and motion picture theaters rose in the 1930s and 1940s even as the number of homes with radio increased. NBC argued that television, the newer broadcast medium, would have a similar positive effect. The network's convenient conclusion: "There is ample reason to believe that the presentation of baseball games via television will not only fail to decrease gate receipts but will actually stimulate greater interest in the American pastime."[22]

In late 1951, Jordan presented the results of a subsequent analysis of 1951 attendance. He found that the nine Major League clubs that increased or maintained extensive television presence had increased attendance by 234,169, while the seven teams that reduced or eliminated or had never televised games lost 1,485,070 paying customers. However, of the nine TV-embracing teams, only four actually showed an attendance increase, as did two of the seven TV-restrictive teams. In addition, two teams had a disproportionate impact on Jordan's results. The White Sox accounted for more than 55 percent of the attendance increase for TV-embracing teams, while the Tigers accounted for 51 percent of the total decrease for the TV-restrictive ones. Jordan also argued that the 20 percent drop in minor league attendance could not reasonably be attributed to television, since "only 40 of the more than 400 clubs were near TV and the decrease was widespread in all areas."[23]

Despite Jordan's analyses, complaints about the negative effects of television games would grow in the 1950s. As the "next big thing," television in the early 1950s was the darling technology of the moment, as radio was in the 1920s and the Internet would be in the 1990s. The emergence of television was an easy causal explanation for any positive or negative change in the culture: a convenient "post hoc ergo propter hoc" rationalization. If television grows and baseball attendance declines, then television must be keeping paying customers at home. In a controlled experiment, this might be a valid conclusion, but television was just one component of a multitude of changes shaping the entire postwar American "experiment."

A Changing America

The U.S. population was on the move in the postwar years, and its migration was almost always away from the existing Major League ballparks. The mode of this urban-to-suburban transport was the automobile. The careful placement of ballparks near mass transit lines during the Progressive Era, the last great era of ballpark construction, was now a failing strategy. Suburbanites wanted parking spaces, not subway platforms. Newly married with expanding families, postwar men also sought home-centered activities rather than the mostly male ballpark hangout. Although the relatively primitive television coverage of the early 1950s was no substitute for being at the game, the mid-century male had much less incentive to cross ever widening distances to see a game in person.

The television-as-threat forces seemed to have a valid argument. Attendance was declining, and the impact of the new medium in the television-saturated market of New York seemed hard to deny. The antibroadcast policy of the 1920s and 1930s was a distant memory. In the prenetwork era, New York television stations seduced all three teams with increasingly lucrative contracts into telecasting all of their home games. With competing programming limited, sponsors were treated to ample audiences for their baseball telecast commercials. After teams had telecast all of their home games during the 1947, 1948, and 1949 seasons, it became difficult for them to reduce coverage. Fans expected the wall-to-wall coverage, and teams became dependent on television revenues to help them produce yearly profits.

Federal Intervention and Team Reponses

As we discuss in detail in chapter 11, the Department of Justice's Anti-Trust Division began to umpire the broadcaster–baseball owner struggle over television. In 1947, the department invalidated MLB's Rule 1(d), which prohibited the broadcast coverage of games within fifty miles of a minor league park without the team's consent. Under continuing pressure from the department, in 1951 baseball repealed Rule 1(d)'s less restrictive alteration, which had allowed MLB games to be broadcast into minor league markets as long as they were not telecast at the same time as a minor league game. Congressional hearings headed by Sen. "Big Ed" Johnson (D-CO) and Rep. Emmanuel Celler (D-NY) failed to reinstate 1(d).

Throughout the 1950s clubs set their own polices regarding baseball. As such, the needs of broadcasters, especially in large markets that had substantial broadcast audiences, usually dictated the club's telecast policy. As attendance declined, broadcasters offered ready cash to offset the owners' losses. If broadcasters were killing the golden goose of ballpark attendance, they were replacing it with a new cash cow: broadcast revenues.

As the decade progressed, legislation that would "protect baseball from itself" never materialized. Major League Baseball's leadership continued to complain of television's negative effect on both the major and minor leagues, but failed to institute any new policies that would restrict the actions of individual teams. Owners propagated widely different television policies based on the characteristics of their particular markets, individual experiences with television, and financial needs (see chapter 3). For some, television was truly a threat. For others it was a savior that kept them afloat while attendance declined.

The Department of Justice intervention also meant that Major League Baseball could not negotiate a national contract for regular-season games. Contracts for national broadcasts in radio and later television were negotiated on a club-by-club basis. The first *Game of the Week* schedule, televised on ABC in 1953, consisted of the home games of only three American League clubs: the White Sox, Athletics, and Indians. At first, participants were weaker teams with low attendance that desperately needed a new source of revenue. During the decade, the *Game of the Week* gained a stronger network, CBS; larger audiences; and then added a competing game on NBC. Its success forced more and more teams to participate. By 1958, eleven of the sixteen MLB teams offered some of their weekend home games on either CBS or NBC.

The Antitelevision Era

Throughout the 1950s, a decade that saw more change for baseball than any since the turn of the century, Major League owners and their print-era commissioner lamented baseball's dependency on television. The print media, both popular and trade, gave voice to these owner complaints. A few headlines from the era convey the print media's predominant point of view:

"Does TV Empty the Ball Parks?" *Business Week*, 1951

"TV Must Go——-Or Baseball Will!" *Baseball Magazine*, 1952

"Baseball Is in Trouble: High Costs, TV Are Blamed," *U.S. News & World Report*, 1952

"Don't Let TV Kill Baseball," *Sport*, 1953

"TV Can Kill Baseball," *Newsweek*, 1953

"Can Baseball Survive TV?," *Business Week*, 1953

"Stop! Killing the Minors," *Baseball Magazine*, 1956

A sharp decline in attendance drove the panic headlines. Major League Baseball attendance dropped from just under 21 million at its postwar peak in 1948 to just under 17.5 million in 1950 and 14.4 million 1953.[24] Almost one-third of MLB's paying customers went AWOL. For many baseball writers, the sharp rise in television penetration from 0.4 percent in 1948 to 44.7 percent by 1953, combined with the extensive TV coverage of the game in many markets, was "proof" that television could "kill" the spectator version of the game.[25]

In August 1951, for the first time since 1946, a Yankees home game was not televised. It was a rainout makeup game with the Red Sox that was not part of the regular schedule. With no TV option, the Monday night game drew 51,005 fans, making it the best-attended night game in a season in which the attendance at night games averaged 30,000. Despite this evidence, Yankee general manager George Weiss questioned if the team could restrict television. With television-driven broadcast revenues now exceeding $500,000, Weiss wondered: "Suppose we did bar the cameras, . . . would the fans repay us for the loss of that revenue?"[26] A possible solution, if television was really the reason for the attendance dive, was to televise only away games. This would tap the promotional power of video without creating a rival for the gate receipts. Although technologically possible by the early 1950s, the cost of renting AT&T's coaxial cable lines made televising all away games prohibitively expensive.

By 1952, both the commissioner of baseball, Ford Frick, and Branch Rickey, considered by many the sharpest mind in the game, were stumped. Rickey said he was "sitting back, watching and studying," but confessed "I don't know about this thing." Frick was even more frustrated, pleading to reporter Dan Daniel, "please don't ask me to give you any definite dope on this television business . . . the picture is changing so fast, it is bewildering to me." Frick noted that surveys in New York and Chicago, conducted only a few months apart, yielded contradictory results.[27] By 1953, Rickey felt he knew "about this thing . . . 'TV Can Kill Baseball.'" For Rickey, "radio created a desire to see something. Television is giving it to them."[28]

Perhaps Frick and Rickey could be dismissed as old men, part of baseball's reactionary past, but Bill Veeck, owner of the St. Louis Browns, was a young Turk if ever there was one, and certainly a progressive voice. Yet Veeck also saw as television a threat, albeit with a typically Veeckian "David versus Goliath" twist. In a 1953 *Sport* article, Veeck argued: "It's dangerous for baseball to lose control of its business to a television sponsor" because "no business man can afford to give away his product."[29] However, he saw television's effect on attendance as even more debilitating to small-market clubs like his own because teams did not have to share broadcast revenues, but did have to share gate receipts. Veeck noted that the original 1901 American League agreement, to reduce the revenue disparity between large- and small-market teams, gave the visiting team 40 percent of the receipts, although inflation in the intervening years reduced that to about 20 percent. Thus, if television took dollars away from the Yankees when the Browns visited the stadium, the Browns lost twenty cents of each dollar. But the Yankees could replace a lost box-office dollar with a TV rights–generated dollar, and they got to keep the whole dollar. As attendance declined in baseball, the TV poor got poorer while the TV rich got still richer.

While the press focused on declining attendance and especially its devastating effect on the Minors, the real bottom line was often ignored. As Veeck lamented, large- and small-market Major League teams were affected much differently by the decline in attendance. Large markets could offset gate losses with rapidly rising local television revenues. As the revenue disparity between large- and small-market clubs increased, the former could use their larger gross revenues to "buy" the best players from struggling teams with poor attendance in weak television markets. And before free agency, large-market clubs could hold on to these elite players indefinitely. Winning ball clubs produced better ratings and higher rights fees, which made it easier to keep that team on top. The dominance of New York teams with substantial television rights revenues in the 1950s (fourteen World Series appearances out of the twenty possible) was likely aided by this imbalance. In addition, teams with declining attendance, often with their TV-based profitability hidden, could use these dramatic figures as evidence for the need for new stadium facilities or even new hometowns. Veeck's lament was to be a recurring theme in baseball. From this time on, the "have" and "have-not" baseball teams were defined in large part by their ability to generate television revenue.

Is It Televised Baseball or Is It Just Too Much Television?

Baseball's magnates also feared that the future impact of television would be even more devastating because the medium was still in its infancy. Dan Daniel noted that "the camera work from ball parks is better ... [and] color television is on the way. Come that day ... the fan will feel there's no use going to the ball game at all."[30] Johnson, the U.S. senator and Western League president with a flair for the dramatic, was even more concerned about the medium's advancement and its impact on baseball: "Forty-and 50-inch screens will be commonplace. Color television which improves the image 100 per cent is out of the laboratory and ready. The three-dimension picture will make the ball game so realistic that you will leap out of your chair and try to grab a souvenir when the ball heads your way."[31]

Although it would take twenty years for color television to become the standard, and we are still waiting for the third dimension to be added to the picture, Johnson gave voice to a prevailing anxiety: that television would produce a mediated experience far superior to the ballpark experience. This anxiety provoked attacks on television coverage as being "too good," thus drawing even more fans away from the park. Pioneering television producer Jim Beach was told at one minor league park that the club's business manager wanted poor positioning of the television cameras because "he doesn't want us to be too good for fear people will stay at home instead of coming to the park."[32] In the late 1950s, both Frick and Weiss tried to restrict the use of the center field camera because it improved coverage too much (see chapter 14).

However, not everyone believed that the televising games meant declining attendance. Some pointed to the medium of television itself, not its coverage of baseball, as the main problem, one that the baseball magnates did not control. Writing in Baseball Magazine, John Drebinger offered an evenhanded analysis: "Television in itself, apart from its baseball offerings, could very easily have made a deep inroad in the game. The novelty of the thing, the fact that it offers many other attractions—the Milton Berles, Jimmy Durantes and the like—could also have contributed much to keeping folks at home evenings, when otherwise they could be going out to the ball park."[33]

Drebinger also suggested that the Majors had a history of shedding "crocodile tears" over the plight of the Minors and might be using the television problem to do so again. Some owners also saw television, not necessarily televised baseball, as the major problem. Although suggesting that the Reds might cut back on televising night games, team president Warren Giles believed that reducing telecasts would not help the attendance slide: "Owners of television sets are not going to turn off their television programs merely because baseball games are not being shown."[34]

We will never know if televising baseball, television itself, television and a variety of other factors (suburbanization, antiquated facilities, and a focus on in-home "family" entertainment), or those other factors alone caused the decline in attendance. But it is clear that the decline in attendance produced dramatic changes in both the major and minor leagues. The Minors saw massive contraction (see chapter 10) during the period of television's ascent. The changes in Major League Baseball were also striking. A fifty-year period of franchise stability stretching from 1903 to 1953 came to an end as five franchises relocated within six years.

At the local level, television coverage of baseball did decline from its peak in the late 1940s both because of the rise of national networks that offered attractive prime-time programming and the antitelevision policies installed by several franchises, most notably the recently relocated teams. However, by 1960, the nationally televised games of the week expanded to three national Saturday games and one Sunday game (see chapter 5).

With the passage of the Sports Broadcasting Act of 1961, baseball and the other professional sports gained the ability to negotiate a national television package that would maximize the benefits of television while limiting its negatives. The National Football League quickly and fully exploited this new tool to manage television. However, in the 1960s, baseball suffered through weak commissioners, allowing local team interests to dominate the game's agenda. Consequently, successful teams had little motivation to share their wealth or pursue a television strategy that might promote the financial health of the entire sport. Indeed, during the following two decades, baseball's leadership focused more on containing labor costs than on maximizing the benefits of television. Only when baseball was "dethroned" as the nation's most popular sport and the reality of free agency finally took hold did baseball's leadership begin to embrace television as a savior rather than a threat.

The Cataclysm of the 1970s

The beginning of the 1970s looked promising for the baseball owners. Although the MLBPA's hiring of veteran labor union official Marvin Miller concerned them, there was little hint of what that hiring would mean in a few years. The decade opened with several events in which MLB moguls could take a great deal of pride:

1. The embarrassing saga of Commissioner "Spike" Eckert ended with the appointment of corporate attorney Bowie Kuhn, who had more media savvy than any commissioner since Happy Chandler.

2. The "Miracle Mets" World Series Championship of 1969 brought baseball back into the spotlight in the nation's media center for the first time since the collapse of the Yankees five years earlier.

3. The new relationship with NBC and the nationalization of the game of the week was producing decent ratings and profits for all. NBC Sports was using MLB and the recent formation of the NFL's American Football Conference following the NFL-AFL merger as its marquee events. While CBS had the National Football Conference and ABC the Olympics, NBA, and college football, NBC was the only member of the Big 3 networks with both of the top-rated sports properties in the nation.

4. New playing fields with many more seats, lots of parking and access to freeways, and such "new" amenities as luxury boxes and dozens of concessions stands and bathrooms were either open or under construction in many MLB cities.

5. MLB had expanded again to twenty-four teams by placing teams in a previously abandoned market (Kansas City), two fast-growing Western cities (San Diego, Seattle), and, for the first time ever, outside the U.S. (Montreal). Even the replacement of the poorly financed Seattle Pilots franchise after one season by Milwaukee was not a negative for MLB. The return to the Brew City redressed the wrong created by the movement of the Braves from Milwaukee to Atlanta in 1966.

By the end of the decade, however, conditions in MLB were far less soothing. Player work stoppages had now become an MLBPA tactic, as had lockouts by the owners, trends that would become far worse in the 1980s and 1990s. Professional football was now consistently cited in polls as the most popular American sport, making baseball's status as the "national pastime" more of an anachronism than a reality. The relative failure of baseball's *Monday Night Baseball* compared to the overwhelming success of *Monday Night Football* marked the diverging fortunes of the two sports. Baseball left the nation's capital for the second time, this time without a replacement team, thus ceding a top-ten television market to the NFL, and later the NBA and NHL. The move did nothing to improve MLB's status with federal lawmakers.

Moreover, attendance stagnated in many cities, prompting a major change in the rules in one league. The American League's "Designated Hitter" rule was despised by purists and made the sport seem even more dysfunctional because the National League shunned it. The unilateral expansion of the AL to Seattle and Toronto in 1977 was poorly received. Now the two leagues had both different rules and a different number of teams. The increasing popularity of the NFL, which absorbed the AFL in 1970, and the rapidly growing NBA and NHL, seemed to herald a new age in professional sports.

The new stadiums (no longer the "fields" or "parks" of the past) did boost attendance in most markets, but that boost was short lived. By the end of the decade, complaints about the new parks were ubiquitous. Critics decried the artificial turf, the symmetrical dimensions, the distance from fan to field, and the "cookie-cutter" sameness of Atlanta-Fulton County, Busch Memorial, Riverfront, Three Rivers, and Veteran's stadiums. The 1960s' civic idea of publicly subsidized multipurpose stadiums to house both MLB and NFL teams backfired for baseball within a little over a decade. The new facilities inherently favored the rectangular nature of a football field. In their baseball configurations, the stadiums increased the distance from fans to the field. They also had so many seats that baseball attendance appeared worse than it actually was. Within ten years the new stadium became an albatross for baseball.

These problems are crucial to understanding why and how baseball and television had to adapt their relationship to changing circumstances. More specifically, they forced MLB to realize that it was no longer as important to the medium as it once had been. From this point on, we see owners far less likely to criticize the medium. Their previous "anti-TV" bias was replaced by a recognition that television revenue was indispensable to the survival of the game.

The Peak of the Big 3

The broadcast television industry on both the national and local levels reached a peak of influence in the 1970s that was never to be duplicated. At the beginning of the decade, over 95 percent of U.S. households had at least one television receiver.[35] A majority of homes also had color television sets and an ever increasing number of homes had more than one television. Over 90 percent of viewing in an average evening was of programming broadcast by the Big 3 networks and delivered by their affiliated or owned and operated stations.[36]

At the beginning of the decade, only a relatively small percentage of households had reasonable alternatives to the Big 3 and their stations. Independent stations, mainly broadcast via hard-to-receive UHF frequencies, were available only in a few of the nation's largest markets and mainly programmed motion pictures and off-network repeats. The newly established Public Broadcasting Service (PBS) was poorly funded, politically targeted, and relegated to a small fringe audience.[37]

Cable television was available only to a small percentage of mainly rural U.S. households. Not until 1972, after promulgation of new Federal Communications Commission rules, would cable gradually start its competition with broadcast television (see chapter 8). The FCC attempted to rein in the power of the broadcast networks in the early 1970s. In 1971, the Commission's Prime Time Access (PTAR) and Financial Interest and Syndication (Fin/Syn) rules went into effect. PTAR limited the networks to offering no more than three hours of programming per evening (except on Sundays), and Fin/Syn forced the networks to get out of the program syndication business. The result was more syndicated game shows at 7:30 Eastern Time, but the rules had minimal impact on rising network profits and power.[38]

ABC Reaches Parity

Federal rules, however, were largely responsible for one of the key television events of the 1970s—the ascendance of ABC to parity with CBS and NBC. Since the beginning of commercial television, ABC had been the third of the three networks and, most of the time, a very weak third. ABC was the 1940s creation of FCC and federal court decisions that forced NBC to divest one of its two networks. With no powerful core of radio industry money to fund its early operations, an asset enjoyed by its rivals, ABC struggled for years to gain the affiliate stations around the country that would give it parity. The FCC's decision to force television receiver manufacturers to integrate UHF tuners in 1964 was of considerable help to ABC in getting its signal across the nation.[39] Similarly, the PTAR and Fin/Syn rules were a boon to ABC because the network could now concentrate on fewer prime-time hours of programming per week. Fox later used this strategy, as did the other new broadcast networks of the 1990s. Losing syndicated operations hurt ABC far less than it stung its larger, older peers, CBS and NBC.

ABC also benefited from a basic change in the way network television ratings were obtained. Advertisers were growing weary of the rural "bias" of national ratings by the end of the 1960s. Local ratings in large cities were showing striking differences in what urbanites watched versus what mainly rural audiences viewed. Much of this difference was related to the more desirable younger age of the urban audiences. In 1970, A.C. Neilsen, then as now the near monopoly provider of television ratings information, changed its sample to better reflect the advertisers' demands for more information on urban viewers. From 1970 to 1972 CBS, usually the number-one network because of its rural and older-skewing programs, was forced to replace such long-running hits as The Beverly Hillbillies, Green Acres, and The Red Skelton Show with more "relevant" programs, including Storefront Lawyers, Headmaster, and The Interns. NBC, although not as rural-skewing as CBS, followed suit with programs such as Name of the Game and NBC Mystery Movie.[40] The transition was not nearly so traumatic for ABC since it had better ratings in urban areas and had always been more successful in creating programs with youth appeal. By the mid-1970s, ABC had parlayed the new demographic touchstone of the Neilsen ratings to first place in the ratings behind such hits as Happy Days, Starsky and Hutch, and, most surprisingly, ABC's NFL Monday Night Football.

ABC's long run as the weakest network among the Big 3 had encouraged it to take chances that CBS and NBC would not. A more innovative corporate culture of risk taking is of course one of the leading characteristics of the smallest entity in an oligopoly.[41] ABC was the first network to make peace with the motion picture studios in the mid-1950s. Its studio collaborations provided the network with many of its first successful series, including Cheyenne, Disneyland, and Maverick. A few years later, ABC was able to take advantage of its structural urban and youth bias with such hits as Naked City, Hawaiian Eye, and 77 Sunset Strip.

ABC also was willing to take chances outside of prime time, many re-lated to sports programming. As detailed in chapter 5, ABC was an early provider of an MLB "game of the week" and broadcaster of the fledgling American Football League. Even after losing such marquee program-ming to its larger rivals, ABC continued to pioneer in sports by allowing the legendary Roone Arledge to introduce and integrate new production techniques such as "instant replays, "slow mo," and the placement of microphones on the sidelines. ABC Sports also built its reputation on anthology programs (*Wide World of Sports*, *The American Sportsman*) that gained strong ratings and sold plenty of advertising by featuring many offbeat, international, and outdoor recreational sports that were ignored by the other networks.[42]

ABC also outbid its rivals for the Olympic Games, making these qua-drennial events a centerpiece of ABC Sports. The Olympics provided the younger network with a chance to demonstrate its technical proficiency along with the gifts of such legendary broadcasters as Jim McKay and Howard Cosell. The ability of the Olympics to gain large audiences over an extended period and to provide a promotional platform for other net-work programming was first discovered and exploited by ABC.[43] This tradition continues today at NBC, which under Arledge acolyte Dick Eb-ersol, has made the Olympics the main ingredient of NBC Sports.

The Significance of Monday Night Football

The willingness to take risks and a paucity of hit programs make it easier to understand why ABC took a chance on prime-time NFL games in 1970. Neither CBS nor NBC were willing to displace successful programming for sports. After all, only boxing had ever proved to be a ratings winner in prime time, and that had been years earlier.

As for the NFL, the ever-canny commissioner Pete Rozelle saw a weekly prime-time game as both a way to create a new revenue stream for the owners and a way of selling the league to a much larger prime-time audience.[44] The story of *Monday Night Football* has been recounted in several sources, including a made-for-TV movie.[45] The program was an immediate success and remained a top-ten rated program for many years to come. ABC pulled out all the stops to ensure its success. The network utilized almost double the number of cameras as in Sunday NFL games, integrated celebrity visits to the broadcast booth, and instituted the first successful three-person announcer team in broadcast history. For football purists, *Monday Night Football* was an insult to the sanctity of the game with its eccentric, colorful, and controversial announcers, particularly Cosell and Don Meredith in the early years, and its unapologetically "show biz" production values. However, the purists were far outnumbered by the millions of viewers, many casual football fans, who tuned into the weekly telecast *regardless* of who was playing in any given week. For the first time ever, the telecast, rather than the teams, was the attraction. The production and programming skills that Arledge had honed with the Olympics and *Wide World of Sports* were now on weekly prime-time display to tens of millions of Americans. National sports coverage was forever changed; sports like MLB looked hopelessly "ancient" by comparison.[46]

Of course, football has certain structural features that make it a near perfect match for the type of television coverage ABC lavished on it. The rectangular playing field is technically easy to cover. The limited number of games makes every contest seem important. Football is played in the fall and early winter, when worsening weather in much of the U.S. increases television-viewing levels. These structural realities do not make the accomplishments of Rozelle or Arledge less significant. They were after all, the first to fully recognize these conditions and exploit them. However, the unique nature of football made it more likely that they would succeed in doing so, a lesson Arledge soon learned as he attempted to do for MLB what he had for the NFL (see chapters 6 and 7).

Labor and Management Conflicts

In the early 1970s, the NFL was riding a crest of popularity from the stunning success of *Monday Night Football*, the continuing popularity of its Sunday afternoon televised games, the government-approved merger of the AFL into the NFL, and such charismatic players such as "Broadway Joe" Namath and O. J. "Juice" Simpson. MLB began to languish in attendance and public attention.

With most of the new, expansive multipurpose stadiums located in

NL cities, the AL was suffering more from a general downturn in attendance. In 1972, for example, the NL drew over a third more fans than the "junior circuit."[47] With average runs per game in the AL games down to less than 3.5, concern was growing that pitching had become too dominant.[48] However, with the NL outscoring and outdrawing the AL, the "senior circuit" saw no reason to change the rules. The result was the American League's adoption of the Designated Hitter (DH) on an "experimental" basis for 1973.[49] Though the DH has now been used by the AL for thirty-five years and is virtually universal in amateur baseball, the fact that only half of MLB adopted the rule in 1973 showed baseball's indecisiveness compared to other sports. By 1974, only 19 percent of respondents in a Harris poll chose baseball as their favorite sport, a stunning decrease from the nearly 50 percent of fans who saw the sport as their favorite just ten years earlier.[50]

Clearly, America's love affair with baseball was "on the rocks," as reflected in public opinion polls, attendance, and declining national television ratings on NBC. Attempts to reverse the game's decline—introducing the DH rule and placing celebrities in the NBC booth for Monday night games—were ridiculed by many observers. To compound the down cycle, the long-simmering dispute between baseball players and owners erupted, fracturing baseball's historical foundations and forever changing the nature of the game.

Miller and the MLBPA Challenge the Owners

Professional baseball players' careers were under the complete control of team owners from the nineteenth century until the 1970s, a period that has been well documented.[51] Its end began when the new Major League Baseball Players Association hired veteran labor union leader Marvin Miller as its executive director in 1966. Early in his tenure, Miller and the MLBPA succeeded in getting a raise in the minimum salary and gaining recognition from the owners with a collective bargaining agreement.[52]

The 1970s witnessed a string of major MLBPA successes that rocked the structural underpinnings of MLB. A failure by the owners and the MLBPA to agree on owners' pension contributions ignited the first union-oriented players strike in U.S. sports history right before the beginning of the 1972 season.[53] Although the dispute was settled in less than two weeks, each team lost between six and eight games. It was now clear that the MLBPA, unlike its weak and ineffective predecessors, was willing to use the tool of a strike to force the owners to negotiate. The players' union could only be ignored at the owners' peril.

MLB was the first professional sports league to endure a strike, and the reaction of many fans and most media members was decidedly negative. The general consensus was that players should be thankful to make a decent living playing a game that many fans would be happy to play for free. The press reminded players that it was a privilege to play the game, and their selfish interest should not interfere with the conduct of baseball.[54] The media trumpeted the "selfless benevolence" of Tom Yawkey, Phil Wrigley, and John Fetzer, among other team owners. Dick Young and his newspaper cronies around the nation perpetuated the myth that owners were "sportsmen" who were more about public benefit than profits.[55]

The owners' most important weapon was the "reserve clause," a part of the standard players' contract that enabled teams to maintain rights to a player for one year after his contract expired. The owners' long-standing position was that the clause could be renewed each subsequent year for as long as the owner wished. Naturally, Miller and the MLBPA felt otherwise. Curt Flood provoked the first test case by attempting to play out his reserve-clause year after being traded from St. Louis to Philadelphia in 1970. Flood said that he did not want to be traded without his consent.[56] Although Commissioner Kuhn ordered Flood to play, and he did return to play for the Washington Senators, his case went all the way to the U.S. Supreme Court. In the 1972 case of *Flood v. Kuhn*, the Court ruled against Flood and the MLBPA by upholding MLB's 1922 exemption from antitrust laws.[57] However, the Court was critical of the exemption and suggested that Congress could overturn it. Most importantly, the Court did *not* uphold the legality of the reserve clause, only MLB's antitrust exemption.

The owners' joy over *Flood v. Kuhn* was short lived. In 1973, after a spring-training lockout failed, the owners agreed to binding salary arbitration for veteran players.[58] Agreeing to salary arbitration turned out to be a huge problem for the owners. With impartial arbitrators compelled to choose either the salary figure submitted by the team or the player (i.e., no splitting the difference) and owners still "lowballing" players because they had always been able to in the past, arbitrators' decisions usually went the players' way. Arbitration opened the door to substantial increases in player compensation.

Free Agency Arrives

Free agency finally arrived for MLB players between the 1975 and 1976 seasons. Andy Messersmith of Los Angeles and Dave McNally of Montreal played the entire 1975 season without signing a contract, taking the position that after that season they were free to sign with any team they chose. This argument was affirmed by arbitrator Peter Seitz in December 1975.[59] Although Kuhn and the owners screamed that such a decision would lead to the economic demise of the game, owners' appeals to the courts failed to get Seitz's decision overturned. After another brief lockout on the part of the owners, a contract was negotiated that provided free agency to players after six years of service.[60]

Although there were many MLB-MLBPA disputes to come, including the truncated and split season of 1981 and the never-completed 1994 season, the Seitz decision was the event that completely altered the game. Concerns about the financial inequalities of teams became particularly resonant in the free agent era. After all, what was to keep a rich team from signing all the best talent?

Not surprisingly, the potential positive benefits of free agency were difficult for the owners to foresee during baseball's cataclysmic 1970s. Many owners and their press sycophants preferred to players as "greedy" and predicted their own financial ruin. Though some owners, including Charlie Finley, Calvin Griffith, and Bill Veeck, did leave the game because of its changing economics, most owners profited from the rising values of their franchises.

The Owners Slowly Face a New Reality

The worst fears of the owners and much of the press about free agency never came to pass. Free agency increased rather than decreased competitive balance in the game. It was now less likely that one team would dominate the sport as the Yankees had from the 1920s until the 1960s. Any team might turn its fortunes around by judiciously signing free agents, which increases interest and attendance in most Major League cities.

Better competitive balance helped baseball maximize its television revenues, which were once again seen as baseball's savior. Baseball's television partner provided new revenues to pay the owners' growing payrolls. National television rights fees, which had been undervalued for years because of MLB's timid approach to the medium, were now leveraged to maximize revenues. For example, the World Series, which had no night games until 1971, became an all-prime-time event. MLB continued to push for more prime-time regular-season games, although with less success.

For the first time, the word *partner* accurately characterized baseball's relationship with television; its application was more than rhetorical. MLB began to cross-promote consistently with the television industry. It was also quick to jump into the emerging cable industry by signing a deal with cable's USA Network (see chapter 8). At the team level, a few teams exported their games nationally through their parent company's superstations.

Fortunately for MLB, the free agency era began just before the cable television boom raised the value of all sports properties. Cable provided a fresh injection of revenue for MLB just as the owners had come down with "free agent flu." For many local clubs, cable money provided revenues that would have been unimaginable in the broadcast era.

There was a downside to the new partnership with television, however. Some teams continued to limit telecasts because they believed it negatively affected attendance. The new revenues from cable were unequally distributed, widening the gap between rich and poor franchises. Congress became increasingly concerned over the migration of sports from "free" (advertiser-supported) to pay (cable) television (see chapter 11). Despite all these problems, there was no going back. Television revenue was now essential to the economic health of MLB. The anti-TV era was finally ending.

Television did not solve all of baseball's problems. Many of the violent upheavals of the 1970s continue to resonate, albeit with much less force after baseball implemented new media and revenue-sharing strategies in the mid-1990s and began to reap the benefits of the Internet in the early 2000s (this book's epilogue discusses these recent events in detail).

However, the owners still had a public relations problem. For over twenty-five years, most owners, MLB executives, and commissioners repeatedly complained about the "terrible" status of the game. MLB's leaders told the public that small-market teams could not compete, players were gluttonous and ungrateful, and the glorious national pastime was tarnished, perhaps beyond repair. Such negative discourse alienates existing fans and drives new ones away. It also discourages television partners. After all, why should the television industry want to devote time and money to telecast a product that its owners are always criticizing?

Despite the self-defeating rhetoric by the games' stewards, baseball rebounded from the cataclysm of the 1970s with the help of television's deep pockets. In the Reagan era, America wanted the best of its past, and baseball was bound up with the country's heritage. Although no longer the only national pastime, baseball prospered in the 1980s. For the owners, television finally seemed less a threat and more a salvation.

Television and the "Death"
of the Golden Age Minors

For its many critics, television is a large, brightly colored target. In the past fifty years the medium has been accused of many social maladies. Critics and many researchers say television reduces attention span and political participation while it increases crime, delinquency, and obesity. Moreover, they say, it fosters perceptions of a mean and scary world.[1] Television is a frequent target because of its ubiquity and extensive use; over 98 percent of U.S homes have a TV, and on average it is on for about eight hours a day.[2]

The rising behemoth of television was also seen by many as an economic change agent. The various mass media that predated television were all radically transformed by it, for example. From the late 1940s to the mid-1960s, the motion picture industry first fought and later reached an accommodation with television to become the major supplier of episodic television programming. As a result, motion picture distribution and exhibition moved from a mass medium to a specialized or niche business. Radio went through a similar adjustment period as it became an industry that appealed to an aggregation of specialized audiences rather than to the mass audience lost to television. Radio's prime time shifted from the evening hours to the morning and late-afternoon "drive time." Print media made the largest adjustment as the diffusion of television essentially destroyed the market for mass-appeal magazines (e.g., *Saturday Evening Post*, *Look*, and *Life*) and evening urban newspapers. In most markets, competition between daily newspapers became a thing of the past.

In addition to its effects on existing mass media, television was also commonly criticized for its impact on live entertainment such as theater (both vaudeville and "legitimate"), music (both "high-" and "low-"

brow), the corner pub, and, of interest here, the ballpark. The old argument against radio broadcasts of baseball games (i.e., that people would stay home to listen rather than go to the game) was revised in a much more intense fashion with the rise of television.

A prime example of the "television was bad for baseball" school of criticism is the frequent accusation that television killed the golden age of the minor leagues. For Happy Chandler, MLB's commissioner at the dawn of televised baseball, TV's negative impact on the minors was fact: "Television did kill the Minor Leagues, especially when they telecast the games into the Minor League territory while the teams were playing."[3] In this chapter, we turn our attention to the struggles of Minor League Baseball from the late 1940s through the early 1960s and the implementation of the Major League Baseball–Minor League Baseball (MLB-MiLB) subsidy plan, which still remains in effect.

Specifically, we will question the traditional argument that the oversaturation of MLB on television starting in the 1950s led to the sharp decline in minor league teams and attendance during that decade. We argue that although growth of television had some negative effect, most of the contraction in the minor leagues was due to other forces. We conclude the chapter with some observations on how Minor League Baseball is thriving in many smaller cities despite ever increasing competition for leisure time and the entertainment dollar.

The Postwar National Association

The immediate post–World War II years were boom times for most segments of the U.S. economy. Although inflation was high, pent-up consumer demand and plenty of industrial capacity fed a growing economy. Leisure-time industries, including baseball and other sports, were one of the many beneficiaries of the boom. Major League Baseball attendance increased, as did that of many of the teams of the National Association (NA, the previous and longstanding name of MiLB). However, unlike MLB, which for a variety of reasons stayed wedded to a sixteen-team, ten-market, eastern and midwest operational scheme until 1953, the Minors expanded to meet the perceived demand. Capturing the exuberance of the era, Lloyd Johnson and Miles Wolff, in their valuable *Encyclopedia of Minor League Baseball*, labeled this 1946–51 period the "Golden Age" of the Minors.[4]

In 1949, minor league attendance reached its highest point ever with over 39.8 million admissions spread among 448 teams in fifty-nine leagues. Only in the past few years has MiLB attendance surpassed that total, albeit with many fewer teams and leagues.[5] The postwar growth in attendance was explosive, rising from approximately 10 million admissions in 1945 to almost 40 million by 1949, as the number of leagues virtually quintupled in that time.[6] The fall was almost as swift as the rise, and the most precipitous drop occurred before television was widely diffused. In 1950 attendance fell by over 5 million, followed in 1951 by a drop of almost 8 million more. This striking 33 percent decline in minor league attendance took place when only 23.5 percent of U.S. households had a television.[7] However, as the diffusion of television accelerated, the Minors continued to contract steadily. By the end of the decade, the twenty-one remaining leagues were dependent on the "Player Development and Promotion" fund of MLB. The failure of this strategy to stabilize the National Association led to the Player Development Plan of 1963. This plan provided an MLB subsidy to guarantee the survival of at least one hundred teams in Classes AAA, AA, A, and Rookie Leagues.[8] In little over ten years, Minor League Baseball had virtually "crashed and burned," while television had become ubiquitous.

Johnson and Wolff recount how minor league operators "loudly protested that the unrestricted telecasting and broadcasting of major league games into minor league markets were killing their game."[9] They briefly discuss other factors that led to the downfall of the Minors' golden age, such as the rise of football and other more "glamorous" television sports, suburbanization, poorly maintained ballparks, air conditioning, and overexpansion of the Minors. Though there is no question that television made other sports more popular, affecting both Minor and Major League Baseball, the social and economic factors deserve far more attention.

Television Love and Hate

Not surprisingly, as television was becoming established it was considered a real benefit to both Minor and Major League Baseball. At the end of the 1948 season, for example, the owners of the AAA Milwaukee Brewers claimed that broadcasting all seventy-seven home games helped "create many new fans, especially women" and generated "just enough interest" to get fans to the ballpark.[10] Major League teams, with a couple of striking exceptions, were quick to embrace the new medium, as were baseball fans. By May 1948, the highest-rated telecast in the New York market was Yankees baseball.[11] Even in the midst of such good times, the baseball press, as exemplified by the *Sporting News*, was already launching an anti-TV screed in the peak year of 1949 (see chapter 9 for a more detailed account of this love/hate relationship).

Once both major and minor league attendance started to decline in 1950, the knives were sharpened in the television attack. By 1952, *U.S. News & World Report* reported that "television is blamed by most minor-league clubs for their reversal of prosperity."[12] By 1954, television was called a "20th Century Cyclops . . . wreaking havoc with us" and guilty of "a clear case of murder."[13] By 1955, the Milwaukee Braves were looking to relocate its AAA Toledo farm club to "a city without expressway links to a major league city, and one that is beyond the range of major-league telecasts."[14]

There is one serious problem with all the antitelevision hysteria of the late 1940s and early 1950s: minimal baseball was on television outside Major League markets during the period of most rapid decline. The beginning of the Minors' decline happened in the middle of the Federal Communications Commission's freeze on new television station applications. For a four-year period, from 1948 to 1952, the FCC issued no new television licenses as it attempted to settle a series of technical issues regarding the allocation of frequencies around the country. By the end of the freeze, only 108 stations were on the air. Most of these were restricted to the largest markets, which varied widely in allocations (e.g., New York and Los Angeles had seven licensees each, and Pittsburgh only one).[15]

Although the end of the freeze led to some expansion of television, the number of stations and the variety of programming in most markets was still very limited. Except for the few markets with non-network-affiliated stations, there was little opportunity for baseball outside of weekend afternoon games.

The FCC's 1952 decision to allow a mixture of VHF (channels 2–13) and UHF stations (originally, channels 14–83) was a failure. UHF stations could not compete because they faced high operational costs and weak signals. They also had small audiences because most televisions did not have the optional tuner needed to receive UHF signals. This situation was not addressed until the 1960s, and it was not "fixed" until the diffusion of cable television made the VHF/UHF distinction irrelevant.

The result of the FCC's failed UHF strategy was a television system dominated by two networks (NBC and CBS) that used both their owned and operated stations and their affiliates, broadcasting on VHF frequencies in the largest markets, to build their audience. The lack of a third VHF signal in most markets until the 1960s and 1970s limited ABC's success and led to the demise of the DuMont network in 1955. Only the nation's largest markets (New York, Chicago, and Los Angeles) had viable nonnetwork or independent VHF stations that could program baseball in prime time.

Even when stations and programming time was available, several Major League franchises restricted or eliminated televised games during the 1950s. In particular, four relocated franchises (the Dodgers, Braves, Giants, and Athletics) allowed virtually no telecasts of home games because they believed overexposure on television had been a major factor in their declining attendance prior to their moves to new cities. In addition, both the Dodgers and the Giants hoped to profit from the demand for television games by selling their video product on pay television (see chapter 3). Thus, although Major League Baseball remained a source of local television programming throughout the 1950s, the number of games telecast declined over the course of the decade.

National network coverage came of age during the decade, but not very quickly. In the 1950s, none of the national networks telecast Major League Baseball in prime time. Even Saturday daytime MLB games did not come to national television until 1953. The original *Game of the Week* telecast originated on the then weak ABC network, which was restricted mainly to major markets and could not be received in much of rural America. It was not until 1955, when the *Game of the Week* shifted to CBS, one of the then "Big Two" networks, that network telecasts were widely viewed in the small and medium markets that were the staple of the minor leagues. By this time, Minor League Baseball was down to thirty-three leagues, and the drop in attendance was continuing.

This is not to say that some minor league franchises were not severely harmed by televised Major League games. Perhaps the best examples are in the New York City metropolitan area. The Jersey City Giants of the AAA International League club saw attendance plunge from 1947's peak of 338,000 (a first-place team) to 174,000 in 1949, when the NA as a whole had its best-ever season. Attendance then plunged to 63,000 in 1950 before the franchise was relocated to Ottawa. League rival Newark had lost its franchise a year earlier after attracting only 88,000 in attendance in 1949.

Clearly the policy of all three New York City Major League teams to telecast all or almost all their home games severely hurt the New Jersey minor league teams. However, most failing teams in the 1950s were not located within the signal range of a Major League city, most cities did not have more than one team, and most teams did not broadcast all home games. The negative impact of televised baseball on these New Jersey teams was an anomaly that was given more attention than it deserved because it occurred in the nation's media center. The fate of these teams became a preferred piece of anecdotal evidence in the case against television.

"War Babies" and the Market Bubble

At the beginning of the 1955 season, Frank "Trader" Lane claimed in *Newsweek* that Minor League Baseball was in "sounder shape" than at any time since the end of World War II. He argued that minor league teams had failed in many towns because they "had no business having [teams] in the first place."[16] They were "war babies." Although the Trader's claim that the Minors were on solid ground was wrong and their decline continued, he was correct about the oversupply of minor league teams in the late 1940s. In 1947, George Trautman, who became head of the National Association, pushed for the inclusion of little more than semipro or even company teams in fully professional leagues. He seemed to be asking, in the words of Johnson and Wolff, "Who was to say that towns of two thousand could not support professional baseball?"[17]

Trautman's push for continuous expansion had some logic in that the end of the war signaled the first period of both peace and relative prosperity since the beginning of the Great Depression in 1929. Baseball, at the time the undisputed national game, was a normalizing activity after the double trauma of depression and war. The number of potential players also greatly expanded after the war ended. Thus, in addition to the normal flow of players reaching their late teens, there was an influx of war-returning players in their early twenties who were anxious to get their shot at making a living playing the national pastime.

This oversupply of potential players combined with plentiful potential capital from wartime savings and a booming economy obviously contributed to the escalation of the minor leagues. For this reason, the shrinking of the leagues in the 1950s can be viewed as the second part of a classic boom/bust cycle.

Certain societal forces set in motion a rapid growth in a particular industry. Initial successes lead to more expansion, until the market is oversaturated with product. The newest participants in the weakest markets are likely to fail first. Even if society remains relatively stable, some financial failures result, leading to a contraction of the overexpanded industry. The failure is likely to be blamed by the industry on external forces (such as television) rather than on the franchise owners' poor judgment. In Minor League Baseball's case, the economic recessions of the middle and later Eisenhower years also caused even more problems for an industry already suffering from contraction.

However, the contraction of the market for Minor League Baseball was too rapid and spectacular to attribute solely to the "inexorable" workings of the market. A more reasonable parallel for Minor League Baseball in the 1940s and 1950s is the "dot-com" boom/bust of the late 1990s and early 2000s. In retrospect, wagering millions that billions might be made selling pet supplies or gift certificates on the Internet is about as farfetched as believing that Newnan, Georgia, or Stroudsburg, Pennsylvania, could support Minor League Baseball without a subsidy.

Another way of providing a context for the overexpansion of the Minors in the late 1940s is to look at the attendance and population figures of the various teams and leagues. Even in the peak minor league attendance year of 1949, the best average attendance (Montreal's 6,153 per game) would not even make the top five of 2006 (led by Sacramento's 10,114).[18] Of the 176 organized minor league teams in operation in 2006, only a handful drew less than a 1,000 per game average, with the lowest being High-A Dunedin, Florida's 411.

A look at the 1949 figures shows dozens of teams below 1,000 in average attendance. There were even entire leagues in which not one team averaged a thousand customers per game (e.g., Class B Colonial, Class C East Texas, and many Class D leagues, including Alabama State, Blue Ridge, Eastern Shore, Far West, Georgia State, Kansas-Oklahoma-Missouri, and Sooner State). Even the abysmal Dunedin attendance of 2006 was ahead of the 1949 attendance of such unlamented teams as the Donna-Robstown Cardinals (286 per game), Nazareth Barons (256), and Newport Canners (226). Even adjusting for today's much greater population would not make the case stronger for the many weak teams and leagues. Attendance would still be too low to sustain a team without subsidy, and the average person today has many more entertainment and sports diversions available than was the case fifty-four years ago.

There are some small cities in organized baseball today (the smallest being Princeton, West Virginia, with a population of 6,347), but most minor league cities are in small- to medium-size metro areas. While virtually every metropolitan area had one or more teams in 1949, one is struck by how many small towns had teams then, from Ada, Oklahoma, to Mayfield, Kentucky, to Wellsville, Pennsylvania.

Obviously such a system of small towns and poor attendance was unsustainable. Combine this with the problem of mixing independent operators and MLB-owned or -affiliated teams in the same league. As the 1950s progressed, it became clear that in most leagues the affiliated teams had an advantage over the independents both financially and in performance. By the time of the 1963 subsidy agreement, independent minor leagues and teams virtually disappeared for almost thirty years.

A Changing Nation

As the Milwaukee Braves realized by the mid-1950s when they wanted to move the AAA Toledo Mud Hens to "a city without expressway links," many other changes were underway in American life during the postwar era. The growth of cities into metro areas of core cities and suburbs was one of them. People by the millions became suburbanites. Hundreds of thousands of miles of new highways, culminating in the beginning of the Interstate Highway System in the mid-1950s, allowed the new suburbanites to commute to their jobs in the city. However, the distance from city to home created a strong barrier to going to or staying in town to seek entertainment, including a ball game.

Almost all baseball parks were located in inner-city areas that were difficult to reach. Increasingly, people who looked, spoke, and acted differently than white suburbanites populated cities, reinforcing cultural stereotypes and fears. Going to watch the "national pastime" presented both physical and psychological obstacles. Movie theaters, located in the same inner-city areas, also experienced a sharp decline, as box-office receipts declined over 40 percent from 1946 to 1962 despite higher ticket prices.[19] Only a move to suburban theaters would eventually reverse the decline of the motion picture industry, although the percentage of Americans who attend the movies has never reached the level of the mid-1940s.

Baseball eventually accommodated the suburbanite by moving out of the inner city or by providing adequate parking and government-subsidized expressways, thus providing worried fans with a fast exit back to the "safe" suburbs. For example, former minor league cities such as Milwaukee and Baltimore both occupied new parks that, while within city limits, were hardly "inner city." In the early 1970s, Cincinnati, Pittsburgh, Philadelphia, and St. Louis would all build new stadiums with freeway access and substantial parking. However, most minor league owners did not have the resources or the inclination to build new parks or upgrade old ones. In the 1950s, minor league cities did little or nothing to assist teams, as they do today. With a booming population and economy, minor league sports were not needed to spur or maintain economic growth. In that era, if professional baseball received public money it was to attract a Major League team, not to perpetuate the city's "minor league" image.

Although the televising of Major League games had minimal impact on the declining fortunes of Minor League Baseball, at least until the second half of the 1950s, it would be a mistake to say that the medium had no effect. Television profoundly changed entertainment in America by moving the locus of entertainment from outside to inside the home. The diffusion of television, combined with suburbanization and the baby boom, led to an extended period of "nesting" and a revolution in home entertainment. When suburbanites returned home from work in the city, they had little interest in returning for an evening game. Even on the weekends, children's activities, including Little League baseball, were much more likely to take up a parent's time and money than a visit to the ballpark. Minor League Baseball, as an out-of-home, evening and weekend activity, was one of many victims of television's vigorous growth in the 1950s. But since there was no hope of containing the general television boom, minor league owners and the press focused their attacks on the televising of Major League Baseball, something they had hopes of controlling. They largely ignored the medium of television—the electronic elephant in the room.

Another important demographic shift was the accelerating movement away from the rural towns and small cities that had long served as market centers for a primarily agricultural economy. Prosperous times in the overall economy typically disguise a poor rural economy. Indeed, for most of us, it is difficult to recall what a prosperous farm-based economy is. Despite our fondness, often expressed in popular culture, for an idyllic rural past, Americans have been leaving the land for decades. This trend accelerated in the 1950s because of industrial agriculture, better highways, and the clearing of farmland for new suburbs. The small market cities and towns that once had their own identities, shaped in part by their own minor league teams, were either becoming depopulated or being absorbed into larger metropolitan areas.

Radio: Another Electronic "Elephant in the Room"

The dysfunctional relationship between baseball and television has antecedents in the problematic baseball-radio relationship. During late 1940s and early 1950s, MLB more or less made peace with the medium, a peace that would be detrimental to the Minors.

Because of the historical bias toward newer media such as television, we often overlook significant changes that affect an established medium. After the Second World War the number of radio stations exploded. In 1946, there were approximately 1,000 commercial stations (948 AM and 46 FM) in the United States. By 1949, there were over 2,600 stations (1,912 AM and 700 FM), a 160 percent increase in only three years.[20]

While the number of stations grew, the number of major national networks supplying programming remained the same (NBC, CBS, ABC, and Mutual). Since these networks already had affiliates in most markets, most new stations had to find nonnetwork sources of programming. During the season, Major League Baseball became an integral part of the supply needed to meet this vast new programming demand. The majority of these new stations were in smaller markets that previously had limited local radio programming. These were the same Class C and D minor league communities that saw the greatest increase in teams after the Second World War.

The increasingly perilous state of the Minors led to federal and legislative action in the late 1940s and early 1950s. As we discuss in detail in chapter 11, the Antitrust Division of the U.S. Justice Department forced, under threat of a lawsuit, the alteration of Major League Rule 1(d), which prohibited Major League broadcasts by either radio or television in markets outside a team's home territory without consent of the club serving that market. MLB altered the rule to restrict out-of-market games only "during the time that such other club is playing a home game."[21] The altered rule was repealed in 1951.

The increasingly precarious state of the Minors was the major impetus for 1953's U.S. Senate hearings aimed at restoring Rule 1(d). Committee chair Ed Johnson (D-CO), himself a minor league official, argued that the restoration of the rule would actually lead to "more telecasting and broadcasting of better baseball than if we continue the present ruinous policy of destroying the minor leagues by the continual invasion of minor-league territory by the majors through radio and TV."[22] His sentiments were echoed by Trautman and several other officials and supporters of the NA. Neither seemed to realize, or more likely they chose to ignore, that there was little possibility that television would ever telecast minor league games or even have stations in the smaller minor league cities.

The legislation put MLB in a precarious situation. In typical fashion, Commissioner Ford Frick failed to take a consistent position on televised baseball. He argued that "unlimited broadcasting and televising of major league baseball in minor league territories is destructive to the minor leagues and is breaking down the very first element that leads to the elimination of baseball." But he also argued that "the idea [of the 1(d) revision] was not that baseball in any sense was going to attempt to limit television or the broadcasting of games beyond what we felt was a reasonable necessity . . . we have no objection to television going into towns that want to see baseball where baseball is not being played or *when baseball is being played*" (our emphasis).[23] Although Frick's syntax is confusing, the positive financial impact of radio and TV revenues was clear. Despite MLB's rhetoric about protecting the Minors as essential to its health, its support for an overly restrictive broadcast policy would have been a poor business decision.

A second event that had a profound impact on the minor leagues was the launching of Liberty Broadcasting System's (LBS) "Game of the Day" broadcasts. In 1947, Gordon McLendon founded LBS. McLendon, a true radio innovator, was later instrumental in developing the top-forty music format. LBS provided programming for the hundreds of new commercial stations going on the air. Initially, stymied by 1(d), McLendon circumvented the rule by developing a "Game of the Day" using recreations based on wire service reports. Liberty's popular broadcasts reached close to four hundred affiliates before closing down in May 1952, after the MLB clubs jointly refused the network any more rights to any games for any market.[24]

McLendon was a broadcast industry maverick who was vilified in the industry's own trade press. A "Baseball 1951" article in *Sponsor*, for example, blamed Liberty for the decline in Minor League Baseball attendance and stated that "Liberty has the distinction of having opened up major league baseball in minor league territory."[25] In the 1953 hearings, McLendon, who was suing MLB for damages, claimed that (1) there was no evidence that his broadcasts hurt minor league attendance, and (2) even if there were such evidence, it would be irrelevant because restricting broadcasts was a violation of antitrust.[26] MLB's decision to cut Liberty off was not primarily aimed at helping the Minors. MLB would not support a nationalized blanket restriction on broadcasts. Indeed, MLB had authorized a "Game of the Day" on the Mutual Broadcasting System (MBS), the fourth national network. Like LBS's stations, many of MBS's affiliates were in smaller markets, providing even more radio competition for the most financially fragile minor league teams.[27]

Though the Liberty and Mutual network broadcasts received most of the attention, regional radio networks for many Major League teams expanded rapidly in the postwar period. The many new program-hungry stations became the basis for the expanding regional radio networks of MLB games. The Cardinals, Reds, and Cubs were particularly adept at leveraging their networks to carve out large regional fan bases (see chapter 3).

Ultimately, the extension of MLB radio broadcasts, both national and local, hurt the minor leagues, particularly in the first half of the 1950s. In rural areas, radio broadcasts certainly had much more impact than baseball telecasts, which were in their infancy. Although televised Major League Baseball had a big effect in Major League cities and their surrounding areas, it was the vast expansion of radio in the latter half of the 1940s and continuing throughout the 1950s that represented the most important form of media competition to minor league teams created during the postwar professional baseball boom.

A Minors Miracle—A Niche, Not a Pastime

The revival of the Minors over the past twenty-five years, including the revival of independent leagues in the past decade, is one of the most important trends in professional baseball. Attendance in "official" Minor League Baseball (the old NA, which does not include the indies) is nearly forty-two million per year, above the 1949 figure though far fewer minor league teams exist.[28] How could this have happened? The factors that led to the demise of the "Golden Age" Minors have only become more prevalent. So how could Minor League Baseball not only survive but thrive in an environment increasingly cluttered with new leisure-time options?

216

Although this is a subject that deserves much more attention than we can give it here, the following is a brief review of some of the major reasons for the revival:

1. The Minors quit competing with the Majors for attention. Instead, they refashioned their marketing appeal as the "non-" or even "anti-" Majors. Most teams promoted themselves as a "throwback" to the time before the players made millions and the owners billions. Low costs and child-friendly policies and promotions made an evening out at the Minors an outing, like going to the movies or to a restaurant.

2. The new Minors capitalized on the mantra of the past two decades, which claims that spectator sports are an important tool for economic development. The economic development argument led to huge subsidies for the construction of new, clean, safe ballparks in many municipalities. Many urban governments and local companies became, in essence, team partners, providing legitimacy and publicity for the teams.

3. Most of the new minor league teams are in metropolitan areas. The model of the small "farm market" town team has never been revived. In fact, one of the most striking trends in both the official and indie minor leagues is the number of successful minor league teams playing in metropolitan areas that have Major League Baseball franchises. Not surprisingly, the Brooklyn and Staten Island teams have garnered much of the publicity from this trend. However, many other Major League markets—Chicago, Boston, the Bay Area, the Twin Cities, St. Louis, Baltimore, Pittsburgh, Cincinnati, Kansas City—have minor league teams.

Being in the "orbit" of an MLB team is an advantage because there is established interest in and press coverage for baseball. This coverage is not simply limited to print and broadcast accounts of games, as an ever increasing number of minor league teams have been able to obtain regular-game coverage on television, radio, or the Internet. Limited coverage can contribute to a team's demise, as in the case of the teams in Pueblo, Colorado, and other relatively isolated markets.[29] In addition, the population in the suburban areas of large metros is greater than the total population of many smaller markets. As another case of "those that have, get more," the proliferation of new minor league teams in the larger cities at the expense of those in more rural areas is predictable.

Verdict: Not Guilty

There is little doubt about the effects of television's diffusion on the media and entertainment industries. However, when it comes to baseball, the direct effect of televised Major League Baseball on the minor leagues appears to have been limited until at least the middle of the 1950s, after considerable minor league contraction had already occurred. With certain highly publicized exceptions (i.e., New Jersey minor teams in the New York City metro area), the teams that declined most rapidly in the 1950s were those in small markets that had little television penetration and almost no televised baseball. This was the case until the middle of the decade, when the CBS *Game of the Week* was widely viewed. Even then, this national coverage of Major League Baseball initially had an impact on minor league attendance only one day per week.

The major factors in the death of the "Golden Age" of the minor leagues were complex economic and cultural forces that precipitated a "market correction" after the boom period of Minor League Baseball in the last half of the 1940s. Of the mass media, radio is likely to have been the greatest contributor to the death of the Minors. The radio industry vastly increased both the number of stations in rural markets and its coverage of baseball during the period when the minor leagues underwent their greatest contraction. Although many critics have justly viewed television as a negative social force, televised baseball is only one of many accessories to the murder of the golden age Minors.

Labeling today the golden age of Minor League Baseball would not be a misnomer. Attendance has never been higher in the official MiLB. Independent leagues continue to proliferate in many parts of North America. Minor League Baseball has carved out a niche in the leisure time of millions of people. The Minors continue their historical purposes of training players and team officials for the Majors and of developing new baseball fans. That the Minors can do this despite the increasing availability of other entertainment and sports options is a testament to their resilience and resonance in American life.

Baseball, Television, Congress, and the Law

Because of its status as the "national pastime," baseball has frequently provoked the interest of the U.S. Congress. Although baseball is no longer the nation's most popular sport, the game's historical stature continues to make it a flashpoint for congressional inquiry.

In the past fifteen years, Congress repeatedly has threatened action against Major League Baseball. MLB's attempt to move its "Extra Innings" package of out-of-market games exclusively to DirecTV generated considerable congressional concern in 2007.[1] After the media-saturated coverage of the steroids issue in March 2005, Congress introduced legislation designed to "clean up" the game.[2] During the work stoppage of 1994–95, Congress held hearings, and members introduced legislation to remove or modify MLB's antitrust exemption.[3] In the early 1990s, the perceived widening of the gap between the rich and poor teams provoked both the House and the Senate to introduce legislation to force a more equitable sharing of local revenues.[4]

Introducing legislation is one thing; passing it is quite another. Congress approved none of this legislation. Although this inertia might reflect an increasing failure of Congress to act on matters of importance, it is "baseball-centric" to regard such legislation as an especially pressing national need. Of course, not every congressional action addresses pressing national needs or "pork barrel" legislation would never get passed. If the "pork" can be passed, why not pass baseball legislation on steroids, contraction, or revenue sharing?

Baseball As a Valence Issue

Politicians often view baseball controversies as valence issues, that is, issues that allow them to stake out a safe position on a matter that interests the public. Donald Stokes has noted that valence issues "merely involve the linking of parties with some condition that is positively or negatively valued by the electorate."[5]

For example, a politician may "fearlessly" support a constitutional ban on flag burning. Although the legislator may not really regard the issue as serious, she or he knows that almost no one is in favor of flag burning. Thus, the politician stakes out a no-lose position on an issue that excites at least part of the electorate.

In the case of baseball, who could have been in favor of steroid abuse? Of the continuation of the work stoppage? Of the growing revenue gap between teams? Of franchise contraction? The answer, of course, is very few. Even if an opposite view is expressed, the argument tends to be more theoretical and complex. In short, much of the congressional action on baseball and other sports has been "grandstanding," that is, appearing to be on the "side of the angels." It has rarely been about actually doing anything to directly control the sport.

In fairness, not all those who have proposed baseball or sports legislation are grandstanders. Though being on the side of baseball fans undoubtedly is good politics, some members of Congress who have proposed new legislation were seriously concerned about the status of professional baseball. Legislation affecting any business, including MLB, has been difficult to pass in a probusiness era. In addition, Congress knows that MLB's antitrust exemption makes it likely that federal courts would overturn its baseball legislation. Nevertheless, MLB's status as the only professional sports entity in the United States with a judicially granted exemption from the nation's antitrust laws is an important justification for congressional scrutiny. In fact, Congress could be accused of abrogating its responsibility if it did not regularly investigate baseball.

Congress and regulatory bodies often gain compliance with their concerns through the method of the "raised eyebrow." That is, instead of passing new legislation, Congress achieves its goal by merely threatening to do so; the organization under congressional review then takes the action on its own. Organizations do not want their business practices altered by government action, nor do they want to spend enormous sums fighting government action in the courts. In most cases, the rational organization conforms, at least somewhat, to congressional demands. Thus, government action "by raised eyebrow" is often a very effective means of regulation.[6]

Congress has often forced MLB to alter its behavior, threatening regulation if it did not. For example, the Players Association agreed to new drug-testing policies under the threat of congressional action in 2005.[7] More recently, former U.S. senator George Mitchell (D-ME), who is employed by MLB as an investigator on the steroids issue, has called for more congressional action on the issue.[8]

Television As Valence Issue

Congress has legal oversight responsibility for television broadcasting. The Radio Act of 1927 and the Communications Act of 1934 established broadcast stations (at first radio and later television) as a licensed media to be operated in the "public interest" because of the scarcity of electromagnetic spectrum.[9] Congress established the Federal Communications Commission to regulate the broadcast and telecommunications industries. But the FCC is "a creature of the Congress" and subject to its ongoing scrutiny. As a result, Congress has more direct oversight of broadcasting than it does of professional baseball.

Congressional concerns about television have also created many valence issues. For example, since the beginning of the medium, politicians have been able to safely oppose "excessive" sex or violence on television. After all, who could be in favor of excessive sex or violence on television? Over the years, television valence issues have included family viewing time, indecency, and political bias. Investigations of the television industry have consumed thousands of hours of congressional hearings and only rarely yielded actual legislation.

Television and baseball's relationship occasionally has been the subject of specific congressional investigation. For example, the Baseball Viewer's Protection Act of 1989 was introduced to limit the number of baseball games that could be moved from broadcasting to cable outlets.[10] This legislation was introduced at the time when a substantial number of regular-season baseball games, long the province of local television stations, were becoming a prominent part of regional sports network programming. Another major concern at the time was the new CBS contract with MLB, which all but ended the broadcast game of the week.

Baseball and the Courts

MLB's legal status and consequent operational parameters have been defined primarily via judicial rather than legislative action. The most prominent case defining baseball's legal status was *Federal Club v. National League*, the 1922 U.S. Supreme Court case that gave MLB an explicit exemption from the antitrust laws by declaring that baseball is "not a business."[11] Although the case law since that time (*Toolson v. New York Yankees, Gardella v. Chandler, Flood v. Kuhn*) has consistently held that the *Federal* case was wrongly decided, the Supreme Court has never overturned its decision, although it has explicitly told the U.S. Congress that it could repeal the exemption.[12]

The professional sports industry was far different in 1922 than it is today. Baseball was the only significant professional sports league in existence. The newly formed NFL had franchises in such markets as Massillon, Ohio; Duluth, Minnesota; and Rock Island, Illinois. There was no NBA, and the five-year-old NHL had not yet expanded to the United States. More importantly, radio was still semiexperimental, and television was about twenty-five years away. Though professional boxing and horse racing had many fans, most individual sports, including Olympic sports, were regarded as avocations of elite amateur sportsmen (and a few sportswomen) rather than as professions. This aura of innocent amateurism had more influence on the Supreme Court in the *Federal* case than the clear evidence that MLB was a fully professional business.

Nonetheless, the *Federal* decision helped canonize baseball as the national pastime—an institution, not a business, worthy of both protection and legislative oversight. MLB's creation of a commissioner who was empowered to act "in the best interests of baseball" regardless of economic consequences reinforced the *Federal* case's view of baseball as a public trust.

This view was not challenged in the radio era, although the new medium was an important new business component for baseball. Radio helped stabilize franchises located in eastern and midwestern markets by providing a new source of revenue and extending the fan base of marginal clubs. Once the owners understood that radio created fans rather than driving them from the ballparks, controversy over radio's negative impact on the sport subsided. The situation was much different with television.

With Television Comes Change

Even more than radio, television promoted nationalization over localization. Television programming was more costly to produce and distribute. The standard television channel requires six hundred times the electromagnetic spectrum space of an AM radio channel. This demand greatly limited the number of television stations. Television coverage required that its stations have a regional focus, especially outside major metropolitan areas. Program costs made national distribution essential for the highest-quality programming once a coast-to-coast network was established in 1951. The national bias of television soon brought it into conflict with the locally focused business of baseball.

Television's perceived effects, including minor league retrenchment and franchise relocation (see chapter 10), were responsible for the substantial congressional interest in baseball and other professional sports in the 1950s and early 1960s. The changes in baseball, the power of television, and the political activism of the day were all part of a climate that was beginning to knock loose baseball's long historical moorings. However, government officials regarded with skepticism the changes that were needed for individual teams to succeed as businesses.

Baseball was both helped and harmed by the myth of nostalgia, the belief that baseball was a unique sport and more important than the others. The sport's "national pastime" status helped MLB in the court decisions that reaffirmed its antitrust exemption, considered by many an anachronism even in the 1940s and 1950s. But the myth of nostalgia limited the ways in which MLB could change. Baseball had to manage change without jeopardizing its uniqueness in American life. How MLB was able to do this is demonstrated in the Johnson and Celler congressional committee hearings of the 1950s, baseball's reaction to the Sports Broadcasting Act of 1961, and MLB's response to the FCC's antisiphoning rules of the 1970s.

MLB Faces Congress in the 1950s

Major League owners recognized the possible impact of televising their games in minor league markets as early as December 1946. They therefore adopted Rule 1(d), which prohibited the telecasting and radiocasting of Major League games in minor league markets without the consent of the minor league team. The market of a minor league team was defined as the area within fifty miles of a ballpark.[13] The rule was intended to protect minor league teams from Major League broadcast competition. Clearly, the rule would limit any MLB owner's attempts to build his own regional networks and completely eliminated any regular-season national broadcasts. Why would the owners do this?

They had at least five reasons. First, the farm system concept had spread from the St. Louis Cardinals and Brooklyn Dodgers to almost every Major League team. Since most teams now also owned minor league teams, many owners believed that Rule 1(d) protected their own interests. Second, many owners were not convinced that regional and national broadcasting would garner significant revenues. Radio had been a great revenue supplement for many Major League teams on the local level, but its significance at the regional or national level was not established. Only the World Series and All-Star Game, broadcast when no minor league games were being played, were national attractions. Third, in 1946 television was a "scary medium" whose effects were unknown. MLB owners regarded Rule 1(d) as a way of exercising control over the new medium before it grew too powerful to contain.

Two other reasons why MLB owners supported the rule involved their fears over national coverage of baseball by radio networks. Both the Mutual Broadcasting Corporation and, by 1948, the Liberty Broadcasting System were making plans to launch a radio "Game of the Day." Though Rule 1(d) did not immediately stop such plans, it forced the networks to use re-creations from wire service information rather than live broadcasts. Eventually, the rule expedited the demise of Liberty, and MLB cut a more favorable deal with Mutual. Finally, in the immediate postwar era local minor league teams were a powerful source of pride in cities ranging in size from Los Angeles to Batesville, Arkansas. Minor league teams played in every state and in almost every congressional district. Team owners in these numerous locations could and did exert considerable pressure on their members of Congress.

The problem with Rule 1(d) was its restraint of trade, which applied to more than just baseball owners. Could baseball use its antitrust exemption to adopt a rule that clearly restrained the trade of broadcasters? Broadcasters clearly saw the near ban on games in minor league markets as a restriction on their requirement to serve the public interest. The National Association of Broadcasters (NAB), then and now one of the most powerful lobbies in Washington, adamantly opposed Rule 1(d), arguing that it prevented its members from giving the public the baseball broadcasts it wanted.[14] Though MLB itself had an exemption from antitrust rules, a challenge to its antitrust exemption was in the courts: the federal courts were considering limiting baseball's antitrust exceptions in the cases of players blacklisted by MLB for signing with teams in the Mexican League.[15]

The end of World War II saw a continuation, and to some extent an expansion, of the New Deal's activist government policies. Those policies had helped win the war and end the Great Depression. The Antitrust Division of the Department of Justice was very active in prosecuting violators of the various antitrust acts. For example, the Justice Department was in the midst of an ultimately successful effort to break up the vertically integrated motion picture industry.[16] Federal courts were also supporting antitrust enforcement at the time. The U.S. Supreme Court upheld the effort led by the Justice Department to break up the motion picture industry. Earlier, the nation's highest court upheld the FCC rules that forced RCA to sell one of its radio networks, NBC Blue. This precipitated the founding of ABC and increased radio network competition.[17]

Given this context, a Justice Department investigation of Rule 1(d) was no surprise. MLB at first reacted by modifying the rule in October 1949. The change limited the broadcast restriction to the times when a minor league game was taking place, unless the minor league team granted permission for the competing Major League broadcast. However, the Justice Department still saw the rule as problematic because of the failure of Liberty Broadcasting, which it blamed directly on the rule.

When the Justice Department pursued its investigation, MLB responded by deleting Rule 1(d) in October 1951.[18]

The Johnson Hearings

A version of Rule 1(d) was in effect for nearly five years, and it did not prevent the Minors from contracting. Even so, its removal by MLB set the wheels of Congress in motion. In May 1953, the minor leagues sought congressional relief. The Senate Committee on Interstate and Foreign Commerce created the Subcommittee on Televising Baseball Games. Led by Sen. Ed Johnson (D-CO), the subcommittee held hearings to consider Johnson's bill exempting MLB from criminal and civil antitrust penalties if it reinstated Rule 1(d). As noted earlier, Senator Johnson was also the president of the Western League, a minor league that, like many others, was suffering declining attendance. This direct conflict of interest did not prevent Johnson from chairing the subcommittee and attacking the few officials who spoke against his bill. Early in the proceedings Johnson made his point of view clear, saying he had "the honor of introducing a bill to protect the weak and helpless elements of America's national game of baseball from a cruel ruthless monopoly, which, strangely enough, was forced upon major league baseball by the Antitrust Division of our own Justice Department."[19]

The hearings turned into a sounding board for other laments about broadcasting's destructive impact on Minor League Baseball. Former baseball commissioner and U.S. senator "Happy" Chandler, for example, told the committee that "thousands of people who can hear a major league game broadcast nationally would not go to see a little home team play."[20] Chandler also reminded the subcommittee that both he and chairman Johnson had been minor league players as young men.

Johnson and his fellow committee members did not accept the NAB position that the restoration of Rule 1(d) would spark a parade of special-interest pleas for new congressional intervention. Subcommittee members mocked the verbose Gordon McLendon, owner of the failed Liberty network, when he suggested that restricting "broadcasts of baseball games in the hope that it will help minor league attendance is like taking aspirin to cure cancer."[21] MLB supported Johnson's assertion that the Justice Department forced it to repeal a rule that MLB thought necessary.

The Celler Hearings

The Johnson hearings were replicated in the U.S. House. Led by Rep. Emmanuel Celler (D-NY) the Judiciary Committee's Subcommittee on the Study of Monopoly Power examined the consequences of Rule 1(d)'s repeal. Celler would become the primary congressional expert on MLB. Ultimately, the Celler Committee recommended that no legislative action be taken until the impact of broadcasting on Minor League Baseball could be more clearly documented.[22] The Senate similarly declined to act.

Rule 1(d) was never revived, and the Minors' decline continued (see chapter 10). Broadcasting's effect on baseball had served as a valence issue. Though nothing really happened as a result of the Johnson or Celler hearings, politicians had the opportunity to express their concerns to all the minor league teams and their fans. The hearings also provided "regulation by raised eyebrow," reminding baseball that "after full review of all of the foregoing facts and with due consideration of modern judicial interpretation of the scope of the commerce clause, it is the studied judgment of the Subcommittee on the Study of Monopoly Power that the Congress has jurisdiction to investigate and legislate on the subject of professional baseball."[23]

MLB could never again claim that its antitrust exemption also exempted it from congressional scrutiny. The debates in the Senate and House constituted a warning shot to MLB that it should protect, or at least appear to protect, the minor leagues. MLB responded by providing more subsidy for the Minors and delaying aggressive exploitation of network-televised regular-season games (see chapter 10).

The Celler Hearings of 1957–58

Celler's Antitrust Subcommittee of the House Judiciary Committee called MLB to Congress again in 1957 and 1958.[24] The main issue was the reserve clause in player's contracts that prevented freedom of movement in the labor market. Celler was well known for his strong prolabor views. The issue raised concerns about whether MLB's antitrust exemption should be modified or revoked. The Supreme Court's split decision in rejecting an appeal of 1953's *Toolson* case provided an impetus for the hearings. In its refusal of certiorari (i.e., refusal to accept the case on appeal), the court revealed a split among its membership on the antitrust exemption. Once again, the Supreme Court recognized the power of Congress to alter the exemption.[25]

Other issues contributed to the House's decision to conduct hearings. Minor League Baseball had continued to shed teams and leagues throughout the 1950s. Franchise shifts had changed the map of MLB for the first time in half a century, angering longtime fans in the deserted cities. Most significantly, the impending move of the Brooklyn Dodgers and New York Giants to the West Coast provided fuel for the hearings' fires.

Here was a situation tailor made for Congress. The nation's largest city was losing two of its three franchises after over sixty-five years of operation. While weakening financial support was a valid reason for the relocation of the Boston Braves, St. Louis Browns, and Philadelphia Athletics, it was not applicable to the New York National League entries, especially the Dodgers.[26] As with the Johnson Senate hearings of the early 1950s, a personal interest was pushing the proceedings. Rep. Celler was a Brooklynite and huge Dodger fan, who, like millions of others, was appalled at what Walter O'Malley intended to do with the borough's beloved "Bums."

By the time of the hearings, there was little the subcommittee could do to prevent New York's loss of its two NL franchises. However, Celler and his colleagues could "shoot a warning arrow" at MLB: relocation was hazardous to its antitrust status. These subcommittee hearings are primarily remembered for the comments of several players and manager Casey Stengel. The comments of Stengel and Mickey Mantle, who both favored keeping the reserve clause, are better remembered than those of Jackie Robinson, Robin Roberts, and others, who argued for its end.[27] Although Congress did not intend to actually modify or scrap baseball's antitrust exemption in 1958, the Celler Committee's "raised eyebrow" made it clear that MLB had better solve its own player contract problems if it did not want Congress to pass legislation. The Celler Subcommittee hearings helped convince MLB to expand and place one of its new teams in New York. In 1962, the "Big Apple" got to "meet the Mets." The hearings also stimulated the creation of the new major/minor league agreement and reclassification system of 1963.

The Sports Broadcasting Act of 1961

The Sports Broadcasting Act (SBA) of 1961 is one of the most important pieces of sports law ever promulgated.[28] The SBA granted all professional sports leagues an antitrust exemption for the purpose of selling the broadcast rights of all league members as packages. The SBA helped promote the nationalization of professional sports, best exemplified by the National Football League.

The SBA was a congressional response to the antitrust suit filed by the U.S. Justice Department against the NFL after the league entered into a joint contract with CBS in 1961. The NFL-CBS contract was preceded by a joint contract between the American Football League and ABC in 1960. After a federal district court found that the NFL's CBS contract was a violation of antitrust, the league lobbied Congress vigorously for antitrust relief.[29] NFL commissioner Pete Rozelle's status as professional sports' smartest leader was forged by his success in getting the SBA enacted. In 1970, Rozelle used his legislative wherewithal to effect a merger with the AFL.

By the end of the 1960s, the NFL was the model for successful exploitation of television by a professional sport. The NFL used television to rival and then surpass baseball as the nation's most popular sport. The league telecast all regular and postseason games. During the regular season, the national rating for NFL telecasts was based on a compilation of all of its local game ratings, while baseball's "national" ratings were based on one game that competed for the baseball audience with other locally televised games. As a result, national ratings for the NFL were dramatically higher than for MLB. The NFL's policy of equally splitting its television revenues created much more economic parity among its franchises compared to their baseball counterparts, where there remained great disparities in local television revenues.[30]

Although the NFL was the primary beneficiary of the SBA, the weaker National Basketball Association and the National Hockey League were able to exploit the SBA to grow their sports nationally. The legislation also allowed MLB to finally consummate a true national television contract, first with ABC in 1965 and then, more successfully, with NBC in 1966 (see chapter 6).

Though the NFL (and NBA) took immediate advantage of the SBA, MLB needed five years to fully exploit the SBA exemption. Many owners still saw television revenues as primarily a local matter. For these owners, competition meant more than winning the pennant and the World Series. It extended to maximizing individual team revenues regardless of the consequences to other teams. MLB had always been split been "have" and "have-not" teams. Sharing, especially for the "have" teams, did not come easily. The NFL had shown that sharing the wealth could ultimately benefit all teams by leveling the playing field among franchises. This would promote better competition, which in turn would produce better overall attendance and broadcast ratings because more teams would have a realistic chance of winning. But imbalance had benefited some of the game's dominant franchises (e.g., Yankees and Dodgers), and baseball's newspaper-era commissioner, Ford Frick, was not one to rock the owners' boat. Although the ground was shifting for the sports industry, MLB was wedded to the past and not well equipped to exploit changes such as the SBA.

Sports Siphoning and Migration

The rise of cable television as a competitor to "free" broadcast television had an enormous impact upon MLB and other sports (see chapter 8). Cable television had two revenue streams: advertising, which also supported broadcast television, and direct payments, including monthly fees and pay-per-view. Thus, cable television was always a form of pay television. For sports industries, cable's direct payments offered a new financial opportunity. A team's core fans might be willing to pay for televised games if that was the only way to get them.

The failure of the early experiments did not kill pay television. There was simply too much money to be made. The new impetus for pay television came from the "new" medium of cable television, which was evolving rapidly in the 1960s. At first, television stations welcomed cable, or "community antenna television" (CATV) as it was known then, because it retransmitted their signals into rural communities that were not adequately served by station signals. However, to improve its product and increase its customer base, cable systems began to import distant stations, increasing competition for local stations. The imported stations also made cable appealing in markets that already had strong broadcast signals. Broadcasters complained to the FCC that cable, while using their signals for free, was unfairly competing for audiences with out-of-market signals. In short order, "pay" cable threatened the health of "free" broadcasting.[31]

Two 1972 FCC decisions were crucial to the development of the cable television industry. In *Third Report and Order on Cable Television*, the commission laid out the "ground rules" by which cable television could begin to enter the nation's urban markets.[32] Though the rules were highly restrictive regarding the types of programming that cable could originate (i.e., no series, no sports events that had been covered by broadcast television in the past two years), cable operators were now legally allowed to originate some programming. Origination was essential to gaining subscribers in urban markets that already had a full complement of broadcast stations.

In its other key 1972 decision, the FCC deregulated domestic satellite usage, making it possible to use satellites to deliver television signals nationally. Reversing its policy from the early 1960s, the FCC now allowed companies to lease transponder space on satellites for purely domestic transmission.[33] Although this option was not realized at the time, the deregulation was a precondition for the growth of new cable networks. Networks no longer had to pay AT&T's mammoth landline charges to transmit a television signal throughout the United States. They could cover the entire country merely by leasing two satellite transponders. While local cable systems clamored for more networks providing original programming to lure new customers, satellites could deliver network signals to any local cable system with a downlink satellite relay. Within a few years, cable pioneers such as the Christian Broadcasting Network, Univision, "Superstation" WTBS (originally WTCG), and HBO would use satellites to reach cable systems all over the nation.

Broadcasters responded to the new cable threat by seeking protection from the FCC and the Congress. Broadcasters argued that they were licensed to operate in the public interest under the Communications Act of 1934. That obligation required them to be protected from unfair competition. Broadcasters also adapted the siphoning position used by the motion picture industry in its successful fight against pay television in California. Broadcasters argued that cable would "siphon" programs away from "free" television.[34]

The siphoning argument had particular resonance for sports telecasts. After all, the Dodgers and Giants had already tried to shift their games to pay television. Many commentators had already predicted the eventual migration of sports from "free" to "pay" television.[35]

As early as the mid-1960s, the FCC adopted antisiphoning rules that severely restricted program origination on cable television.[36] However, the 1972 decisions on cable and satellite are what set the parameters for the future growth of the cable industry and facilitated its ability to contest the FCC's programming rules.

In 1977, the U.S. Court of Appeals for the District of Columbia held that the commission's antisiphoning rules for series, movies, and sports were unconstitutional. The court found the rules to be overly restrictive and a violation of the cable industry's First Amendment rights.[37] The appeals court's decision opened the floodgates for sports on television. Now cable could secure rights to sports events regardless of their previous broadcast history. The number of hours of sports available to the average U.S. television household exploded. The HBO v. FCC decision led to the birth of ESPN in 1979 and the creation of regional sports networks in the 1980s.

The court's decision kicked off the "deregulatory era" for communications industries in which the government regulations once seen as necessary to protect the "public interest" were repealed. In the deregulation era, corporate interests and the public interest are often seen as the same because of the strong belief of government officials in the efficacy of markets. Regulations were believed to limit competition and industry growth. For example, the Cable Communications Policy Act of 1984 severely restricted the ability of municipalities to regulate cable rates and programming in their communities.[38] The cable industry has argued that the removal of these local regulations was a major factor in the rapid diffusion of cable. However, the 1984 act also allowed cable systems, usually local monopolies, to increase their rates without municipal approval, leading to increases in the cost of cable to consumers.

Congress Gets Involved . . . Again

The rapid expansion of sports on cable television eventually attracted the attention of Congress. In the early 1990s, Sen. John McCain (R-AZ) and Representatives Peter Kostmayer (D-PA) and Gerry Sikorski (D-MN) each introduced bills that would reserve major sports events, such as the World Series and Super Bowl, for the broadcast television that was available to almost every American family.[39] But as is often the case with proposed sports legislation, no bills were actually passed. However, as part of the Cable Television Consumer Protection and Competition Act of 1992, Congress did require the FCC to conduct a study on the migration of sports television.[40]

The commission's subsequent interim and final reports on *Sports Programming Migration* found that, contrary to popular belief, the major broadcast networks had actually increased the amount of time devoted to sports in the 1980s.[41] In comments collected during the investigation, all the major sports leagues and the NCAA applauded cable's contribution to televised sports since the end of the antisiphoning rules. MLB argued that cable was now a necessity for its fans because broadcast networks were increasingly reluctant to air baseball's regular-season games due to declining ratings. The FCC concurred and stated that the new television environment had forced MLB "to accept more risk than other professional sports leagues."[42] Although the FCC's report did not result in new legislation, it did reaffirm that both sports and television are of interest to lawmakers. Both are regarded as public "trusts," and both have highly vocal, powerful defenders.

MLB's Nightmare: A Cable World Series

High-profile events such as the World Series and the All-Star Game are not likely to migrate to cable or other forms of pay television. Such siphoning by cable would create a public relations nightmare for MLB and force Congress to act. Pure economic considerations are also at work. The World Series remains a popular national television event, despite declining ratings, and is a major promotional platform for both its broadcast network and MLB. Broadcast networks are still willing to pay millions more than cable networks for these rights because they still have the greatest potential audience for the games. Even MLB owners are not so foolish as to jeopardize that asset. As long as there is broadcast television, the World Series will remain a national broadcast tradition.

However, this does not mean *only* broadcast television. The Internet era gives MLB and the other major sports leagues the ability to both have their cake and eat it, too. MLB may offer a "new and improved" pay telecast of the World Series *in addition to* the "free" telecasts. Nothing prevents MLB from creating new revenue streams by offering "enhanced" (e.g., no commercials, more interactivity) versions of its product over the Internet for a fee. This scenario is much more likely than migration to cable.

Siphoning from Local Broadcasters

For regular-season games, the siphoning picture is quite different. Local and regional telecasts of MLB games have all but disappeared from broadcast stations in many markets. By 2003, broadcasting of home-team games had disappeared in Cincinnati, Cleveland, Montreal, Pittsburgh, and Toronto and had been sharply curtailed in many other markets.[43] The creation of team-owned RSNs, including co-ownership deals with Comcast, and Fox's aggressiveness in maintaining its leading position in the RSN business have continued to remove games from local stations and the syndicated broadcast networks that used to be common. RSNs are a much more lucrative source of revenue generation for MLB teams. League Division Series and League Championship Series games are migrating to cable. The most recent national MLB television contracts moved the four LDS and one of the two LCS (annually alternating between the AL and NL) to Time Warner's TBS basic cable network in 2007.[44] Despite cable's approximately 10 percent smaller delivery capability as compared to a broadcast network, it provides a more effective promotional and marketing platform. This is because the contracts guarantee a level of cross-promotion with MLB that is not available on broadcast.[45] Other major professional and collegiate sports have seen a similar migration. Even the mighty NFL has increased the number of regular telecasts that are presented exclusively on cable.

Future Legal Issues

The relationship between sports and television will continue to trigger congressional hearings, much proposed and a small amount of actual legislation, limited regulatory action, and the court decisions that usually follow. As powerful economic and cultural entities, they deserve oversight. But the popularity of sports on television also makes them a frequent source of valence issues, whether steroid abuse or competitive balance, that politicians can exploit. For baseball, the potential loss of MLB's antitrust exemption will continue to bolster congressional power over the sport. The antitrust hammer is likely to be wielded whenever a franchise threatens to relocate.

The migration of baseball to pay television has been normalized, so siphoning from advertiser-supported to pay television is not likely to be a major issue in the future. The concern will likely resurface only if MLB foolishly shifts the World Series and All-Star Game away from broadcast television. Maintaining the current broadcast approach and adding enhanced pay versions of these games, delivered on the Internet, gives MLB a better opportunity to maximize the value of its premier television products without provoking the wrath of the federal government.

Baseball and Television Synergy

As rights fees for Major League Baseball and all other major sports leagues exploded in the 1970s and 1980s, the nature of the relationship between sports and television providers changed. Media companies and major sports began to realize that working together, rather than just for their own interests, could produce even more revenue. The bigger income pie benefited both parties. The word *partnership* increasingly became the main descriptor of the relationship.[1] Sports rights became a key branding strategy for national, regional, and local television. A sports coverage brand differentiated one network from its increasing number of competitors for audience attention. For the regional sports networks that developed in the 1980s, local sports teams were their raison d'être. Indeed, local teams sometimes forced RSNs to become "partners" or lose their sports product to other distributors.

Synergy in the Deregulation Era

In addition to branding, synergy became a key sports television concept in the 1980s. Successful synergy means that two or more entities working together are greater than the apparent sum of their parts. The diffusion of new media technologies, beginning in the 1970s and accelerating in the 1980s, stimulated interest in synergy. The old television oligopoly (ABC, NBC, CBS) was losing control over its audience because of the public's rapid acceptance of cable satellite television delivery. The established Big 3 networks tried to strengthen their declining position through new strategic alliances. The U.S. government's move to "deregulate" communications industries, beginning in the late 1970s and rapidly advancing since, removed the regulatory boundaries that had once made certain forms of synergy antitrust violations.

Deregulation by the Reagan-era FCC made it possible for broadcast television networks to become major investors in both the cable television industry and television program production. In addition, the gradual loosening of ownership restrictions, which had limited the number of television or radio stations any company could control, spurred a major media industry consolidation. In the 1980s, the Loew's-CBS, General Electric–NBC, and Capital Cities–ABC mergers as well as the creation of the News Corp.'s Fox network constituted the largest media deals of all time. Within about a decade, the Paramount-Viacom-CBS, Disney-ABC-ESPN, NBC-Universal-Vivendi, and Time Warner–AOL mergers eclipsed these former megadeals. In a relatively short time, television networks underwent historic changes. The Big 3 were no longer modestly regulated domestic businesses, restrained in their relations with program suppliers. They were now part of minimally regulated, multibillion-dollar international businesses that had dramatically increased control over program production and distribution. In addition, they could profit from special access to the program products of "sister" companies within their mega-conglomerates.

These deals benefited MLB and the other major professional sports leagues. New competition for both broadcast and television viewers spurred consistent increases in rights fees. The deregulation-era creation of the Fox network and many RSNs, most under the control of News Corp., was especially significant. News Corp.'s corporate policy focused on sports as a key programming strategy. Aggressive application of this policy made the fledgling "fourth network" and its RSNs primary buyers of sports programming by the 1990s. This led to Fox's acquisition of national broadcast rights to MLB and the acquisition by News Corp.'s RSNs of local television rights.

Vertical Integration

Successful branding and synergy both rely on vertical integration, one of the oldest operational goals in capitalist economics. Essentially, it is the control of all levels of the supply chain from ownership to consumer.[2] For media corporations, this means the control of (1) production, (2) distribution, and (3) exhibition (P-D-E). Despite multinational corporations' current conventional wisdom that vertical integration is necessary for companies to "compete," until quite recently vertical integration was regarded as something to be avoided because of its negative effects on the consumer.

For decades, U.S. government policies assumed that a vertically integrated market structure is anticompetitive and therefore bad for the public. The control of each element of the P-D-E chain leads to a market that presents high barriers to entry for new competitors. The negative implications of vertical integration have been the rationale for antitrust actions against many corporate schemes. In the 1948 *Paramount* decision, motion picture studios had to divest their ownership of theaters.[3] In the 1960s, the Justice Department refused to allow International Telephone and Telegraph to acquire ABC.[4]

Today, these Department of Justice actions seem like ancient history. The prevailing zeitgeist is that vertical integration is essential if large corporations are going to compete in a global marketplace. A rhetoric of corporate consolidation has replaced "the public interest" as the mantra for government regulators. The 1980s ushered in not only the age of deregulators and "free-market" advocates who ignored, revoked, or redefined the rules, but also an age of technological convergence and economic consolidation that would make the media industries a far more powerful force than was once the case.

The advantages of vertical integration to the parent corporation are well established. It gives the owning corporation control of costs, a steady stream of products to distribute, and guaranteed access to the audience. In the late 1950s and early 1960s, before the age of deregulation, Major League Baseball experimented with vertical integration. Control of the Detroit Tigers guaranteed that the team's owner, John Fetzer, would have popular Tiger broadcasts for his radio station group in the upper Midwest. Analysts attributed Gene Autry's acquisition of the expansion Angels in 1961 to his desire to control an MLB team's television rights after he failed to secure Dodger broadcast rights for his Los Angeles television station.[5]

A False Start: CBS Buys the Yankees

In the most publicized and ultimately least successful television-baseball integration, CBS purchased the New York Yankees in August 1964

28. *The sale of the Yankees to* CBS *would hasten Yogi Berra's departure as the Bombers' manager.* © *Bettmann/Corbis.*

for $14 million. The network was already the owner of the number-one national television and radio networks, highly rated New York radio and television stations, and many other prosperous large-market stations. Many critics saw its purchase of the nation's most popular team as a disturbing harbinger of the future of sports' ownership.

The *Sporting News* saw "promotional gimmicks flourish[ing] under the new regime."[6] Other team owners were leery of the deal because it put baseball's most successful franchise in the deep pockets of one of the world's largest media corporations. CBS and the Yankees consummated their marriage just as owners were contemplating the potential impact of pay television experiments on the West Coast.[7] The CBS-Yankees deal and pay television raised concerns about the erosion of the economic balance in baseball. For most owners, the relationship between baseball and television appeared to be entering a new and disturbing stage.

These owner concerns led Commissioner Ford Frick to seek and receive a letter from CBS assuring that "any rights or privileges accruing to CBS would be accrued on a competitive bidding basis and not by reason of stock ownership or club control."[8] CBS needed to assuage owners' fears that it would use the Yankees to develop a network television package without bidding for a package in competition with other teams so as to gain approval for the Yankee purchase. In addition, as a broadcaster, CBS was subject to considerable governmental oversight.

More than today, the 1960s was a time of vigorous regulatory oversight of many businesses. Because of its ubiquity, influence, and status as a public resource, broadcasting was particularly subject to regulation by both the Federal Communications Commission and the Congress. CBS could not afford to jeopardize the FCC-granted licenses of its radio and television stations, the network's primary revenue stream, by violating antitrust rules. Antitrust infractions would give the FCC legal grounds for not renewing the licenses of CBS stations that were to be operated in the "public interest."

CBS did leverage its purchase briefly by creating a *Yankee Game of the Week* in 1965 to compete with ABC's game of the week. The Yankees had a contract with CBS that predated their purchase by the network. This and a prior television commitment by the Phillies prevented MLB from adopting a national television policy that encompassed all of the then twenty teams. After these contracts expired, MLB was able to sign its first truly national contract with NBC in 1966 (see chapter 6).

Ultimately, the CBS-Yankees combination failed, best symbolized by the network's 1973 sale of the team to a George Steinbrenner–led group, which resulted in a multimillion dollar loss for CBS.[9] This was one of the few times in MLB history when a franchise was sold at a loss. CBS's willingness to dump the Yankees means that it both overpaid for the franchise in 1964 and, by 1973, was very motivated to end its baseball ownership.

CBS had the misfortune of buying a great team just at the moment of its collapse: not what the network anticipated when it purchased the "Bronx Bombers." CBS was not able to use its substantial corporate resources to turn around the failing franchise. The new amateur draft meant it could not corral the best young players simply by paying them more than other franchises. In addition, the reserve clause meant there were no free agents for CBS to sign. The new national contract with NBC also helped level the financial playing field by giving each franchise an equal share of national television revenue.

In retrospect, CBS's purchase of the Yankees was a business venture before its time. While continuing on-the-field success would have benefited its local stations' revenues, baseball games were just a small part of a broadcast schedule. Games were broadcast during warm-weather months when viewing levels were at their lowest. Evening games would interrupt the network prime-time schedule. In this pre-cable era, distribution channels were limited and all-sports stations (television or radio) were impossible to implement. Finally, baseball soon entered a period of serious stagnation, culminating in professional football's ascendancy as the nation's most popular sport. For a television network, all of these conditions limited the value of owning a baseball team.

The Superstation Formula

The first postcable, postderegulation television baseball merger was Ted Turner's purchase of the Atlanta Braves in 1976. Turner, a true media pioneer, was already the owner of a weak UHF station in Atlanta (WTCG). But early on, he recognized that the FCC's 1972 deregulation of satellite transmission for television signals would be the major impetus for the development of a competitive cable industry. Turner acquired a satellite transponder position for WTCG and proceeded to turn it into the nation's first superstation, WTBS. Turner even coined the term *superstation*.[10]

A key strategy in building TBS was acquiring sports franchises: the Atlanta Braves and, later, the NBA's Hawks and NHL's Thrashers. Telecasts of the Braves and Turner's other sports teams gave TBS hundreds of hours of cheap original programming with no ongoing acquisition costs or rights fees, except when needed as a corporate bookkeeping maneuver. Turner billed the Braves as "America's Team." Both TBS and the Braves gained popularity around the nation, despite the latter's non-contention until its dominance in the 1990s and early 2000s.

As detailed in chapter 8, the superstation banner was later taken up by New York's WOR, Los Angeles's KTLA (the Autry station), and Chicago's WGN. WGN-TV, owned and operated by the (Chicago) Tribune Company, ever since the advent of television in the late 1940s, was the longtime television home of the Cubs and, sometimes, the White Sox. Turner's success with the Braves was a clear impetus for Tribune Company to purchase the Cubs from the Wrigley family in 1980. The Tribune Company now controlled the rights to a team it had long televised and that provided many hours of programming to its television and radio stations in Chicago. The *Chicago Tribune*'s newspaper sports section also teemed with stories on the Cubs.

In the 1980s and 1990s, baseball team ownership by media corporations was a growing concern in MLB because teams became increasingly stratified between the local television "haves" and "have-nots." MLB even took action to prevent more teams from being "swallowed" by the superstations.[11] However, MLB did not prevent other media owners from becoming sports owners. The two primary examples were Disney's 1996 acquisition of the then Anaheim Angels and News Corp.'s 1998 purchase of the Los Angeles Dodgers. Paralleling this was Time Warner's absorption of all of Turner's interests, including the Atlanta Braves. To most observers, it appeared that corporate media ownership of MLB and other professional sports teams was the wave of the future.[12]

A Strategy Shift

By 2003 and 2004, the new watchword seemed to be sports team divestiture rather than acquisition. Frank McCourt became the new majority owner of the Los Angeles Dodgers after he purchased the team from News Corp. (i.e., Rupert Murdoch). In 2003, the Walt Disney Company, one of News Corp.'s primary rivals in the global media business, sold the reigning world champion Anaheim Angels to Arturo Moreno, who soon created the unwieldy moniker "Los Angeles Angels of Anaheim." Time Warner put the Atlanta Braves on the seller's block and radically cut the team's payroll to attract a buyer.[13]

This trend away from the joint ownership of media and sports is not limited to baseball. Time Warner sold the Atlanta Hawks (NBA) and

Thrashers (NHL). Disney sold the NHL's Mighty Ducks of Anaheim, now the Anaheim Ducks. Even in the nation's largest and most lucrative media market, YankeeNets, the brainchild of Steinbrenner, and another source of millions of dollars of revenue for the Yankees, sold the New Jersey Nets to a Brooklyn developer.[14]

Why has there been a reversal of what seemed a logical trend: the joint ownership of media and sports? Does the shift signal a return to the individual ownership mythologized by the mainstream media and most baseball fans? Or do these deals reflect new kinds of relationships between corporate media and sports franchises?

Problems with Vertical Integration

Professional sports leagues and their member teams really never had to deal with significant antitrust issues, even before the market mania of the past twenty to twenty-five years. MLB has enjoyed an explicit exemption from most antitrust concerns since 1922.[15] The Sports Broadcasting Act of 1961 further granted all the professional leagues an antitrust exemption for developing policies on television and radio.[16] Combine these longstanding exemptions with a new tolerance of vertical integration and it is not surprising that sports leagues, a legalized cartel, and media firms, a semilegalized cartel, would make a series of deals to enhance their relationships.

One unique feature of the integration of media and sports firms is the presence of backward vertical integration. Unlike the more conventional model of a producer acquiring distribution and exhibition, the sports-media integration consisted of mammoth media companies with distribution and exhibition channels adding a programming product: MLB and other sports. For instance, the Tribune Company already owned the WGN superstation as well as other television and newspaper outlets at the time it purchased the Cubs. Backward integration was even stronger for News Corp. and Disney, as they added a team to an even larger portfolio of distribution and exhibition entities.

For these corporations, sports teams were the last piece of the vertical integration puzzle. In some cases, they were merely an afterthought to the economic vibrancy of the mid-1990s. This integration helps to explain why these arrangements were so easily terminated when the economy changed. Instead of "last hired, first fired," it was "last bought, first dumped."

Disney and News Corp. clearly expected the acquisition of sports teams to contribute positively to their corporate coffers. Though the relationship can also mean a positive balance sheet for the ongoing operation of the team, it is just one of several money-making possibilities. Control of a team by a television distributor and/or exhibitor means that it has a guaranteed source of programming at a fixed price. In the case of MLB, with its 162-game season and minimum three-hour-per-game telecasts, this can mean almost five hundred hours a year of original exclusive programming. In addition, ownership of the team means that rights fees paid to the team become an in-house revenue shift, allowing corporations to play (and win!) various tax games. Other tax savings are realized through the depreciation rules available to all professional sports franchise owners.

In addition to providing hundreds of hours of original and exclusive programming, corporate-owned sports teams also help to attract the elusive male audience that is valued by advertisers and difficult to reach with non–sports programming. Thus, televised sports can often demand premium rates for advertising because of the desirability of its audience. With household ratings becoming less important in the calculations of advertisers and television continuing to divide into a series of niches, the more homogeneous audience for sports has made it a premium television product.

Regional sports networks are the best example. Unlike local broadcasters or most cable-satellite networks, RSNs must have team television rights in order to exist. As developments in several MLB markets show, one way to ensure the survival of a lucrative RSN is to share joint ownership of the network with one or more of the teams in the market that provides the bulk of the RSN's programming. The Red Sox (NESN), Yankees (YES), Royals (RSTN), Indians (SportsTime Ohio), Mets (SportsNet New York), and Phillies (Comcast SportsNet) are among the teams that either control or share ownership interests with RSNs.[17] The growing importance of RSNs can be seen in the creation of the Mid-Atlantic Sports Network (MASN) in the Washington-Baltimore area. The network, which telecasts both Nationals and Orioles games, is largely owned by Orioles' owner Peter Angelos. Angelos allegedly won his large stake in MASN as part of his agreement not to legally contest the relocation of the Montreal Expos to Washington in 2005.[18]

In short, there are many reasons for large media firms to own professional sports teams. Vertical integration that allows ownership of sports teams guarantees programming to media channels with no additional costs incurred outside of the corporation rights fees. Thus, ownership integration of two cartels appears to be a "win-win" for the team and the media company. So why would Disney sell the Angels and News Corp. sell the Dodgers? Why is Time Warner trying to dump the Braves? Why the urge to purge?

Dance of the Cartels

The public relations releases detailing these fairly recent sales do not reveal the reasons for them. They simply say how happy the selling corporation was to be part of the game and how happy they are to see the team in the capable hands of the new owner. Not surprisingly, investment analysts have provided the clearest explanations of the motivations behind these deals. Our analysis of the present state of the media and sports allows us to suggest the following reasons for divestiture:

1. Macroeconomic conditions
2. Costs of sports programming
3. Implemented and failed plans
4. The "price" of partnerships

These four factors are indicative of emerging new patterns in the media sports dynamic.

Macroeconomic Conditions

The general state of the economy strongly affects corporate behavior. The Disney-Angels, News Corp.–Dodgers, and Time Warner–Turner–Braves deals all took place in an economically robust time. Although the corporate economy began trending upward again in the mid-2000s, the slump of the early 2000s is at least partially responsible for the drive to sell teams.

The urge to purge should be expected. Throughout history companies have concentrated resources on their "core" assets during troubled economic periods. For example, in the early 1970s, CBS divested such assets as the Wurlitzer piano company and the Yankees.[19]

A corollary to this reversion to "core assets" in times of economic trouble is the "overextension" of corporations when times are flush. Time Warner, Disney, and News Corp. provide three examples. Time Warner acquired the Braves, Hawks, and Thrashers as a consequence of its acquisition of Ted Turner's business and not because the world's largest media company was seeking to own sports teams. The situation was much different with Disney and News Corp., since these companies made aggressive bids for their sports franchises.

In Disney's case, the Angels and the Mighty Ducks were key to both synergistic media deals and a commitment to Anaheim at the time when the company was investing hundreds of millions of dollars in a refurbished Disneyland including the new California amusement park section. The reason for Murdoch's acquisition of the Dodgers was less clear to analysts. The franchise was never leveraged in ways that would have made it a key source of programming for News Corp.'s extensive Asian television holdings. Despite having one of baseball's highest payrolls, the Dodgers, under News Corp.'s management, lost much of the team's onetime luster.

Perhaps the way to explain Murdoch's purchase of the Dodgers is as a deal for the sake of dealing: the modern corporate equivalent of Frank "Trader" Lane's player-swapping reputation as a general manager. Michael Wolff, a media business author-analyst and former dot-commer, reminds us that giant corporations do not necessarily make rational decisions. In fact, in Wolff's estimation, they rarely do so. For the giant media corporations in an era of continuing economic consolidation and technological convergence, the largest "sin" is to sit still.[20] In a time of minimal regulation and flux in the media-telecommunications industry, the clear impetus is to try new things, even if they turn out to be mistakes, rather than appear left behind in the new digital world. The News

Corp.–MySpace and Google-YouTube deals are recent examples of the same corporate behavior.[21]

Costs of Sports Programming

Despite the almost constant hand wringing over the escalating costs of rights fees, sports traditionally have been a relatively low-cost programming option. Sports are appealing television programming. They provide many hours of live programming, they appeal to hard-to-reach demographics, and they provide a promotional-branding platform. However, the continuing proliferation of new television networks under fewer owners is leading to a new oligopoly. For these new configurations, professional sports, and especially baseball, may not be as cost efficient as they were a few short years ago.

For example, note the reduced number of Atlanta Braves games on Superstation TBS in the past few years and the similar reduction of Cub and White Sox games on WGN. TBS is part of the Time Warner media colossus. Often, even reruns of programs controlled by Time Warner will attract an audience as economically viable as televised Braves games, without the latter's programming or production costs. In addition, Braves games have been diverted from TBS to build the Turner South RSN, a highly specialized and lucrative cable-satellite service. The value of Braves games is much lower than in the 1970s and 1980s, when Turner used the Braves and Hawks to build a local television station and then the first superstation.

In Chicago, the affiliation of the Cubs' owner, the Tribune Company, with the CW television network necessitates the broadcast of fewer evening ballgames. The Tribune Company's WGN may still bill itself as "Chicago's Very Own," but the station is no longer a true independent. It must provide clearance for CW evening programming if it is to maintain a healthy partnership with the network. Thus, for WGN, baseball is a less important programming element in its basic cable or broadcast operations.

A media problem for baseball has always been too much product. Though this oversupply enabled local broadcast stations to become the first cable superstations, it is now an albatross for them. In the current era of television, hard-core fans can turn to RSNs, or digital cable-satellite services (e.g., "Extra Innings"), or the Internet (e.g., MLB.com) while the more casual fan moves onto abundant niche programming more to his or her tastes.

As superstation baseball coverage of a single team's games begins to fade, those stations' emphasis on sports has, in large part, shifted to RSNs. RSNs play to the traditional source of baseball's fan base: the fan of a local or nearby team. Although on a much larger scale in most markets, MLB understands, with the NBA and NHL, the importance of regionalization. People are fans of a specific team rather than a specific league. With the exception of the postseason and the All-Star Game, most viewers prefer "their" team. RSNs were designed for the "hometown" fans, both in these networks' game coverage and in the other programming they design for their service area, such as local sports news and analysis and call-in programs.

Implemented and Failed Plans

Although much of the media commentary on the recent spate of corporate divestiture of teams has suggested that the companies did not know what they were doing, this is not necessarily the case. Some of the companies did benefit from team ownership before cashing out. Braves games were key to the development of Time Warner's Turner South RSN. There is little doubt that the corporation will keep those television rights for the long term. Similarly, on a regional and national level, News Corp.'s Fox network and RSNs continue to be partners of MLB despite selling the Dodgers. In both cases, owning a specific team was likely a short-run means of creating or maintaining a relationship with baseball rather than a core asset that needed to be sustained.

Conversely, there are the deals that did not work out. At the time of the Angels purchase, Disney, through its just completed acquisition of ESPN, hoped to create a major Southern California RSN (ESPN West).[22] But Fox prevented Disney's entry by its earlier development of Fox Sports Net's RSNs there and throughout the nation. In fact, one of the reasons for News Corp.'s purchase of the Dodgers was to curry favor with the other MLB owners, as its Fox Broadcasting network was bidding for exclusive broadcast rights, and its Fox Sports Net's RSNs were becoming the dominant regional baseball television outlets throughout the nation.[23]

In addition to supporting an RSN, News Corp.–Fox had another plan for the Dodgers—one that failed. News Corp. planned to leverage the team to its television services (Star TV) in Asia, because parts of Asia are baseball hotbeds and have a rising level of satellite television penetration.[24] However, Murdoch's companies seemed to have misread the interests of both the national and international baseball audience. First, any individual baseball team is a regional phenomenon. Even the New York Yankees or the Chicago Cubs have a relatively small fan base outside of their core cities, spring-training sites, and a few retirement communities. Just as CBS misread the baseball market in the 1960s when it purchased the Yankees, so Fox could not leverage the Dodgers domestically to the degree they hoped. As for the Asian television market, News Corp. seems to have fallen into a neocolonial mindset in its plans for global television. The expectation that millions of Japanese, Korean, Malaysian, or Chinese viewers would flock to Dodger games via Star TV ignores the reality that these nations have their own sports entities, including baseball, with passionate followings.

The idea that the Dodgers could somehow become the Manchester United of baseball or, more accurately, a continental Yomiuri Giants simply ignores local cultures, the regional appeal of baseball, and the power of programming rather than distribution in media success. In addition, the failure of the Murdoch-owned Dodgers to market themselves in Asia through off-season tours and other promotions also reflects a serious miscalculation. Indeed, the best messenger for MLB in Asia may be the Asian corporation. The Seattle Mariners offer the best example of a U.S. team that created interest in Japan because the team is owned by a Japanese corporation and signed the iconic Ichiro Suzuki.

The "Price" of Partnerships

In the United States, professional sports leagues are legalized cartels exempt from even the increasingly lax antitrust standards applied to U.S. corporations. Though the economic consolidation of the media industries creates new oligopolies that work in legal concert to produce salable content, these industries differ from sports leagues in one key way. The nonsports corporate world creates, consumes, and discards partners at will. With few exceptions, such as the attempted contraction of the Expos and Twins, sports do not work this way. The individual teams in MLB or any sports league have no business without the other teams that are their partners.

Because owning a team is a minor part of large media firms' portfolios and because baseball operates under a very different business culture from media, baseball teams can quickly become more trouble that they are worth. For example, Rupert Murdoch has used sports from baseball to soccer to rugby to build his television empire, but he has no special affinity for these games. Is it any surprise that News Corp. would be much more interested in acquiring DirecTV (later also discarded), the largest player in the fastest-growing distribution system in the United States, or the MySpace social networking web site than in trying to reinvigorate the Dodgers?[25]

Sports partnerships also pose special problems for media conglomerates. News Corp. was constrained in how it could use the Dodgers as a source of media programming. To create a Dodgers network on any but a regional level would violate partnership rules and most likely lead to unwanted scrutiny of the entire corporation. This in turn could lead to new regulations by MLB, a corporate board on which News Corp. had only one of thirty votes and led by a CEO who is a former car dealer from Milwaukee. In addition, there are payroll taxes that limit excess spending (investment) in individual teams. This reduces the advantage that deep-pocket corporations have over the financially weaker competitors. This might or might not be good for the sports leagues and their fans, but it makes absolutely no sense for a giant media firm. Why bother with such a small entity that greatly restricts your ability to maximize your profits? There are those like Steinbrenner who are willing to pay the luxury tax penalty for spending above the "soft cap." However, his reasons for doing so are an interesting mix of both financial acumen and, perhaps more importantly, psychological need, a motivation disdained in the modern corporate world.

The spending typical of baseball team owners is anathema to the mind-set of the conventional publicly traded corporation. Most corporations exist to generate a positive return on investment on a quarterly basis. Institutional investors and major stockholders expect nothing less. To deficit-spend on a baseball team, which is only one relatively small part of a corporation, makes no sense. While the Steinbrenners or Morenos in MLB answer to no one other than their partners, they are free to spend money on the team as they please. They do not answer to stockholders, do not have to present quarterly statements to the government and business press, and are much more free to alter their operational behavior if they choose. Perhaps the only media mogul of recent times who had similar latitude was Ted Turner, and even he eventually ran into financial problems and ultimately surrendered his interest to Time Warner.

The Tribune Company's ownership of the Cubs is instructive. Owning the Cubs was critical to turning WGN-TV into a superstation with value beyond the metropolitan Chicago area. The popularity of the team generated box-office and broadcasting profits and gave *Chicago Tribune* writers much to discuss. Note that only in the past few years has the Tribune Company begun to raise the Cubs' payroll to figures reflective of Chicago's status as the nation's third-largest television market. Is there any doubt that the Cubs were a "cash cow" for many years?

The reason for the recent increase in payroll is tied to the breakup of the Tribune Company's many assets. A competitive team will likely fetch a much greater return than one that has had one failure after another. In other words, the Tribune Company was frugal (if not stingy) when it owned the team, knowing that huge profits were guaranteed anyway. Whether or not the Tribune Company cares about the team's success on the field, there is little doubt that the Cubs were a relatively low-spending club for years. After all, winning teams generate more revenue but also cost much more to maintain. The worth of the team to corporate coffers is revealed now that Tribune Company has been sold and the Cubs are being divested.[26]

It is widely assumed that sports teams, particularly baseball clubs, have a responsibility to their fans as well as to their owners. This "fan responsibility myth" has affected the law (Sports Broadcasting Act of 1961,

NFL blackout rules) and could easily move Congress to action under certain circumstances. For example, any attempt to move postseason baseball to pay television would engender much congressional posturing and threats of new legislation. Thus, while the fan responsibility myth is vital to team owners pursuing public subsidies for new parks, it does restrain the actions of leagues and individual teams.

The public nature of sports is alien to many mammoth corporations. Perhaps CBS executives expected to be chewed out by Congress over Janet Jackson's exposed right breast as a result of network's public interest obligations, though even so the network fought back with legal action. Yet most corporations in the era of deregulation expect little congressional scrutiny. Sports are different, however. Any labor dispute or structural change is local and national news to tens of millions of fans.

Vertical Integration: Back to the Future?

The divestiture of sports team ownership by media conglomerates is not evidence of a decline in the importance of sports to media and media to sports. In fact, there appears to be a movement back to a traditional form of vertical integration in which teams (producers) control the distribution and exhibition of their own product. New York's YES network is the exemplar of this trend. YES feeds millions of dollars of revenue into the coffers of its majority owner: the Yankees.[27] The Yankees do not have to share revenue with another company such as Fox, the dominant owner-operator of RSNs.

The multiple distribution systems provided through satellite, cable, and Internet transmission offer realistic ways for sports teams to become their own producers, distributors, and exhibitors. This infrastructure makes it possible for them to offer game coverage targeted to different types of viewers at different prices. Coverage can be in high or standard definition, with or without digital enhancements, in packages focusing on only one team or featuring all of the league's televised games. With pay-per-view or full-season premium packages, a relatively small core of fans could generate huge amounts of new money for popular teams, even as most fans continue to get their coverage through established cable and broadcast networks.

Of course, as the new team-owned RSNs and their related businesses begin to generate substantial revenues, teams may again become acquisition targets for major media firms. The sports-media business cycle we seem to be leaving could reemerge. In sum, the recent divestitures do not in any way represent a trend toward the separation of big media and big sports. Major sports offer major benefits to scores of television and other media entities, including branding, demographic appeal, and, to a limited degree, international marketing (e.g., the Yankees have a co-marketing arrangement with Manchester United).[28] The development of new team-owned RSNs is just the latest permutation of the dynamic marriage of big media and big sports.

How the Game
Was Covered

4

The Announcer in the Television Age

The story of announcers and their struggle to capture baseball on both radio and television has been well documented. In his 1970 book, *The Broadcasters*, announcing legend Red Barber wrote the first extensive history of the baseball announcing craft. But the most lasting contribution to our understanding of that craft is Curt Smith's *Voices of the Game* and his subsequent books, *The Storytellers* and *Voices of Summer*.[1] Smith has chronicled the experiences of virtually every Major League Baseball announcer. In addition, because of their popularity with fans, our most important baseball announcers have left no shortage of oral histories documenting their personal experiences. Our task in this chapter is not to retell those individual stories but to focus on the special challenges that baseball presents to the television announcer and how announcers, over the decades, have addressed them. But first we ask: What makes one announcer more successful than another? What leads to legendary stature for those "voices of the game?"

"MAT" Makes for Greatness

For the successful baseball announcer, familiarity breeds, not contempt, but friendship. The everyday relationship that an announcer has with a fan necessitates a personality that wears well over time. But what makes one announcer a legend and a candidate for the announcers' wing of the Baseball Hall of Fame, while another has only a successful career? We believe that "superstar" baseball announcers often are engendered by an interaction of three elements: the nature of media they use, the announcers' own talents, and the quality and location of teams they cover. This is what we will call the "MAT" (medium, announcer, team) theory of announcing fame.

The superstar announcer emerges from the intersection of just the right combination of MAT. Legendary announcers often come to prominence after special conditions are introduced into the media environment. Red Barber and Mel Allen capitalized on the end of the radio embargo in New York to become that city's most beloved announcers of the radio era. Dizzy Dean's immense popularity was partially a product of the creation of a national baseball game of the week two years after the completion of the first national television networks. His rural appeal was perfectly suited to the small-market audience created by blackout rules that excluded cities with Major League franchises from the telecasts.

Vin Scully's superior skills as a radio announcer were well suited to the needs of the new Los Angeles Dodgers franchise, whose television policy severely restricted telecasts into the 1980s. In the 1950s and the 1960s, Scully would become the voice of the Dodgers and the fans' window to the team, just as his mentor Barber had been in the 1940s. He even profited from the Dodgers' first few years in cavernous Los Angeles Coliseum, where fans often listened to Scully on their transistor radios, so they could "see" the game from their distant seats.

Harry Caray exploited two media transformations. He benefited first from the rapid expansion of the Cardinals' radio network in the 1940s and 1950s to become a voice recognized throughout the southern and western United States at a time when MLB had no franchises in those regions. His career bloomed a second time with the creation of the cable television superstation WGN. Starting in 1982, Caray's fan-friendly style entertained a now national audience for the Chicago Cubs.

However, changes in the media environment are not enough to ensure legendary stature. Each of these announcers had special talents well suited to the new media configuration. Red Barber and Vin Scully had the superior language skills characteristic of the best radio announcers. Mel Allen and Harry Caray announced with flamboyant style and infectious enthusiasm. Dizzy Dean brought a larger-than-life personality and his own version of the English language to his down-home audience. Other announcers without the necessary talent were unable to exploit the new media environment. After his retirement in 1951, Joe DiMaggio, the most popular player of his era, flopped as television performer because of his reserved personality and inability to improvise (even DiMaggio's interviews had to be fully scripted). Announcers' talents remain a key component of their success. They add the "A" to our MAT theory.

Finally, legendary announcers often have the good fortune of calling the games of some legendary teams: the "T" in our theory. Barber and Scully benefited from the long run of great Dodger teams, starting in the late 1940s and running through the mid-1960s. Scully also was positioned to receive the affection of enthusiastic Los Angeles fans excited when Major League Baseball finally arrived in 1958. Allen presided over a Yankee dynasty that appeared in fifteen World Series and won ten world championships between 1947 and 1964. Caray covered championship Cardinals teams in the late 1940s and 1960s. In his third year with the Cubs, he had the great fortune of watching the long-dormant franchise win the 1984 NL Eastern Division Championship and come within one game of their first World Series appearance since 1945. Successful teams bring national attention to their players, managers, and even announcers, making it possible for talented voices to be more widely recognized. The location of a successful team in a major media market (New York, Los Angeles, Chicago) also makes it much more likely that the announcer's gifts will receive national acclaim.

Television versus Radio

In one sense, the difference between television and radio is obvious. Since television offers pictures and radio does not, the announcer in television must acknowledge the role of the picture in constructing the baseball telecast. For some, this means that the announcer's role is diminished because the picture is the primary attraction and the primary source of information about the game. But for others, television enhances the role of the announcer by freeing him from simply describing the game. In radio, silence or "dead air" is considered a taboo. But in television, brief periods of silence are hardly noticed because the picture can sustain the broadcast. In fact, announcers have often been critically acclaimed because they know exactly when to "shut up" and "let the picture tell the story." Words-delivered-per-minute, often cited as a rough measure of a radio announcer's skill, was no longer relevant in the television age. In fact, radio sports legend Ted Husing, who was once clocked at four hundred words per minute, was criticized for talking too much during telecasts.[2] Conversely, Hall of Fame announcer Vin Scully won acclaim for his response to Hank Aaron's recorded-breaking 715th home run. He simply stepped away from his microphone and poured himself a fresh cup of coffee, letting the sounds of the crowd and the pictures on the screen carry the scene. Years later, reflecting on his role in one of baseball's most historic moments, Scully mused, "What am I supposed to say? He hit a home run?"[3] Television releases the radio announcer from the burden of describing all significant on-field activity and the pressure of filling every moment of the broadcast with an uninterrupted flow of words.

The earliest television announcers, who had learned their craft in the radio age, commented extensively on how television was changing their descriptions of the on-field activities. For Dizzy Dean, television coverage of Yankee games on WABD was not a major adjustment: "Only difference between television and radio is they ain't so much to talk about in television. If a batter is taking his stanch [sic] at the plate, all you got to do is name him. They ain't no point in saying he is taking his stanch at the plate."[4]

Mel Allen saw TV as "tough on the announcer" because he had to monitor both the live action and game monitor at the same time. However, Allen thought that the medium would "breed a more accurate group of sportscasters in the future" because "there is a large, critical audience listening to—and watching."[5] Allen also saw an end to "time-honored clichés as 'Here's the wind-up and the pitch,'" thus allowing the announcer more time to teach fans "the intricacies of the game." But many listeners accused Allen of offering too much "idle chatter," or as the verbally challenged Yogi Berra put it, using "too many woids."[6]

In 1948, Jack Brickhouse, who announced both Cubs and White Sox games and most other televised sports, expressed the difference between television and radio as a percentage of the words used by a radio announcer in reporting a contest. Televised boxing required only 50 percent of the "wordage" used for a radio description of the same contest, while basketball required 60 percent. Televised baseball required 80 per-

29. *In the radio age, the announcer was the show. Here a young Mel Allen shows how simple radio could be. National Baseball Hall of Fame Library, Cooperstown NY.*

cent of words used for the radio version of the game. Brickhouse gave no indication of where these figures came from, saying only that they "are accepted generally at this time." Like Allen, Brickhouse believed that television would force announcers to improve their accuracy, claiming "if television forces an inaccurate announcer out of the sports field . . . it's probably something that should have happened to him long ago."[7]

Clearly, radio-era announcers needed to adjust to the demands of the visual image. One way to think of the announcer's role is to examine how he shapes his commentary to complement the visual portion of the

30. Throughout his long career, radio-trained Vin Scully knew when to stop talking and let the picture tell the story. *Herald Examiner Collection, Los Angeles Public Library.*

telecast. Lindsey Nelson, NBC's first game-of-the-week play-by-play announcer, saw himself "at the mercy of what pictures the producer and director show. . . . Your destiny is in someone else's hands."[8] For Vin Scully that meant following the director's vision as represented on the announcer's monitor. "In radio you're leading all the time, but in television you're a counterpuncher."[9]

But to get to the crux of the announcer's role, we need to ask what he contributes to our understanding and enjoyment of a baseball game regardless of the medium. In the history of televised sports, only one game has been telecast without an announcer, a 1980 NFL contest in Miami between the Dolphins and the New York Jets, scheduled primarily as a publicity stunt. Why does the visual medium of television seem to require announcers while the visual experience of attending the live event does not? Announcers are needed because they deliver to viewers three major elements: descriptions of game and game-related activities, analyses of those activities, and emotional responses to what is unfolding before their eyes.

Describing the Game

Describing on-field activities is clearly a major part of the announcer's job. The zenith of descriptive announcing was the game re-creation, when announcers used the sparse data offered by the Western Union telegraph wire to reconstruct an entire game with their own "word pictures." From the 1930s, re-creations were used primarily for away games that were far too costly to broadcast live in the era of limited radio networking. They gradually disappeared in the 1950s, as networking facilities improved. In 1955, the Pirates were the last Major League team to do away with road-game re-creations.[10]

Although certainly more important in radio where there is no picture, descriptions of on-field activities are a staple of baseball telecasts and a necessary one. As Jack Brickhouse observed: "The relatively small area covered by the camera often is not so sharp as the announcer may believe. A few words will help complete the picture."[11] Calling the balls and strikes and briefly describing the play and its outcome are common in television. The redundancy between the visual and audio channels is a factor in much of television and welcomed by viewers who are often monitoring the sound feed of a telecast while doing other things. One early study of television viewing found that viewers actually gave the screen their full attention only about 50 percent of the time.[12] The fact that one of televised baseball's standard two sportscasters is called a "play-by-play announcer" validates the centrality of describing on-field action.

The television announcer's description certainly differs from the radio announcer's. The television announcer will try to highlight key activities with minimal language, while the radio announcer must provide a "word picture" description from the same observation. Red Barber argued that "radio demands a fellow with a fluency of words and just a smattering of the game." The radio announcer also has more time to compose his description: "he can get around the ticklish spots . . . fence around until a decision comes through. But in television, you've got to be able to tell them what happens when it's happening."[13] Lindsey Nelson found television "much more stressful" than radio because in radio, "you can get out of trouble . . . because there's no picture; *nobody knows* it."[14] For the television announcer, descriptions should be short, enhance what the viewer can see, and coincide with what is on the screen at that moment. Speed and accuracy are paramount.

In 1956, Senators announcer Bob Wolff provided *Baseball* magazine with an action-by-action comparison of how to call a game sequence on radio and television:

> 1. RADIO: Jones looks in to get the sign. Here's the windup—and the pitch. TELEVISION: No comment necessary. (Sometimes during the game the sportscaster may comment on Jones' unusual windup, if he has one, or on any particular noteworthy mannerism which he displays on the mound.)
>
> 2. RADIO: Smith swings and misses for strike 2. TELEVISION: That's strike 2. (If the batter took a particularly hard cut at the ball, a comment might be added to the effect that "Smith was really trying to powder that one, wasn't he?" Or, "That was a mighty good curve ball that Jones dished up that time.")
>
> 3. RADIO: There's a hard hit ground ball going two hops to the shortstop, Johnny Brown. There's the throw to first and Smith is out on a close play. There are two away. TELEVISION: That's Brown making the throw. Two out.[15]

Wolff's comparison illustrates how the radio announcer must describe the action, while his television counterpart needs to highlight key information and provide analysis of action that the viewer cannot see.

Because of the verbal dexterity required, play-by-play announcers, particularly in the radio age, tended to come from the ranks of professional announcers rather than ex-players. Many of these radio-trained announcers (Red Barber, Mel Allen, Jack Brickhouse, and Harry Caray) were hired as staff announcers and then quickly gravitated to sports assignments. Red Barber claimed that his first announcing assignment for the University of Florida's educational radio station was to read a professor's paper entitled "Certain Aspects of Bovine Obstetrics."[16] However, there were exceptions. Hall of Fame pitcher Dizzy Dean, perhaps the most popular announcer of his era, was hardly a candidate for staff announcer. When asked only to read the sponsors' commercials as written, Dean balked, saying "if them sponsors wants me to sell their stuff, they ain't no use for them to write out pieces for me to read. If they'll leave me alone I'll really sell that stuff just as fast as a monkey can shin up a tree."[17]

Analyzing the Game

Though play-by-play is frequently the province of the professional announcer, the role of analyst or color commentator is usually the realm of the ex-player, and occasionally ex-manager or even ex-umpire. The reason is obvious. The professional announcer is supposed to excel at verbal descriptions of the game, but the analyst at his side has the direct experience with the contests that no outsider can ever fully understand. There has always been tension between the player analyst and the professional announcer over who really contributes the most to the coverage of the game. This schism is probably best summed up in the title of one of Howard Cosell's most successful books, *I Never Played the Game*. No matter how articulate, well prepared, or insightful, the professional announcer can never fully understand what is happening on and off the baseball field. From the ex-player–analyst's point of view, the professional wordsmith may be able to express eloquently what is easily observable on the field, but he can never provide a full explanation of why it is happening in just that way. From the announcer's point of view, on the other hand, the player-analyst certainly brings experience to the table, but cannot eloquently articulate his pearls of wisdom. Players have often gained access to the broadcast booth because of their name recognition rather than their ability to contribute to a telecast. Harry Caray advised aspiring announcers to first "become an all-American football or a baseball player. Get into the professional ranks, play ten years, and then they'll put you in the television booth."[18]

In practice, the dichotomy between the professional announcer and experienced player-analyst is not nearly so severe. The professional announcer occasionally flubs even a simple description, and his vast experience of the game culled from hundreds or even thousands of broadcasts means his analysis is hardly superficial. From the analyst's side, the truly inarticulate ex-player rarely lasts as a color announcer. One summer in the Fox television booth taught veteran MLB manager Lou Piniella just how tough announcing can be: "The amazing thing about the booth that people don't realize is that things happen a lot quicker up there than they do in the dugout. And you have to be able to articulate it. And they're talking in your ear when you're speaking."[19]

Though the typical announcing team still combines a professional announcer with many years of announcing experience and a player with many years playing experience, there are exceptions. If not always lauded for their verbal skills, several successful play-by-play announcers were ex-players, including Dizzy Dean, Waite Hoyt, Jerry Coleman, Bob Uecker, and Ken "Hawk" Harrelson. In recent years, ex-Cardinals and Phillies catcher Tim McCarver has been lauded as one of baseball's finest announcers, and Hall of Fame second baseman Joe Morgan has become a mainstay of ESPN's national cablecasts.[20] Many Cubs fans still lament the loss of the articulate, witty, and insightful Steve Stone, the 1980 American League Cy Young Award winner, after he left superstation WGN's booth.

The role of the analyst is to provide historical context for the game, educate fans about its finer points, provide statistical information about the players and the events on the field, and analyze the strategies being employed by the players and the opposing managers. Baseball, more than any other sport, provides substantial time to reflect on the relatively small number of events actually unfolding. The consensus among announcers is that there are only about two minutes of sustained action in every sixty minutes of play, with only one in four pitches being put into fair play. Buddy Blattner, Dizzy Dean's first *Game of the Week* sidekick and a longtime Kansas City announcer, outlined the temporal challenge a baseball announcer faces: "There's an average interval of 15 seconds between pitches. You've got to fill some of that dead air. You can't keep saying over and over that 'the pitcher gets set on the mound, tugs at his cap, etc.'"[21]

Because there is less need for description and more time for analysis, the color commentator is more important in television than in radio. Early regular-season radio broadcasts often used only one announcer; the additional color commentary did not become standard until the 1950s. For playoffs, All-Star Games, and World Series contests today, television booths often feature two analysts and a play-by-play announcer. Although critics will lament the wall-to-wall words that flow from the crowded booth, networks still approach these special contests with a "more is better" philosophy.

The player-turned-analyst also faces the challenge of staying current as his own vivid personal experiences slide into the past. A fifty-five-year-old ex-player extolling the virtues of teammates long retired is a good vehicle for alienating younger fans. By the end of his run in the mid-1960s, even the legendary Dizzy Dean's fans were starting to tire of the stories of his flamboyant 1930s Cardinals teammate Pepper Martin, "the Wild Horse of the Osage." By the mid-1970s, Joe Garagiola's stories about "Mr. Rickey" (Branch Rickey) were wearing thin on baseball's baby-boomer fans. Today's fans may lament Tim McCarver's frequent references to Cardinal pitching legend Bob Gibson. In addition, analysts must address the ever-widening knowledge gap among fans. Though new fans, especially children, need to be taught the basics of a very complex game, the most knowledgeable fans today have access to an ocean of information about the national pastime. With dozens of new baseball books published each season, a steady supply of newspaper and magazine articles, and an ever expanding mass of current information available on Internet sports news sites and fan blogs, the baseball "fan" can become the self-taught baseball "expert." The analyst must entertain and inform these sophisticated baseball fanatics without totally alienating the novice or casual customers. For the color commentator, knowing what to say and when to say it has never been more challenging.

Tapping Emotions

Beyond description and analysis, the baseball announcer brings an emotional presence to the game. These emotional responses are what fans most remember, most cherish, and, occasionally, are most offended by. As longtime Pirate announcer Rosy Rowswell told his radio pupil Bob

Prince, "It's not just the play-by-play that matters. It's what you say between the pitches that counts."[22] Announcers develop signature "calls" to sum up the games most intense moments. For most announcers, the home run call is the most well known. Harry Caray's "It might be, it could be, it is!"; Hawk Harrelson's "You can put it on the board, Yesss!"; Bob Prince's "You can kiss it good-bye!"; Jack Brickhouse's "Hey, Hey!"; and Chris Berman's "Back, Back, Back" are just a few of the many memorable labels for the homer. The signature home run call is so ubiquitous that when it isn't forthcoming it catches viewers by surprise. In game seven of the 1965 World Series, Twins announcer Ray Scott's call of Dodger outfielder Lou Johnson's critical fourth inning four-bagger contained just two flatly delivered words: "home run."

But home run calls are hardly the only announcing catch phrases. Most announcers have a trademark exclamation that fits an array of on-field events. For Harry Caray and Phil Rizzuto, "Holy Cow!" could denote both the most positive and most negative moments, from great plays in the field to errors in critical situations. Mel Allen's "How about that?" captured his amazement at the latest Yankee heroics. For Hawk Harrelson, "Mercy" expresses the angst of the moment, while for Ron Santo a simple "Oh, no" does the job. Rosey Rowswell, forced to report the failings of the many last-place Pirate teams in the 1940s and early 1950s, developed many catch phrases: "FOB" for "the bases are full of Bucs," "dipsy-doodle" for a Pirate pitcher's strikeout, "doozie marooney" for an extra-base hit, "Oh, my aching back" after a loss, and "Put on the lamb chops. I'll be home soon" for a Bucco victory.[23] Rowswell's Pirate announcing progeny, Bob Prince, continued the verbal tradition with "closer than a gnat's eyelash" (close play), "bug on the rug" (ground ball hit on artificial turf), "we had 'em all the way" (Pirate victory), and many others. Red Barber adapted Rowswell's FOB to mean "full of Brooklyns" and created some of his trade's most famous expressions, including "rhubarb" for an argument and "catbird seat" for his own privileged perch. Most catch phrases capture the emotions of the moment while colorfully communicating what is happening on the field.

Announcers also bring interest to the game by adopting a persona that readily evokes particular emotions. First Joe Garagiola and then Bob

Uecker became renowned as baseball humorists, using the comic story-telling skills they developed on baseball's banquet circuit. Garagiola's first book, the bestseller *Baseball Is a Funny Game* published in 1960, established him as a national figure and paved the way for his long career at N BC. Uecker's skill as a jokester led to a successful situation comedy in the mid-1980s, *Mr. Belvedere*; a string of commercials for Miller Lite beer; and film roles, including the whiskey-sipping baseball announcer Harry Doyle in the feature film *Major League*.

At the opposite end of the emotional scale from the humorist are the provocateurs: announcers who stir controversy and provoke anger at their club or even themselves. Harry Caray had many run-ins with players, managers, and owners over his long career because he was willing to openly criticize players. In *The Pennant Race*, one of baseball's first "insider" books, relief pitcher Jim Brosnan's summed up the struggling player's point of view on Caray's carryings-on. "To hell with Tomato-Face. He's one of those emotional radio guys. All from the heart, y'know? I guess he thinks I'm letting the Cardinals down, and he's taking it as a personal insult."[24] But Caray was quick to justify his provocative approach: "The trouble with the players is they feel the fan is so dumb he won't notice their shortcomings unless an announcer calls attention to them. Well the fan isn't that stupid. The announcer doesn't create a player's weaknesses."[25] Foreshadowing the combative atmosphere of contemporary sports talk radio and television, Caray teamed with volatile ex-player Jimmy Piersall to create perhaps the most openly critical announcing team ever as they covered the White Sox from 1977 to 1981. Even controversial White Sox owner Bill Veeck, no stranger to criticism, found Caray difficult to take at times. "Frankly, I hate to listen to him when we're losing because he can put the greatest degree of contempt in what he's saying."[26]

Although not primarily a baseball announcer, perhaps the most extreme provocateur was Howard Cosell, who appeared on ABC's *Monday Night Baseball* and postseason telecasts from the mid-1970s to the mid-1980s. Cosell's job, established first on *Monday Night Football*, was to provoke controversy by "telling it like it is," which helped to make the weekly telecasts "special" events worthy of prime-time placement. The conflict could come with his fellow announcers, with players and managers, or even with the sport itself. In the mid-1970s, his savage criticism of baseball, a game he viewed as "boring," made him an outcast in the sport, a role he seemed to enjoy. By the end of his life, Cosell had become one of televised sports most vocal critics (see chapter 6).

Announcers also tap viewers' and listeners' emotions by developing a strong personal friendship with the fans. During his time in Chicago, Harry Caray become the unofficial "Mayor of Rush Street" because he so enjoyed partying with White Sox and, in later years, with Cubs fans after the games. During the broadcasts, he saw himself as the voice of the fan. Fittingly, Caray's Hall of Fame plaque photo shows him calling a game surrounded by fans in the Comiskey Park bleachers. But the announcer who most intimately connected to his fans was Dizzy Dean. In the 1940s and 1950s, Dean became the virtual spokesperson for rural America. His notorious problems with the English language were a source of endearment to his many small-town fans.

Also tapping viewer emotions are announcers who are unabashed fans of the teams they cover. Their emotional power comes from the empathy they express for teams and especially their players. These "homers" are generally less critical of their teams, although they do not totally overlook poor play. However, their delight in their team's successes and disappointments in its failures are perceived by fans as genuine. Mel Allen, considered a classic homer, believed that the announcer needed to distinguish between "partisanship," which is fine, and "prejudice," which is not. For Allen, rooting for your team was no problem, but distorting your description in its favor was a sin. One Allen listener told him that "all I have to do is listen to the tone of your voice when I tune in, and I know instantly whether the Yankees are winning or losing."[27]

Many critics saw Bob Prince as baseball's most pronounced homer. For *Voices of the Game* author Curt Smith and many Pirates fans from the 1950s to the 1970s, "*Bob Prince* was the Pirates."[28] Prince would openly cheerlead, inventing hexes, for example, such as the "green weenie," to jinx the opposition and boost the Buccos' chances. Because of his close identification with the Pirates, Prince could not make a successful transition to the national stage for ABC's 1976 edition of *Monday Night Baseball* (see chapter 6).

Although homers have gradually become more accepted, announcers who viewed themselves as reporters first and fans second have been critical of the "Mid-west Cheerleading School" of baseball announcing.[29] In particular, Red Barber often expressed concern about the "trend of broadcasters being unabashed rooters for their own clubs."[30] The critics of homers are concerned that their "partisanship" will shift to "prejudice," and they will overlook their teams' flaws. But what is the appropriate level of "objectivity" for the baseball announcer? Are they reporters or are they promoters?

Announcer as Reporter, Announcer as Promoter

As a reporter, the television announcer must report the events on the field with a high degree of accuracy because the audience can see his errors if he does not. But an announcer's commentary moves beyond simple description, providing an interpretation of the events on the field. Interpretation is inherently subjective. Two analysts will often interpret the same events very differently. What factors can influence that interpretation? Clearly, the announcer's own values, beliefs, and experiences with the game will have a strong impact on his interpretation. One of the stronger arguments for increasing ethnic and gender diversity in announcing booths predominantly staffed with white males is that different groups will provide a different perspective on the game based on their own personal baseball history. What about influence from above (the administrative type, not the divine), however? How much independence can announcers have as they "report" on the very teams that employ them?

Some of the most respected radio-era announcers thought of themselves as reporters first and promoters second. Socialized in the era when objective, socially responsible journalism was becoming the norm for major metropolitan newspapers, Red Barber and his most famous pupil, Vin Scully, demanded independence from their employers. In Barber's obituary in *Sports Illustrated*, distinguished baseball writer Robert Creamer reminded readers that "Barber thought of himself as a reporter, not a showman or a shill."[31] Barber's honest reporting of the paltry attendance of 413 for a Yankee home game during the end of a disastrous 1966 season was widely seen as a major reason for his firing by the Yankees. After his request for the cameras to show the nearly empty stands was refused, Barber told his viewers, "I don't know what the paid attendance is today—but whatever it is, it is the smallest crowd in the history of Yankee stadium . . . and this smallest crowd is the story, not the ball game."[32] Within a week, the Yankees let Barber know that his services were no longer needed. Harry Caray's popularity with fans gave him special clout with management and the latitude to criticize players and managers. Vin Scully claimed that the Dodger brass never interfered in his broadcasts. "Many a time I've said the Dodgers blew the game or it was a bad play on somebody's part. We're strictly reporters."[33] Most announcers did not have that kind of freedom.

Early on, baseball writers noted problems with team interference. Brooklyn sportswriter Michael Gaven called baseball broadcasts "government radio," comparable to broadcasts controlled by communist governments that disseminated "official propaganda": "Some broadcasters call themselves 'Reporters on the Air,' but they are not reporters as long as they . . . can lose their jobs at a whim of the club owner."[34] In one sense, baseball writers were defending their turf; only they, independent of the clubs, could honestly report on the sport. The writers conveniently ignored the fact that clubs gave them ready access to players and managers, not to mention free press-box meals, hoping for favorable treatment in exchange.

Even announcers employed by sponsors instead of the teams were not expected to criticize the product on the field. In 1952, Indians television announcer Bob Neal "violated what appears to be an unwritten law in this trade," Baseball Digest reported, by criticizing an Indians pitcher on the air. His sponsor promptly "slapped Neal's wrist in public." Neal's crime was to conclude that "a pitcher who can't get the ball over the plate doesn't belong in major league baseball."[35]

Some teams were very clear about their promotional expectations. The flamboyant Charlie Finley, longtime owner of the Athletics, made it clear that the announcer's job was to promote the team. As a result, A's announcers could be fountains of fluff. Oakland announcer Red Rush was cited in a 1971 Sports Illustrated article for offering these niceties:

"This is some kind of ball game."

"This Sal Bando is some kind of player."

"This Rick Monday can sure pick 'em up and lay 'em down."

"Hey, the crowd is on the edge of its seats. This is some kind of crowd."

And that was some kind of puffery. Finley was not the only owner pressuring announcers. The Reds "expect their announcers to refrain from saying anything negative," while Phillies vice president Bill Giles proclaimed that the announcer's role was "to make us look as good as possible."[36]

Onetime Washington Senators owner Bob Short told announcer Shelby Whitfield not to give the scores of the rival National League's games, not to report that the Senators had left men on base, and to avoid saying that it was raining at the game because it might discourage fans from coming to the contest. Whitfield appropriately entitled one of the chapters of this "tell-all" book "Radio Moscow Has More Freedom."[37] Short felt no reason to apologize for his interference: "I don't think a man broadcasting your games should be deprecating the product, and the best way to make sure he doesn't is to see that you're in a hire-and-fire situation."[38]

Even if the owners did not apply direct pressure, announcers, particularly ex-players, often found it difficult to criticize their own teams. Announcers traveled with the team, appeared at team promotions with players, and became friends with both players and owners, making it difficult to offer objective analysis. For a while, Cubs announcer Jack Brickhouse even served on his team's board. Yankee announcer Phil Rizzuto would gently note the poor fielding of Yankee players, but "I try not to overdo it. I played baseball and I know that errors are part of the game."[39] Fans often assumed that the announcer was part of the team, not an independent voice. Lindsey Nelson reported that "if I walk down Fifth Avenue I'm stopped by people asking, 'What are you going to do about the Mets?'"[40]

National telecast announcers, although not as directly affiliated with any particular team, were also criticized for promoting the glories of the game and their network while remaining silent about its problems. In an article bylined "Cyclops," *Life* magazine found problems with NBC's coverage of the 1971 All-Star Game in Detroit. Curt Gowdy and Tony Kubek were criticized for ignoring Tiger fans' snubbing of Orioles manager Earl Weaver during pregame introductions. Tiger fans were upset because Weaver had been reluctant to add Tiger first baseman Norm Cash to the American League All-Star team. Among Gowdy and Kubek's other apparent oversights was failing to note that for the first time the All-Star Game's two starting pitchers were African American and to report the excessively large strike zone of the home plate umpire. As *Life* put it, for baseball's TV talkers, "the game we're watching exists wholly outside of any social or historical context."[41]

The ambiguity surrounding the sports announcers' real loyalties came to a head in 1974. The FCC took the position that viewers need to know just who was paying the salaries of their team's announcers. At the time, twenty-four of the eighty professional sports teams hired their own announcers. In August, the FCC told broadcasters: "Licensees and networks are hereby notified that, effective October 16, 1974, they will be required to disclose clearly, publicly and prominently during each broadcast of an athletic event, the existence of any arrangement whereby announcers broadcasting that event may be directly or indirectly, chosen, paid, approved and/or removed by parties other than the licensee and/or network upon which that event is broadcast."[42]

As a result of the FCC's action, announcers now read disclaimers during telecasts to make it clear who employs them.

Controlling the Telecast: Announcer versus Director

Both radio and television announcers have always faced some degree of interference from owners or sponsors, but the television announcer must also share the telecast with many production partners. As noted earlier, television announcers must follow the visual leads given by the directors and producers who are in charge of the production. Although he would fight it for several years, Red Barber had to share command with, and eventually lost command to, an anonymous "technician" squirreled away in the depths of Ebbets Field. That technician was the television director.

31. *Red Barber covering the Yankees. "The Old Redhead" would try to keep the announcer in charge of the telecast. National Baseball Hall of Fame Library, Cooperstown NY.*

In radio, Red and his fellow announcers called the game and the shots. Like famed umpire Bill Klem, who often reminded batters that, until he called it, a pitched ball was nothing at all, Barber knew that the action on a baseball field was nothing at all until he made the call. For the radio listener, Red Barber *was* the game and with that came the fame. In television, Red could still call the game, but the director was calling the camera shots. Barber understood television better than any other baseball announcer. The "old redhead" called the first televised Major League game on August 26, 1939, at Ebbets Field (see chapter 1). It was also the first game covered by two cameras, which meant that the director would have a choice of what to show and when to show it.

At first, there was little coordination between picture and sound: the announcer called his game and the director called his. Barber could see that this situation would have to change. And a monitor was introduced. The monitor turned out to be the director's Trojan horse. It brought a different view of the game, and it wasn't Barber's view, an eye sharpened by more than a decade of training. It was the view of an outsider and one that he, the best-loved announcer in baseball, was supposed to follow. Barber and all his announcing colleagues were unhappy about it. However, unlike his peers, Barber fought back.

After the 1949 season, Red Barber developed, employed, and ultimately abandoned the signal panel. This was a shallow box with a two-foot square surface area. On the grass-green surface, sketched in bright white lines was a baseball field with clearly defined infield, dugouts, and bullpens. At each of these areas on the field and at each player's position was a bubbled light and an on/off toggle switch lever. In the director's control room, wedged in with all of the other equipment, was an identical signal box connected by cable to Barber's in the announcer's booth.

The operation was simple. When Barber threw a lever at, say, left field to the "on" position, the amber light glowed in left field on the director's signal box. Barber's command was clear: focus a camera on the left fielder because Barber had something to say about that player. The signal box was Barber's mongoose set to kill the director's video cobra, the monitor. Whenever he wanted he could direct the director. Red Barber was back in control.

But the signal box was not the answer. Despite the age-old criticism that baseball games move too slowly, the game often moved much too fast for the signal box to be of much use. When the action was slow, it worked well. But when things picked up, Barber had to decide what to ask for and then flip the switch to ask for it. Then the harried director had to see the amber light, tell the cameraman to shift his focus, wait for the cameraman to adjust the focus, and tell the video switcher to cut to Barber's requested camera. It all took too much time.

After an initial period of experimentation, Barber used the signal board less and less. The television director and his producer inevitably gained exclusive control of the picture. From that point on, televised baseball became a directors' game. In our next chapter, we explore how those directors changed their approaches to covering baseball over the next forty years.

14

Innovations in Production Practices

The evolution of the production practices used in televised baseball is a rich topic that merits book-length treatment. In the past seven decades, the changes have been dramatic. NBC's first televised game in May 1939 featured only one camera, while Fox's coverage of the 2006 World Series employed 28.[1] Although there have been periods of relative stagnation, today's high-definition digital telecasts have as much in common with the first World Series coverage in 1947 as the Internet has with the telegraph. As we noted earlier, until the mid-1960s, baseball owners sought to limit innovations in television's coverage of the game out of fear that high-quality television would erode attendance. But the creation of the first truly national contracts with ABC in 1965 and NBC in 1966 forged a partnership between MLB and the television industry—at first dysfunctional, but gradually growing stronger. Since the first national contracts, networks and stations have actively promoted the quality of their work. Formally faceless technicians, such as NBC's longtime director Harry Coyle and Chicago superstation WGN's director Arne Harris, have been applauded in the national and local press.

At its heart, the goal of television production is rarely artistic expression, but the efficient, flawless creation of a telecast on a rigid schedule within a prescribed budget using professional standards. Like any mass-audience production process, once the technology and technique are sufficiently developed to produce an acceptable product, there is minimal incentive to innovate. Television producers accept the axioms that you "don't mess with success" and "if it ain't broken, don't fix it." However, as we shall see in this chapter, innovations do happen, and the "product" does improve over time. But what promotes that improvement? What motivates networks and stations to make a better "ballcast?"

The Roots of Innovation

First, improvements in television technology promote innovations in baseball's coverage. Although new technologies are increasingly developed specifically for sportscasts (e.g., the telestrator, disc recorders for instant replay), most innovations spring from larger developments in television and related technologies. Color television was first applied to studio programs and gradually introduced into remote telecasts, making its first national baseball appearance at the 1955 All-Star Game. Forty-two years later, digital high-definition television (HDTV) baseball was introduced at Baltimore's Camden Yards.[2] Videotape technology premiered in the mid-1950s, allowing networks to replay programs in order to adjust for time zone differences. Videotape then became the first technology used for instant replay in the 1960s. Portable cameras first used to cover political conventions were quickly applied to sports. Later, miniature cameras developed for surveillance spawned on-the-field cameras, including catcher and diamond cams. Ever since the 1970s, the rapid development of personal computer technology has led to increased use of graphics on baseball telecasts.

Typically, new technology is introduced in sports telecasts relatively quickly, since sports are high-profile programs with costly rights fees and more technologically interested viewers. Because the rights fees are so high, the extra expense associated with using the newest technologies represents a small addition to the overall cost of the telecasts. As the television industries retool with newer technologies, they become part of sports productions simply because the technology is available and technicians are excited to use the latest "toys."

This technological push from the television industry does not account for the timing of an innovation's introduction, however. Premier sports events, such as baseball's World Series, playoffs, and All-Star Game, promote innovation. This trend has become even more pronounced as the rights fees paid by networks to cover these events have skyrocketed (see chapter 7). Color television, split-screen images, in-the-stands interviews, cameras embedded in the ground, even the center field camera, were introduced to national audiences at baseball's spotlight games. In some cases, the introductions were gimmicks that faded quickly, while others, such as colorcasts and the center field camera, gradually became standard practice in network and local telecasts. The All-Star Game is frequently used to try out new techniques before their multigame use in the postseason. Since the All-Star Game is an exhibition and does not affect the pennant races or Championship Series, MLB has been willing to let the contests serve as televised baseball's experimental laboratory.

As in most industries, competition among television networks promotes technical innovation. This is especially true of sports coverage, where the basic game remains the same regardless of which network or station telecasts it. Thus, networks must offer some variation in their coverage to differentiate themselves from their rivals. When NBC challenged CBS with a competing game of the week in 1957, CBS installed a miniature (for its day) "videon" camera behind home plate, offering viewers an umpire's view of the proceedings. CBS may have gotten the idea from the Brooklyn Dodgers, who introduced a low home camera during their 1956 games in Jersey City.[3] But CBS's tinkering was minor compared to ABC's alterations when it captured the weekly telecasts in 1965. Having built its reputation as sports television's most innovative network, ABC brought striking advances to the MLB telecast table, including isolated instant replay, field microphones, and a separate camera for each base runner.[4] Although ABC held the game-of-the-week contract for only a year, it forced NBC to dramatically alter is coverage. NBC's 1965 coverage of the World Series featured videotaped replays, prerecorded audio analysis from key players, and enhanced animated graphics.[5]

When ABC and NBC began sharing the national contract in 1976, competition led to a camera "arms race." After NBC used eleven cameras for the 1978 World Series, ABC raised the number to fourteen for the 1979 fall classic.[6] When CBS wrestled the national contract away from them, it increased the number of All-Star Game cameras to sixteen, including one embedded in the first base bag and two in blimps.[7] Fox has proved the most innovative of the competing broadcast networks, however, adding FoxBox graphics, more embedded cameras, improved sound, and FoxTrax strike-zone graphics that brought critical acclaim to its telecasts, including a 1996 Emmy Award for its World Series coverage.[8] In short, competition among networks sharing the national contract and the shifting of the national contract to a new network promote innovation in production practices.

Although local stations conducted the first experiments in baseball coverage, in more recent times innovations have typically trickled down from the national to the local game. The development of national networks and game-of-the-week broadcasts starting in the early 1950s made it possible for producers and directors from across the nation to see the latest network advances. Local broadcast stations and regional cable sports networks operate with much more restricted budgets than national networks, forcing some economies in production. National networks introduce innovations to enhance their products, and these are gradually adopted by most game producers. For example, the FoxBox graphics that summarize key game information were introduced by the network in 1996 and are now a standard part of game coverage. The center field camera, nationally introduced by NBC in its World Series and All-Star Game telecasts of the mid-1950s, gradually became universal and replaced the high home camera as the most common televised perspective on the game. Even when a technology is first introduced at the local level, such as WGN's use of the center field camera at a 1951 Little League game or the colorcasts of 1951 Brooklyn Dodgers contests, the technique or technology does not disseminate widely until it becomes established practice at the national level.

The Challenge of Baseball

Most popular sports play on a rectangular field in which the action moves horizontally or in a ring or court where it is contained in a relatively modest-sized space. Football, basketball, ice hockey, and soccer, among others, provide broadcasters with action that moves from left to right or right to left. One camera panning right to left can cover the essential horizontal game action. Boxing, wrestling, and tennis all confine the action to a limited space in which most moves can be covered by a single camera in a fixed position. All of these sports are now covered by multiple cameras, but the basic action on the field, rink, or ring can be conveyed successfully with only one camera using a simple horizontal

32. The earliest games often used two press-box cameras like these in Yankee stadium.
National Baseball Hall of Fame Library, Cooperstown NY.

movement and lens zooms. This is not the case in baseball. A director
can present a wide-angle shot that would show the entire field, capturing
all of the game action, but the individual actions of the players would be
difficult to see and the ball almost impossible to locate. In most sports,
the basic action is predictable. A football, soccer, basketball, or hockey
team's offense will be moving, or at least trying to move, in one direction.
When possession of the ball or puck is lost, the other team will always be
moving in the opposite direction. As once former baseball director put
it: "My first sport was hockey. I was a complete nonfan but it turns out
to be one of the easiest games to do, as opposed to baseball. Any court
game where the puck or ball is going back and forth is easier. . . . If I had
walked fresh into a baseball game, it would have been a whole different
story."[9] Similarly, a boxing, wrestling, or tennis contest features fast action, but always within a restricted space.

In baseball, the director only knows that action will usually start with the ball being thrown from the pitcher toward the catcher; after that it could fly or bounce in any direction, land in the catcher's glove, or roll to the backstop. Of course, even the pitcher's initial toss isn't perfectly predictable; he might ignore the batter and try to pick a runner off on first, second or even third.

The size of its field and unpredictability of its action gave baseball telecasters a huge handicap, particularly in television's formative years (see chapter 2). The relative popularity of televised baseball during this period is a testimony to the public's appetite for the sport even when it was covered with just two or three cameras, one or two of them high behind home plate and one in the upper deck on the first base side of the field. As early as 1946, one critic argued that stations would need at least five cameras to cover the game adequately.[10] Once regular telecasts of games began in 1947, coverage improved steadily. By 1951, WOR was covering Brooklyn Dodger games with five cameras: one from the press box behind home, and two on both first and third base sides of the field (one in the upper deck stands and one by the dugout). This basic configuration, with the addition of a camera in center field, is still in use today (see figure 35 showing placement at a 2006 Chicago Cubs game).

Though most sports could be covered adequately with two or three cameras, the director of televised baseball had to oversee twice as many, each assigned to cover different aspects of a visually volatile game. More cameras meant more shot changes and, thus, more split-second decisions. A short thirty-seven-second sequence from the sixth game of the 1975 World Series between the Reds and Red Sox shows just how fast the pace could be. In the bottom of the first inning, Fed Lynn hits a three-run homer into the right-field stands at Fenway Park. This single act is recorded in a sequence of nine shots using six cameras:

1. The center field camera has a loose shot of the runner on second, the pitcher, Lynn, the catcher, and the umpire as Lynn hits the ball.
2. The high home camera picks up the ball in flight and follows it into the right-field stands.
3. The high third base camera shows Carl Yastrzemski scoring.

4. The high first base camera shows Lynn rounding second base.

5. The lower third base camera shows the crowd cheering.

6. The high third base camera shows Lynn approaching home.

7. The high first base camera shows Lynn touch home as three teammates greet him.

8. The camera in Fenway's left-field "Green Monster" shows Red Sox dugout and fans above it cheering.

9. The high third base camera shows a closer shot of Lynn being congratulated by his teammates in the Red Sox dugout.

The sequence is followed by a slow-motion, stop-action close-up replay of Lynn's swing covered by a seventh camera, an additional one in center field. There is nothing extraordinary in this sequence; it is just one wave of action in a sea of events that unfolded in a twelve-inning game that was ended by Carlton Fisk's dramatic and often replayed home run. The NBC crew even "missed" one significant moment: Fisk scoring the second of the three runs just after Yastrzemski. Directors calling the camera-shot changes and their technical directors making them on video switchers must concentrate intensely for three or more hours with only commercial breaks offering rest for the weary.

Using "PLS" (personal lines), directors maintain constant communication with their camera crews. But if directors are lucky, they rarely need to supply verbal direction because their camera operators instantly follow the changing action, offering directors the shots they need just as they realize they need it. Directors often remark on their complete dependence on their camera operators' talent. With skill and luck the director and crew give the viewer the essential action, missing nothing of significance. To improve his crew's skills and reduce its need for luck, NBC's Harry Coyle wrote a fourteen-page manual detailing each camera operator's assignment during the game's most common plays. "Harry's Bible" of baseball was the blueprint for NBC's national telecasts.

When things went well, Coyle, other directors, and their crews usually were rewarded with anonymity, since the best coverage did not call attention to itself or intrude on the game. Harry Coyle insisted that his job was "to be a reporter first. That's why the public tuned in—to see a ball game, not a vaudeville show." Although pitching perfection is possible

33. Harry Coyle was the most recognized director of televised baseball.
NBC used his reputation to differentiate its coverage from ABC's.
National Baseball Hall of Fame Library, Cooperstown NY.

even in a World Series, Coyle saw missed shots as a given in his reporting assignment, lamenting, "I don't think anyone will have a perfect game as a director."[11] When the crew's work is noticed, it was usually because a crucial play was missed, leaving viewers frustrated. For Coyle, the television director's experience of a fast-paced, high-pressure environment featuring constant headset communication was familiar; he was a pilot during the Second World War.

In 1950, Red Barber wrote that "the most interesting picture in all TV is that of the turmoil and tenseness and confusion which reigns behind the picture the public sees." Barber thought that the "director of baseball had the toughest job in TV." Directors of televised baseball worked in a cramped, intense, and often hot remote truck cut off from action on the field. Their cameras and headphones provided their only contact with the game. They were in charge of balancing the images from four cameras and coordinating a nineteen-member crew that had to keep up with the game's unpredictable changes.[12] If the baseball director of 1950 felt challenged by four cameras and a crew of nineteen, the twenty-first-century director must be truly stressed: he or she faces as many as twenty-eight camera monitors and oversees a crew numbering in the hundreds.

Camera Innovations: Clearer, Closer, and More

The developmental pattern for television cameras since the inception of televised baseball has been to produce images that are clearer, closer, and more focused on specific events. The first televised game on May 17, 1939, used only one iconoscope tube camera. It produced an image so fuzzy that it was almost impossible for viewers to follow the ball (see photograph in chapter 1). The second televised game and first televised MLB game that August used two iconoscope cameras, which produced a more coherent, if not necessarily clearer, coverage of the game's events. Image clarity improved as iconoscope tubes gave way to orthicon and then image-orthicon tubes in the mid-1940s. This improvement was especially noticeable in the lower light conditions produced by night and overcast day games. By the mid-1950s, black-and-white image orthicon cameras produced acceptable day and night images in stadiums that had been developed for spectator viewing during the pre-TV era. However, color television, introduced in the mid-1950s, produced new changes. The first-generation color cameras could not cover night games effectively. Moreover, the strong shadows cast in late-afternoon day games, common at the time, produced color shifts (see the section on color telecasts later in this chapter). As stadium lighting and color camera tubes improved in the 1960s, color replaced black-and-white telecasts entirely.

Camera images continued to improve gradually during the next three decades, but the basic standards for broadcast television set by the FCC in 1941—a 525-line interlaced analog signal—made dramatic improvements in picture clarity. The phased-in adoption of digital television standards using high-definition signals, begun in 1998 by stations in major markets, has led to dramatic improvements in image clarity. HD pictures rival projected 35-millimeter film, and their superior resolution is especially evident on large-screen LCD, plasma, and projection televisions. Because of FCC mandates, broadcast stations and networks have led the way in developing HD programming, including sports programming. A larger screen combined with a much sharper picture especially benefits baseball, where a wide-angle camera view is often required to capture the basic on-the-field action once the ball is put into play. Though baseball may not have been the ideal sport for television in the era of the small screen, the clearer, big-screen future appears more accommodating. The first high-definition MLB game, a contest between the home-team Orioles and visiting Indians, was broadcast on September 16, 1997 by Harris Corporation to an audience of executives and journalists on a 16-by-9-foot screen at the National Press Club. Harris's CEO, Phillip W. Farmer, argued that HDTV was "tailor-made for baseball" because fans would be "able to see a third more of the playing field in every shot with more than twice the clarity."[13] The Harris demonstration was timed to concur with congressional hearings urging broadcasters to offer more HD programming. The popularity of HD sports has forced both digital satellite and cable systems to expand their capacities for transmitting HD signals. Now all national network and most home games covered by local stations and regional sports networks are presented in both high and standard definition.

Getting Closer All the Time

The pursuit of clarity has persisted throughout the seventy-year history of broadcast television, but the quest for greater image magnification took only two decades. The iconoscope camera covering the first televised game in May 1939 had no lens magnification, and the results were disappointing. By the second TV game in August, NBC had already

34. At the 1959 All-Star Game in the cavernous LA Coliseum, a fan gets a better view of the game on television. National Baseball Hall of Fame Library, Cooperstown NY.

added a telephoto lens to get closer to the action. Throughout the 1940s lenses got longer, with a multi-lens rack of wide-angle, normal view, and telephoto lenses becoming common by end of the decade. Throughout the 1950s, stations and networks replaced these multi-lens turrets with much more flexible Zoomar or "zoom" lenses. The zoom lens was a boon to televised baseball because it was designed to start on a wider shot of action and then zoom quickly as the ball flies or bounces in an unpredictable direction. As we've seen, by 1959 directors had added special 80-millimeter-long lenses that provided magnifications from the center field camera so large that the commissioner of baseball objected because viewers, and possibly opposing managers, could see the catchers' signs.

Field camera lenses continued to improve levels of magnification until full-screen closeups of objects as small as a player's hand were possible. Recent memorable examples of extreme closeups include pinch runner Dave Roberts's hand beating the ball to second base during a critical steal in game four of the Red Sox's dramatic come-from-behind win over the Yankees on the way to the 2004 World Series. Another unforgettable image is the smudge of "dirt" on Tiger pitcher Kenny Rogers's hand during game two of the 2006 World Series, which provoked suspicions that Rodgers was "doctoring" the ball.

Quantity Improves Quality

Effective coverage of specific events on the field is contingent on three factors: the number of cameras, the skill of each camera operator, and the proficiency of the director and his technical director at switching camera shots as each play in the game unfolds. The first camera operators had been trained in television studio production, and some knew little about the game. Bernie London, who directed CBS's telecasts of Dodgers games in 1947, complained that "camera men in those days of TV would often ask, 'Where's first base?'" After one director requested a shot of the bullpen, his baseball-challenged operator asked, "Where are the bulls?"[14] Directors of televised baseball and their camera operators lost no time improving their craft, however. Baseball's daily telecasts in many markets spurred rapid improvement. For example, in only the first few seasons of televised baseball, crews in the New York market produced hundreds of games.[15] Camera operators received specific training in their responsibilities for any game event, and they were expected to understand the game's nuances. Although Harry Coyle's "bible" is the most famous training manual, it was not the only one. In the mid-1940s, P. K. Wrigley, owner of the Cubs, commissioned Capt. William Eddy of pioneer station WBKB to produce a manual for baseball telecasts.[16] As a result of increasingly professional training and experience, "the human factor" in game coverage would have less of an impact on the quality of telecasts.

As differences in experience and skill narrowed, effective game coverage increasingly depended on just how many cameras a director had at his disposal. With more cameras available to him, the director could assign each camera less responsibility for the game action, making it less likely that any significant event would be missed by all the cameras. Camera operators could take more risks, such as shooting tighter shots, because other cameras would still have the basic action covered if they "blew" the shot. Ric LaCivita, coordinating producer for CBS's 1990s baseball coverage, believed more cameras were part of a generational shift in baseball coverage. LaCivita argued that first-generation directors like Harry Coyle used cameras to cover the ball, while his camera followed the base runners. "Those guys from the 50's weren't risk-takers. I'm a risk-taker."[17] More cameras also meant more opportunities to cover off-the-field activities: celebrities in boxes behind home plate, emotional reactions from players' family members, the manager staring out of the dugout, and bench jockeys adjusting their rally caps.

Cameras could also be assigned to highlight shots that might not be needed to cover the on-field action but could provide dramatic emphasis during a replay sequence. For example, at the 2005 World Series, an isolated replay camera showed former president George H. W. Bush and wife Barbara's expressions of disappointment as the final out of the Series ended the championship hopes of their hometown Houston Astros. But perhaps the most famous, and frequently rerun, isolated replay is Carlton Fisk's twelfth-inning home run that won game six of the 1975 World Series for the Red Sox. Despite instructions to follow the ball, the NBC camera operator lodged in Fenway Park's left-field "Green Monster" stayed on a full-screen shot of Fisk as he waved his arms to summon the psychokinetic forces needed to keep his long drive fair. As it turns out, the camera operator's decision to stay on Fisk was not a decision at all, but a manifestation of rat phobia. A nearby rodent living in the Green Monster had distracted him from his job. The accidental shot

35. *The arrangement of* HDTV *cameras at a recent Chicago Cubs game. Clockwise from the left side: Lower third base camera, Cubs announcers watch their* HDTV *monitors, high home, lower first base, high first base cameras. In center, the center field camera in its own hut. Photographs by James Walker.*

proved so sensational that NBC director Harry Coyle revised his book, suggesting that camera operators hold their positions for an additional five seconds to allow for reaction shots.[18] When it came to cameras for televising baseball, more definitely seemed better.

One of the most striking differences between regular-season and playoff coverage is the number of cameras used. Although these differences were minimal through the early 1960s, as competition heated up among networks to produce the best sportscast, the number of cameras increased dramatically. NBC's 1957 World Series telecasts used only four color cameras for Yankee Stadium games and six black-and-white cameras for games at Milwaukee's County Stadium. In 1970, NBC assigned ten cameras for its All-Star Game coverage, four more than during its regular-season games.[19] For the 1974 All-Star tilt, NBC used nine field cameras (plus one for visuals), including two roving, hand-held cameras linked by microwave to its production truck.[20] The fixed field cameras included six in the double horseshoe arrangement, with cameras at third, home, and first on two levels, in addition to the center field camera. When NBC and ABC began alternating coverage of the World Series in 1976, the number of cameras increased sharply. NBC used eleven cameras for the 1978 World Series.[21] ABC bumped that number to fourteen for the 1979 Fall Classic.[22] For the 1983 All-Star Game, NBC used nearly as many: thirteen cameras, including ten fixed-position, two mobile, and one in the Goodyear blimp.[23] By the 1997 All-Star Game, Fox had increased modestly to sixteen, including a ten-ounce catcher-cam.[24] Developments in miniaturization and robotics would soon make these numbers seem modest. For the 2006 World Series, Fox employed twenty-eight cameras, including super-slow motion, diamond cams, and cable cams.[25]

Although the number of cameras in use has grown dramatically for postseason and All-Star Games, this profusion has not spilled over to regular-season games produced locally. As early as 1951, local stations were assigning five cameras, but by 1997 that number had grown to only six or seven for locally produced Mets games: high home, high first, low first, high third, low third, and two center field cameras.[26] A late-season HD telecast by WGN in 2006 used only five manned cameras (see figure 35).

For network regular-season games, the quantity of cameras increased over time. Networks experimented with additional smaller cameras as early as 1957. CBS positioned its small videon camera behind home plate, and NBC announced that it would use a small "cigar box"–size camera that "can even be carried into the dugout to get a picture of Casey Stengel twitching."[27] When NBC assumed the exclusive national contract in 1966, it typically used six or seven field cameras. Although locations varied with each home ballpark, NBC usually featured two high home cameras, one low home behind the foul ball screen, two third base side (high, low), one first base side, and one center field camera.[28] Because color cameras were less reliable then, NBC favored two "cover shot" high home cameras, the most used at the time, in case one had problems. Eventually, the second high home camera was abandoned in favor of a second on the first base side of the field, creating a double horseshoe arrangement. Thirty years later, Fox was using a minimum of eight manned cameras and three robotic cameras, one in each bullpen and one over home plate.[29] In addition to the double horseshoe, manned cameras were located to the left and right of home plate so balls traveling down either the right- or left-field foul lines could be followed, as could runners going to first or trying to score from third.

Raw numbers weren't the only basis on which networks competed with cameras. For its 1984 playoff coverage, ABC added a "Super Slo Mo" camera to track pitches as they came toward home plate, allowing viewers to see the spin on the ball. For that year's World Series, NBC countered with its own version of the camera, facetiously named "Super Duper Slo Mo."[30] The cameras work by tripling the number of frames used, from the thirty per second used in standard television to ninety per second, allowing action to be seen with greater clarity at slow speeds. Super slow-motion cameras have become a standard part of the specialty cameras that are assigned specific tasks in postseason games.

The Center field Camera

The center field camera's perspective on the pitcher, batter, catcher, umpire, and sometimes a runner at second is the most common shot in a baseball telecast. Fox announcer Tim McCarver estimates that "the shot over the pitcher's right shoulder as he looks in at the batter is probably on the screen 65 percent of time."[31] Although this might be an exaggeration, the center field shot is without doubt the most frequent image on the screen. The shot's ubiquity is tied to the rhythms of the game. Much of the game takes place between pitcher and batter. Most thrown balls are taken as balls or strikes or swung at and missed by the batter. Only when contact is made does the director need to cut to another camera to follow its path. The center field camera has replaced the high home perspective as the basic cover shot of the game: the image that remains on the screen until game events force a change in perspective. However, this was not always the case.

The story of the center field, or at least outfield, camera starts with the

36. Currently, baseball games are covered by as many as three center field cameras.
Photograph by James Walker.

1949 World Series, when young Harry Coyle experimented with placing a camera in right field at Yankee Stadium. Center field was not considered because the cable connecting the camera to the production truck would be too long to carry an acceptable signal. The right field camera was not particularly well received (see chapter 4) and missed its most noteworthy opportunity to impress when a distracted camera operator, attempting to catch the ball, failed to follow Tommy Henrich's home run as it came directly at the camera.[32] WOR-TV considered adding a center field camera to its 1951 Dodger coverage, but was concerned that it "would be asking too much to expect the video-viewing fan to be sitting vicariously behind home plate one instant and then out back of the outfielders the next."[33] WGN director Jack Jacobson made the earliest claim for using a true center field camera. He recalled using one while covering a Little League game at Thillins Stadium in Chicago in 1951. The main cover shot camera would not fit behind home plate. "The field was so small that if you went between third base and home plate there would be so much panning everyone would get dizzy, so I walked around out in center field, and I saw the pitcher pitching batting practice. I took the framer out with me and said, 'Let's try a camera here.'" Jacobson claimed that the new camera position was used the next day at Wrigley Field.[34]

Though WGN's claim to having the first center field camera seems credible, Harry Coyle is widely attributed with the TV baseball first of introducing the camera to a national audience at the 1955 All-Star Game. Coyle claimed he got the idea, not from WGN, but from watching the umpire in a softball game call balls and strikes from behind the pitcher rather than the catcher.[35] Although baseball was not ready for such a radical shift in the umpire's perspective, Coyle thought televised baseball would profit from the change. He began using the shot in most of NBC's World Series and All-Star Games when they were carried in black and white. Since fewer cameras were used at games telecast in color, the center field camera disappeared. During the 1957 Series directed by Coyle, the *Sporting News* commented on NBC's "spectacular photography, including an unusual camera angle at Milwaukee that enabled viewers to look directly over the pitcher's shoulder toward home plate." The reporter noted that the first attempts to use a portable camera in center field were unacceptable, forcing NBC to construct a twenty-five-foot platform for the new camera.[36] However, the camera won widespread acceptance only gradually.

For the 1957 season, WPIX considered using a center field grandstand camera, but was wary because "the camera can steal the catcher's signals."[37] Jack Murphy, director of Yankee telecasts in the 1950s and 1960s, claimed that Yankee GM George Weiss thought the camera would make "the telecasts too good, which would keep people away from the park." Weiss imposed restrictions on the number of times the center field camera could be used in each game. Murphy reported that this was the "only censorship ever imposed upon me."[38] Because of concerns over sign stealing in 1959, Commissioner Ford Frick convinced NBC to eliminate the shot temporarily out of fear that the game's integrity would be compromised. These concerns apparently had a chilling effect. The kinescopes of a Yankee telecast from 1958, a CBS *Game of the Week* from 1961, and the last two innings of WGN's coverage of Cub Don Cardwell's May

15, 1960, no-hitter show limited use of the center field camera. The camera shot is used frequently for some batters and not at all for others. The viewer sees only a distant shot of the pitcher and home plate area with no zooming.[39] By the 1965 World Series, the center field perspective was starting to emerge as televised baseball's most important shot. Footage from the 1968 and 1969 World Series confirms the growing popularity of the shot. By the 1975 World Series, the shot had become so essential that NBC was employing two center field cameras: one tight shot of the pitcher/batter confrontation and one looser shot that included the runner at second base. NBC's camera plan for the 1983 All-Star Game also reveals a second center field camera as well as cameras behind both left and right field walls of Comiskey Park.[40]

The Growth of Color Television

Although the first color telecast of Major League Baseball is often ascribed to NBC's 1955 World Series between the Brooklyn Dodgers and the New York Yankees, the credit should go to an earlier 1951 Dodgers venture with CBS that used an entirely different color television system. Unlike the poorly documented experiments that predated NBC's "first" baseball broadcast in May 1939, the CBS experiments with color were a widely publicized part of their campaign for FCC adoption of a hybrid electronic-mechanical color television system. CBS had transmitted experimental color programs, including other sports events such as boxing, since 1946 to generally positive reviews.[41] Although adopted by the FCC briefly in 1952, the CBS system, which required a separate converter attached to an existing black-and-white television, was rejected by both the television industry and later the FCC. RCA lobbied the FCC for adoption of its all-electronic system, which was fully compatible with existing black-and-white televisions. In 1953, the FCC approved the RCA system that became the U.S standard. But in August 1951, CBS's system had a full head of steam and needed publicity.

As they had in 1939, broadcasters turned to Major League Baseball, the Brooklyn Dodgers, and Red Barber for a public display of their technological prowess. In his position as CBS's director of sports, Barber became a color enthusiast. He claimed that color would add "that final touch of realism" to television and that "it is not difficult to visualize how wonderful sports on color television will be."[42]

The CBS color experiment played out over three Saturday day games on August 11 and 25 and September 8, 1951. Although CBS's estimate that ten thousand viewed the game on one thousand home-made converters was likely an exaggeration, the press was generally positive about the games it had seen on color receivers at CBS headquarters or Gimbels department store. Red Smith wrote that in the two-camera color broadcast of the August 11 game between the Dodgers and the Boston Braves, the ballplayers "all came out as spectacularly beauteous critters, except for Roy Campanella who had neglected to shave. The reproduction was excellent, striking, and only faintly phony." Smith did complain that the athletes had "magnificently bronzed complexions glowing with not quite believable health." But "like a picture postcard, everything was just the least bit brighter, more colorful, neater and prettier than life itself."[43] CBS continued its color sports telecasts by broadcasting nine NCAA football games during the fall of 1951.

Although CBS experiments with baseball and other programming were fairly successful, ultimately it was RCA's fully compatible color system that would win the color TV battle. NBC became the major player in color television, with CBS and ABC offering few broadcasts until the mid-1960s. Though it was the network of the World Series, NBC became the network of color television. It broadcast the World Series every year from 1947 through 1976, and it was the first to offer the Fall Classic in color. Although there was some speculation that the 1955 All-Star Game in Milwaukee would be the moment NBC would debut baseball and color on the national stage, the network waited for another all-subway series that fall.[44] Thus, the first World Series win for the "bums" from Brooklyn was the first in "living" color.

The 1947 World Series had been a boon to black-and-white television sales, and RCA hoped the 1955 Series would stimulate the lagging sales of costly color receivers, which ranged from $700 to $1,000 ($5,100 to $7,250 in 2006 dollars). The interest in color TV was widespread. The 1955 Bowman baseball cards had each player's photo inset in a television frame with the words *Color TV* below the picture. *Newsweek* even featured the World Series on the cover of its October 3rd issue, asking "Color TV: Is '56 the Big Year?"[45] However, NBC's colorcast fell only slightly short of being a failure. The network had featured color "spectaculars" and other studio programs since 1954, but its color technology was not well suited for outdoor scenes, especially with harsh shadows. The afternoon World Series games produced deep shadows as the contests wore on. RCA's four color cameras could be adjusted if they moved from complete sunlight to complete shadow, but the results were poor from the high home camera that showed most of the field, some of which was in sunlight and some in shadow. As Jack Gould reported in the New York Times, "most shots of the field suffered from noticeable harshness of tints and assorted overcasts. Over a prolonged stretch the variations in color reproduction proved wearing on the eye, and this viewer ultimately was glad to return to the black and white."[46] Variety was even more critical, suggesting that the games looked like they were played on Kentucky's bluegrass rather than the traditional green. "The tints were not true, the contrast was inadequate and the close-ups of the players lacked the sharp definition of the black-and-white sets."[47] The color cameras' bulk reduced their mobility, and their cost restricted the number used, further limiting the coverage. Although CBS used only two cameras in its 1951 experiment, by the mid-1950s World Series fans expected at least six cameras, not the four used by NBC in its colorcast.

The 1957 and 1958 contests between the Yankees and Milwaukee Braves produced split coverage: the New York games were in color, and the Milwaukee contests in black and white.[48] Color coverage was still not well received, however. Variety preferred the six-camera black-and-white coverage of the 1957 games in Milwaukee, particularly their use of the center field camera, to the four-camera color fare in New York. It noted that the color camera still presented "considerable color distortion in some of the shots" and had problems adjusting between sunlight and shadows.[49] Sports Illustrated gave many examples of color distortion and even reported that one New York bar whose advertising read "See the World Series in Color" switched from its very expensive color receiver to a black-and-white set at its customers' request.[50] Time was a bit more positive, but still noted the occasional "Kentucky blue" grass and "shaded areas filled with indigo murk." However, the magazine did report that better equipment had "averted the blind shadows that plagued the first color Series in 1955."[51] By 1959, color remote equipment was available, and the World Series became a permanent color event, as color quality improved with a new generation of camera tubes produced by RCA.

Color coverage of baseball in local markets proceeded much more slowly. For example, it was 1968 before the Philadelphia Phillies offered their first local games in color.[52] This followed the pattern for other local broadcasts. Most stations deferred their investment in color television until there was wide acceptance of color by the networks and significant increases in the sales of color receivers, neither of which occurred until the mid-1960s. Two early exceptions were stations that had a strong commitment to both color television and baseball: WLW in Cincinnati and WGN in Chicago. WLW was owned by Crosley Broadcasting and was part of the larger Crosley Corporation, which owned both radio and television manufacturing facilities and the Cincinnati Reds. It invested in color facilities as early as 1954 and aired its first local color programs in August 1957, prompting RCA to label Cincinnati as "Colortown, U.S.A."[53] Recalling the introduction in the late 1940s of monochrome television, the station installed color receivers in local department stores and bars. In 1959, WLW telecast its first color day baseball games, featuring twelve Saturday and Sunday games over its five-station network during the summer. WLW's coverage employed three cameras: one behind home and one on both the first and third base sides of the infield. Although it's difficult to substantiate, WLW claimed that the Reds' color coverage increased sales of color televisions, improved game ratings, and even helped ballpark attendance.[54] In May 1960, the station telecast the first-ever night baseball game in color, using RCA's new, more sensitive color camera tubes. By 1962, WLW was presenting twenty-two of its fifty-three televised Reds games in color.[55]

WGN's commitment to color was almost as intense as WLW's, and its commitment to televised baseball was even more pronounced. As an independent (non-network-affiliated) station responsible for producing much of its own programming, WGN had invested heavily in both color equipment and baseball broadcasts. In 1960, it used the newly introduced RCA 4401 camera tube to telecast 120 games in color, alternating between Wrigley Field and Comiskey Park, and claimed the title of baseball's leading colorcaster.[56]

Improved color camera tubes made night colorcasts possible, but high-quality color television also required changes in existing stadium lighting. In 1967, the three major networks (ABC, CBS, and NBC) proposed major improvements to stadium lighting at virtually every major stadium in the United States. They asked for "three times as much light" and much more uniform illumination of the playing area to avoid problems caused by variations in light intensity. The networks argued that current lighting made the tight player shots common in black-and-white television impossible in color coverage.[57] But a newer generation of color cameras introduced in the later 1960s made these radical changes less necessary. By 1967, WHDH in Boston was using four of RCA's TK-43 "Big Tube" cameras to cover Red Sox games. The telecasts demonstrated strong improvements in capturing nighttime games and better handling of contrasts between sunlight and shadow during daylight.[58] In 1966, as part of its first national contract, NBC became the first network to offer its game-of-the-week telecasts in color, establishing it as the standard for the highest-quality regular-season broadcasts.[59]

High-quality day and night game color coverage required a decade to develop. Broadcasters overcame near failure at the first color World Series in 1955 to achieve acceptable standards by the late 1960s. During the same period, color television itself moved from an expensive novelty to center stage in the American home. CBS and ABC joined NBC in offering extensive programming in color, and the costs of receivers gradually dropped to levels that most consumers were willing to pay.

Major League Baseball responded to the growth in color television by switching to more colorful uniforms, mascots, and even ballpark seating. Athletics' owner Charley Finley was particularly aggressive in "colorizing" his team's wardrobe with bright green and gold uniforms. He even proposed that MLB change the baseball from white to bright yellow for the benefit of television's color cameras. Although his fellow owners quickly dismissed the idea, baseball became a more "colorful" sport in the 1970s.

Today, as televised baseball approaches its seventh decade, a similar transition is underway. Networks and stations are moving from standard definition television, based on technical requirements introduced in 1941, to high-definition TV. Fox and ESPN offer all of their games in HD, while most local stations and regional sports networks, as we noted earlier, now telecast home games in HD. After a slow start, the transition of televised sports to high definition has picked up speed because of high rights fees, increasing HDTV sales, and stronger competition for the audience, mirroring the accelerated transition from black-and-white to color starting in the mid-1960s.

Graphics: From Flip Cards to FoxBox

For the first two decades of televised baseball, graphics relied on a primitive technology. Directors used black cards (or slides) with white letters that could be captured by a television camera (or telecine) and then superimposed (or "supered") over a game image generated by another camera. Other graphic information came from shots of the game scoreboard viewed by the fans at the park. Superimposing lettering required that both cameras be transmitting at approximately half strength, which made the background image from the game look washed out. But an even greater limitation was the fixed nature of flip-card graphics: professional-looking lettering had to be created in advance, limiting the information to what was known before the game. If directors wanted to update batting averages or the starting pitchers' strikeout total, they had to have a production assistant use crude paste-up graphics, or, worse, white-chalk hand lettering on a blackboard. As such, graphics information presented during the game was limited to players' names and occasionally season statistics—batting average, home runs, RBIS—which were supered below the player's image. These first-generation telecasts relied primarily on the announcers to supply most player or team information. The game's progress was communicated by shots of the scoreboard at the end of each inning. For special games such as the 1956 World Series, photographs or sketches of players would be shot from a flip card and integrated into the game coverage.

As late as the 1961 World Series, these primitive graphics were the norm, but as the decade progressed simple electronic imagery began to appear. Where the kinescoped segments of a 1958 Yankee game show only the players' names superimposed over the lower third of the screen, a 1961 CBS *Game of the Week* added the player's batting average just above the supered name. For that year's World Series, NBC superimposed game summary (runs, hits, errors) data between innings in addition to player names. By the 1965 World Series, NBC was employing animated graphics to dramatically enhance the opening of its telecasts, a far cry from the opening of earlier series telecasts—a high home shot of the field with no graphics. Graphics were now matted over field images, allowing both the graphics and background images to be shown at full intensity and eliminating the washed-out background images inherent in the superimposition process. The batter's name appeared for virtually every plate appearance; balls, strikes, and number of outs were provided more frequently; each inning ended with a game summary graphic, including the NBC logo; and crawls (lettering moving horizontally across the screen) were occasionally used to give information about the batter.

The primitive electronic character generator facilitated these improvements. It enabled producers to store dozens of pages of information that could be drawn at will from the device's memory. Producers could now type in more information about players, teams, ballparks, and the game's history than they could possibly use during the telecast. Graphics information was increasingly used to prompt announcers. Information could be entered in real time as events unfolded, and basic player statistics could be updated throughout the game. The first character generators were expensive but still within the budget of national, and soon even local, baseball telecasts. Newer character generators and video switchers allowed for color graphics—single colors at first and then multiple color graphics with design elements as well as numbers and letters. NBC's coverage of the 1971 All-Star Game featured white electronic graphics, including the NBC logo. The 1975 World Series between the Reds and Red Sox offered yellow graphics that were updated during the game. For example, a summary of the batter's previous appearances ("0 for 2") could be included with his name. The game summary at the end of each half inning was matted over a freeze frame of the game action and sported a stylish NBC World Series logo. Upgraded game graphics relied upon the microprocessor technology that soon would fuel the personal computer revolution. As processing and storage power increased, so did the quality and variety of graphic information in baseball telecasts. In addition, computing technology made updating player statistics easy and accurate.

The hand calculations of Allan Roth, longtime Dodger and NBC statistician, were replaced first by the digital calculator and then by the personal computer. The computational power that the PC put into consumer hands meant that more fans could crunch the numbers as well. The rise in the 1980s of more complex "sabrmetric" analyses, facilitated by home computers, changed how both fans and professionals analyzed the game. The explosion of statistical information fostered an interest in fantasy games that were based on individual players' statistics but divorced from the actual outcomes of the Major League games themselves. The digital revolution came to televised sports, including baseball, and produced an increasing array of visual information displayed with eye-catching graphics wizardry. It also ushered in a new digital age for televised baseball (see this book's epilogue).

By 1998 Mets announcer Tim McCarver was reporting that local broadcasts used about two hundred graphics per game, which was only about 30–40 percent of graphics stored for the game. In addition to the game monitor, announcers used a special graphics monitor that could help direct their commentary. Graphics operators could either lead the announcer or follow his lead, but coordination between the two was paramount. "When you're on the same wavelength," McCarver said, "you know you're really clicking."[60]

As graphics became more sophisticated, producers increasingly used them to convey visual information beyond words and numbers. For example, Fox's coverage has employed "Hit Zone" graphics to show the hitter's relative strength in different parts of the strike zone, "Spray Charts" to show where a batter tends to hit the ball, and "FoxTrax" to show the location of pitches relative to the strike zone.[61] Video segments and animations are now included in the graphics presentations, creating dynamic displays and blurring the distinction between live-action video and graphics.

The FoxBox, which summarizes key game information on the top or bottom of the screen, was a major innovation in the 1990s and has become standard in almost all sports telecasts. The increasing size of the average viewing screen in U.S. homes made it easier for viewers to see multiple boxes of displayed information. In addition, many viewers' experience navigating web pages, which often group content into different boxes, has made it easier for them to process information from an increasingly segmented television screen. Indeed, the modern telecast's constant barrage of on-screen information allows many baseball fans to multi-task, following the game on screen, the action in the rest of MLB, and the exploits of their fantasy team's players at the same time.

Instant Replay

At first, televised games could only be recorded on kinescopes, special films made from the images projected on a television monitor. The earliest known kinescope was a one-minute-and-fifteen-second sample of a 1948 Giants-Braves game at the Polo Grounds, which NBC made to demonstrate its new "television transcription" technology.[62] Kinescopes of televised games are rare, and the oldest complete examples are games six and seven of the 1952 World Series. These film copies were made primarily for viewing by armed forces personnel overseas and secondarily as historical records. Since the film they were recorded on had to be processed, they could not be used to replay events within the telecast they originated from. For instantaneous recording, telecasters needed a different technology.

The Ampex Corporation introduced the first videotape recorders (VTRs) in 1956 at the National Association of Broadcasters convention. Despite their obvious advantages (instant copying, reusable tape), both the machines and the tapes they used were extremely costly. Consequently, VTRs diffused slowly during the next decade, first to networks and then to stations.

Videotape provided a means of replaying an entire game for presentation to baseball-starved fans during the off-season. In Chicago, WGN replayed games from the previous summer. Milwaukee station WISN-TV planned to air videotapes of games from Cuba because of "widespread demand for TV presentation of winter league games."[63] Networks also used videotape occasionally to move games to a more convenient time. For example in 1965, ABC used a videotape of its game from the East or Midwest as a backup in case its later West Coast game was rained out.[64]

Almost as soon as Ampex created a sensation at the 1956 NAB convention with its VTR, however, telecasters anticipated its use in sports to replay action. In a review of an early 1956 Dodgers game, Jack Gould of the *New York Times* reported that television engineers had already discussed the possibility of replaying a tape a few seconds after an umpire's call to see if he "blew a close one" and "reassure the city's beer-drinkers of their superior wisdom."[65] However, instant replay was pioneered not in a baseball telecast but in a CBS telecast of the Army-Navy football game on December 7, 1963. When Army quarterback Rollie Stichweh ran the ball in from the two-yard line, CBS director Tony Vera called for the videotape recording of the touchdown. The replay ran flawlessly, causing Vera to exclaim, "Oh my God, it works!"[66] Instant replay was here to stay.

Instant replay was especially well suited to football, a game that alternates between intense, sometimes spectacular action that cannot be fully comprehended in real time, and periods of inaction when players walk back to the huddle, call the next play, and line up. The lulls in action provide a perfect opportunity to insert one or more replays, and slowing down the action makes it much easier to absorb and fully appreciate. Both college and professional football telecasts began to use instant replay starting in the early 1960s. ABC Sports received special recognition for its creative use of the technique.[67] The network worked with Ampex to develop an instant-replay technology based on a recordable videodisc that produced replays of up to thirty seconds in length within four seconds. The Ampex system had three speeds of slow motion and allowed for freeze frames.[68]

Baseball's dance with instant replay followed a slower beat. Despite instant replay's wide use in football, footage of the 1961 and 1965 NBC coverage of the World Series shows no use of the technique. Yankee baseball director Don Carney recalled Mel Allen requesting a videotape replay of a bloop hit that ended a no-hit bid by Ralph Terry. (Carney did not mention the year, but Terry played for the Yankees from 1959 to

1964.) The ball "came so close to being caught that Mel wanted the viewers to see it again. . . . It took a couple of minutes to get it done, but that was the beginning of instant replay."[69] Of course, the several-minute lag time meant the replay was hardly "instant." It is also possible that other television directors were providing something similar to replays since videotape was already in use in baseball postgame highlight programs. The first use of instant replay in baseball that received extensive press appears to be ABC's 1965 game-of-the-week telecasts. A *New York Times* review of ABC's first game of the season commented on frequent, but not effective, use of isolated camera replays. The critic claimed that, while the technique was well suited to the "diversified nature of the action" in football, it was not useful in baseball, where "the spectator needs only to follow the ball."[70] However, even the *Times*' reviewer found the isolated instant replay effective on one play, a successful first base pick-off of the Giants' Jim Hart by Mets catcher Chris Cannizzaro. For the 1968 and 1969 World Series, NBC used replays sparingly and usually at the break before commercials rather than during the inning.

As replays became a more frequent feature of baseball telecasts, commentators debated their potential impact on umpires. Some suggested that umpires, fearing criticism when replays made a call questionable, would become more cautious and resentful of television's intrusion. But Mets announcer Ralph Kiner countered the criticism by asserting that he "never saw the camera yet that could countermand an umpire, considering that the camera angle is just as prone to error as anything else. In fact, video tape seems to show how few mistakes umpires make."[71] Lou Boudreau, the Cubs' television announcer, reported that WGN refrained from replays on "judgment calls" to avoid the problem. However, instant replays also had the potential to correct obvious umpire errors, if they could be consulted. Umpires rejected that possibility, however, preferring to work with each other when plays were ambiguous. Umpire Tom Gorman emphatically expressed the umpire's reaction: "If a man can't see a play clearly, he ought to ask somebody's advice, but never on a judgment play or for any reason related to cameras. We just can't operate that way."[72]

By the mid-1970s, instant replays from isolated cameras with slow motion had become an established part of baseball coverage. For the 1975 World Series, NBC used six replay devices (four disc recorders and two VTRS). The network outlined how instant replay would happen:

(1) A commentator in NBC's broadcast booth, and producer Roy Hammerman or director Harry Coyle in the control truck, anticipate a play, or players, to be isolated for Instant Replay.

(2) The director in the control truck then assigns a camera, or cameras, to isolate on a player, or players.

(3) The picture, or pictures, are fed into one of the mobile units and recorded on disk or videotape machine.

(4) The producer picks the isolate he considers most appropriate for a playback to the viewing audience. The commentator is so advised and there you have Instant Replay.[73]

NBC's attention to replays was noted by *Sports Illustrated*, which applauded the network's use of multiple replays from multiple angles during key Series moments.[74]

However, multiple replays were not always welcome. As improved digital technology and additional cameras made it possible to include ever more replays, some critics complained that the networks had regressed to little boys with a new toy. For networks, nearly every play seemed to require an instant replay. When CBS used 133 replays in game six of the 1991 League Championship Series, Richard Sandomir of the *New York Times* argued that "routine groundouts and pop flies need not be replayed" because each replay required an explanation from analyst Tim McCarver, "opening McCarver to criticism that he talks too much." For Sandomir, "baseball should not become MTV because you're endowed with extra video ammo. . . . TV the medium, is not the message. The game is."[75] But replays continued to grow in number and complexity. The ability to digitally store and retrieve instantly an almost unlimited number of video clips from a computer's hard drive made multiple replays even more popular. By 1998, Tim McCarver could ask his producer for a "sequence"—a collection of related replays, such as all of the pitches in a single at bat or a pitcher striking out the side.[76] In thirty years, the instant replay had evolved from a once-a-game event to an instant highlight reel, edited on the fly.

Sound: No Longer an Afterthought

In radio, sound is everything. Its role became ancillary, however, when television arrived. As broadcasters focused considerable resources and directorial attention on the picture, in its formative years televised baseball's sound included little more than microphones for each announcer and field mikes to capture crowd responses to the action. The chief concern of the audio engineer was to ascertain the appropriate volume level for the announcers and to effectively blend ambient stadium sounds as a background for the announcers' commentary. By 1966, NBC had added directional mikes to pick up the sound of the bat on the ball and the ball hitting the glove at first base. There was also an audio connection to the ballpark's public address system.[77] In the 1970s, bulky table microphones gave way to headset microphones that allowed producers to communicate with announcers about upcoming action. This interaction was especially critical when instant replay became a standard part of the telecast in the mid-1960s. Producers needed to alert their announcers instantly which replays would be shown. In the process, they advanced the gradual shift in telecast control from the announcer in the booth to the producer and director in the remote truck.

As high-quality microphones became smaller and, through wireless technology, more mobile, baseball telecasts began to feature interviews from various ballpark locations. At the 1969 World Series, NBC assigned Tony Kubek to interview some of the many politicians and celebrities attending games at New York's Shea Stadium. Not all critics were impressed. For the 1970 All-Star Game telecast, the *Sporting News* argued that NBC's "interviews with show biz 'celebrities,'" along with an excessive number of commercials and network promos, made it difficult for fans to follow the game.[78] In 1971, Kubek was also sharply criticized for interviewing Oriole relief pitcher Bob Bolin in the bullpen, thus lengthening his warmup time and delaying the game. Newspaper reporters were especially concerned that their rival medium was now being allowed to interfere with on-field events as the game was in progress, a transgression never tolerated for their reporters. For game two of the 1984 World Series, NBC miked Padre manager Dick Williams and some of his coaches and played their comments during game three's pregame show. Williams grumbled about a failed drag bunt by Steve Garvey, but little else of interest was forthcoming.[79]

Television sound began to change in the 1980s, when stereo was introduced by networks and broadcast stations. At the same time, new compact disc technology using digital recording and reproduction technology helped raised consumer awareness of the importance of sound quality. Networks responded with wireless microphones placed strategically around the ballpark to pick up sounds that matched the on-screen action: the crack of the bat, the umpire's ball or strike call, the runner's foot hitting the base, the ball hitting the first baseman's glove, even the outfielder hitting the wall as he tried to steal away an extra-base hit. By the late 1980s, even local telecasts were using a dozen microphones, with many placed down the left and right field lines to improve the stereo effect.[80] These carefully positioned microphones were turned on in anticipation of a play and then quickly muted after the action to avoid picking up unwanted sounds. Audio operators now needed to be as "baseball savvy" as their video counterparts.

The network that demonstrated the strongest commitment to sound enhancement in baseball telecasts was Fox, which started its national broadcast contract in 1996. Fox covered the entire infield using three microphones and transmitters embedded in first, second, and third bases. Two parabolic reflector microphones (one aimed at left-handed and one at right-handed hitters) were located behind home plate to pick up the ball's impact on the bat or the catcher's glove. Pressure zone microphones were used in the right, center, and left field walls to capture outfielders running after fly balls and occasionally crashing against the wall. The outfield mikes also could pick up "the crack of the bat 400 feet away and home runs pinging off foul poles."[81] Fox even branded its audio innovations as FoxVox, echoing its FoxBox graphics trademark. For its 1997 weekly games, Fox used fourteen field microphones. Because they are relatively cheap and do not usually require a dedicated operator, the number of microphones used in baseball telecasts, especially in the postseason, has exploded. By the 2006 World Series, Fox was employing eighty microphones and capturing "the ball popping into the catcher's glove or chest protector; the first base coach hollering, 'Back!' or Carlos Delgado and Carlos Beltran high-fiving each other after a home run."[82]

Building a Better "Ballcast"

Over a more than seventy-year history, baseball telecast productions have improved dramatically. Modern productions use more cameras, microphones, replays, and graphics than ever before. Baseball is a demanding sport for the television director, and the expanse of technology has made it possible to adequately cover a vertical game never designed for the horizontal bias of the television frame. With each additional camera, microphone, graphic, and replay, the probability that a baseball telecast will miss critical action decreases.

In television production, innovation needs stimulation. The demanding routine of live production requires a process that is comfortably familiar to all those involved, and change opens opportunities for errors. Most viewers think little about how the game is covered; they are concerned mostly with what game is covered. As a result, production processes will tend to stagnate over time unless innovation is provoked. Innovations tend to follow changes in the competitive structure of television. As new networks take on the challenge of televising baseball, they introduce new production techniques. For "ballcast" innovation, competition is essential.

Today, competition for the television medium comes from an emerging system of video distribution: the Internet. As broadband becomes common in U.S. households, as digital compression improves, and as the Internet's capacity to transfer data grows, television, including broadcast, cable, and satellite distribution, loses its monopoly over the presentation of live and recorded video. As we will see in our epilogue, Major League Baseball has already seized the day, gaining a stronghold in what MLB calls "advanced media."

Epilogue: Baseball in the Advanced Media Age

Nobody knows how big [MLBAM will] be. Certainly if the past is the pro-logue, the new delivery mechanism is going to be more important than the old delivery mechanism. Radio replaced newspapers, TV replaced radio. All survived, but television is now dominant.

Bob Bowman, President and CEO,
Major League Baseball Advanced Media[1]

Tradition is not a business.

Tim Brosnan, Executive Vice President,
Business, Major League Baseball[2]

Our history of televised baseball has found that often the positive ben-efits television brings baseball can have a corresponding negative side. Increasing television revenues were distributed in an unbalanced way, leading to greater disparity between "have" and "have-not" teams. Dis-agreements over television money also contributed to the destructive la-bor/management disputes that affected baseball from the mid-1970s to the mid-1990s.

Television extended baseball to a much greater audience than previ-ous media had. However, television coverage revealed that baseball is not an aesthetically pleasing television sport. The long season and large number of games have also been a problem for baseball. Baseball has an excess inventory so few individual regular season games are significant enough to attract a large national audience.

Television exposure, while expanding and nationalizing baseball, also has increased scrutiny on professional baseball's operations. The game's special status as the national pastime has been eroded by this scrutiny and by the exposure television has brought other major sports. Whether from fear of franchise relocation or that pay television will take the game away from fans, or simply because of politicians' posturing, Congress has been much more likely to call hearings on baseball issues than it once did.

As we have documented, most of the problems in baseball's rela-tionship with television are self-imposed. Baseball was popularized in a pretelevision era and was slow to adapt to the nationalizing effect of television. For too many years, baseball's owners did not consider other teams to be business partners. They did not understand that national television thrives on competition and innovation, not just on tradition. They refused to pool their national television efforts until several years after the Sports Broadcasting Act of 1961 legalized such arrangements for professional sports leagues, which contributed to the N FL's surpassing MLB as the most popular sport in the United States.

The owners continued to fight with the Major League Baseball Players Association and, in doing so, seemed to take a perverse pleasure in criticizing the players and, by extension, the game itself. The owners were slow to develop a rational approach to the emerging medium of cable television. This allowed individual teams to become adjuncts of superstations or regional sports networks, exacerbating revenue disparity.

Our history, then, exposes the failure of owners and MLB officials to come to terms with the most powerful mass medium. Today, however, changes in television and the organization of baseball are ushering in a new era.

Baseball since the 1970s

The organization of professional baseball is much different than it was before television. The major leagues expanded and relocated to every region of the United States and into Canada even before the important events of the 1970s (see chapter 9). The events and alterations since that time are even more striking. By 2000, MLB had expanded to thirty teams and reduced the once independent National League and American League to mere organizational labels like the conferences of other professional sports. MLB became the manager of the major leagues. Divisions were realigned to more accurately reflect geography and create more competitive races in six divisions. The introduction of a "wild card" and new round of postseason play, the League Division Series, heightened the competition.

The myth of an independent commissioner operating in "the best interests of baseball" faded with the appointment of a team owner, Bud Selig, as commissioner. Although widely criticized, Selig's ascension clearly indicated that MLB wanted a commissioner who represented the owners; the independent and non–baseball executives of the past need not apply.

The minor leagues also instituted changes that helped to revive their fortunes. The historic name *National Association* was changed to the more descriptive *Minor League Baseball*. Most minor league teams developed new identities with catchy nicknames. They made substantial investments to market themselves as an affordable, family-friendly, leisure-time option. The moves paid off in minor league attendance records. The growing attendance stimulated the growth of independent leagues in the 1990s.

Television since the 1970s

Television has been radically altered since the 1970s. Cable or satellite television now reaches 90 percent of U.S. television households. Traditional definitions of pay television have been altered as most everyone now pays for television service. The Big 3 oligopoly of the broadcast networks (NBC, CBS, and ABC) has seen its onetime 90 percent market reach in prime time halved.[3]

The technological convergence and corporate consolidation of the past thirty years have altered the operational and conceptual framework of television. The audience can no longer be conceptualized as relatively passive viewers of whatever programming and advertising is presented to it by a limited number of channels. The explosion in the number of television viewing options, combined with the ubiquitous remote control devices and VCRs, DVDs, and DVRs, have turned the passive viewer into an increasingly active user of television.[4] Though the industry is countering this new viewer power by further consolidating channel ownership and integrated advertising into programming, the relationship of viewer to medium has been radically altered.

The television industry is much more competitive today. With more channels competing for the same audience, the ratings for most programming, including baseball, have declined. For media companies, ratings are just the start; the development of a brand identity is also of paramount importance. A television network or channel must be distinctive to attract new audiences and maintain existing ones. Consistently, sports have helped television networks build strong brands. Sports' branding power is reflected in the continuing growth of RSNs and ESPN's products. However, sports still have considerable value to providers of more general-interest television.

Sports can consistently generate an audience of young males that is difficult to reach with any other programming. The television industry also sees sports programming as a valuable promotion tool. Even the inattentive viewer will encounter promos for Fox network programming within the regular-season and postseason baseball games it carries. The Fox Broadcasting network, now one of the Big 4 broadcast networks, has strategically used sports to achieve its current level of success.[5]

MLB has been a large part of Fox's strategy in that the network controls the broadcast rights for a regular-season game of the week, the All-Star Game, and some of the postseason, including the crown jewel: the World Series. In addition, a "sister" company of Fox Broadcasting within the News Corp. media empire controls about two-thirds of RSNs' rights for local cablecasting.

Baseball and Television Coming Together

Television needs major sports such as MLB more than ever. This demand had produced higher rights fees, despite the general decline in overall ratings for most types of programming. With very few programs attracting the mass audience that broadcast television once sustained, the desirable demographics and built-in audience appeal of sports give it more value than ever. MLB is now operating in a buyer's market.

More importantly, MLB has finally adopted a business approach that can exploit the growing demand for its product. Negotiations are now conducted in private with little of the well-publicized animosity that characterized bargaining in earlier decades. Recently, Fox and ESPN renewed their contracts for national telecasts and offered a substantial increase in guaranteed money. These deals were concluded relatively quickly and without the extended negotiation "dance" that was once so common.

MLB's new leverage over television has given it the power to create its own network, The Baseball Channel, which plans to launch no later than

2009.[6] Following earlier NFL- and NBA-specific channels, baseball's effort will likely succeed in a television universe that has expanding channel capacity. A "24/7/365," all-baseball channel is particularly important for "hard-core" fans, enabling them to stay connected to the game in or out of season. During the season, the channel will join ESPN and TBS as a national cable carrier of MLB games. In the off-season, games from spring training and the fall, winter, and international leagues, perhaps including future World Baseball Classics, will provide constant promotion for MLB. It will be able to create and control a plethora of new programming series, including analyses, reruns of classic games, and personality profiles. The new network will be a permanent "hot-stove league" for baseball's most devoted fans.

In traditional network programming, where single-program ratings are paramount, MLB's excess inventory was a problem. With so many televised games, it was difficult to generate a large national audience for any single game. As MLB begins to develop its own network and exploit emerging media, that excess product inventory becomes a positive. Industry officials see the vast amount of inventory as a strategic advantage. As one business analyst explained, "Baseball, with its every-night schedule and a relatively large percentage of fans pulling for teams outside the market in which they live, is an ideal sport to draw viewers, and advertisers, to its Web site."[7]

MLBAM: Cooperation in the Digital Age

Owners who signed deals that maximized television benefits to their own clubs epitomized MLB's early television negotiations. But this approach changed dramatically in the Internet age. For MLB, Internet revenues are shared equally. Analysts now believe that MLB has the most lucrative and innovative web presence of any professional sport.

Major League Baseball Advanced Media (MLBAM, pronounced "M.L.-BAM") was created as a joint venture of the thirty franchises in June 2000, with each team providing $1 million to fund MLB.com's start-up operations. MLBAM was profitable within two years and within five years saw revenues increase from $5 million to $265 million.[8] It streams more live content than any other web site and is considered to be the most profitable Internet sports retail site.[9] It owns Tickets.com, manages the web sites for most MiLB and Major League Soccer teams, and has stakes in such entities as World Championship Sports Network, an Internet source of Olympics-style sports such as gymnastics and track and field, and Signatures Network, a music promotion site.[10]

In late 2005, MLBAM CEO Bob Bowman estimated that MLB.com generated about $40 million in nonbaseball revenues in 2006.[11] MLB.com is second only to NFL.com in web traffic among all sports web sites but bests NFL.com in page views.[12] Most impressively, MLBAM had an estimated market value approaching $3 billion at the end of 2006, from an initial investment of about $75 million from the teams.[13] If MLB was to have an initial public offering for MLBAM, even selling 30 percent of MLBAM would generate at least $25 million per team.[14]

MLBAM has been a huge success for MLB, generating millions of dollars per team. With projections of 30–35 percent revenue growth in the near future, MLBAM has given baseball owners an entirely new revenue stream.[15] This new money has helped finance a new round of MLB player salary increases. After the 2006 season, several free agents with marginal statistics received eye-popping contracts, including Jason Marquis (Cubs), Juan Pierre (Dodgers), and Gary Matthews Jr. (Angels). This new money also helped promote smoother negotiations between MLB and the Players Association during their most recent bargaining. The money flowing from television and MLBAM is simply too great for MLB to allow another disruptive lockout or strike. Although the owners and players have a history of painful conflict, money heals all wounds.

One of MLB.com's key features is the access it provides to a variety of audio and video (i.e., radio and television) services. This encompasses many free offerings of highlights and talk-analysis programs, including fantasy baseball information via BaseballChannel.TV. The MLB.com web site also offers audio and television subscriptions to regular-season, postseason, spring-training, and international games (e.g., the Caribbean Series). Radiocasts of all games are also are packaged with video highlights, ring tones, and wallpapers for mobile phones.

Providing television and radio content has accounted for a substantial portion of MLB.com's success. The web site is a baseball source for displaced or traveling fans, as well as for viewers subject to blackout restrictions. As broadband Internet connections become standard, the number of subscribers is sure to increase from the less than one million at the end of 2004 to many millions.[16] However, the rise of MLBAM is generating conflict with traditional television rights holders, triggering legal action.

MLBAM and Television Rights

MLBAM is in charge of all MLB's Internet businesses and other so-called advanced media, including mobile and hand-held devices. It also controls all of MLB's video streaming of live games, a fact that became an issue during the renewal of the ESPN contract. Like all television entities, ESPN wants some streaming rights to support its own web sites. It agreed to pay baseball $30 million a year for some Internet rights, namely, to use video streams as part of a service that distributes all of its programming over the Internet. It may not create a separate baseball package; only MLBAM can.[17] MLBAM's ownership of web rights preempted a move by the team to webcast Dodger games on a video-on-demand basis.[18]

As the Internet becomes an increasingly important source of television content and revenue, such disputes are likely to increase. The boundaries separating advanced media, television, and radio are fading. Prime-time broadcast and cable programs are now available through network web sites. AOL has created a "channel" of free streams of older network series.[19] Tim Brosnan, executive vice president of MLB's business unit, has said that the commissioner's office, responsible for broadcasting and cable, "can do what we do, and they [MLBAM] do what they do." He cautions that MLBAM's relationship with the rest of MLB is evolving as technological conditions change.[20]

Gaming, Fantasy, and Intellectual Property

MLBAM is an unknown entity to the average fan. Its activities are the backbone of MLB.com, but it does not even have a separate web site. However, this relative anonymity is disappearing as MLBAM begins an aggressive push to defend MLB's intellectual property rights.

MLBAM's most publicized property rights case to date sprang from its partnership agreement with the Players Association. In January 2005, MLBAM paid a reported $50 million to the player's union for five years of "exclusive rights to use, and to sublicense to others, Major League Baseball player group rights for the development and creation of on-line games, all other Online content, including fantasy baseball and interactive games."[21] MLBAM claimed that it now owned rights to the player statistics used by fantasy game businesses and could demand payment from those who wanted to use them. CDM Fantasy Sports sued MLBAM over the right to use player statistics. In August 2006, U.S. District Court Judge Mary Ann Medler granted CDM's motion preventing MLBAM and the MLBPA from interfering with fantasy games. The judge concluded that statistics were not a property owned by MLBAM.[22] MLBAM and MLBPA have appealed this ruling.[23] Whatever the ultimate decision, baseball owners and players clearly are asserting property rights more aggressively.

MLBAM had more success with other fantasy and video-game producers, who have accepted its ownership of these property rights. For example, Yahoo! pays MLBAM about $3 million a year, and Take-Two Interactive paid between $80–$150 million for the exclusive rights to publish and distribute MLB video games.[24] The Big 3 of game console manufacturers, Microsoft, Nintendo, and Sony, are the only other video-game companies that have the right to develop games with MLB content.[25] With an estimated sixteen million fantasy sports players in the United States and millions more video-game players, both revenue and rights disputes are likely to increase.[26]

Other Audio and Video Initiatives

Neither the broadcast and cable contracts nor MLBAM exhaust MLB's sources of media revenue. In 2007 MLB attempted to make its "Extra Innings" satellite package of out-of-market games available exclusively to DirecTV for $700 million over seven years.[27] Critics saw the deal as a shortsighted "money grab" by MLB, and congressional pressure led MLB to change its position and continue "Extra Innings" availability on cable.[28] The result is that MLB will get both (1) more money from DirecTV and the cable industry than in the previous contract and (2) guaranteed coverage for its new "Baseball Channel."

The interest of members of Congress in promoting access to televised baseball games and preventing the siphoning away of baseball from cable to another form of pay television (satellite) is another instance of the valence issues that congressional members find so irresistible. The DirecTV debate is also a reminder that the issue of where televised baseball appears is as important today as it was when the debates focused on siphoning baseball from "free" to pay television (see chapter 8).

MLB's new Baseball Channel is guaranteed to be carried by DirecTV and many of the major cable systems in the United States.[29] This will gain the new channel substantial national clearance, a necessity when generating advertising revenue. As a new cable-satellite channel, the Baseball Channel will have the benefit of DirecTV's subscription base, making a successful launch more likely. MLB's approach in the DirecTV deal is reflected in an even older medium: radio.

Although television is this book's topic, radio coverage of baseball is also changing in the rapidly evolving media industry. In 2005, MLB contracted with XM Satellite Radio to provide subscription satellite broadcasts of every Major League game, earning MLB $650 million over eleven years.[30] Using this new medium, MLB generated more new revenue that will be split equally among the thirty teams.

Many radio station owners complained about the XM deal, arguing that the value of their local radio rights would be compromised. Stations noted that the FCC never intended for satellite radio to compete with local broadcasters.[31] This latter complaint had a familiar ring; broadcast television operators used the same argument to bottle up cable television in the 1960s and 1970s.

MLB executive Brosnan suggests that the first two seasons of the deal (2005–6) prove that there has been no "dilution of values" for local radio rights holders because local ratings "have never been stronger. The XM audience is composed mainly of displaced fans. Local listeners still tune to their local stations for their team's games. XM's retransmission of local broadcasts actually benefits local sponsors who now have a national audience for their advertising."[32] Now that game audio is also available on mobile devices, perhaps XM will begin to complain about losing its audience to an even newer competitor.

A final change affecting radio is the migration of local broadcasts from powerful AM stations. Many teams keep their rights, purchasing station time and selling advertising for their broadcasts. Other teams sell the rights to sports-only stations.[33] The 50,000-watt powerhouse stations, like KDKA in Pittsburgh or KMOX in St. Louis, are no longer baseball's radio home. Today, a less powerful station, often FM, is likely to use the games as a station-branding tactic, increasing its credibility as the local "source for sports." Although the number of baseball telecasts has strongly declined on local broadcast stations, radio broadcasts are not likely to fade because of radio's lower cost structure and the popularity of the all-sports format.

The Future of a Dysfunctional Marriage

Anyone who reads, hears, or sees preseason baseball predictions knows that they rarely reflect the final season standings. In both baseball and television, the future is difficult to predict accurately. Nevertheless, like rushing fools, we will forecast what might happen over the next few years.

First, we believe that baseball will continue to thrive in the new television-media environment. Baseball's long season and daily play produce a huge inventory of games. MLB can exploit this surplus of product on the Internet, the coming Baseball Channel, and multiple national television partners. After years of lagging behind in the broadcast and cable eras, baseball is now on the "cutting edge" of the new television era.

New media revenues, equally shared, will lessen the economic imbalances that have long plagued the game. Chris Isidore, a senior writer for CNNMoney.com, predicts that "in 20 years, MLBAM could make the sport the share-the-wealth socialist paradise that has been long entrenched in the [NFL]."[34] The huge disparities that once existed are being flattened by the new media deals and MLB's aggressive revenue-sharing plans. As Brosnan states, "parity is still the goal."[35]

In 2006, MLB had an estimated $300 million in shared revenues, and the standard deviation of team payrolls fell for the first time since 1994.[36]

The gap between baseball's "haves" and "have-nots" is narrowing. The narrowing revenue gap, combined with shrewd resource management, should make more teams competitive.

Changes in media technology are creating an "on hand and on demand" media environment in which our personal media content choices can come with us wherever we are.[37] Direct consumer payment will bear the costs of this technology. Although the medium was once viewed for free, Americans now routinely pay a monthly fee for better television service. Paying for what used to be "free" is no longer a political issue. However, marketing and political realities will keep baseball's most popular events, the World Series and the All-Star Game, on broadcast television. However, enhanced versions of televised baseball will be available for a fee. Want to watch a condensed version of a classic game? Want to hear a live game on your cell phone? Want to play an online fantasy game with up-to-the-second statistics? Want to watch the spring training games of multiple teams without going to Arizona or Florida? All of this is available now.

The rapid diffusion of broadband will bring more baseball, in all its mediated forms, to those who can afford it. Fans with open wallets will be able to choose camera angles and generate custom stats for the game they are watching in high definition. For these fans, the advanced media era of television will be the best of baseball times.

On the other hand, perhaps the future will simply confuse some fans, overloading them with too much information and too many options. For those fans, there is a simple solution: turn off the television, power down the notebook, silence the cell phone, and go to the ballpark.

Appendix A
Televised Baseball Games, 1949–81

American League – Televised Games, 1949–66

Teams	1949	1950	1951	1952	1953	1954	1955
ATHLETICS	77	54	54	42	42	42	0
road games	0	0	0	0	0	0	0
BROWNS/ORIOLES	5	5	5	5	5	56	59
road games	0	0	0	0	0	30	31
INDIANS	77	77	77	77	77	77	25
road games	0	0	0	0	0	77	25
RED SOX	77	77	77	77	74	77	71
road games	0	0	0	0	0	18	18
SENATORS/RANGERS	77	77	21	26	38	50	57
road games	0	0	0	0	14	26	29
TIGERS	35	35	35	35	35	42	42
road games	0	0	0	0	0	7	13
WHITE SOX	77	54	54	54	54	54	54
road games	0	0	0	0	0	0	0
YANKEES	77	77	77	77	72	77	77
road games	0	0	0	0	0	0	0
ANGELS							
road games							
TWINS							
road games							
ROYALS							
road games							
PILOTS/BREWERS							
road games							
BLUE JAYS							
road games							
MARINERS							
road games							
TV Games Average	63	57	50	50	49	59	48
TV Road Games Average	0	0	0	0	2	20	15
TV as % of Games	41%	37%	32%	32%	32%	39%	31%
Road as % of TV Games	0%	0%	0%	0%	4%	33%	30%

American League – Televised Games, 1949–66 (continued)

1956	1957	1958	1959	1960	1961	1962	1963	1964	1965	1966
0	0	0	10	10	30	30	41	40	40	25
0	0	0	10	10	30	30	40	35	35	20
55	58	53	54	46	50	50	50	50	47	50
29	37	32	33	35	39	46	44	45	39	42
54	54	54	53	54	57	56	52	51	46	48
27	27	27	36	37	45	43	28	26	27	28
51	55	55	51	55	56	56	55	57	56	56
17	20	20	24	25	19	21	22	26	26	22
51	48	48	13	24	30	30	30	33	35	35
27	24	24	5	12	17	19	19	22	24	24
44	37	39	41	42	41	41	41	41	40	40
19	27	28	29	30	30	30	31	32	29	29
54	54	53	54	55	56	57	56	56	55	78
0	0	0	0	12	12	13	13	13	13	13
77	77	140	123	124	127	127	127	124	123	110
0	0	63	46	47	46	46	46	47	47	45
					20	20	20	20	20	20
					10	20	20	20	20	20
					50	50	50	50	50	50
					45	45	46	46	46	46
48	48	55	50	51	52	52	52	52	51	51
15	17	24	23	26	29	31	31	31	31	29
31%	31%	36%	32%	33%	32%	32%	32%	32%	32%	32%
31%	35%	44%	46%	51%	57%	61%	59%	60%	60%	56%

American League – Televised Games, 1967–81

Teams	1967	1968	1969	1970	1971	1972	1973
ATHLETICS	20	25	25	25	25	25	22
road games	15	25	25	25	25	25	22
BROWNS/ORIOLES	52	50	52	52	52	52	52
road games	45	44	45	45	46	44	44
INDIANS	46	46	45	48	48	48	33
road games	27	27	25	29	29	29	33
RED SOX	56	56	56	56	56	62	62
road games	26	26	23	30	30	35	36
SENATORS/RANGERS	35	35	35	30	40	24	22
road games	24	24	24	30	40	19	22
TIGERS	40	40	40	40	40	40	43
road games	29	29	30	29	29	29	31
WHITE SOX	63	144	135	135	135	135	30
road games	13	63	54	54	54	54	15
YANKEES	112	112	95	86	96	78	76
road games	47	47	41	37	47	35	32
ANGELS	22	24	24	24	25	26	25
road games	22	24	24	24	25	26	25
TWINS	55	50	50	50	50	50	30
road games	51	46	46	46	46	46	30
ROYALS			26	24	26	26	28
road games			26	24	26	24	28
PILOTS/BREWERS			0	0	25	33	30
road games			0	0	16	26	20
BLUE JAYS							
road games							
MARINERS							
road games							
TV Games Average	50	58	49	48	52	50	38
TV Road Games Average	30	36	30	31	34	33	28
TV as % of Games	31%	36%	30%	29%	32%	31%	23%
Road as % of TV Games	60%	61%	62%	65%	67%	65%	75%

American League – Televised Games, 1967–81 (continued)

1974	1975	1976	1977	1978	1979	1980	1981
0	37	27	25	25	30	30	30
0	27	20	20	20	23	20	20
52	52	51	52	50	51	51	50
43	43	42	44	42	45	45	45
40	40	40	40	40	40	70	60
15	25	25	25	25	30	45	45
67	86	92	95	93	93	97	97
41	63	67	65	62	62	67	67
22	23	24	24	25	27	27	27
22	23	24	24	25	27	27	27
41	50	46	46	41	46	52	52
30	36	34	34	24	29	36	38
125	125	125	125	125	125	125	64
49	49	49	49	50	50	50	52
72	68	68	68	78	100	95	101
30	29	29	29	37	60	55	59
25	26	26	28	30	30	30	30
25	26	26	28	30	30	22	24
30	50	50	50	50	50	50	50
30	46	46	46	46	46	46	46
35	35	35	40	45	45	41	41
35	35	35	40	45	45	41	41
30	30	30	30	30	37	40	60
20	20	22	22	22	31	34	60
			16	22	18	16	22
			9	13	8	7	10
			17	18	18	20	20
			17	18	18	20	20
45	52	51	47	48	51	53	50
28	35	35	32	33	36	37	40
28%	32%	32%	29%	30%	31%	33%	31%
63%	68%	68%	69%	68%	71%	69%	79%

American League – Average Televised Games by Time Period

Teams	1949–53	1954–60	1961–68	1969–81	1949–81	1949–81 Road %
ATHLETICS	54	9	31	25	28	57%
road games	0	3	29	21	16	
BROWNS/ORIOLES	5	54	50	51	45	78%
road games	0	32	43	44	35	
INDIANS	77	53	50	46	53	51%
road games	0	37	31	29	27	
RED SOX	76	59	56	78	68	43%
road games	0	20	24	50	30	
SENATORS/RANGERS	48	42	33	27	35	58%
road games	3	21	22	26	20	
TIGERS	35	41	41	44	41	59%
road games	0	22	30	31	24	
WHITE SOX	59	54	71	116	83	29%
road games	0	2	19	48	24	
YANKEES	76	99	120	83	94	34%
road games	0	22	46	40	32	
ANGELS			21	27	25	95%
road games			20	26	23	
TWINS			51	47	48	92%
road games			46	44	45	
ROYALS				34	34	100%
road games				34	34	
PILOTS/BREWERS				29	29	78%
road games				23	23	
BLUE JAYS				19	19	47%
road games				9	9	
MARINERS				19	19	100%
road games				19	19	
TV Games Average	54	51	52	46	44	
TV Road Games Average	0	20	31	32	26	
TV as % of Games	35%	33%	32%	28%	27%	
Road as % of TV Games	0%	39%	59%	69%	58%	

National League – Televised Games, 1949–66

Teams	1949	1950	1951	1952	1953	1954	1955
BRAVES	77	77	54	54	0	0	0
road games	0	0	0	0	0	0	0
CARDINALS	30	5	5	5	5	77	77
road games	0	0	0	0	0	77	77
CUBS	77	77	77	77	77	77	77
road games	0	0	0	0	0	0	0
DODGERS	77	77	77	77	77	77	102
road games	0	0	0	0	0	0	25
GIANTS	77	77	77	77	77	77	77
road games	0	0	0	0	0	0	0
PHILLIES	77	54	54	54	42	40	62
road games	0	0	0	0	0	0	33
PIRATES	0	0	0	0	0	36	0
road games	0	0	0	0	0	36	0
REDS	77	77	26	26	27	26	26
road games	0	0	0	0	0	0	0
ASTROS							
road games							
METS							
road games							
EXPOS							
road games							
PADRES							
road games							
TV Games Average	62	56	46	46	38	51	53
TV Road Games Average	0	0	0	0	0	14	17
TV as % of Games	40%	36%	30%	30%	25%	33%	34%
Road as % of TV Games	0%	0%	0%	0%	0%	28%	32%

National League – Televised Games, 1949–66 (continued)

1956	1957	1958	1959	1960	1961	1962	1963	1964	1965	1966
0	0	0	0	0	0	15	25	30	17	18
0	0	0	0	0	0	15	20	18	17	18
65	64	30	41	40	39	20	21	21	24	22
65	64	30	41	40	39	20	21	21	24	22
77	77	77	77	82	82	86	86	86	86	86
0	0	0	0	5	5	5	5	5	5	5
102	102	0	11	11	11	10	9	9	9	9
25	25	0	11	11	11	9	9	9	9	9
77	77	0	0	0	11	9	9	9	9	17
0	0	0	0	0	11	9	9	9	9	17
74	75	70	64	60	56	60	54	51	51	62
52	51	40	33	36	36	35	30	30	30	43
0	24	25	27	30	33	33	33	33	34	38
0	24	25	27	30	33	33	33	33	34	38
53	53	53	53	50	51	50	47	44	38	41
30	30	30	30	27	29	29	30	26	28	29
						14	14	12	13	12
						14	14	12	13	12
						133	128	126	122	126
						52	52	45	41	45
56	59	32	34	34	35	43	43	42	40	43
22	24	16	18	19	21	22	22	21	21	24
36%	38%	21%	22%	22%	23%	27%	26%	26%	25%	27%
38%	41%	49%	52%	55%	58%	51%	52%	49%	52%	55%

National League – Televised Games, 1967–81

Teams	1967	1968	1969	1970	1971	1972	1973
BRAVES	18	20	20	20	20	20	52
road games	18	20	20	20	20	20	52
CARDINALS	22	24	26	26	26	26	29
road games	22	24	26	26	26	26	29
CUBS	86	144	144	144	148	148	148
road games	5	63	63	63	67	67	67
DODGERS	9	9	18	21	21	22	21
road games	9	9	18	21	21	22	21
GIANTS	17	17	17	17	17	17	20
road games	17	17	17	17	17	17	20
PHILLIES	58	59	60	60	67	68	70
road games	39	41	39	39	53	50	46
PIRATES	38	38	38	37	38	38	38
road games	38	38	38	37	38	38	38
REDS	42	42	40	40	35	35	35
road games	30	34	35	35	30	30	30
ASTROS	14	12	14	14	14	14	20
road games	14	12	14	14	14	14	20
METS	117	117	117	117	117	117	106
road games	42	42	46	42	42	49	56
EXPOS			15	15	18	21	19
road games			5	5	5	7	6
PADRES			4	20	22	22	0
road games			4	20	22	22	0
TV Games Average	42	48	43	44	45	46	47
TV Road Games Average	23	30	27	28	30	30	32
TV as % of Games	26%	30%	26%	27%	28%	28%	29%
Road as % of TV Games	56%	62%	63%	64%	65%	66%	69%

National League – Televised Games, 1967–81 (continued)

1974	1975	1976	1977	1978	1979	1980	1981
60	50	64	74	98	97	97	147
60	50	64	74	74	74	76	70
29	30	29	31	33	40	40	40
29	30	29	31	33	40	40	40
148	148	145	142	137	141	148	148
67	67	64	61	56	60	67	67
21	21	21	26	22	22	24	50
21	21	21	26	22	22	24	50
20	20	20	20	23	31	31	30
20	20	20	20	23	31	31	30
70	68	70	68	71	71	70	70
46	44	52	54	55	55	56	56
38	38	38	44	40	40	46	42
38	38	38	44	40	40	46	42
35	34	35	40	40	40	45	48
30	32	32	37	37	37	42	45
20	28	28	45	46	72	79	67
20	28	28	45	46	72	79	67
117	120	113	116	117	99	98	100
61	59	59	61	58	46	44	45
20	20	22	20	17	20	18	32
7	7	8	7	6	7	6	32
0	0	0	14	22	26	39	42
0	0	0	14	22	26	39	42
48	48	49	53	56	58	61	68
33	33	35	40	39	43	46	49
30%	30%	30%	33%	34%	36%	38%	42%
69%	69%	71%	74%	71%	73%	75%	72%

National League – Average Televised Games by Time Period

Teams	1949–53	1954–61	1962–68	1969–81	1949–81	1949–81 Road %
BRAVES	52	0	20	63	37	65%
road games	0	0	18	52	24	
CARDINALS	10	54	22	31	32	95%
road games	0	54	22	31	30	
CUBS	77	78	94	145	108	26%
road games	0	1	13	64	28	
DODGERS	77	52	9	24	36	41%
road games	0	14	9	24	15	
GIANTS	77	40	12	22	33	35%
road games	0	1	12	22	12	
PHILLIES	56	63	56	68	62	57%
road games	0	35	35	50	36	
PIRATES	0	22	35	39	28	100%
road games	0	22	35	39	28	
REDS	47	46	43	39	43	59%
road games	0	22	29	35	25	
ASTROS			13	35	28	100%
road games			13	35	28	
METS			124	112	116	42%
road games			46	51	49	
EXPOS				20	20	42%
road games				8	8	
PADRES				16	16	100%
road games				16	16	
TV Games Average	48	44	43	51	46	
TV Road Games Average	0	19	23	36	25	
TV as % of Games	31%	29%	27%	32%	29%	
Road as % of TV Games	0%	42%	54%	70%	54%	

Notes

Introduction

1. Seth Livingstone, "The Top 100 Things That Impacted Baseball in the 20th Century," *Baseball Weekly*, January 5, 2000, 16–17, 21.
2. Robert V. Bellamy Jr., "The Evolving Television Sports Marketplace," in *MediaSport*, edited by Lawrence A. Wenner, 73–87 (London: Routledge, 1998).
3. "World Series TV Ratings," Baseball Almanac.com, http://www .baseball-almanac.com/ws/wstv.shtml (accessed December 18, 2006).
4. "All-Star Television Ratings," Baseball Almanac.com, http://www .baseball-almanac.com/asgbox/asgtv.shtml (accessed December 18, 2006).
5. "MLB, Fox, and Turner Reach New Television Agreements," press release, Major League Baseball, July 11, 2006, http://mlb.com/news/press_releases/ press_release.jsp?ymd=20060711&content_id=1552548&vkey=pr_ mlb&fext=.jsp&c_id=mlb.
6. Curt Smith, *Voices of the Game* (New York: Simon & Schuster, 1992).
7. Tom Duncan, *Principles of Advertising and IMC*, 2d ed. (New York: McGraw-Hill, 2005).
8. Robert V. Bellamy Jr. and James R. Walker, "Foul Tip or Strike Three? The Evolving Marketing Partnership of Major League Baseball and Television," *NINE: A Journal of Baseball History and Social Policy Issues* 3, no. 2 (1995): 261–75.
9. Charles Dexter, "The Staley Story," *Baseball Digest*, August 1960, 67, 72.
10. Ed Rumill, "Is TV Ruining Catchers?" *Baseball Digest*, August 1965, 69–70.
11. Smith, *Voices of the Game*, 1992.
12. See, for example, Jack Buck with Rob Rains and Bob Broeg, *That's a Winner!* (Champaign IL: Sports Publishing, Inc.); Harry Caray with Bob Verdi, *Holy Cow!* (New York: Villard, 1989); and Chuck Thompson with Gordon Beard, *Ain't the Beer Cold!*, new ed. (Baltimore: Diamond Communications, 2002).

1. The Experimental Years

1. *New York Times*, "Notes on Television," May 7, 1939; *New York Times*, "Televised Baseball Due First Time Wednesday," May 15, 1939; *New York Times*, "Television Game Today," May 17, 1939.
2. H. Winfield Secor, "Strike One! Greets Japanese Visualists," *Television News*, November-December 1931, 331.
3. Jeff Kisseloff, *The Box: An Oral History of Television 1920–1961* (New York: Viking, 1995), 11.

4. "Connie Mack and Boake Carter Stage Air's First Large-Scale Television Test," *Sporting News*, February 18, 1937, 10.

5. "New Touch Given Old Game," *Sporting News*, March 30, 1939, 4.

6. National Broadcasting Company. *Television's First Year* (New York: NBC, 1940).

7. Harry Gordon, "The 1940 Report on Television Reaction . . . Second and Concluding Study of a Survey of New York World's Fair Visitors," NBC Archives, Wisconsin Historical Society, Madison, Wisconsin (hereafter "NBC Archives").

8. Michael Ritchie, *Please Stand By* (New York: Overlook Press, 1994), 128.

9. Orrin E. Dunlap Jr., "Collegians Play Ball As Television Mirrors the Game," *New York Times*, May 21, 1939.

10. Dunlap, "Collegians Play Ball," May 21, 1939.

11. "First Television of Baseball Seen," *New York Times*, May 18, 1939.

12. Ben Bodec, "Baseball Televizes Blurringly," *Variety*, May 24, 1939.

13. William O. Johnson Jr., *Super Spectator and the Electric Lilliputians* (Boston: Little, Brown, 1971), 37.

14. Dunlap, "Collegians Play Ball," May 21, 1939.

15. Bodec, "Baseball Televizes Blurringly."

16. "First U.S. Sports Event Is Televised by NBC," *Life*, June 5, 1939, 70.

17. "Estimated 38 Million Will See World Series on Television," *Washington Post*, October 4, 1950.

18. Bill Stern with Oscar Fraley, *The Taste of Ashes* (New York: Henry Holt, 1959), 72.

19. Smith, *Voices of the Game*, 40.

20. A. H. Morton to John F. Royal, July 15, 1936, interdepartmental correspondence; Red Barber to Alfred H. Morton, September 5, 1936; John F. Royal to A. H. Morton, October 6, 1936, interdepartmental correspondence. NBC Archives.

21. R. H. Stewart, "The Development of Network Television Program Types to January, 1953," vol. 1; 2 vols. (PhD diss., Ohio State University, 1954).

22. Jim Beach, "The Television Producer," in *Baseball Is Their Business*, edited by Harold Rosenthal, 105 (New York: Random House, 1952).

23. Bob Lardine, "TV Baseball Is 25 years old," *New York Sunday News*, August 23, 1964.

24. Red Barber, "We Were Making History—Flying Blind," *TV Guide*, August 24, 1974, 17; "First Workout for Commercials on Television," *Variety*, August 30, 1939; "New Dodger Stunt—Twin-Bill Televised," *Sporting News*, August 31, 1939, 3.

25. "See Big League Baseball" (advertisement), *Brooklyn Eagle*, August 24, 1939.

26. Gabriel Paul to Michael Maher, March 6, 1987, Television File, National Baseball Hall of Fame Library, Cooperstown, New York.

27. Harry Craft to Michael Maher, February 25, 1987, Television File, National Baseball Hall of Fame Library, Cooperstown, New York.

28. "Watching a Televised Baseball Game," *New York Times*, September 3, 1939.

29. *Sporting News*, August 31, 1939, 3.

30. Red Barber and Robert Creamer, *Rhubarb in the Catbird Seat* (Garden City NY: Doubleday, 1968), 57.

31. Ritchie, *Please Stand By*, 133.

32. Red Barber, *The Broadcasters* (New York: Dial, 1970), 135.

33. "Baseball Telecast," *Broadcasting*, September 1, 1939, 17.

34. "First Workout for Commercials on Television," *Variety*, August 30, 1939.

35. "Pacific Coast League Ushers in the 1940 Campaign, But Two Openers Are Set Back by Dying March Lion," *Sporting News*, April 4, 1940, 5.

36. "Television Notes," *Broadcasting*, May 1, 1940, 63.

37. "Radio Today," *New York Times*, June 11, 1941.

38. "Televise First Game—And the Results Are Amazingly Good!" *Radio & Television*, August 1941, 204.

39. "Novel Commercials in Video Debut," *Broadcasting*, July 7, 1941, 10.

40. "Adam Hat Shows Its Faith in Television by Signing for All NBC Sports Events," *Broadcasting*, August 25, 1941, 56.

41. Christopher H. Sterling and John Michael Kittross, *Stay Tuned: A History of American Broadcasting*, 3d ed. (Mahwah NJ: Erlbaum, 2002), 169.

42. "NBC Will Televise Events in the Garden, Chiefly for Wounded in Service Hospitals," *New York Times*, October 12, 1943.

43. NBC Television Department, "Summary Outline of Television Program Activities Station WNBT National Broadcasting Company June 1942 to Date," February 26, 1945, NBC Archives.

44. "American to Film Game," *Broadcasting*, August 27, 1945, 4.

45. T. R. Kennedy Jr., "Television in Action," *New York Times*, June 24, 1945.

46. "N.Y. Yankee–Detroit Baseball Game," *Variety*, July 6, 1945.

47. "Chi Cubs Telecast Hits Elevator Snag," *Variety*, April 24, 1946.

48. "Cubs Home Games Now Regular WBKB Remote Television Feature," press release, WBKB, July 15, 1946, 1–2.

49. "Championship Fight," *Life*, July 1, 1946, 22.

50. "Live Color Show Televised by CBS," *New York Times*, September 16, 1946.

51. "235,000 See Game Telecast," *New York Times*, December 1, 1946.

52. "Giants vs. Braves Baseball," *Variety*, May 29, 1946.

53. *Variety*, May 29, 1946.

54. "Baseball—Red Sox vs. Yanks," *Variety*, August 21, 1946.

55. "Possibility of Televising World Series Is Studied," *Sporting News*, August 21, 1946, 34.

56. "Radio Today," *New York Times*, October 3, 1946; "Playoff Telecast," *Broadcasting*, October 7, 1946.

57. Dan Daniel, "Television Clause Snags Player Contract, *Sporting News*, September 25, 1946, 1.

58. "CBS Will Telecast Dodgers Next Year," *Broadcasting*, November 11, 1946, 78.

59. "DuMont to Televise Yankees Baseball and Football Games," *Broadcasting*, December 9, 1946, 84.

60. "Television Rights to Yank, Giant Home Games Sold," *Sporting News*, December 11, 1946, 29.

2. The First Seasons of Televised Baseball

1. Otis Freeman, "How WABD Handles Remotes," *Tele-Tech*, March 1948, 42.

2. "TV Rights Free," *Broadcasting*, May 3, 1948, 30.

3. "TV Baseball," *Broadcasting*, January 31, 1949, 31.

4. John P. Taylor, "Camera Placement and Switching for Baseball Broadcasting," *Broadcast News*, September 1947, 57–58.

5. Sterling and Kittross, *Stay Tuned*, 864.

6. Sterling and Kittross, *Stay Tuned*, 864.

7. John P. Taylor, "Baseball Television: 1949," *Broadcast News*, September 1949, 19–27.

8. "Baseball More Coverage Announced," *Broadcasting*, April 25, 1949, 31.

9. Quoted in Leonard Koppett, *Koppett's Concise History of Major League Baseball* (New York: Carroll & Graf, 2004), 231.

10. "Sports Programs Lead New York Fare," *Broadcasting*, January 16, 1950, 11.

11. Interdepartmental correspondence, National Broadcasting Company, January 10, 1949, NBC Archives.

12. "Bat, Beer & Camera," *Time*, April 26, 1954, 104.

13. Pete Coutros, "Don Wiltsbooth," *New York Post*, March 4, 1988.

14. "Radio and TV Highlights of 1950," *Broadcasting*, January 8, 1951, 32.

15. Bill Garden, NBC Television Field Program Director, to Noel Jordan, March 25, 1948, NBC Archives.

16. Beach, "The Television Producer," 106.

17. Sterling and Kittross, *Stay Tuned*, 834.

18. Carleton D. Smith to Sidney N. Strots, May 25, 1948, NBC Archives.

19. Bill Garden to Noel Jordan, May 26, 1948, NBC Archives.

20. Reynold Kraft, NBC Television Sales Manager, to Newell-Emmett Company, July 6 and 7, 1948, NBC Archives.

21. Carleton D. Smith to Niles Trammell, April 19, 1949, NBC Archives.

22. Jack Murphy, "How to Televise Baseball," *Broadcasting*, May 18, 1953, 78.

23. "Baseball TV," *Broadcasting*, May 15, 1950, 4.

24. "Baseball Packs," *Broadcasting*, March 5, 1951, 24.

25. Televised game totals compiled from the *Sporting News* summaries of radio and television coverage published each April.

26. Sterling and Kittross, *Stay Tuned*, 864.

27. John Thorn, Pete Palmer, Michael Gershman, and David Pietrusza, *Total Baseball*, 6th ed. (New York: Total Sports, 1999), 107–8.

28. Kisseloff, *The Box*, 132.

29. Bill Garden to Larry Bruff, February 10, 1948, NBC Archives.

30. Jim Ogle, "Murphy Made All Stops in 20 Years As Yank TV Boss," *Sporting News*, August 24, 1968, 17.

31. *Newsweek*, "Via Video," August 30, 1948, 46–47.

32. Noran Kersta to Trevor Adams, October 1, 1948, NBC Archives.

33. Kisseloff, *The Box*.

34. Taylor, "Baseball Television," 11.

35. Noel L. Jordan to W. Wade, May 14, 1948, NBC Archives.

36. Ted Vernon, "Around the TV-Radio Circuit," *Sport*, April 1952, 9.

37. Taylor, "Baseball Television," 15.

38. Vernon (Red) Thornburgh, "Sports: The WLWT Touch," *Broadcasting*, July 25, 1949, 46–48.

39. Beach, "The Television Producer," 109.

40. Murphy, "How to Televise Baseball," 80.

41. "Baseball Tops TV," *Broadcasting*, May 31, 1948, 30.

42. "Half of First Ten Pulse Ratings Taken by Sports," *Broadcasting*, July 12, 1948, 14.

43. "Philly TV Survey on Night Baseball," *Broadcasting*, August 9, 1948, 60.

44. "Video Outshines Radio with Chi. Baseball Fans," *Broadcasting*, January 23, 1950, 67.

45. "Chicago Pub Patrons Like Baseball on TV," *Broadcasting*, July 12, 1948, 68.

46. Edward P. Morgan, "Fifty-Mile Bleachers," *Collier's*, September 27, 1947, 30.

47. "It's the Taverns That Still Worry Baseball Chiefs," *Variety*, June 16, 1948, 32.

48. "Playground TV," *Broadcasting*, March 29, 1948, 24.

49. "Bets Ride on Every Pitch As Video 'Casinos' Boom," *New York Times*, July 2, 1949.

50. Red Smith, "TV Peep Show," *Baseball Digest*, February 1951, 91.

51. Richard Ben Cramer, *Joe DiMaggio: The Hero's Life* (New York: Touchstone, 2001), 263.

52. John Crosby, "Here's How It Is over Television," *Baseball Digest*, August 1947, 21–22.

53. "Take Me Out to the Ball Game," *Variety*, April 23, 1947.

54. "Inside Stuff—Television," *Variety*, May 28, 1947.

55. "No Runs, Few Hits, What Errors!" *Variety*, May 5, 1948,

56. William Garden, "Some Runs, Hits, Few Errors!" *Variety*, May 19, 1948.

57. "Baseball—A Dim View," *Variety*, April 27, 1949.

58. Stewart, "Development of Network Television Program Types."

3. Team Approaches to Television in the Broadcast Era

1. Andrew Zimbalist, *Baseball and Billions* (New York: Basic Books, 1994), 148.

2. Paul D. Adomites, "Baseball on the Air," in Thorn and Palmer, *Total Baseball*, 654–56 (New York: Warner Books, 1991).

3. Bellamy, "The Evolving Television Sport Marketplace."

4. Phillip M. Cox II, "Flag on the Play? The Siphoning Effect on Sports Television," *Federal Communications Bar Journal* 47, no. 3 (April 1995); Federal Communications Commission, *Sports Programming Migration Interim Report*, 8 FCC Rcd. 4875 (1993).

5. Bellamy, "The Evolving Television Sport Marketplace."

6. Andrew Zimbalist, *May the Best Team Win: Baseball Economics and Public Policy* (Washington DC: Brookings Institution Press, 2003).

7. Vic Gregovits, Vice President of Marketing, Pittsburgh Pirates, personal communication with Robert V. Bellamy Jr., October 21, 1999.

8. Gregovits, October 21, 1999.

9. Adomites, "Baseball on the Air," 654.

10. Adomites, "Baseball on the Air," 654.

11. David Brugnone, Director of Affiliate Sales and Marketing, Prime Sports KBL, Pittsburgh, personal communication with Robert V. Bellamy Jr., May 18, 1995; Gil Lucas, Director of Operations, KBL Sports Network, Pittsburgh, personal communication with Robert V. Bellamy Jr., April 16, 1992.

12. Jeff Passan, "Selig's Promise," Yahoo! Sports, July 11, 2006, http://sports.yahoo.com/mlb/news?slug=jp-blackouts071106&prov=yhoo&type=lgns.

13. David Brugnone, Director of Affiliate Sales and Marketing, Prime Sports KBL Pittsburgh, personal communication with Robert V. Bellamy Jr., October 7, 1999.

14. Bob Smizik, "Bettman Deserves Applause," *Pittsburgh Post-Gazette*, February 1, 2005, C1.

15. Brugnone, October 7, 1999.

16. Tom Barnes, "Pirates Balk at Restaurants' Pitch," *Pittsburgh Post-Gazette*, December 4, 2001, C3.

17. Adomites, "Baseball on the Air," 1991.

18. John Helyar, *Lords of the Realm* (New York: Villard, 1994); Smith, *Voices of the Game*.

19. Figures from the annual "Baseball" rights report in *Broadcasting* and its successor, *Broadcasting & Cable* magazine.

20. Lucas, April 16, 1992; Brugnone, May 18, 1995.

21. Adomites, "Baseball on the Air," 1991.

22. Smith, *Voices of the Game*, 458.

23. St. Louis Cardinals (official team web site), http://www.stlcardinals.com (accessed June 23, 1998).

24. Helyar, *Lords of the Realm*, 1998, 98.

25. David Whitson, "Circuits of Promotion: Media, Marketing and the Globalization of Sport," in *MediaSport*, edited by Lawrence A. Wenner, 57–72 (London: Routledge, 1998).

26. Smith, *Voices of the Game*, 14.

27. Russ Hodges and Al Hirshberg, *My Giants* (New York: Doubleday, 1963), 31.

28. Kisseloff, *The Box*, 87–88.

29. Larry Wolters, "W-G-N Video Station Orders $300,000 Units," *Chicago Tribune*, June 2, 1947, 1.

30. Smith, *Voices of the Game*, 148.

31. Kisseloff, *The Box*, 137.

32. Daniel D. Calibraro and John Fink, *WGN: A Pictorial History* (Chicago: WGN, Inc., 1961).

33. "Baseball Revenue Levels Off," *Broadcasting*, March 4, 1963, 66–70.

34. Helyar, *Lords of the Realm*, 365.

35. Fox Sports Biz.com, "MLB Team Owners," http://www.foxsports.com/business/resources/owners/mlb.sm (accessed June 24, 2000).

36. Forbes.com, "Baseball Team Valuations," http://www.forbes.com/lists/2006/33/Rank_1.html (accessed January 21, 2007).

37. James Elsener, "Baseball Is More Than a Sport, It's a Business Too," *Chicago Tribune*, August 14, 1977, 1, 14.

38. Katherine Q. Seelye, "2 Billionaires Make Offer for Tribune," *New York Times*, March 30, 2007. http://www.nytimes.com/2007/03/30/business/media/30tribune.html?_r=1&ref=media&oref=slogin; David Greising, "Cubs for Sale, But Is Wrigley Field?," *Chicago Tribune*, April 2, 2007, 1.

39. Sterling and Kittross, *Stay Tuned*, 864.

40. Robert V. Bellamy Jr., "Constraints on a Broadcast Innovation: Zenith's Phonevision System, 1931–1972," *Journal of Communication* 38, no. 4 (1988): 8–20.

41. Ted Leitzell, Zenith Radio Corporation, to Walter F. O'Malley, January 29,

1953. Archives, National Baseball Hall of Fame and Museum, Cooperstown, New York.

42. Joe King, "O'Malley Wants to Test Pay-at-Home Baseball TV," *New York World-Telegram & Sun*, January 27, 1953.

43. Bellamy, "Constraints on a Broadcast Innovation," 1988.

44. David Gunzerath, "'Darn That Pay TV': STV's Challenge to American Television's Dominant Economic Model," *Journal of Broadcasting and Electronic Media* 44, no. 4 (2000): 655–73.

45. Gunzerath, "'Darn That Pay TV'"; David H. Ostroff, "A History of STV, Inc. and the California Vote Against Pay Television," *Journal of Broadcasting* 27, no. 4 (1983): 371–86.

46. *United States v. Paramount Pictures, Inc.*, 334 U.S. 131 (1948).

47. Gunzerath, "'Darn That Pay TV.'"

48. See, for example, "Stark Calls Pay TV a 'Monster,'" *Broadcasting*, July 1, 1957, 91–92; and "TV & Baseball," *Wall Street Journal*, October 31, 1957, 1.

49. "Dodgers' President Backs Pay-As-You Television for Baseball," *Wall Street Journal*, May 5, 1955; Arthur Daley, "It's His Own Description," *New York Times*, October 14, 1957, 26.

50. "Bill to Ban Fee TV Offered by Rep. Cellar," *Broadcasting*, June 20, 1955, 7; "The Pay-TV Debate (Continued)," *Broadcasting*, July 22, 1957, 31.

51. "Pay TV for Giants," *Chicago Daily News*, September 9, 1958.

52. Bob Hunter, "O'Malley Taps New Mother Lode—Fee Teevee," *Sporting News*, August 1, 1964, 2.

53. Gunzerath, "'Darn That Pay TV'"; *Time*, "Death of STV," November 13, 1964, http://www.time.com/time/magazine/article/0,9171,898247,00.html (accessed January 12, 2007).

54. Ostroff, "A History of STV."

55. Encyclopedia of Company Histories, "Anaheim Angels, Baseball Club, Inc.," Answers.com, http://www.answers.com/topic/anaheim-angels -baseball-club-inc (accessed January 17, 2007); Ross Newhan, *The Anaheim Angels: A Complete History* (New York: Hyperion, 2000).

56. Jack Sands and Peter Gammons, *Coming Apart at the Seams* (New York: Macmillan, 1993).

57. Noah Liebman, "MLB's Internet Plans May Cut into Web Cash," *Street & Smith's SportsBusiness Journal*, March 6–12, 2000, 13.

4. Televising the World Series

1. Erik Barnouw, *The Golden Web: A History of Broadcasting in the United States 1933–1953* (New York: Oxford, 1968).

2. "Possibility of Televising World's Series Is Studied," *Sporting News*, August 21, 1946, 34.

3. "Radio-TV Draw Huge Series Audience," *Broadcasting*, October 6, 1947, 83.

4. "Gillette, Ford Sponsor Series Telecasts," *Sporting News*, October 8, 1947, 33.

5. "Gillette, Ford Sponsor Series Telecasts," *Sporting News*.

6. "The News of Radio," *New York Times*, September 24, 1947.

7. "Short Stops on Video," *Variety*, October 8, 1947.

8. Jack Gould, "The News of Radio," *New York Times*, September 30, 1947.

9. Jack Gould, "The News of Radio," *New York Times*, August 29, 1947.

10. Jack Gould, "The News of Radio," *New York Times*, September 4, 1947.

11. "Series to Be Televised; 2 Sponsors Pay $65,000," *New York Times*, September 27, 1947.

12. Jack Gould, "The News of Radio," *New York Times*, September 10, 1947.

13. "Series Television Plugs Show 5 O' Clock Shadow," *Sporting News*, October 15, 1947, 26.

14. R. W. Stewart, "Baseball on Video," *New York Times*, October 5, 1947.

15. *Variety*, October 8, 1947.

16. *Variety*, October 8, 1947.

17. "Radio and Television," *New York Times*, September 18, 1948.

18. *New York Times*, September 18, 1948.

19. "Stratovision Plan for Series Bright," *Broadcasting*, October 11, 1948, 67.

20. "TV Pitchers Curve," *Broadcasting*, October 18, 1948, 26, 64; "Attempt to Telecast Series Contest Using Airplane Relay Fails," *Chicago Tribune*, October 12, 1948.

21. "Stratovision Plan for Series Bright," 67.

22. "World Series Televised Free," *New York Times*, October 3, 1948; "World Series on Boston Common—by Television," *Business Week*, October 16, 1948, 54.

23. "Chicago Gets Series Seat Thru Video," *Chicago Tribune*, October 9, 1948; "Chicago to See Series Games from Cleveland," *Chicago Tribune*, October 6, 1948.

24. "Train Television Shows Ball Game," *New York Times*, October 8, 1948.

25. "Video Cameras Turn in Dull Story of Big Game," *Variety*, October 7, 1948.

26. "World Series Roundup," *Variety*, October 13, 1948.

27. "Television Takes Its Eye Off Ball in World Series Opener," *Washington Post*, October 7, 1948; "World Series Roundup," *Variety*, October 13, 1948.

28. "It's Series Time," *Broadcasting*, October 3, 1949, 23.

29. Jack Gould, "Video to Get No Fee for World Series," *New York Times*, September 20, 1949.

30. Sterling and Kittross, *Stay Tuned*, 864; "Millions to See World Series via Television," *Chicago Daily Tribune*, October 5, 1949.

31. "Barkley, Senate View World Series thru Video," *Chicago Daily Tribune*, October 6, 1949.

32. "Video Allocations Issued by Admiral," *New York Times*, September 24, 1949.

33. Thomas M. Pryor, "Theatre Televising of World Series Games," *New York Times*, October 16, 1949.

34. "Beer Nursers Jam Bars Having Video," *New York Times*, October 6, 1949.

35. "Key TV Cities Blow Hot and Cold on World Series Camera Techniques," *Variety*, October 12, 1949.

36. "TV Strikes Out on Two Innings of World Series," *Chicago Tribune*, October 5, 1950; "Millions of Fans to Watch Series on Television Sets," *Los Angeles Times*, October 4, 1950.

37. "$500,000 Bid for World Series TeeVee Rights," *Los Angeles Times*, August 3, 1950; "Best Series Video Bids Hit $650,000," *Los Angeles Times*, August 17, 1950; "$1,000,000 Video-Radio Series," *Washington Post*, August 22, 1950.

38. "Gillette Plays Up Series TV—with Tears in Its Eyes?," *Business Week*, September 16, 1950, 84–86.

39. "Chandler Brushes Off Players on TV Split," *Washington Post*, October 3, 1950; "Want Broadcast Share," *New York Times*, September 15, 1950; "Players May Cut Television Melon," *New York Times*, September 22, 1950.

40. "Marty Marion Says That Chandler Refused Conference on Players' Television Rights," *New York Times*, October 3, 1950.

41. "Broadcast Money Discussed Again," *New York Times*, October 8, 1950.

42. "Players O.K. TV Cash for Pension Fund," *Chicago Tribune*, November 9, 1950; "Agree on Series Money," *New York Times*, November 9, 1950; "Pension Fund Gains TV Money," *Chicago Tribune*, November 17, 1950.

43. "Happy's Last Stand," *Life*, March 26, 1951, 107.

44. Irving Vaughan, "Majors Vote to Name New Commissioner," *Chicago Daily Tribune*, December 13, 1950.

45. Vaughan, "Majors Vote to Name New Commissioner."

46. Albert B. Chandler to Michael Maher, March 25, 1987, Television File, National Baseball Hall of Fame Library, Cooperstown, New York.

47. John Drebinger, "Majors Fail to Buy Contract of Chief," *New York Times*, December 13, 1950.

48. "6-Year TV Rights Sold to Gillette," *New York Times*, December 27, 1950.

49. Sterling and Kittross, *Stay Tuned*, 2002, 864.

50. Dan Parker, "Poor Reception for TV Deal," *Baseball Digest*, March 1951, 52–53.

51. "Baseball's TV Contract Stirs Cub Owners," *Chicago Daily Tribune*, December 27, 1950.

52. "Saigh Tells Why He Voted Against Chandler," *Washington Post*, January 7, 1951.

53. John F. Royal to Joseph H. McConnell, November 15, 1949, interdepartmental correspondence; Easton C. Woolley to Charles R. Denny, November 16, 1949, NBC Archives.

54. John Drebinger, "Rejection Is Seen for Elevation Bid," *New York Times*, December 11, 1947.

55. "World Series' Coverage Answers All Questions; Reflectar Lens Standout," *Variety*, October 11, 1950.

56. "Kinks in TV Kick Up for World Series," *New York Times*, October 5, 1950.

57. "Nation-Wide Video Likely by Sept. 30," *New York Times*, August 4, 1951.

58. "NBC Neatest Trick of Year in Gillette Sports Swap Deal," *Variety*, September 12, 1951.

59. Koppett, *Koppett's Concise History*, 247.

60. "TV Industry Plays Ball in N.Y. Playoff on Dodgers-Giants," *Variety*, October 3, 1951.

61. "TV's Slick Performance on World Series, with Minimum of Frills," *Variety*, October 10, 1951.

62. "TV's Slick Performance," *Variety*.

63. "70,000,000 See Series on TV," *Variety*, October 8, 1952.

64. "The World Series Stare," *Life*, October 20, 1952, 47.

65. "TV Turns in a Solid Workmanlike Job on Series, Sans Gimmicks," *Variety*, October 7, 1953.

66. "World Series," *Variety*, October 6, 1954.

67. *World Series 1952: Game 6*, October 6, 1952, Catalog ID: T86: 1626, Museum of Television and Radio, New York.

68. "World Series," *Variety*.

69. From 1959 to 1962, there were two All-Star Games each summer. In 1970, the game moved permanently to the evening hours.

70. Walter W. Mulbry to John F. Royal, May 4, 1948, NBC Archives.

71. John F. Royal to Walter W. Mulbry, May 11, 1948, telegram, NBC Archives.

72. Carleton D. Smith to John F. Royal, May 11, 1948, MLB Archives.

73. "Gillette Has Video at All-Star Contest," *Broadcasting*, July 12, 1948, 30.

74. Jimmy Dolan to Carleton D. Smith, June 7, 1949, NBC Archives.

75. Thorn, Palmer, Gershman, and Pietrusza, *Total Baseball*, 291.

76. John F. Royal to Sylvester Weaver, May 9, 1950, memorandum, NBC Archives.

77. William F. Brooks to George Frey, June 16, 1950, memorandum, NBC Archives.

78. Thorn et al., *Total Baseball*, 292.

79. Lalia Pleadwell to Steve Flynn, June 22, 1951, NBC Archives.

80. Jimmy Dolan to Bob Ritter, July 12, 1951, NBC Archives.

81. Maxon Inc. Advertising, "Opening of Telecast . . . All-Star Baseball Game," July 10, 1951, NBC Archives.

82. Paul Simpson to Robert Sarnoff, telegram, received September 30, 1955; Michael Horton to Paul Simpson, October 7, 1955, NBC Archives.

83. "World Series Pays Off with Dip in Crime Rate," New York Times, October 4, 1955.

84. "News of the Advertising and Marketing Fields," New York Times, September 10, 1956.

85. "Dulles at U.N. Watches World Series on TV," New York Times, October 10, 1956; "World Series Clicks on His Meter," Chicago Daily Tribune, October 5, 1956; "Bell Rings Now That World Series Is Over," Chicago Tribune, October 11, 1956.

86. Sterling and Kittross, Stay Tuned, 864.

87. "Ballplayers Rebuffed," New York Times, February 2, 1956; "Owners Hold Purse Strings; Just Ask 'em!" Chicago Tribune, February 2, 1956; "Major Ballplayers' Plea for Salary Raise Refused," Los Angeles Times, February 5, 1956.

88. "N.B.C. to Televise 5 World Series," New York Times, July 3, 1956.

89. "20 Million TV-Radio Pact Made," Chicago Tribune, February 25, 1960.

90. Sterling and Kittross, Stay Tuned, 864.

91. "Presenting the World Series," Washington Post, October 6, 1966.

92. Washington Post, October 6, 1966; "Baseball Is Sticky Wicket to Britons Watching the Telly," New York Times, November 5, 1966; "Spain Ignores 'World' Series," Los Angeles Times, October 8, 1966.

93. "Series, All-Star Game TV Pact Up 68 Per Cent," Washington Post, May 3, 1966.

94. Sterling and Kittross, Stay Tuned, 864.

95. Washington Post, May 3, 1966.

96. Leonard Koppett, "Sacrifice Sign Is On," New York Times, June 5, 1966.

97. "Baseball Owners Accused of Greed," Los Angeles Times, August 27, 1966.

98. Leonard Koppett, "Baseball Pension Fund Is Increased," New York Times, December 2, 1966.

99. "Baseball to Collect $50 Million in New 3-Year Pact with NBC," Washington Post, August 5, 1967; "Baseball, NBC Sign 50 Million TV Deal," Chicago Tribune, August 5, 1967.

5. Origins of the Game of the Week

1. Pete Axthelm, "Will Success Spoil Baseball?" New York Herald Tribune," January 21, 1966.

2. Charles Maher, "Baseball's Death Greatly Exaggerated," *Los Angeles Times*, March 6, 1972.

3. "Sen. Johnson's Warning on Majors' Video Policy," *Sporting News*, February 11, 1953, 18.

4. "Major 'Game of Week' Shaping Up on TV Net," *Sporting News*, February 18, 1953, 15.

5. James R. Walker and Douglas A. Ferguson, *The Broadcast Television Industry* (Needham Heights MA: Allyn & Bacon, 1998), 21–22.

6. John Drebinger, "President Will Make First Pitch at Re-Scheduled Capital Opener," *New York Times*, April 14, 1953.

7. "Bits and Bites, Begged, Borrowed and Bagged," *Sporting News*, March 4, 1953, 16.

8. "Baseball Bill Dead for '53; NFL Threatens Radio-TV Ban," *Broadcasting*, July 20, 1953, 48.

9. "TV Games of the Week Listed for Remainder of Season," *Sporting News*, July 1, 1953, 38.

10. "Variety Reveals Wide Scope of TV Game of Week," *Sporting News*, October 27, 1954, 16.

11. *Sporting News*, October 27, 1954, 16.

12. Smith, *Voices of the Game*, 155.

13. "CBS-TV Telecasts, NBC-TV Telecasts," *Sporting News*, April 17, 1957, 32.

14. "Lippy vs. Dizzy—TV 'Games of Week' Offer Contrasts," *Sporting News*, May 22, 1957, 20.

15. "CBS Plans Sunday TV Game of the Week," *Washington Post and Times Herald*, December 17, 1957.

16. "Sunday Baseball TV Plan Proceeds Despite Minors' Pleas," *New York Times*, December 17, 1957.

17. George Trautman, President-Treasurer, National Association of Professional Baseball Leagues, to league members, December 12, 1957, the *Sporting News* archives, St. Louis, Missouri.

18. "Congress Action to Aid Minors in TV Fight Is Held Unlikely," *New York Times*, January 15, 1958.

19. Smith, *Voices of the Game*, 247.

20. Smith, *Voices of the Game*, 246.

21. Robert V. Bellamy Jr. and James R. Walker, *Television and the Remote Control: Grazing on a Vast Wasteland* (New York: Guilford Press, 1996).

22. "Sponsor Shifts to New Network," *New York Times*, March 17, 1960.

23. "ABC Telecast Maris' Miss, Yankees' Pennant-Clincher," *Sporting News*, September 27, 1961, 9.

24. Louis Effrat, "Special Lens for Baseball TV Shuttered by Frick's Request," *New York Times*, July 14, 1959.

25. Effrat, "Special Lens for Baseball TV."

26. Effrat, "Special Lens for Baseball TV."

27. Red Smith, "TV Baron Knows What's Best for Baseball," *New York Herald Tribune*, May 2, 1964.

28. Jim Murray, "TV Should Clean Own House First," *Los Angeles Times*, April 25–26, 1964.

29. Red Smith, "TV Baron Knows What's Best."

30. Jack Gould, "Baseball Clubs Propose TV Deal," *New York Times*, February 12, 1964.

31. "Invitation for Bids for the 1965 Monday Night Major League Baseball Spectacular," August 24, 1964, the *Sporting News* archives, St. Louis, Missouri.

32. Leonard Koppett, "Yanks Excluded from A.B.C. Deal," *New York Times*, December 16, 1964.

33. Koppett, "Yanks Excluded from A.B.C. Deal."

34. C.C. Johnson Spink, "Spectacular TV Plans," *Sporting News*, January 30, 1965, 12.

35. C.C. Johnson Spink, "TV Stimulates Baseball," *Sporting News*, March 27, 1965, 14.

36. Smith, *Voices of the Game*, 276.

37. Frank Quinn, ABC Television Network, to Jim Gallagher, Baseball Office of the Commissioner, October 26, 1965, letter and exhibit B, Television File, Baseball Hall of Fame Library, Cooperstown, New York.

38. Quinn to Gallagher, October 26, 1965.

39. Pete Axthelm, "ABC's Baseball Loss May Be NBC's Gain," *New York Herald Tribune*, January 20, 1966.

40. Pete Axthelm, "Will Success Spoil Baseball?" *New York Herald Tribune*, January 1966.

41. Smith, *Voices of the Game*, 281.

42. Val Adams, "NBC in Baseball Package Deal," *New York Times*, October 24, 1965.

43. Michael Katz, "TV's Isolated Camera Proves No Substitute for the Umpire," *New York Times*, April 18, 1965.

44. "ABC-TV's Baseball Bow," *Variety*, April 21, 1965.

45. Shirley Povich, "Lush TV Fees Send Value of Big League Franchise Soaring," *Baseball Digest*, March 1965, 33–34.

46. Joseph Durso, "Frick, in Last Year, Warns Big Leagues," *New York Times*, January 3, 1965.

6. The National Television Package, 1966–89

1. Helyar, *Lords of the Realm*, 76.

2. Koppett, *Koppett's Concise History*, 303.

3. Smith, *Voices of the Game*, 280.

4. Helyar, *Lords of the Realm*, 76.

5. "Airmen Tagged Him 'Stone Face,'" *Chicago Tribune*, November 18, 1965.

6. Joe Falls, "Owners Find Right Channel in Tuning in on TV Receipts," *Baseball Digest*, February, 1966.

7. "Baseball Teams Ask TV for Bids," *New York Times*, October 16, 1965; "Majors Seek TV Bids for 1966," *Washington Post*, October 18, 1965; "Game of the Week Up for Grabs," *Chicago Tribune*, October 18, 1965; "Major League Baseball Sells NBC TV Rights for $30.6 Million Bid," *Wall Street Journal*, October 20, 1965; "N.B.C Will Pay $30.6 Million for Baseball TV in New Pact," *New York Times*, October 20, 1965; "NBC Will Pay Baseball $30.6 Million," *Chicago Tribune*, October 20, 1965; "Holiday Baseball Planned at Night," *Washington Post*, October 22, 1965; "NBC in Baseball Package Deal," *New York Times*, October 24, 1965.

8. Smith, *Voices of the Game*, 294.

9. Smith, *Voices of the Game*, 293.

10. Smith, *Voices of the Game*, 295.

11. Smith, *Voices of the Game*, 276.

12. Smith, *Voices of the Game*, 296.

13. Smith, *Voices of the Game*, 310.

14. Ralph Ray, "Baseball Delighted; Video Ratings Jump 58 Per Cent in 1966," *Sporting News*, January 7, 1967, 42.

15. Pete Axthelm, "ABC's Baseball Loss May Be NBC's Gain," *New York Herald Tribune*, January 20, 1966.

16. Smith, 1992, 298.

17. "Koufax Ends TV Career," *Washington Post*, February 23, 1973.

18. Smith, *Voices of the Game*, 310.

19. "'The Thief' Steals His Way into TV," *Chicago Tribune*, May 6, 1973.

20. Smith, *Voices of the Game*, 310.

21. "Baseball to Collect $50 Million in New 3-Year Pact with NBC," *Washington Post*, August 5, 1967; "Major League Baseball," press release, NBC Sports, August 7, 1967.

22. Leonard Koppett, "Victim of Circumstance," *New York Times*, December 7, 1968.

23. Leonard Koppett, "Kuhn Voted 4-Year Term," *New York Times*, August 13, 1969.

24. Red Smith, "Kuhn in Hot Seat over TV," *Washington Post*, May 9, 1971.

25. "Players Complain on Hidden TV Pact," *New York Times*, July 6, 1971.

26. Red Smith, "Owners Refuse to Own Up," *Washington Post*, July 9, 1971.

27. Jerome Holtzman, "Owners Yield, Players Get TV Data," *Sporting News*, November 20, 1971.

28. "Entertainers to Pinch Hit on N.B.C.-TV Baseball," *New York Times*, April 20, 1973.

29. Dave Brady, "Garagiola Picked for Spelling Out NBC's TV BB," *Washington Post*, February 20, 1974.

30. Smith, *Voices of the Game*, 387.

31. Hal Bock, "Kuhn 'Bullish' Despite Contraction in Economy," *Los Angeles Times*, April 15, 1975.

32. Sterling and Kittross, *Stay Tuned*, 871.

33. "Kuhn Says Cable TV Doesn't Pay," *Washington Post*, October 26, 1974.

34. Gary Deeb, "Cosell Shut Out of ABC Plans for Baseball TV," *Chicago Tribune*, March 11, 1975.

35. "ABC Unveils Monday Baseball As Frozen Fans Get Ueckered," *Variety*, April 14, 1976.

36. Smith, *Voices of the Game*, 389.

37. Gary Deeb, "Cosell on Monday Night Baseball, Despite Kuhn," *Chicago Tribune*, February 8, 1977.

38. Deeb, "Cosell on Monday Night Baseball."

39. "Old, New Sponsors Follow Audience Upsurge," *Television/Radio Age*, January 31, 1977, 29–30.

40. Leonard Koppett, "World Series After Dark: Nightmare or Dream Come True?" *New York Times*, October 5, 1976; Shirley Povich, "This Morning . . . ," *Washington Post*, April 11, 1971.

41. Dean A. Sullivan, ed., *Late Innings: A Documentary History of Baseball, 1945–1972* (Lincoln: University of Nebraska Press, 2002), 184.

42. "63 Million, a Record, Saw Series Night Game," *New York Times*, October 15, 1971.

43. "Bowie Kuhn, October 28, 1926—March 15, 2007", *USA Today*, March 20, 2007.

44. Charles Maher, "Are the World Series Lights Going on for Good? Kuhn Has Doubts But . . . ," *Los Angeles Times*, October 23, 1976.

45. Barry Lorge, "Drysdale Pleasant, But Not ABC Coverage," *Washington Post*, April 14, 1978.

46. Shirley Povich, "ABC-TV Scores Despite Cosell," *Washington Post*, June 25, 1977.

47. Andrew Beyer, "Watch the Series on TV, But Listen to Your Radio," *Washington Post*, October 11, 1979.

48. Deeb, "Cosell on Monday Night Baseball."

49. Paul Henniger, "NBC Plays Angles," *Los Angeles Times*, April 7, 1979.

50. "Baseball!: Rights Go Out of the Park," *Broadcasting*, March 10, 1980, 33.

51. Sterling and Kittross, *Stay Tuned*, 871.

52. Baseball Almanac, http://www.baseball-almanac.com/ws/wstv.shtml.

53. Norman Chad, "NBC's Adjustments Improve Baseball Coverage," *Washington Post*, April 14, 1985.

54. *Broadcasting*, March 10, 1980, 33.

55. Society for American Baseball Research, Business of Baseball Committee, http://www.businessofbaseball.com/data.htm.

56. Skip Myslenski, "Majors' TV Package Worth $1.2 Billion," *Chicago Tribune*, April 8, 1983.

57. Jim Spence, *Up Close and Personal* (New York: Atheneum Publishers, 1988), 223.

58. Spence, *Up Close and Personal*, 217.

59. Chad, "NBC's Adjustments Improve Baseball Coverage."

7. National Broadcasts in the Cable Era

1. Koppett, *Koppett's Concise History*, 376–77.

2. Figures derived from MLPA information, SABR Business of Baseball Committee, http://bob.sabr.org/data.htm, December 2006.

3. Sharon Strover, "Cable Television: United States," in *Encyclopedia of Television*, 2d ed., vol. 1, edited by Horace Newcomb, 393–95 (New York: Fitzroy Dearborn, 2005).

4. *Broadcasting & Cable Yearbook 2007* (New Providence NJ: R.R. Bowker, 2006), A-15.

5. Norman Chad, "Shifting Playoffs to Cable Discussed," *Washington Post*, December 8, 1988.

6. Joseph Durso, "A Billion-Dollar Bid by CBS Wins Rights to Baseball Games," *New York Times*, December 15, 1988.

7. Jeremy Gerard, "A Last-Place Team Gambles on a Billion-Dollar Contact," *New York Times*, December 19, 1988.

8. Durso, "A Billion-Dollar Bid by CBS."

9. Sterling and Kittross, *Stay Tuned*, 871.

10. Jeremy Gerard, "ESPN Will Pay $400 Million for Baseball-Game Rights," *New York Times*, January 6, 1989.

11. George Vecsey, "The Uebie Years: A Retrospective," *New York Times*, February 19, 1989.

12. Curt Smith, "It's Going, Going, Going. . . ," *Sports Illustrated*, April 17, 1989, 104.

13. Curt Smith, "Fight Baseball's TV Fadeout," *New York Times*, October 1, 1989.

14. Curt Smith, "Goodbye to the Beloved 'Game,'" *Newsweek*, April 30, 1990, 8.

15. Smith, "Goodbye to the Beloved 'Game,'" 8.

16. William Oscar Johnson and William Taaffe, "A Whole New Game," *Sports Illustrated*, December 26, 1988, 34.

17. Richard Sandomir, "Baseball Broadcasts and the Bottom Line," *New York Times*, May 17, 1991.

18. Sandomir, "Baseball Broadcasts and the Bottom Line."

19. Bill Carter, "CBS Earnings Fall 30%; Sports Costs Cited," *New York Times*, October 11, 1990; Bill Carter, "Big Cuts Expected for CBS," *New York Times*, April 5, 1991.

20. "Baseball Throws CBS a Curve," *Broadcasting*, August 26, 1991.

21. James Deacon, "Ball-park Figures," *Maclean's*, October 21, 1991.

22. T. Tyrer, "World Series Lags in Prime Ratings," *Electronic Media*, November 1, 1993, 2.

23. T. Wendel, "Baseball Owners' Overhaul Is Overkill to the Fans," *Baseball Weekly*, May 26, 1993, 5.

24. T. Tyrer, "New Deal Reshapes Baseball on TV," *Electronic Media*, June 7, 1993, 10.

25. "Baseball Wants More Buck for Its Bang," *Broadcasting*, February 24, 1992, 24.

26. C. Muskat, "Deal Devised to Appeal to Broader Fan Base," *Baseball Weekly*, May 19, 1993, 6.

27. Steve McClellan, "Baseball Approves Deal with ABC, NBC," *Broadcasting & Cable*, May 31, 1993, 11.

28. Steve Nidetz and Jerome Holtzman, "Baseball Strikes Bold TV Deal," *Chicago Tribune*, May 9, 1993.

29. Wendel, "Baseball Owners' Overhaul Is Overkill."

30. Muskat, "Deal Devised to Appeal to Broader Fan Base."

31. Rich Brown, "More Post-season Games for MLB," *Broadcasting & Cable*, September 13, 1993, 15.

32. J. Jensen, "Ken Schanzer: NBC Exec Teams Up His Network with ABC, Major League Baseball in New Ad Venture," *Advertising Age*, August 9, 1993, 24.

33. Wendel, "Baseball Owners' Overhaul Is Overkill."

34. Richard Sandomir, "On a Roll," in *The 1994 Information Please Sports Almanac*, edited by M. Meserole, 514–20 (Boston: Houghton Mifflin, 1993).

35. Leonard Koppett, "Self-Destruction in Prime Time," *Los Angeles Times*, July 9, 1993; Wendel, "Baseball Owners' Overhaul Is Overkill."

36. Curt Smith, "Baseball Is Destroying Itself through the Lack of Consistent National TV Coverage," *Broadcasting & Cable*, October 4, 1993, 76.

37. Nidetz and Holtzman, "Baseball Strikes Bold TV Deal."

38. M. Dodd, "Congress Tracks Cable, Pay-Per-View Changes," *USA Today*, July 23, 1993.

39. Steve McClellan, "Two Ways to Go on Baseball—CBS vs. ABC-NBC," *Broadcasting & Cable*, May 17, 1993, 67.

40. Zimbalist, *May the Best Team Win.*

41. Steve Rosenbloom, "Tell a Vision, Sell a Vision," *Chicago Sun-Times*, May 10, 1993.

42. "Fox, CBS Swinging for Baseball," *Broadcasting & Cable*, October 23, 1995, 8.

43. Richard Sandomir, "Account Running Dry for Baseball Network," *New York Times*, September 2, 1994.

44. Richard Sandomir, "As TV Fades to Black, Networks Point Fingers," *New York Times*, June 24, 1995.

45. Richard Sandomir, "All Are to Blame for Baseball Network's Demise," *New York Times*, June 27, 1995.

46. Richard Sandomir, "Billion-Dollar Bonus Baby; Networks Ante Up," *New York Times*, November 7, 1995.

47. Jim McConville, "MLB Sews Up Deal with Fox, NBC," *Broadcasting & Cable*, November 6, 1995, 8.

48. Joe Schlosser and David Carter, "TV Sports: A Numbers Game," *Broadcasting & Cable*, April 2, 2001, 32.

49. Kim McAvoy, "Baseball Gets the Bucks," *Broadcasting & Cable*, April 2, 2001, 27.

50. Tim Brosnan, Executive Vice President, Business, Major League Baseball, personal communication with authors, January 19, 2007.

51. "TBS Joins Fox As Major Players in TV Deal," *Chicago Tribune*, July 12, 2006; Richard Sandomir, "TV Lineup Is Changed for Postseason Games," *New York Times*, July 12, 2006; "Fox Sports and Major League Baseball Reach New Seven-year Rights Agreement," http://msn.foxsports.com, July 11, 2006; "Fox, TBS Have Seven-year, $3 Billion TV Deal with MLB," http://sports.espn.go.com, July 11, 2006.

8. The Pay Television Era

1. Neil deMause and Maury Brown, "You've Got the Brawn, I've Got the Brain, Let's Make Lots of Money," in *Baseball Prospectus 2007*, edited by Christina Kahrl and Steven Goldman (New York: Plume, 2007), 559.

2. Michael Spence and Bruce Owen, "Television Programming, Monopolistic Competition, and Welfare," *Quarterly Journal of Economics* 91, no. 1 (1977): 103–26.

3. "Dann v. Klein: The Best Game in Town," *Time*, May 25, 1970, http://www.time.com/time/magazine/article/0,9171,909291-1,00.html (accessed March 23, 2007).

4. Alison Alexander, James Owers, Rod Carveth, C. Ann Hollifield, and Albert N. Greco, eds., *Media Economics: Theory and Practice*, 3d ed. (Hillsdale NJ: Erlbaum, 2003).

5. Susan Tyler Eastman and Douglas A. Ferguson, *Media Programming: Strategies and Practices*, 7th ed. (Belmont CA: Wadsworth, 2005); and Eric Rothenbuhler, "Demographics," in *Encyclopedia of Television*, 2d ed., vol. 2, edited by Horace Newcomb (New York: Fitzroy Dearborn, 2005), 680–81.

6. Eastman and Ferguson, *Media Programming*.

7. *Home Box Office, Inc. v. FCC*, 567 F.2d 9 (D.C. Cir., 1977).

8. Sterling and Kittross, *Stay Tuned*.

9. Megan Mullen, "Pay Television," Museum of Broadcast Communications, http://www.museum.tv/archives/etv/P/htmlP/paytelevision/paytelevision .htm (accessed January 12, 2007).

10. Federal Communications Commission, *Third Report and Order on Docket 18397*, 24 RR2d 1501 (1972).

11. Dwight L. Teeter Jr. and Bill Loving, *Law of Mass Communications: Freedom and Control of Print and Broadcast Media*, 11th ed. (New York: Foundation Press, 780).

12. Brosnan, January 19, 2007.

13. Katherine Q. Seelye, "2 Billionaires Make Offer for Tribune," *New York Times*, March 30, 2007. http://www.nytimes.com/2007/03/30/business/ media/30tribune.html?_r=1&ref=media&oref=slogin.

14. *Home Box Office v. FCC*, 567 F.2d 9 (D.C. Cir. 1977).

15. Ronald Garay, "USA Network," in *The Cable Networks Handbook*, edited by Robert G. Picard, 203 (Riverside CA: Carpelan, 1993).

16. Garay, "USA Network," 205.

17. Garay, "USA Network," 205.

18. Charlie Warner and Michael O. Wirth, "Entertainment and Sports Programming Network (ESPN)," in *The Cable Networks Handbook*, edited by Robert G. Picard, 86 (Riverside CA: Carpelan, 1993).

19. Warner and Wirth, "Entertainment and Sports Programming Network (ESPN)," 88.

20. Warner and Wirth, "Entertainment and Sports Programming Network (ESPN)," 88.

21. Paul D. Staudohar, "The Impact of Baseball's New Television Contracts," *NINE: A Journal of Baseball History and Culture* 10, no. 2 (2002): 102–9.

22. Staudohar, "The Impact of Baseball's New Television Contracts," 2002.

23. "Baseball, ESPN Settle Suit at Eve of Trial," *Mark's Sportslaw News*, December 9, 1999, http://www.sportslawnews.com/archive/articles%201999/ MLBESPNsettle.htm (accessed January 14, 2007).

24. Andy Bernstein, "Flexibility a Key in New MLB-ESPN Deal," *Street & Smith's SportsBusiness Journal*, September 19, 2005, 3.

25. Bernstein, "Flexibility a Key in New MLB-ESPN Deal," 3.

26. Bernstein, "Flexibility a Key in New MLB-ESPN Deal," 3; "MLB Announces iN DEMAND deal," press release, Major League Baseball, April 4, 2007, http://mlb.mlb.com/news/press_releases/press_release .jsp?ymd=20070404&content_id=1879904&vkey=pr_mlb&fext=.jsp&c _id=mlb.

27. Brosnan, January 19, 2007.

28. Robert V. Bellamy Jr. "Regional Sports Networks: Prime Network and SportsChannel American," in The Cable Networks Handbook, ed. Robert G. Picard (Riverside CA: Carpelan, 1993), 163.

29. Bellamy, "Regional Sports Networks," 164.

30. Bellamy, "Regional Sports Networks," 164.

31. Bellamy, "Regional Sports Networks," 164.

32. Richard Tedesco, "Cable Play: Deregulation Means Viewers for Regional Sports Networks," Electronic Media, February 16, 1987, 1, 27.

33. Bellamy, "Regional Sports Networks," 165.

34. Bellamy, "Regional Sports Networks," 165.

35. Bellamy, "Regional Sports Networks," 166.

36. Bellamy, "Regional Sports Networks," 169.

37. William Shawcross, Murdoch: The Making of a Media Empire (New York: Touchstone, 1997).

38. Bellamy, "Regional Sports Networks," 169.

39. Ronald Grover and Tom Lowry with William C. Symonds, "Rumble in Regional Sports," Business Week, November 22, 2004, http://www .businessweek.com/magazine/content/04_47/b3909143_mz016.htm (accessed January 14, 2007).

40. Grover and Lowry, "Rumble in Regional Sports."

41. Grover and Lowry, "Rumble in Regional Sports."

42. Grover and Lowry, "Rumble in Regional Sports."

43. Grover and Lowry, "Rumble in Regional Sports."

44. Robert V. Bellamy Jr., "The Evolving Television Sports Marketplace."

45. Brosnan, January 19, 2007.

46. Robert V. Bellamy Jr., "Sports Media: A Modern Institution," in Handbook of Sports and Media, ed. Arthur R. Raney and Jennings Bryant, 63–76 (Mahwah NJ: Erlbaum, 2006).

9. Television As Threat, Television As Savior

1. W. O. McGeehan, "Another Menace to Sports," in Wake Up the Echoes, edited by Bob Cooke (Garden City NJ: Hanover House, 1956), 229.

2. Curt Smith, Voices of the Game, 39.

3. "Bob Boosts Television," Sporting News, December 25, 1946, 16.

4. "Wrigley to Bat for Video Ball," *Variety*, September 10, 1947, 30.

5. "Baseball Boxoffice Hit by Video, Stoneham Says," *New York Times*, November 15, 1948.

6. Tom Meany, "Game Challenged by Television's Growth," *Sporting News*, May 21, 1947, 2.

7. Ed McAuley, "Clubs Seek Answer to Television Problem," *Sporting News*, July 2, 1947, 11.

8. Stan Baumgartner, "Crack-Down Seen on Major Telecasts," *Sporting News*, June 8, 1949, 1.

9. Ed James, "TV and the Gate," *Broadcasting*, June 13, 1949, 36, 66.

10. John P. Taylor, "Camera Placement and Switching for Baseball Broadcasting," *Broadcast News*, September 1947, 57–58.

11. "Record Baseball Crowds Are Attributed to Video," *Broadcasting*, September 13, 1948, 72.

12. Bill Veeck, "Don't Let TV Kill Baseball!" *Sport*, June 1953.

13. Jack Gould, "The News of Radio," *New York Times*, August 29, 1947.

14. Arthur Daley, "When the Ringside Becomes the Fireside," *New York Times*, March 27, 1949.

15. Jerry N. Jordan, *The Long Range Effect of Television and Other Factors on Sports Attendance* (Washington DC: Radio-Television Manufacturers, 1950).

16. Jordan, *The Long Range Effect of Television*.

17. "Sports Gate," *Broadcasting*, July 24, 1950, 57.

18. Sterling and Kittross, *Stay Tuned*, 864.

19. Sterling and Kittross, *Stay Tuned*, 864.

20. "Sports Gate," *Broadcasting*, August 21, 1950, 63.

21. "The TV Habit," *Broadcasting*, February 13, 1950, 15.

22. National Broadcasting Company, "Baseball and Television," 1950, NBC Archives.

23. "Clubs Televising All Games Had Increases, TV Declares," *Sporting News*, December 12, 1951, 18.

24. Thorn, Palmer, Gershman, and Pietrusza, *Total Baseball*, 107–8.

25. Sterling and Kittross, *Stay Tuned*, 864.

26. Dan Daniel, "TV Must Go—Or Baseball Will!" *Baseball Magazine*, November 1952, 6.

27. Daniel, "TV Must Go," 37.

28. "Branch Rickey: TV Can Kill Baseball," *Newsweek*, June 8, 1953, 67.

29. Veeck, "Don't Let TV Kill Baseball!", 10.

30. Daniel, "TV Must Go," 37.

31. Veeck, "Don't Let TV Kill Baseball!", 79.

32. Beach, "The Television Producer," 114.

33. John Drebinger, "Radio and Television," *Baseball Magazine*, February 1951, 324.

34. Tom Swope, "Giles Hints TV Cut in Reporting 24 Pct. Drop in Reds Gate," *Sporting News*, November 29, 1950, 17.

35. Sterling and Kittross, *Stay Tuned*, 864.

36. A good overview of the peak years and subsequent decline of the Big Three era can be found in Ken Auletta, *Three Blind Mice: How the TV Networks Lost Their Way* (New York: Random House, 1991).

37. Patricia Aufderheide, "Public Television," in *Encyclopedia of Television*, 2d ed., vol. 3, edited by Horace Newcomb, 1856–57 (New York: Fitzroy Dearborn, 2004); Robert M. Pepper, *The Formation of the Public Broadcasting Service* (New York: Arno Press, 1976).

38. Robert G. Finney, "Prime Time Access Rule," in *Encyclopedia of Television*, 2d ed., vol. 3, edited by Horace Newcomb, 1818 (New York: Fitzroy Dearborn, 2004).

39. Christopher Anderson, "American Broadcasting Company," in *Encyclopedia of Television*, 2d ed., vol. 1, edited by Horace Newcomb, 87 (New York: Fitzroy Dearborn, 2004); Leonard H. Goldenson, *Beating the Odds: The Untold Story Behind the Rise of ABC* (New York: Scribner, 1991).

40. Goldenson, *Beating the Odds*.

41. Richard E. Caves, *Switching Channels: Organization and Change in TV Broadcasting* (Cambridge MA: Harvard University Press, 2005).

42. Goldenson, *Beating the Odds*; Roone Arledge, *Roone: A Memoir* (New York: HarperCollins, 2003).

43. Jennifer Holt, "Olympics and Television in the United States," in *Encyclopedia of Television*, 2d ed., vol. 3, edited by Horace Newcomb, 1685–87 (New York: Fitzroy Dearborn, 2004).

44. Arledge, *Roone: A Memoir*.

45. Arledge, *Roone: A Memoir*; Goldenson, *Beating the Odds*; Gunther and Carter, *Monday Night Mayhem: The Inside Story of ABC's Monday Night Football* (New York: Quill, 1989). *Monday Night Mayhem* was made into a made-for-television movie, which originally aired on TNT on January 14, 2002. See the Internet Movie Database (IMDb) at http://www.imdb.com/title/tt0268466/.

46. Arledge, *Roone: A Memoir*.

47. Steve Treder, "The Year That Changed Everything," *NINE: A Journal of Baseball History and Culture* 13, no. 2 (2005): 1–18.

48. Figures retrieved from the Baseball Reference.com web site, http://www.baseball-reference.com/.

49. Treder, "The Year That Changed Everything."

50. Treder, "The Year That Changed Everything."
51. See, for example, Robert F. Burk, *Much More than a Game* (Chapel Hill: University of North Carolina Press, 2001); Kenneth M. Jennings, *Balls and Strikes: The Money Game in Professional Baseball* (New York: Praeger, 1990); Lee Lowenfish, *The Imperfect Diamond: A History of Baseball's Labor Wars*, rev. ed. (New York: DaCapo, 1991); and Marvin Miller, *A Whole Different Ball Game: The Sport and Business of Baseball* (New York: Birch Lane Press, 1991).
52. Burk, *Much More than a Game*, 157
53. Burk, *Much More than a Game*, 176–77.
54. Burk, *Much More than a Game*, 165.
55. Burk, *Much More than a Game*, 162–63.
56. Curt Snyder, *A Well-Paid Slave: Curt Flood's Fight for Free Agency in Professional Sports* (New York: Viking, 2006).
57. *Flood v. Kuhn*, 407 U.S. 258 (1972).
58. Burk, *Much More than a Game*, 185–86.
59. Burk, *Much More than a Game*, 193–206.
60. Burk, *Much More than a Game*, 199; Miller, *A Whole Different Ball Game*, 255–66.

10. Television and the "Death" of the Golden Age Minors

1. Jennings Bryant and Dolf Zillman, *Media Effects: Advances in Theory and Research* (Hillsdale NJ: Erlbaum, 1994); James R. Walker and Douglas A. Ferguson, *Broadcast Television Industry* (Boston: Allyn & Bacon, 1998).
2. Sterling and Kittross, *Stay Tuned.*
3. Albert B. Chandler to Michael Maher, March 25, 1987, Television File, National Baseball Hall of Fame Library, Cooperstown, New York.
4. Lloyd Johnson and Miles Wolff, eds., *The Encyclopedia of Minor League Baseball*, 2d ed. (Durham NC: Baseball America, 1997), 347.
5. MiLB.com, "Minor League Baseball History," http://www.minorleaguebaseball.com/milb/history/ (accessed March 28, 2006).
6. Johnson and Wolff, *Encyclopedia of Minor League Baseball*, 347.
7. Sterling and Kittross, *Stay Tuned*, 864.
8. Johnson and Wolff, *Encyclopedia of Minor League Baseball*, 411.
9. Johnson and Wolff, *Encyclopedia of Minor League Baseball*, 411.
10. "Record Baseball Crowds Are Attributed to Video," *Broadcasting*, September 14, 1948, 72.
11. "Baseball Tops TV," *Broadcasting*, May 31, 1948, 30.
12. "Baseball Is in Trouble: High Costs, TV Are Blamed," *U.S. News and World Report*, May 30, 1952, 16.
13. "Jimmy Jemail's Hotbox," *Sports Illustrated*, October 4, 1954, 2–3.

14. "Toledo Ball Club May Move; Owners Seek TV-less Haven," *Business Week*, September 24, 1955.
15. Sterling and Kittross's *Stay Tuned* provides a valuable overview of the early television era. For more information on the early history of the MLB-television relationship, see Robert V. Bellamy Jr. and James R. Walker, "Baseball and Television Origins: The Case of the Cubs," *NINE: A Journal of Baseball History and Culture* 10, no. 1 (2001): 31–45; and James R. Walker and Robert V. Bellamy Jr., "Baseball and Television the Formative Years," *NINE: A Journal of Baseball History and Culture* 11, no. 2 (2003): 1–15. Information on minor league franchises in the 1940s and 1950s is from Johnson and Wolff, *Encyclopedia of Minor League Baseball*.
16. "Where's Baseball Headed?" *Newsweek*, April 18, 1955, 90.
17. Johnson and Wolff, *Encyclopedia of Minor League Baseball*, 347.
18. "2006 Minor-League Attendance by Average—Affiliated," *Ballpark Digest*, http://www.ballparkwatch.com/features/attendance_by_average _affiliated_2006.html (accessed January 23, 2007).
19. Gerald Mast, *A Short History of the Movies* (Indianapolis: Bobbs-Merrill, 1976).
20. Sterling and Kittross, *Stay Tuned*.
21. Senate Subcommittee on Televising Baseball Games of the Committee on Interstate and Foreign Commerce, *Broadcasting and Televising Baseball Games*, May 6, 1953, 13.
22. Senate, *Broadcasting and Televising Baseball Games*, 7.
23. Senate, *Broadcasting and Televising Baseball Games*, 9–12.
24. Old Radio: The Broadcast Archives (web site), "Liberty Broadcasting System," http://www.oldradio.com (accessed January 7, 2002); Senate, *Broadcasting and Televising Baseball Games*, 93–118.
25. *Sponsor*, "Baseball 1951," April 9, 1951, 135.
26. Senate, *Broadcasting and Televising Baseball Games*, 95.
27. Old Radio, "Liberty Broadcasting System"; Senate, *Broadcasting and Televising Baseball Games*, 93–118.
28. MiLB.com.
29. Jon C. Stott, *Leagues of Their Own* (Raleigh NC: McFarland, 2001).

11. Baseball, Television, Congress, and the Law

1. SI.com (*Sports Illustrated* online), "Kerry Wants DirecTV Deal Delayed," March 27, 2007, http://sportsillustrated.cnn.com/2007/baseball/ mlb/03/27/bc.bbo.tvpackage.ap/index.html (accessed March 27, 2007).
2. *Clean Sports Act of 2005*, S 114, 109th Cong., 1st sess., May 24, 2005; *Drug Free Sports Act (Reported in House)*, HR 3084, 109th Cong., 1st sess., June 28,

2005. Accessed via Library of Congress Thomas system, http://thomas.loc
.gov.

3. *National Commission on Major League Baseball Act of 1994*, S 2401, 103d Cong.,
1st sess., August 17, 1994. Accessed via Library of Congress Thomas system, http://thomas.loc.gov.

4. *Major League Baseball Equity Act*, S 1729, 102d Cong., 1st sess., September 19,
1991; *Major League Baseball Equity Act*, HR 3368, 102d Cong, 1st sess.,
September 19, 1991. Accessed via Library of Congress Thomas system,
http://thomas.loc.gov.

5. Donald E. Stokes, "Spatial Models of Party Competition," *American Political
Science Review* 57, no. 2 (1962): 373.

6. Erwin G. Krasnow, *The Politics of Broadcast Regulation*, 2d ed. (New York: St.
Martin's Press, 1978).

7. "MLB, MLPA Announce New Drug Agreement," press release, Major
League Baseball Players Association, November 15, 2005, http://mlbplayers
.mlb.com/pa/releases/releases.jsp?content=111505.

8. "Mitchell Warns Baseball Owners Congress May Intervene in Steroids Investigation," USA Today, January 18, 2007, http://www.usatoday.com/
sports/baseball/2007-01-18-mitchell-warning_x.htm.

9. Dwight L. Teeter Jr. and Bill Loving, *Law of Mass Communications: Freedom
and Control of Print and Broadcast Media*, 11th ed. (New York: Foundation
Press, 2004), 706–11.

10. *Baseball Viewer's Protection Act of 1989*, HR 2593, June 8, 1989. Accessed via
Library of Congress Thomas system, http://thomas.loc.gov.

11. *Federal Baseball Club v. National League*, 292 U.S. 200 (1922).

12. *Toolson v. New York Yankees*, 346 U.S. 356 (1953); *Gardella v. Chandler*, No.
98, Docket 21133, U.S. District Ct. (S.D.N.Y., 1949); *Flood v. Kuhn*, 407 U.S.
258 (1972).

13. Senate, *Broadcasting and Televising Baseball Games*, 5.

14. Senate, *Broadcasting and Televising Baseball Games*, 69.

15. *Gardella v. Chandler*.

16. *United States v. Paramount Pictures, Inc.*, 334 U.S. 131 (1948).

17. Sterling and Kittross, *Stay Tuned*, 231.

18. Senate, *Broadcasting and Televising Baseball Games*, 5.

19. Senate, *Broadcasting and Televising Baseball Games*, 2.

20. Senate, *Broadcasting and Televising Baseball Games*, 146.

21. Senate, *Broadcasting and Televising Baseball Games*, 93.

22. House Subcommittee on Monopoly Power of the Committee on the Judiciary, *Organized Baseball*, 82d Cong., 2d sess., H. Rep., May 25, 1952.

23. House, *Organized Baseball*.

24. House Subcommittee on Antitrust of the Committee on the Judiciary, Hearings, 85th Cong., 1st sess., August 1, 7–8, 1957. Accessed via http:// www.bizofbaseball.com/index (November 17, 2006).
25. *Toolson v. New York Yankees*, 346 U.S. 356 (1953).
26. Brooklyn Dodger attendance was above the league average every season from 1938 to 1956, and was above one million per year from 1945 to 1957 (the teams' last season in New York). Baseball Almanac: The Official Baseball History Site, http://www.baseball-almanac.com/teams/laatte.shtml (accessed March 26, 2007).
27. House, Hearings, August 1, 7–8, 1957.
28. *Sports Broadcasting Act*, Public Law 87–331, 75 Stat. 732 (1961).
29. *U.S. v. National Football League*, 196 F. Supp. 445, 446 (E.D. Pa., 1961).
30. John Fortunato, *Commissioner: The Legacy of Pete Rozelle* (New York: Taylor, 2006).
31. Teeter and Loving, *Law of Mass Communications*, 726–32.
32. FCC, *Third Report and Order on Docket 18397*.
33. Teeter and Loving, *Law of Mass Communications*, 780; Federal Communications Commission, *Domestic Communication Satellite Facilities*, 35 FCC2d 844, 1972.
34. Phillip M. Cox II, "Flag on the Play? The Siphoning Effect on Sports Television," *Federal Communications Bar Journal* 47, no. 3 (April 1995).
35. Cox, "Flag on the Play?"
36. Federal Communications Commission, *Commission's Rules and Regulations to Provide for Subscription TV Service*, 15 FCC 466, 1968.
37. *Home Box Office, Inc. v. FCC*, 567 F.2d 9 (D.C. Cir. 1977).
38. *Cable Communications Policy Act*, 47 USC 521, 1984.
39. Cox, "Flag on the Play?"
40. *Cable Television Consumer Protection and Competition Act of 1992*, Public Law 102–385, 106 Stat. 1460 (1992).
41. FCC, *Sports Programming Migration Interim Report*; Federal Communications Commission, *Sports Programming Migration Final Report*, FCC 94–149 (July 6, 1994), http://www.fcc.gov/Bureaus/Cable/Orders/1994/orcb4014.txt (accessed April 3, 2007).
42. FCC, *Sports Programming Migration Final Report*, 46.
43. Grover and Lowry, "Rumble in Regional Sports."
44. Brosnan, January 19, 2007.
45. Brosnan, January 19, 2007.

12. Baseball and Television Synergy

1. Bellamy, "The Evolving Television Marketplace"; Bellamy and Walker, "Foul Tip or Strike Three?"; Bellamy, "Sports Media: A Modern Institution."

2. Alexander et al., *Media Economics*, and David Croteau and William Hoynes, *The Business of Media: Corporate Media and the Public Interest* (Thousand Oaks CA: Pine Forge Press, 2001).

3. *United States v. Paramount Pictures, Inc.*, 334 U.S. 131 (1948).

4. Goldenson, *Beating the Odds*.

5. Encyclopedia of Company Histories, "Anaheim Angels"; Newhan, *Anaheim Angels*.

6. Til Ferdenzi, "Topping and Webb to Remain in Posts As Bombers Execs," *Sporting News*, August 29, 1964, 2.

7. *Broadcasting*, "Stark Calls Pay TV a 'Monster,'" July 1, 1957, 91-92; and *Wall Street Journal*, "TV & Baseball," October 31, 1957, 1.

8. Frick discussed the CBS agreement in a meeting with a representative of the U.S. Department of Justice in a September 9, 1964, memo (Baseball Hall of Fame Archives, Cooperstown, New York). More information on the controversy over and politics of the sale of the Yankees to CBS can be found in Roger Angell, "Two Strikes on the Image," *New Yorker*, October 24, 1964, 224–36.

9. Maury Allen, *All Roads Lead to October: Boss Steinbrenner's 25-year Reign over the New York Yankees* (New York: St. Martin's, 2000).

10. Ken Auletta, *Media Man: Ted Turner's Improbable Empire* (New York: W.W. Norton, 2004), 13.

11. Robert V. Bellamy Jr., "Impact of the Television Marketplace on the Structure of Major League Baseball," *Journal of Broadcasting & Electronic Media* 32, no. 1 (1988): 73–87.

12. Richard Hack, *Clash of the Titans* (New York: New Millennium, 2003); Michael A. Hiltzik, "Playing by His Own Rules," *Los Angeles Times*, August 25, 1997, 1; and Sallie Hofmeister, "Murdoch Deal Sets Stage for Fox Challenge to ESPN," *Los Angeles Times*, June 24, 1997, 1.

13. Associated Press, "Angels Success Could Hasten Sale of Team," *Slam! Sports Baseball*, September 20, 2002, http://slam.canoe.ca/Slam20920/mlb_ana-ap.html; Alec Klein, *Stealing Time: Steve Case, Jerry Levin, and the Collapse of AOL Time Warner* (New York: Simon & Schuster, 2003); Aaron Moore, "Big Media Go Back to Basics," *Street & Smith's SportsBusiness Weekly*, January 19–25, 2004, 22; Nina Munk, *Fools Rush In: Steve Case, Jerry Levin, and the Unmaking of AOL Time Warner* (New York: Harper Business, 2004); Reuters, "News Corp. Signs Deal to Sell L.A. Dodgers," Forbes.com, January 20, 2004, http://www.forbes.com/newswire/2003/10/10/rtr1106442.html, and Zimbalist, *May the Best Team Win*.

14. Associated Press, "Ratner Reaches Agreement to Buy Nets," CBS Sportsline.com, January 21, 2004, http://www.fcrc.com/full_newsrelease.asp?brief=27 (accessed April 3, 2007).

15. *Federal Baseball Club v. National League*, 292 U.S. 200 (1922).

16. *Sports Broadcasting Act*, Public Law 87–331, 75 Stat. 732 (1961).

17. Grover and Lowry, "Rumble in Regional Sports."

18. Thomas Heath, "Angelos Willing to Share MASN with Comcast," *Washington Post*, April 8, 2006, E10.

19. Sally Bedell Smith, *In All His Glory: The Life and Times of William S. Paley and the Birth of Modern Broadcasting* (New York: Simon & Schuster, 1990).

20. Michael Wolff, *Autumn of the Moguls* (New York: Harper Business, 2003).

21. Australian Broadcasting Corporation, "News Corp. Buys MySpace.com," ABC Online, July 19, 2005, http://www.abc.net.au/news/newsitems/200507/ s1417139.htm (accessed April 3, 2007); Associated Press, "Google Buys YouTube for $1.65 Billion," October 10, 2006, http://www.msnbc.msn .com/id/15196982/ (accessed April 3, 2007).

22. Thomas R. Umstead, "ESPN Drops Plans for Regional Service," *Multichannel News*, July 1998, 1.

23. Associated Press, "Angels Success Could Hasten Sale."

24. Sallie Hofmeister, "Deal Shows Use of Teams to Build a Global TV Empire," *Los Angeles Times*, March 20, 1998, 1.

25. Australian Broadcasting, "News Corp. Buys MySpace.com."

26. Greising, "Cubs for Sale, But Is Wrigley Field?"

27. Allen Kreda, "Cablevision to Show YES Network to All Subscribers," *Bloomberg News*, March 24, 2004, http://www.thejournalnews.com/ newsroom/032504/d01a25cablevision.html and YES Network web site, http://www.yesnetwork.com (accessed March 28, 2004).

28. "Man Utd and Yankees Team Up," BBC Sport, February 7, 2001. http:// news.bbc.co.uk/sport1/hi/1159026.stm (accessed April 3, 2007).

13. The Announcer in the Television Age

1. Barber, *The Broadcasters*; Smith, *Voices of the Game*; Curt Smith, *The Storytellers* (New York: Macmillan, 1995); Curt Smith, *Voices of Summer* (New York: Carroll & Graf, 2005).

2. "New Medium Demands New Tricks," *Sport*, March 1951, 33.

3. Steve Rushin, "The Most Artful Dodger," *Sports Illustrated*, August 19, 2002, 17.

4. Frank X. Tolbert, "Dizzy Dean—He's Not So Dumb!" *Saturday Evening Post*, June 14, 1951, 104.

5. Mel Allen, "TV Is Tough on the Announcer," *Sport*, April 1951, 34.

6. Bill Davidson, "Mel Allen: Baseball's Most Controversial Voice," *Look*, September 27, 1960, 98.

7. Jack Brickhouse, "Sportscaster Finds Rules of Game Changed," *Chicago Tribune*, April 4, 1948.

8. Smith, *Voices of the Game*, 191.

9. Jerry Kirshenbaum, "And Here, to Bring You the Play by Play . . . ," *Sports Illustrated*, September 13, 1971, 34.

10. Smith, *Voices of the Game*, 335.

11. Brickhouse, "Sportscaster Finds Rules of Game Changed."

12. R. B. Bechtel, C. Achelpohl, and R. Akers, "Correlates between Observed Behavior and Questionnaire Response on Television Viewing," in *Television and Social Behavior*, vol. 4, edited by E. A. Rubenstein, G. A. Comstock, and J. P. Murray, 274–344 (Washington DC: Government Printing Office, 1972).

13. "The Reckoning," *Time*, June 7, 1948, 60.

14. Smith, *Voices of the Game*, 191.

15. Bob Wolff, "Behind the Mike," *Baseball Magazine*, October 1956, 36.

16. Richard G. Hubler, "The Barber of Brooklyn," *Saturday Evening Post*, March 21, 1942, 61.

17. Tolbert, "Dizzy Dean—He's Not So Dumb!" 104.

18. Charles P. Miller, "Holy Cow! It's Harry Caray," *Saturday Evening Post*, October 1989, 105.

19. Chris De Luca, "Cubs Ready to Introduce Piniella As Manager," *Chicago Tribune*, October 16, 2006.

20. Roger Angell, "The Bard in the Booth," *New Yorker*, September 6, 1999, 28–32; Pete Dexter, "Of Pigeons and Catchers," *Esquire*, April 1985, 46, 48.

21. Kirshenbaum, "And Here, to Bring You the Play by Play . . . ," 43.

22. Smith, *Voices of the Game*, 76.

23. Smith, *Voices of the Game*, 76.

24. Jim Brosnan, *The Long Season* (New York: Harper, 1960), 132.

25. Ron Fimrite, "The Big Wind in Chicago," *Sports Illustrated*, September 18, 1978, 39.

26. Fimrite, "The Big Wind in Chicago," 39.

27. Davidson, "Mel Allen," 98.

28. Smith, *Voices of the Game*, 331.

29. Smith, *Voices of the Game*, 75.

30. "Where Are They Now? The Ol' Redhead," *Newsweek*, October 2, 1972, 11.

31. Robert Creamer, "The Ol' Redhead," *Sports Illustrated*, November 2, 1992, 13.

32. Barber, *The Broadcasters*, 218.

33. Kirshenbaum, "And Here, to Bring You the Play by Play . . . ," 43.

34. Gerry Hern, "It's 'Government Radio,'" *Baseball Digest*, November 1948, 71.

35. Jerry Nason, "House Announcer Blows a Tube," *Baseball Digest*, September 1952, 39–40.

36. Kirshenbaum, "And Here, to Bring You the Play by Play . . . ," 35.

37. Kirshenbaum, "And Here, to Bring You the Play by Play . . . ," 38.

38. Shelby Whitfield, *Kiss It Goodbye* (New York: Abelard-Schuman, 1973).

39. William Leggett, "Testing a Not-So-Golden Rule," *Sports Illustrated*, September 30, 1974, 59.

40. Kirshenbaum, "And Here, to Bring You the Play by Play . . . ," 35.

41. "They Hardly Ever Knock the Product," *Life*, August 13, 1971, 12.

42. Leggett, "Testing A Not-So-Golden Rule," 59.

14. Innovations in Production Practices

1. Dave Darling, "FOX Breaks the Sound Barrier with Baseball Telecasts," *Orlando Sentinel*, October 21, 2006.

2. MLB, "First Live Digital High Definition Television Broadcast of MLB," press release, September 15, 1997.

3. Jack Gould, "Jersey City Stadium Offers New Point of View for Television," *New York Times*, April 20, 1956.

4. "Spectacular TV Plans," *Sporting News*, January 30, 1965, 12.

5. For this chapter, the authors reviewed videotape recordings of eight televised games from 1952 to 1975. The specific games are noted in the text.

6. Bob Addie, "Usual Huge Audiences for World Series," *Washington Post*, October 8, 1978.

7. Richard Sandomir, "Blimps and BaseCams Cause Fans to Lose Sight of the Game," *New York Times*, July 14, 1992.

8. Darling, "FOX Breaks the Sound Barrier."

9. Mike Bryan, *Baseball Lives* (New York: Pantheon Books, 1989), 227.

10. Dan Daniel, "Five Cameras Required in Televizing Ball Game," *Sporting News*, September 25, 1946, 2.

11. Neil Amdur, "NBC and Harry Coyle's Book," *New York Times*, October 4, 1983.

12. Red Barber, "The Turmoil Behind the Baseball Telecast," *New York Times*, April 30, 1950.

13. MLB, "First Live Digital High Definition Television Broadcast." It should be noted, however, that the 16-by-9 aspect ratio used in HD is actually better suited to the horizontal movements of football, basketball, ice hockey, and soccer than baseball's more vertically oriented action.

14. Gay Talese, "Better Baseball Coverage Promised for New Season," *New York Times*, April 14, 1957.

15. Jack Murphy, "How to Televise Baseball," *Broadcasting*, May 18, 1953, 78.

16. Kisseloff, *The Box*, 87–88.

17. Sandomir, "Blimps and BaseCams Cause Fans to Lose Sight of the Game."

18. Skip Myslenski, "He's a Master of Direction," *Chicago Tribune*, July 5, 1983.

19. Jack Craig, "An Epic Telecast," *Sporting News*, August 1, 1970.

20. NBC Sports, press release, July 15, 1975, Television File, National Baseball Hall of Fame Library, Cooperstown, New York.

21. Addie, "Usual Huge Audiences for World Series."

22. Jane Leavy, "Pictures Worth a Million," *Washington Post*, October 13, 1979.

23. Myslenski, "He's a Master of Direction."

24. Tim McCarver with Danny Peary, *Baseball for Brain Surgeons and Other Fans* (New York: Villard, 1998), 14.

25. Darling, "FOX Breaks the Sound Barrier."

26. McCarver, *Baseball for Brain Surgeons*, 14.

27. Talese, "Better Baseball Coverage Promised."

28. *1966 Major League Baseball Television Manual*, NBC Sports, 50–87, Television File, National Baseball Hall of Fame Library, Cooperstown, New York.

29. *Broadcast Guide*, Fox Sports, 1997, 69, in authors' possession.

30. Lawrie Mifflin, "In Fine Series Coverage, Less Was More," *New York Times*, October 16, 1984.

31. McCarver, *Baseball for Brain Surgeons*, 16.

32. Bob Lardine, "A Diamond-studded Show," *New York Sunday News*, October 2, 1960.

33. Beach, "The Television Producer," 109.

34. Kisseloff, *The Box*, 137.

35. Richard Sandomir, "Harry Coyle, 74, TV Director; Pioneered Coverage of Baseball," *New York Times*, February 21, 1996.

36. Clifford Kachline, "New Camera Angles Give TV Viewers Choice Seats," *Sporting News*, October 16, 1957, 14.

37. Talese, "Better Baseball Coverage Promised."

38. Jim Ogle, "Murphy Made All Stops in 20 Years as Yank TV Boss," *Sporting News*, August 24, 1968, 17.

39. The Yankee telecast and CBS footage are available from Rare Sportsfilms, Inc., http://www.raresportsfilms.com; videotape of Don Cardwell's no-hitter, WGN-TV, Item No. TV-01482, Museum of Broadcast Communications, Chicago.

40. Myslenski, "He's a Master of Direction."

41. "Live Color Show Televised by CBS," *New York Times*, September 16, 1946.

42. "Air Lanes," *Sporting News*, June 20, 1951, 32.

43. Red Smith, "How Colorful Can They Get?," *Sporting News*, August 22, 1951, 10.

44. "Color Telecasts Not Far Off," *Sporting News*, June 1, 1955, 16.

45. "Color in Baseball: The World Series Is a Television 'First,'" *Newsweek*, October 3, 1955, 1.

46. Jack Gould, "TV: Multi-Hued Series; First Coverage of Games in Color, Like the Dodgers, Is Not a Winner," *New York Times*, September 29, 1955.

47. "Playing World Series on Kentucky's Blue Grass—That's the Story of Tint," *Variety*, October 5, 1955.

48. "NBC Will Offer Full Classic in Color TV for Fourth Time," *Sporting News*, September 28, 1960, 28.

49. "M'waukee Camera Shots Zing Up World Series Telecasts; Tint a Poser," *Variety*, October 9, 1957.

50. "Color Added," *Sports Illustrated*, October 14, 1957, 31.

51. "Best Seat in the House," *Time*, October 14, 1957, 57.

52. "61 Phil Tilts to Be TVed in Color for First Time," *Sporting News*, March 2, 1968, 32.

53. "Crosley Pioneers in Programming Color," *Broadcasting*, Crosley Supplement, April 2, 1962, 26–27.

54. "Color Baseball Telecasting," *Broadcast News*, September 1959, 6–12.

55. *Broadcasting*, April 2, 1962, 26.

56. "New Low-Light-Level Camera Tube Expands Indoor and Outdoor Color Programming," *Broadcast News*, April 1961, 5.

57. "U.S. Stadiums Need New Lighting for Proper Color TV Sports Coverage," *Sponsor*, April 3, 1967, 21.

58. Philip Baldwin, "Baseball in Color . . . Night and Day at WHDH-TV, Boston," *Broadcast News*, August 1967, 26–33.

59. Ralph Ray, "Baseball Delighted; Video Ratings Jump 58 Per Cent in 1966," *Sporting News*, January 7, 1967, 42.

60. McCarver, *Baseball for Brain Surgeons*, 13.

61. *Broadcast Guide*, 1997, 67.

62. NBC, *A Demonstration of Television Recording*, March 1949, Catalog ID: T77:0375, Museum of Television and Radio, New York.

63. "TV Tape Bolsters, WISN-TV's Sports Schedule," *Broadcast News*, September 1959, 31.

64. "ABC Presents Major League Championship Baseball," Procedure Manual, ABC Sports, 1965, Television File, National Baseball Hall of Fame Library, Cooperstown, New York.

65. Gould, "Jersey City Stadium Offers New Point of View."

66. John Hall, "Instant Verna," *Los Angeles Times*, December 5, 1980.

67. Leonard Shecter, "Why It's Better to Watch the Game on TV," *New York Times Magazine*, March 3, 1968.

68. J. Peter Kane, "Instant Replay," *Electronics World*, November 1968, 39.

69. Pete Coutros, "Don Wiltsbooth," *New York Post*, March 4, 1988.

70. Michael Katz, "TV's Isolated Camera Proves No Substitute for the Umpire," *New York Times*, April 18, 1965.

71. Joseph Durso, "The Magic Eye," *New York Times*, August 3, 1965.
72. Durso, "The Magic Eye."
73. NBC Sports, "Instant Replay—How It Will Work in the 1975 World Series" (press release), 1975, Television File, National Baseball Hall of Fame Library, Cooperstown, New York.
74. "Replays and Rapprochement," *Sports Illustrated*, October 27, 1975, 60.
75. Sandomir, "Blimps and BaseCams Cause Fans to Lose Sight of the Game."
76. McCarver, *Baseball for Brain Surgeons*, 9.
77. *1966 Major League Baseball Television Manual*, 50.
78. "Mystery Show on TV," *Sporting News*, August 1, 1970, 16.
79. Mifflin, "In Fine Series Coverage, Less Was More."
80. Bryan, *Baseball Lives*, 228.
81. *Broadcast Guide*, 1997, 66.
82. Darling, "FOX Breaks the Sound Barrier."

Epilogue

1. Quoted in Chris Isidore, "Baseball's Secret $uccess $tory," CNNMoney.com, December 25, 2005, http://money.cnn.com/2005/12/23/commentary/column_sportsbiz/sportsbiz/index.htm.
2. Brosnan, January 19, 2007.
3. Eastman and Ferguson, *Media Programming*.
4. Bellamy and Walker, *Television and the Remote Control*.
5. William Shawcross, *Murdoch: The Making of a Media Empire* (New York: Touchstone, 1997).
6. Brosnan, January 19, 2007.
7. Isidore, "Baseball's Secret $uccess $tory."
8. Isidore, "Baseball's Secret $uccess $tory."
9. Isidore, "Baseball's Secret $uccess $tory."
10. Isidore, "Baseball's Secret $uccess $tory"; David Lieberman, "MLB Ready to Play Ball with Musicians," *USA Today*, April 9, 2006, D1; Ryan Naraine, "MLBAM Goes Beyond Baseball Diamond," Internetnews.com, May 5, 2004, http://www.internetnews.com/bus-news/article/php/3349891; Jon Surmacz, "In a League of Its Own," *CIO Magazine*, April 15, 2005, http://www.cio.com/archive/041505/baseball.html.
11. Isidore, "Baseball's Secret $uccess $tory."
12. Isidore, "Baseball's Secret $uccess $tory."
13. Tim Arango, "Baseball's Cash Stash," Yahoo! Finance, November 21, 2006, http://biz.yahoo.com/hftn/061121/102906_8393081.html.
14. Russell Adams, "Is MLB Extending Its Reach or Overreaching?," *Street & Smith's SportsBusiness Journal*, March 28, 2005, 21.

15. Jorge L. Ortiz, "Offseason Is Field of Green," USA Today Sports Weekly, December 20–27, 2006, 8–10.

16. Russell Adams, "Is MLB Extending Its Reach?"

17. Andy Bernstein, "Flexibility a Key in New MLB-ESPN Deal," Street & Smith's SportsBusiness Journal, September 19, 2005, 3.

18. Bill Shaikin, "Dodgers Told TV Deal Breaks Rules," Los Angeles Times, September 7, 2006, http://www.bizofbaseball.com/index (accessed January 15, 2007).

19. In2TV. http://video.aol.com/video-category/in2tv/2120.

20. Brosnan, January 19, 2007.

21. Jeff Passan, "The Reality of Fantasy," Yahoo! Sports, April 21, 2006, http://ca.sports.com/mlb/news?slug=jp-fantasy042006&prov=yhoo&type=lgns.

22. Staci D. Kramer, "Federal Court Says MLBAM Can't Halt Use of Player Names, Stats," paidContent.org, August 9, 2006, http://www.paidcontent.org/entry/federal-court-says-mlbam-cant-halt-use-of-player-names-stats.

23. Maury Brown, "MLBAM and MLBPA: Formal Appeals in Fantasy Stats Case," Business of Baseball (web site), December 18, 2006, http://www.bizofbaseball.com/index.php?option=com_content&task&id=540.

24. Passan, "The Reality of Fantasy."

25. Curt Feldman, "Take-Two Bulks Up on Baseball; Adds MLBP, MLBAM to Partner Lineup," Gamespot.com, January 30, 2005, http://www.gamespot.com/xbox/sports/espnmajorleaguebaseball2k5/news.html.

26. Passan, "The Reality of Fantasy."

27. Brian Borawski, "MLB Close to Deal with DirecTV over Extra Innings," The Hardball Times (web site), January 24, 2007, http://www.hardballtimes.com/main/article/business-of-baseball-report240/.

28. "MLB Announces iN DEMAND Deal," press release, Major League Baseball, April 4, 2007, http://mlb.mlb.com/news/press_releases/press_release.jsp?ymd=20070404&content_id=1879904&vkey=pr_mlb&fext=.jsp&c_id=mlb.

29. Maury Brown, "The Monopolizing of MLB's Extra Innings Package," Baseball Prospectus (web site), January 8, 2007, http://www.baseballprospectus.com/article.php?articleid=5796; Richard Sandomir, "Extra Innings Exclusively on DirecTV," New York Times, January 20, 1997, http://www.nytimes.com/2007/01/20/sports/baseball/20base.html.

30. Adams, "Is MLB Extending Its Reach?"

31. Adams, "Is MLB Extending Its Reach?"

32. Brosnan, January 19, 2007.

33. Adams, "Is MLB Extending Its Reach?"; "Pirates End 51-year Partnership with KDKA," The Biz of Baseball (web site), September 12, 2006, http://www.bizofbaseball.com/index.

34. Isidore, "Baseball's Secret $uccess $tory."

35. Brosnan, January 19, 2007.

36. Chris Isidore, "Baseball's Flatter Playing Field," CNNMoney.com, October 7, 2006, http://money.cnn.com/2006/10/06/commentary/sportsbiz _baseball/index.htm.

37. James B. Chabin, President and Chief Executive Officer, PROMAX International, personal communication with Robert V. Bellamy Jr., December 10, 2004.

Index

2